SOWERBY'S
BOOK OF
SHELLS

SOWERBY'S
BOOK OF
SHELLS

CRESCENT BOOKS
New York

Originally published 1852 by
Henry G Bohn, York Street, Covent Garden
as A Conchological Manual.
This edition includes additional
prints taken from
Dictionnaire Universel d'Histoire Naturelle
by Charles d'Orbigny

This 1990 edition published by Crescent Books
distributed by Crown Publishers, Inc., 225 Park Avenue South,
New York, NY 10003

Printed and bound in Czechoslovakia

ISBN 0–517–02199–4

h g f e d c b a

FOREWORD

The Sowerby family was distinguished during the eighteenth and nineteenth centuries for its contributions to the literature of natural history. The Sowerbys are remembered now chiefly for the several thousand hand coloured plates they produced, many of them being the corporate efforts of the family working as a team. The author of *A Conchological Manual* was the second and the most prolific of three members of the family who successively bore the name George Brettingham and added significantly to the literature of natural history. He was very knowledgeable about conchology, wrote extensively about the subject and illustrated his writings with accurate engravings.

The first edition of his *Conchological Manual*, to which his father made important contributions, was first published in 1839. The fourth and last edition, extensively revised and illustrated with extra plates, appeared in 1852. Sowerby's book was intended for the shell collector rather than the serious scientific student and as such had popular appeal. The illustrations show typical examples of the various genera and are, as they always were, the book's principal attractions. He would have been the first to admit that his knowledge of conchology was more wide ranging than profound.

This re-issue of the fourth edition differs in several respects from the 1852 issue. In the original there were two folding tables comparing the conchological systems of De Blainville and Lamarck. These tables have been omitted as irrelevant and of little interest to the modern student. The woodcut vignettes, illustrating shell features, were originally presented in groups of two, three, four or more. Here they have been placed adjacent to the relevant portions of the text. Except for the frontispiece the 29 hand coloured plates were originally grouped together, but in this edition they have been distributed evenly through the text. The most substantial innovation, however, is the addition of a dozen hand coloured plates of shells culled from the multi-volume *Dictionnaire Universel d'Histoire Naturelle*, edited by Alcide Charles Victor Dessalines d'Orbigny and published at Paris between 1839 and 1849.

Each volume of this work is comparable in format to *A Conchological Manual*, the illustrative plates being hand coloured etchings. The exquisite illustrations of shells are based on original drawings by Jean Gabriel Prêtre, a highly talented artist who specialized in the very difficult art of shell portraiture. They make an attractive supplement to the hand coloured lithographs of G.B. Sowerby Junior and allow us to compare French and English styles of conchological illustration. Clearly the French favoured a more delicate and more highly coloured style. Also they seem to have preferred their gastropod (or univalve) shells to be shown upside-down. The orientation of these shells as shown by Sowerby is the one now adopted almost universally, although even today some French conchologists adopt the 'upside-down' style in their publications.

No useful purpose would be served by trying to make Sowerby's original text conform with modern linguistic and scientific requirements. It is now appreciated as a period piece and would gain nothing from drastic revision. In its original published form *A Conchological Manual* is now a costly item obtainable only from the antiquarian book trade. This attractively designed and augmented re-issue of its 1852 edition is a handsome substitute.

S. PETER DANCE
January 1990

NAMES OF AUTHORS ABBREVIATED

Adans. Adanson. Author of "Voyages du Senegal".

Bl. Blainville. Author of "Manuel de Malacologie et de Conchyliologie", &c.

Brod. W.J. Broderip, Esq. Author of various descriptions of shells in the Zoological Journal, &c.

Brongn. Brongiart. Author of "Memoire sur les terrains du Vicentin, d'Italie, de France, et d'Allemagne," &c.

Brug. Bruguière. Author of "Dictionaire des Vers testacés, dans l'Encyclopédie," &c.

Cuv. Baron Cuvier. Author of "Regne Animal," &c.

Defr. Defrance. Contributor to the "Annales des Sciences Naturelles," &c.

Desh. Deshayes. Author of "Coquilles fossiles des environs de Paris," &c.

D'Orb. D'Alcide d'Orbigny.

Drap. Draparnaud. Author of "Histoire Naturelle des Mollusques terrestres et fluviatiles de la France," &c.

Fer. De Ferussac. Author of "Histoire Naturelle des Mollusques terrestres et fluviatiles," &c.

Flem. Fleming.

Gmel. Gmelin. Author of an edition of Linnæus's "Systema Naturæ," &c.

Guild. Rev. Lansdowne Guilding.

Hübn. Hübner.

Humph. The late George Humphrey.

Lam. Lamarck. Author of "Animaux sans Vertebres," &c.

Lin. Linnæus. Author of "Systema Naturæ," &c.

Mont. Montague. Author of "Testacea Britannica," &c.

Montf. Montfort. Author of "Histoire Naturelle des Mollusques," &c.

Müll. Müller. Author of "Vermium terrestrium et fluviatilium Historia," "Zoologia Danica," &c.

Ranz. Ranzani. Author of "Considerations sur les Balanes," &c.

Schum. Schumacher.

Sow. Sowerby. The late and present James. Authors of "Mineral Conchology," &c. George Brettingham, Senr., "Genera of Shells," "Species Conchyliorum," &c. G. B. Jun. "Conchological Manual," "Conchological Illustrations," "Thesaurus Conchyliorum," Description of New Shells in the Zoological Proceedings, &c.

Sw. Swainson. Author of "Zoological Illustrations," "Exotic Conchology," and Treatises in "Lardner's Cabinet Cyclopedia," &c.

Turt. Turton. Author of "British Shells."

PREFACE TO THE FIRST EDITION

Iᴛ may be necessary in introducing this little volume, to state, that it is strictly conchological, and that it is compiled for the use not only of those who wish to acquire an elementary acquaintance with the subject, but also of authors and others, who, desirous of extending their knowledge and pursuing their researches, require a book of reference, containing a general outline of what has been done by those who have trodden the same path before them. It has been thought advisable, for general convenience, to arrange the principal part of the information in alphabetical order; adding tables of the systems of Lamarck and De Blainville, to facilitate the systematic pursuit of the science [these tables have been omitted from this reprint].

Persons of the class first alluded to, will find great assistance in the explanation of technical words, their application being further illustrated, in most cases, by a reference to the figures; and, although they might have been multiplied, it is trusted that enough are given for every useful purpose.

The definition of the Classes, Orders, Families, and Genera, in the system of De Blainville, and a tabular view, are presented for the use of those who prefer it, or who wish to compare it with that of Lamarck.

In the explanation of the figures will be found a systematic arrangement of shells, according to Lamarck, including the names of genera established or proposed since the publication of his system. The descriptions of established genera have been rendered as concise and clear as possible. It is hoped that no essential characters are omitted, and that those living authors, whose proposed generic distinctions have been passed over in a few words, will not have to complain of want of justice in the attempt to interpret their meaning.

In most cases the generic name will be found accompanied by its derivation. This has been done, in the hope of assisting the memory by associating the meaning of a term with some peculiarity in the thing described. At the end of each description of a genus, some general observations occur, pointing out the principal character which distinguishes it from others, to which it is nearly allied; and also stating the geographical or geological distribution and habits of the animal.

The above descriptions and definitions are illustrated by a series of plates, containing above 500 etchings of nearly as many proposed or established genera, arranged in Lamarckian order, so as to show at a glance all the generic forms of each family. And, although from their number, they could not be very highly finished, it is hoped that they will be found characteristic.

The compiler cannot replace his pen without acknowledging, with filial gratitude, the kind assistance of one who has sacrificed much of his time in bringing his knowledge and experience to bear upon the correctness and utility of this humble attempt to remove some of the difficulties to which the commencement of this, as well as of every other study, is exposed.

PREFACE TO THE FOURTH EDITION

Iɴ this edition many synonyms have been rectified, some dates have been given, a few doubtful or unnecessary definitions have been altered or expunged; descriptions of many additional genera, illustrated by new figures, have been inserted, and the work made as complete as its purely conchological character will admit.

July, 1852   G. B. S.

INTRODUCTION

The Science of Conchology affords a very delightful and instructive amusement for the leisure hours of those who, retiring occasionally from the more active pursuits of life, seek pleasure in the quiet contemplation of some of the smaller, but not less wonderful operations of creative wisdom. And, although the study of shells would be more complete, and rank higher in the scale of philosophical pursuits, were it always accompanied by that of the animal inhabiting them, it nevertheless presents means of intellectual gratification, to many who cannot follow it beyond the cabinet and the boudoir. These may examine with admiration and mental improvement, the beautiful colouring and architecture of these wonders of the deep, they may exercise their taste and judgment in the selection and arrangement of specimens, and their discrimination in detecting and appreciating the distinctions upon which the arrangement is founded.

It is but little that can be known of the subject without forming a collection of greater or less extent; for, as it would be uninstructive merely to delight the eye with the bright colours and elegant form of shells, without possessing correct information respecting them, so it would be insipid and useless to learn technicalities without being acquainted, by personal observation, with the subjects to which they are applied. The first endeavour should, therefore, be to obtain a few shells as examples of the larger divisions, and, when these are understood, to proceed with the smaller groups, until a collection be formed to represent as many generic forms as possible. It may be as well here to advise those who are forming a collection to be very particular, in every practicable instance, to have the shells properly named at the time of purchasing; as it will save much trouble, and materially assist in the attainment of the desired object. To this end, recourse should be had to those naturalist tradesmen, who unite the attainment and diffusion of real scientific knowledge with their commercial pursuits.

Supposing, however, that the person who desires to learn the science, possesses a small parcel of unarranged and unnamed shells, without any previous acquaintance with the subject, the following introductory explanations, are drawn up with the view of enabling him, without further assistance, to obtain a general insight into its principles, equal to that of those who have studied it long and laboriously. To effect this, he must read them, carefully comparing the descriptions with the figures referred to, and with the specimens which he may have at command.

After describing the nature of the science and defining its objects, we shall proceed to explain the structure of those objects, and the manner of their growth. We shall then enter somewhat minutely into the principles of classification, the distinctions upon which they are founded, and some of the technical terms used to express them. After which we shall pass through the arrangement of Lamarck, defining the general divisions adopted under the terms of "*Classes, Orders, and Families,*" as far as they are capable of definition. The subdivisions of the latter into *genera* will only be entered into so far as to enumerate the principal of them, the more minute descriptions being reserved for the alphabetical part of the work.

Let none be discouraged by the number of generic distinctions proposed and adopted in modern times; for *if well defined*, they will be found to facilitate rather than encumber the science. The knowledge of species must be the foundation of every system, and the greater their number, the more necessary it becomes to subdivide them; if, for instance, all the species now known were to have been included in the 50 genera of Linnæus, a single genus would have contained many hundreds of incongruous species, in which case it would be much more difficult to remember them, than if they were to be divided into a far greater number of genera. Every well marked division, tends to simplify the subject, and to facilitate the researches of the student.

NATURE OF THE SCIENCE

Conchology is the study of shells, viewed and described as to what they are either in themselves, or in relation to the soft, inarticulate animals which produce them, and of which they form a part. These animals are called Mollusca, and perhaps the best general description of them will be found in De Blainville's "Manuel de Malacologie et de Conchyliologie." The following is a translation, "Animal in pairs, the body and its appendages soft, inarticulate (not jointed), enveloped in a muscular skin, commonly called the mantle, which is extremely variable in form, and has developed either within or upon it a calcareous portion, consisting of one or several pieces, commonly called a shell."

The term Mollusca was formerly restricted to those soft animals which were destitute of shells, although possessing in other particulars, the characters described above, and it was used in order to distinguish them from the TESTACEA, which were covered or internally supported by calcareous parts. In the system of Linnæus, the soft portions are first arranged under the general designation of "Vermes Mollusca," and described without regard to the presence, absence, or character of the shells; and then the shells are separately characterized under the appellation of "Vermes Testacea," without any further notice of the animal, than an indication of the genus to which it belongs; thus the animal of Cypræa is said to be a Limax, and that of Tellina a Tethys.

The nearest approach to correctness, and the most philosophical method of study will be found in the modern system, adopted by Lamarck and his followers, of observing these animals as a whole, and arranging them according to the assemblage of characters which they present; of course taking into consideration the existence or non-existence, the form and structure of the shell, on the same principle, which, in arranging the vertebrated animals would lead us to study the hair, hoof, nails, claws, &c. as well as the other parts.

At the same time, it must be admitted that there are many private collectors of Shells who would find it a difficult, if not impossible task to study minutely and successfully the soft parts of the Mollusca. Ladies, for instance, could not be expected to handle with pleasure and perseverance, these bodies, which in order to be preserved from putrefaction, must be kept in spirits; and yet such persons may, with improvement and advantage to their own minds, enjoy the interesting and scientific amusement of studying and arranging the clean and beautiful shells which are so easily preserved, and so exquisitely beautiful in their structure. Let it also be remembered, that if shells had not been rendered commercially valuable, by the zeal and emulation manifested by *mere* Conchologists for the possession of rare specimens, few travelling merchants and sea captains would have thought them worthy of a corner in their cabins. In this case, few specimens being brought to the country, the more Philosophical Naturalist would have been left without the means of obtaining materials to work upon, or of attracting public attention to his favourite pursuit.

On account of these and other considerations, it has been thought advisable that the present work should bear a purely conchological character. The peculiarities of the shells alone being detailed for the assistance of those who collect and study them, while at the same time, in deciding upon their affinities and places, in the arrangement, it will be necessary sometimes to adopt conclusions arrived at by those who have studied the animal in all its parts. And the conviction must be expressed, that if ever a complete Natural System shall be formed it will result from the labours of the last mentioned class of naturalists.

DEFINITION OF A SHELL

Before entering minutely into the description of shells, it will be necessary to distinguish from the true testaceous Mollusca two kinds of animals, which have formerly been associated with them. Of these, the first is the class of CRUSTACEA, consisting of crabs, crayfish, &c. These differ from shell-fish, not only in structure and chemical composition, but also in the fact that the animal has jointed limbs, and that the substance of the flesh is inseparable from the hard external covering, which invests each particular joint as with a sheath; whereas the Molluscous animal is but partially attached to its shell, from which it possesses the power of partly withdrawing and returning. The second class is that to which the sea-urchin, or Echinus, belongs, of which there are many genera and species. The testaceous covering of Echini is composed of a number of small pieces, placed edge to edge, forming a more or less globular external covering to the flesh, which is supported in the centre by a number of bones leaning upon each other in a pyramidal form. The *test* is of a fibrous texture, guarded on the outside with moveable spines, which turn on ball and socket joints.

A true shell is composed of one or more calcareous pieces, commonly called valves, each piece formed by a series of layers, applied obliquely upon each other, in such a manner that each new layer begins within, and terminates a little in advance of the one before it.

The Cirripedes, however, although their testaceous pieces will correspond with this definition, are otherwise so connected with the crustacea, that they do not enter into the study of Conchology.

STRUCTURE AND GROWTH

We shall now endeavour to describe the manner in which the growth of each separate valve, or each regularly formed shell, proceeds from the nucleus.

Before the young animal has left the egg, if it be an *oviparous* species, or the body of the parent if *viviparous*, the nucleus of the shell is generally formed, and specimens are sometimes preserved in which the young shell is seen within the egg, as in the cut, fig. 1, 2; or adhering to the inner surface of the full-grown shell by the dried mucus of the animal, as seen in fig. 3.

1. Egg of a Bulinus. 2. The same broken, shewing the young shell. 3. The young of a Paludina, as seen in the aperture of the shell.

In both cases, the nucleus is generally of a more horny and transparent composition than the parts subsequently produced. As soon as the animal is hatched, or, in other words, leaves the egg or body of the parent, of course it begins to increase in size, and to require a corresponding enlargement in the shell. To effect this, a small quantity of mucous substance, secreted by the mantle of the animal, is deposited on the edge of the aperture. When this is dry and become sufficiently hard, it is lined by a more calcareous secretion; and these together form a new layer, which is followed by others in succession; each new layer being larger than the one that preceded it until the whole being complete, the full-grown animal is invested with a shell commensurate with its own proportions. Thus from the apex or nucleus the formation proceeds, as it were, downwards, taking the shape of the part which secretes it, on which it is in a manner moulded.

The nucleus, or first formed portion, may for technical purposes be considered, mathematically, as the apex of a spiral cone. And here it must be observed, that whether the shell consists of one or several pieces, each piece has a distinct nucleus, and the process of formation is separately repeated with each. The word *cone* is used for convenience, and its meaning extended so as to include all those structures which commencing at a point enlarge downwards.

From the apex, the next layer is deposited on its edge, and advancing beyond it necessarily adds to its extent. Thus, suppose for the sake of illustration, the part marked *a* in the diagram, fig. 4, to represent a nucleus, the cross lines (*l*) will shew the consecutive layers which enlarge their circle as they add to their numbers. This disposal of shelly matter into layers is marked externally by concentric striæ, or *lines of growth*,

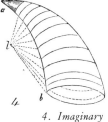

4. Imaginary cone. a. Apex. b. Base. l. Lines of growth.

while on the inside, the edges of the laminæ are consolidated into a kind of enamel. If a perpendicular section of a solid portion of a shell were magnified, it would present, in many instances, an appearance resembling the diagram, fig. 5; *a* may be taken to represent the horny part of the layers which form the outer coating, named "*Periostaca*," or "*Epidermis*;" the undulating line *b*, is formed by the edges of the calcareous layers, and causes the striæ, or lines of growth, which are often distinguishable

5. Supposed section of a part of a solid shell.

6. Section of an oyster shell enlarged.

on the surface of the shell; the space *c* is the middle part of those layers, and at *d* they are consolidated into the enamel which lines the interior.

In some species the layers are irregularly grouped together, and their edges overlap each other, so that they are easily separable, and advancing beyond each other, give a leafy appearance to the external surface. This structure is termed *foliaceous*. A very familiar instance

of this may be observed in the common oyster. If a specimen of this shell be broken, the substance will be seen to exhibit a degree of looseness, and a magnifying glass will enable the student to trace distinctly the laminæ of which it is composed. The accompanying representation of a magnified section (fig. 6) will shew at *a*, the external surface, with the foliations or leaves; at *b*, the parcels of layers which form them; and at *c*, the pearly structure produced by their consolidation, and by the subsequently deposited enamel which covers their external surface.

CLASSIFICATION

The classification of shells, that is, their systematic arrangement into *classes*, *orders*, *families*, *genera* and *species*, cannot be made to depend entirely upon the characters observable in them, viewed by themselves; for this reason, that many similarly formed shells belong to animals perfectly distinct, and that many molluscous animals are found to agree with each other in every respect but in the form of their testaceous support. There are, however, many important distinctions to be observed in the shells themselves, leading to the establishment of many of those very divisions, which would afterwards be confirmed by an examination of the soft parts. It is desirable to attend, as far as means and opportunity will allow, to *all* the points of difference, in order to form, or even to appreciate, a generic or wider distinction. It will therefore be our endeavour to explain the general principles upon which those distinctions are formed, and the manner in which they are applied and expressed in detail by scientific writers.

NUMBER OF PIECES, OR INDEPENDENTLY FORMED PARTS

The first, most simple and obvious division of shells, is that which results from the number of separate pieces composing them. Hence the distinction implied by the terms UNIVALVE, or consisting of a single piece; BIVALVE, or composed of two pieces; and MULTIVALVE, or composed of more than two. For an example of *univalve*, take a common whelk; for a *bivalve*, take a muscle or scallop; and for a *multivalve*, the *chiton*.

But although this arrangement may appear at first sight perfectly easy and plain, some explanation will be necessary in order to guard the student against understanding the above expressions in their strictest sense, without qualification. Thus the univalves are said to consist of a single piece, or spiral cone; but it would be more correct to speak of this piece as forming either the whole or principal part of the shell: for there is in many instances, a much smaller flattened piece attached to the foot of the animal, which being drawn in when it retires, closes the aperture as with a kind of door, to which in fact the word valve might be very properly applied; it is called, however, the *operculum*, of which the little horny plate, frequently drawn out by means of a pin from the aperture of a periwinkle, will present a familiar example.

The same may be said respecting the bivalves; for besides the principal portions or valves of which the shell is composed, there are in many species, one or two smaller separate portions, named "*accessary plates*" by some authors. They are fixed by means of cartilages, on the back of the hinge.—The engraving, fig. 7,

7. Accessary valves of a Pholas.

represents the accessary valves of a species of Pholas, which was on this account arranged by Linnæus with the Multivalves. Nearly allied to the Pholades is a set of shells to which De Blainville has given the name "*Tubicolæ,*" or inhabitants of tubes. In this case, the bivalve shell is connected with a testaceous tube or pipe, to which it is attached either by one or by both valves, or in which it lies attached only by the cartilages of the animal. In the genus Aspergillum, the two small valves are soldered into the sides of the tube in such a manner as to constitute a part of it. One of these shells, called the Water-spout, might be taken up by a person not aware of its real nature, and regarded as a pipe or tube prettily fringed, and nothing more; but upon a closer examination, he would find the two valves, the points of which are visible from the outside of the tube.

HABITS – *Land, Fresh-water, or Marine Shells*

Another distinction, leading to important results in classification, is that which is derived from the nature of the element breathed by the Mollusc. And although this consideration belongs more especially to the study of the animal itself, yet the habits of the animal materially influence the structure of the shell.

The TERRESTRIAL or LAND Molluscs live on land, breathe air, and feed on plants and trees.—Those who find pleasure in horticultural pursuits will at once call to mind a too familiar example of these Molluscs in the common garden snail. The Land-shells are all univalves, and constitute a family in the Lamarckian system under the name "*Colimacea*" or snails, corresponding with the Linnean genus Helix.—They are generally light in structure and simple in form.

The AQUATIC, or Fresh-water Molluscs, such as the Planorbis, commonly called the Fresh-water Snail; the Unio—known by the name of Fresh-water Muscle, is found in ponds, ditches and rivers. The *epidermis* of these is generally of a thick, close-grained character, and they are subject to corrosion near the umbones.

The MARINE, or *sea-shells*, belong to all the classes and orders, and include by far the greater number of species. They vary in the habits of the animal, and consequently in the situations in which they

are found. Some are found buried in sand and marine mud, and are named "*Arenicolæ*" or inhabitants of sand; others in holes of rocks and other hard substances, then they are named "*Petricolæ,*"—some of these latter form the holes in which they live by corroding or eating away the stone. A section of these form the family of "*Lithophagidæ,*" or stone-eaters, of Lamarck. Others, again, take up their parasitical abode in the bodies of animals, and feed upon their substance; as for instance, the Stylifer, which is found in the vital part of star-fish, and Coronula, and Tubicinella, found buried in the skin of the whale.

LOCOMOTION – *Attached, Unattached*

A much more subordinate source of distinction arises from the freedom or attachment of the shells. Some of them float or walk freely in their natural element; others are fixed or attached to foreign bodies. Among those which are attached, there is again a difference as to the *mode* of attachment. Some are united to foreign bodies by means of a glutinating substance, secreted by the animal, and joining part of the surface of the shell to that of the stone, coral or other substance. In this way shells are fixed to each other in groups; this is the case with the Spondyli among bivalves, and the Serpulæ among univalves. M. de Blainville applies the term "*Fixæ*" to these shells. Others are kept in a particular place by means of a *Byssus* or Tendinous fibrous line or bunch of silky hairs, acting as a cable, and allowing the Mollusc to ride as it were at anchor. This Tendon is connected with some part of the animal from which it passes through an opening or hiatus in the shell, as in the Terebratula and the Mytilus.

In the former, represented by the cut, fig. 8, the tendon passes through a perforation in the upper valve; and in the latter, Mytilus, fig. 9, the byssus passes out between the valves.

Before proceeding to explain the characters of the different groups, according to the modern system of classification, it may be desirable to explain the terms by which the different parts and characters are described, and to shew the manner in which the shells are measured. For this purpose we shall treat of the general divisions separately. We begin with

UNIVALVE SHELLS

In considering Univalves merely with reference to their mathematical construction, the first point demanding our attention is, whether they are symmetrical or non-symmetrical, or, in other words, whether a straight line drawn through the shell would divide it into two equal parts. The greater part of univalves are non-symmetrical, being rolled obliquely on the axis; but many are symmetrical, being rolled horizontally on the axis. The Nautilus presents an illustration of the latter; the Snail is a familiar example of the former.

Symmetrical Univalves

In describing these it will be well to commence with the most simple form, such as the Patella,—taking a conical species as an example. In this it will be observed that there is no winding or curvature, but a simple depressed cone, and that the line *a, p,* divides it into two equal parts.

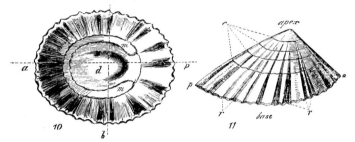

The *anterior, a, (cut,* fig. 10) is known by the interruption of the muscular impression which surrounds the central disc (*d*). This interruption of the muscular impression is in the place where the head of the animal lies in the shell. The impression itself is caused by the fibrous muscle which attaches the animal to the shell. The apex (*a*) in Patella, generally leans towards the anterior (*a*) part of the shell, and away from the posterior (*p*); and this circumstance has caused some mistakes, because in Emarginula the apex leans towards the posterior; and students, instead of examining the muscular impression, which is the only criterion, have only noticed the direction in which the apex turned, and concluded that to be the anterior, towards which it inclined. The lines or ribs running from the base to the apex of the shell, in the direction *r*, are called *radiating* lines; and those which encircle the cone in the direction *c c,* from front to back, are very properly described as *concentric.* The *length* is measured from front to back in the line *e*; the breadth, from side to side, in the line *b*; and the depth from the apex to the base.

Let it be observed that patelliform, or limpet shaped shells are not all symmetrical; Umbrella, Siphonaria, Ancylus, &c. will form exceptions, of which we have yet to speak. And the learner may also be reminded that the Limpets themselves are not *all* regular in their form: for as they adhere to rocks and other rough surfaces, and are so little locomotive, in many instances they partake of the inequalities of the surface, and conform to its irregularities. This adherence is not affected by any agglutinating power in the animal, nor by any

12. Dentalium Elephantinum.

tendinous process like that described above; but simply by means of the foot of the animal acting as a sucker.

The next variation in symmetrical univalves is to be observed in the tubular, curved form, the example of which will be the Dentalium, fig. 12.

This has an opening at the anterior termination *a*, called the aperture. The opening at the posterior end (*p*) is named a fissure, or perforation. The ribs running along the sides of the shell are *longitudinal,* or radiating. And the lines round the circumference are *lines of growth,* or *concentric*—each one having in succession, at earlier stages of growth, formed the aperture. They are described as concentric or transverse.

Symmetrical Convolute Univalves

The Nautilus, the Spirula, the Scaphite, and the Ammonite are the leading types of this form; but when we use the term symmetrical, in reference to these, the word must not be understood in its strictest sense, for no shell is *perfectly* symmetrical: but it means that there is no perceptible difference in the proportion of the two sides; as in the human body, the right side is larger and more powerful than the left, yet to a degree so small that it gives no apparent bias to the figure.

CHAMBERED SHELLS

Many of the shells now under consideration are chambered, that is, the internal cavity is divided into separate compartments by plates reaching across it, named *Septa*; and the only connection between the chambers is formed by the small pipes passing through them, to which the name of Siphon is attached.

Septa

The septa are *simple* in some species, as in the Nautilus, fig. 13. In others they are undulated, having waved edges, as in some species of Ammonites; in others they are *angulated,* as in Goniatites, fig. 480 in the plates; and in the greater number of instances, among the Ammonites, they are *arborescent,* or branched.

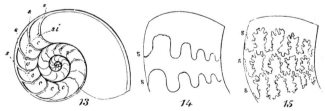

13. Section of Nautilus.—14. Undulating Septa.—
15. Arborescent Septa.

In the above section of a Nautilus, fig. 13, diminished in size, shewing the whorls and chambers (*c*), it will be seen that the edges of the septa (*s*) are formed in one simple curve. In fig. 14, the upper part of an Ammonite, the undulating line will be seen; and in fig. 15 a specimen is given of the arborescent septa.

Siphon

The Siphon is *dorsal* when placed near the outside of the whorls; *central* when near the middle; and *ventral* when near the inside of the whorl, or that part which leans against the last volution. When it passes uninterruptedly from one chamber to another, it is described as *continuous*, as in the case of Spirula; when, on the other hand, it only passes through the septum a little distance, and opens into the chamber, as in Nautilus, it is *discontinuous*.

Whorls of Symmetrical Univalves

They are *disunited* when they do not touch each other, as in the case of Spirula (fig. 471 in the plates); but in the contrary case they are said to be *contiguous*. In some species of Nautilus the whorls overwrap each other in such a manner that the early whorls are entirely covered by the last, the edges of which reach to the centre of the disk; the spire is then said to be *hidden*; as in the Nautilus Pompilius. In Nautilus umbilicatus the spire is nearly hidden, the whorls not quite covering each other; but in the greater number of the Ammonites, the largest part of the preceding whorl is seen. To express the degree in which the whorls overwrap each other, has caused much difficulty in concise descriptions. Perhaps it would be well to apply the term *spiral disc* to so much of the shell as is seen besides the last whorl, and to describe it as large or small in diameter, compared with the whole: or to say that the whorls of the spire are half, or one-third, or one-fourth covered, as the case may be.

Aperture of Symmetrical Univalves

In Ammonites Blagdeni and some others the aperture is of an oblong square; it is then said to be *sub-quadrated*; in Nautilus triangularis it is *angulated*; in Ammonites Greenoughi it is of an interruped oval shape, described as *elliptical*. In the greater number of Orthocerata, it is rounded or *circular*. The entrance of the last whorl into the aperture of some rounded species of Nautilus causes it to take a *semi-lunar* form; if rounded at the sides it is said to be *reniform* or kidney-shaped: if pointed at the sides it is *semi-lunar*; and in some species of Ammonites, it is five-sided or *quinquelateral*.

Measurement of Symmetrical Conical Univalves

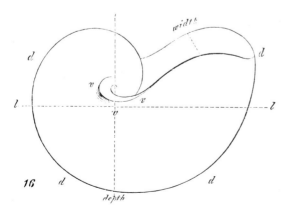

The *width* is measured across the aperture, which is the widest part of the shell. The *length* (*l*) from the dorsal part (*d*) of the aperture to the dorsal part of the *whorl* (*d*) on the opposite part of the shell. The *ventral* part of the whorls is that nearest to the axis, and the *dorsal* that which forms the outline of the figure.

NON-SYMMETRICAL UNIVALVES

These are *conical, irregular, spiral*, or *convolute*. The *conical* form is when there is no enrolment of the apex. Although the Patellæ were described as symmetrical, there are several species of Patelliform shells which are not symmetrical. In Umbrella, for instance, the apex is oblique, the shells being placed obliquely on the animal. In the genus *Siphonaria*, there is a grove on one side, where the brachia or gills of the animal rest. In the genus Ancylus, it will be observed that the apex bends on one side, and the animal is like the Limnæa, which has a spiral shell. The cup and saucer Limpets, or Calyptræ-dæ, present a group which requires to be described differently from the symmetrical or true Limpets. Their structure is very curious, and they vary considerably among themselves, some of them being simply conical, others nearly flat, or discoidal, and others more or less spiral. But their principal peculiarity consists in their having a small internal process or plate, commonly named their *septum*, variously shaped.

Septa of Limpets

The septa of Limpets assume a variety of forms, the principal of which will be seen in the accompanying engravings.

The form from which the group derives its generic appellation is that of the cup-shaped or *Cyathiform* species (fig. 17). In the Crepidulæ, or Slipper-Limpets, the septum is flat, reaching across the opening, like the deck of a vessel; it is then described as *transverse* (fig. 20). In Calyptræa Equestris, it has two prominent points, and is described as *bi-furcated* (fig. 18). In another species, it is a three-sided plate rather spiral at the apex (fig. 19).

Measurement of Cup and Saucer Limpets

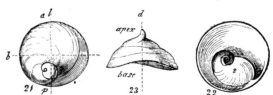

The line marked *a, p, l l*, indicates the direction in which the shell is to be measured for *length*. *a* indicates the *anterior*, *p* the *posterior*. The line *d* (fig. 23), from the apex to the base, is the *depth*. The line *b* (fig. 21), is in the direction of the breadth.

Irregular non-symmetrical Univalves

Serpuliform shells are irregularly twisted hollow tubes, which were formerly considered to have been secreted by a kind of worm, but now known to be the shells of true Molluscs, of a kind not very widely differing from those which have regularly spiral shells. The greater part of these are attached to foreign bodies, or to each other in groups. Some are attached by the whole length of the shell, they are then said to be *decumbent*. Some of these are coiled round like the Spirorbis, the little white shell seen on the carapace of the Lobster or on leaves of sea-weeds; they are then said to be discoidal; others again, such as the *Vermetus*, approach more nearly to the spiral form. The deviation from the regular spire only taking place after the first few first volutions.

SPIRAL NON-SYMMETRICAL UNIVALVE

As these constitute the largest class, it will be necessary to dwell upon them in detail. First as to *measurement*.

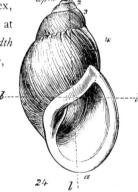

The length is measured from the apex, to that part of the aperture *a* (fig. 24), at the greatest distance from it. The *breadth* is in the opposite direction. The *anterior*, or front part of the aperture, is marked *a*, where the head of the animal protrudes.

Spire of non-symmetrical Univalves

In counting the whorls of which the spire consists, we commence at the apex, and reckon downwards to the last, or body whorl. The spire is described as being long or short in relation to the aperture: in which case, all that is above the aperture is measured with the spire. Its apex requires particular notice, as the character of the whole shell frequently depends upon the particulars observable in this part. It is sometimes *obtuse*, or blunt; sometimes *acute*, or sharp. In the Cones it is frequently flat, and in Planorbis it is concave. It is sometimes of a different structure from the rest of the shell, retaining the horny and transparent appearance which characterized it when the animal was first produced. The Tritons present an instance of this, although it is not always observable, owing to the tenderness of the substances which causes it to break or fall away in many specimens. A very remarkable instance also occurs in Bulinus decollatus (cut, fig. 27,

28), so named, because the apex, to the depth of several whorls, falls off, and the shell is *decollated*. In this, and many more instances, among Pupæform land shells, the occurrence of this circumstance seems to be by no means rare or accidental, a provision having been made for filling up the opening by a septum. A *papillary apex* is one

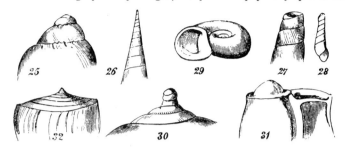

Fig. 25, obtuse; 26, acute; 27, 28, decollated; 29, concave; 30, papillary; 31, mammellated; 32, discoidal.

which is swelled at the extremity into a little rounded knob, or nipple; and a *mammellated* apex is one which is rounded out more fully.

Whorls

The spire is described as consisting of *numerous* or *few* whorls, and sometimes the number of them is particularly stated. A whorl consists of one turn of the spiral cone. The whorls are described as *flattened*, when their sides are not much bulged out: when the contrary is the case, the whorls are said to be *ventricose*, and either *rounded* or *angulated*. The degree of rapidity with which the whorls become enlarged presents an important source of distinction. The *suture*, or seam, which separates one whorl from another is also noticed as being *distinct* or otherwise; *canaliculated*, or grooved; or covered by an enamel, which in some instances is even *tumid* or swelled into a ridge.

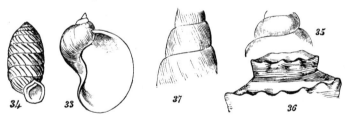

Fig. 33, few; 34, numerous; 35, rounded, ventricose; 36, angular, ventricose; 37, flattened.

Suture.

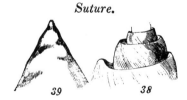

Fig. 38, canaliculated; 39, enamelled.

Varices

Varices are caused by periodical rests or stoppages in the growth of the shell, when the edge of the aperture thickens, and renders the shell as complete as when full grown. Again, after an interval, another check takes place, and another thickened edge is formed, and so on in succession, until the animal arrives at maturity, and the shell is full-grown. The thickened edges successively forming the aperture, remain visible on the outside, through all the subsequent stages. When these rests take place at frequent periods, the varices will of course be numerous, as in Harpa and Scalaria. They occur at regular or irregular distances, varying in shape and other characters. When the varices occur at regular intervals, and form a connected ridge from whorl to whorl up the spire, they are said to be *continuous*, as in Ranella; when on the contrary, the varix on one whorl does not come in contact with that on the other, they are described as *discontinuous*. In order to distinguish a regular varix from a mere external ridge, it will be sufficient to notice whether its edge overlaps the external surface, and whether it resembles the open edge of the aperture, which true varices do.

Fig. 40, numerous; 41, few, continuous; 42, few, discontinuous.

Aperture

The aperture or opening of the spiral tube, was formerly called the "mouth;" a term calculated to convey an erroneous impression, when applied to a part of the shell which has no correspondence with the mouth of the animal. The word *aperture* is used by modern writers in a general sense, including the cavity, its edges, and the canals. The cavity itself is distinguished in various shells as to its shape, which depends much upon the degree of modification produced by the last whorl. In some cases, as in Cyclostoma, where the aperture stands apart from the last whorl, the shape is round, or nearly so. The Scalaria presents a good example of this. In others, where the inner edge or lip, wrapping over the body whorl is nearly straight, the aperture is *semi-lunar*, or half-moon shaped: this is remarkable in the "*Neritacea*" of Lamarck, named, on that account, "*hemi-cyclostomata*" by De Blainville. In a great number of instances, the lower part of the body whorl enters obliquely into the upper part of the aperture, the result being a *pyriform*, or pear-shaped opening. The aperture is described as *long* when it is largest in the direction of the axis, and *wide*, in the contrary case. The *anterior* is the part at the greatest distance from the apex, and the body whorl; the *posterior*, the part nearest to the apex. Thus some apertures are described as *posteriorly contracted* and *anteriorly widened*, or the reverse. A *linear* aperture is one contracted in its whole length, as in Cypræa. When the whorls are angulated, a *trigonal* aperture is the result, as in many species of Trochus. Some are *transversely oval*, that is in an opposite direction to the axis, and others *longitudinally oval*. When the whorls

are formed with two outer angles, a somewhat quadrated aperture is formed. There are other variations too numerous to mention.

Apertures

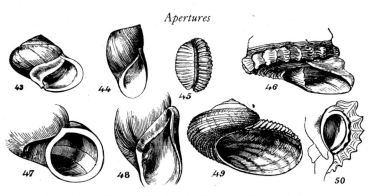

Fig. 43, Helicina, semilunar; 44, Pirena, pyriform; 45, Cypræa, linear; 46, Trochus, trigonal; 47, cyclostoma, rounded; 48, Chilina, posteriorly contracted; 49, Stomatia, transversely oval; 50, Murex, longitudinally oval.

The entire edge of the aperture described generally, is named the *Peritreme*, but this term can only be conveniently applied in cases where, in some at least of its characters, it is the same all round, so that one descriptive term is applicable to the whole. As, however, this is of rare occurrence, it is found convenient in descriptions to separate the inner from the outer lip. In a great number of instances, this is done naturally, by a canal, or notch at the anterior or lower extremity, and by the posterior union of that part which overlays the body whorl with the other portion. At these two points the outer and inner lips separate from each other: we therefore describe the

Canals of the Aperture

When there is neither notch nor canal, anteriorly or posteriorly, interrupting the edge of the aperture, it is described as *entire*. When there is a notch or sinus at the anterior extremity, it is said to be *emarginated*. When the edge of this notch is expanded, and drawn out in the form of a beak, it is said to be *canaliferous*, or to have a *canal*. When, in addition to this, the lips are thickened and contracted posteriorly near their junction, and drawn out so as to form a groove, it is said to be *bi-canaliculated*, or to have two canals. The *anterior canal* is said to be long or short, according to the proportion which it may bear to the rest of the shell. Thus the canal of Ranella ranina (fig. 393 in the plates), may be described as *short*; while that of Murex haustellum, (fig. 396, pl.) is *long*. When it is wide near the aperture, and becomes gradually contracted towards its termination, it is said to be *tapering*, as in Pyrula (fig. 388, pl.); when the termination is sudden, it is described as *truncated*. If, on placing the shell upon a plane, with the aperture downwards, the canal is seen to rise upwards, it is *recurved*. In Buccinum and Nassa it is turned suddenly over the back, and forms a short, curved elevation; it is then described as *recurved* and *varicose*. If the edges meet, so as to form a tube, it is said to be closed, as in some species of Murex and Typhis. The posterior canal is, in some cases, *free*, or standing out from the spire, as in some species of Ranellæ; while in others it is *decumbent*, running up the sides of the spire, as in Rostellaria (fig. 402, pl.).

Canals

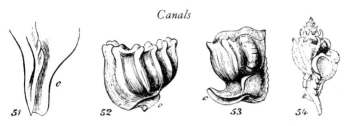

Fig. 51, *Fasciolaria, truncated*; 52, *Nassa, recurved, varicose*; 53, *Cerithium, recurved*; 54, *Typhis, closed*.

Lips, or edges of the Aperture

The part of the edge of the aperture next to the body whorl is named the *inner*, or *columellar* lip. Posteriorly it commences at the point of union with the outer lip, where that touches the body whorl, the junction being generally marked by an angle, and sometimes by a canal. Anteriorly it terminates where there is generally seen a notch or canal, or sudden angle from which the outer lip proceeds. The part which setting out from the body whorl, and proceeds outwards at a distance from the axis, till it reaches the anterior canal or notch (or its place in case of absence) is named the *outer lip*. In many cases the edges are united in such a manner, that it is difficult to distinguish where the inner lip terminates, and the outer lip commences: when this is the case, it is usual to describe the margin or peritreme, as a whole, without distinguishing the parts. The *outer* lip, sometimes called the *right* lip, or *labrum* of continental writers, is sometimes *acute*, not being of thicker substance than the remainder of the shell. In other cases it is *obtuse*, or thickened and rounded at the edge. When thickened and turned backwards it is described as *reflected*; when, on the other hand, it is turned inwards towards the axis, as in the Cypræd æ, it is *inflected*, or involute. When it is *toothed*, a distinction must be observed as to whether the dentations are external or internal. If the teeth are small and numerous, it is *denticulated*; if larger, it is *dentated*; when expanded into a kind of wing, as in some species of Strombus and Rostellaria, it is described as *alated*; and a family in Lamarck's system is named "Alatæ," from this very circumstance. In some of those which are expanded, the expansion is divided into separate, attenuated portions, they are then said to be digitated.

Outer Lips

The *inner* lip, sometimes named the *columellar* lip, or "*labium*," is subject to similar variations as to thickness, dentition, &c. That portion of it which lies upon the body whorl is frequently distinguished from that which intervenes between it and the notch or canal. De Blainville, restricting the term *lip* "bord gauche" to the former portion, applies the term "columella" to the latter; and in some instances this may be the more convenient method of describing the part in question. The columellar lip is sometimes *detached* entirely

from the body of the shell, as in Murex haustellum; in others it is *decumbent*, or lying over the last whorl, although quite distinct, and in some cases, *thickened, callous*, or *tumid*.

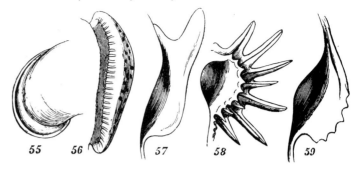

Fig. 55, *Helix, reflected*; 56, *Cypræa, involute, denticulated*; 57, *Seraphs, alated*; 58, *Murex, digitated*; 59, *Rostellaria, dentated*.

At the lower or anterior part, sometimes called the *columella*, there are in many instances flattened, laminated folds; these are particularly conspicuous in the genera Cymba and Melo, where, being obliquely spiral and laminar, they are extremely elegant, presenting to the eye graduated repetitions of the line of beauty. In other cases, as in the Turbinellæ, they are more horizontal and thickened.

In some cases the columella is swelled into a varicose mass; as in Oliva, Ancillaria, &c.; it is then described as *tumid* or *varicose*. It is sometimes *tortuous*, and sometimes straight, and is susceptible of many variations, too minute and particular to be described in this part of the work.

Columellar Lips

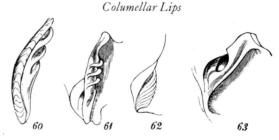

Fig. 60, *Melo, obliquely plaited*; 61, *Turbinellus, horizontally plaited*; 62, *Ancillaria, varicose, tortuous*; 63, *Natica, straight*.

OPERCULUM

The aperture of many species of shells remains constantly open; but in a great number of species it is occasionally closed, whenever the animal is retracted within the shell, by a calcareous or horny piece called the operculum. This must be distinguished in the first instance from another kind of calcareous covering, which in some univalve shells serves to close the aperture during a certain portion of the year. This piece, named the *epiphragm*, although hardened and shelly in appearance, is no real part of the animal or of the shell; being only a secretion temporarily hardened, for the purpose of defending the animal from external influences during the *hibernating or torpid* season, to be dissolved when the season is at an end. On examining this piece, it will be observed that it is not formed in regular layers like the rest of the shell; while the true operculum is of a regularly laminated structure, having a nucleus and receiving obliquely deposited additions, either in a lateral, spiral or concentric direction. It is attached to the posterior part of the foot on the upper surface; and when the animal retires within its shell, that part of the foot enters last, drawing the operculum after it, and thus closing the aperture.

Opercula of Spiral Univalves

The opercula of various shells differ in the first place as to their chemical composition. They are sometimes formed principally of calcareous matter, like the rest of the shell, as in Neritina, Nerita, and some others. They are *corneo-calcareous*, when upon an internal lamina of horn there is a thickened layer of shelly matter. This is the case with shells of the genus Turbo and Phasianella, which are on this account distinguished from those of the genus Trochus; the opercula of the latter being horny or *corneus*.

The size of the operculum is distinguished by comparison with the rest of the shell; thus, those of Strombus, Cassis, &c. are small; while those of Cyclostoma and others are large, filling up the cavity at its outer edge.

The direction in which the successive layers are deposited, forms another ground of distinction. The disc is formed in some instances of a series of whorls, the apex or nucleus being more or less central; if these whorls are numerous, the operculum is described as *multispiral*, as in shells of the genus Trochus; if few, as in Cyclostoma, it is *paucispiral*. In some instances the flattened spire consists of but one whorl, it is then *unispiral*; and when scarcely one turn is completed, it is described as *subspiral*. When the layers are applied upon each other in such a manner that the nucleus is central, and the edges of the subsequent layers are extended beyond each

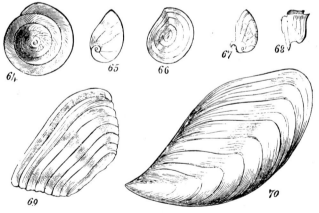

Fig. 64, *multispiral*; 65, *paucispiral*; 66, *concentric*; 67, *articulated*; 68, *radiated*; 69, *lammellated*; 70, *unguiculated*.

other all around, so as to form rims, the operculum is described as *concentric*; if the nucleus is lateral, or at one side without being spiral it is *lammellated*; and when it forms a terminal point, enlarging in the form of a finger-nail or claw, it is *unguiculated*. In the operculum of a Neritina, there is a lateral process, by means of which it is locked into the columella, the term *articulated* is then applied. In that

of Navicella, there is also a process which appears to radiate from the nucleus, it has therefore been described as a *radiated* operculum.

BIVALVE SHELLS

Bivalve shells, named Conchacea by Lamarck, are those which consist of two principal portions united to and folded upon each other by means of a hinge. The pieces united compose the shell, while each piece separately is called a valve. Considering the bivalve shell as a whole, it will be necessary, in the first instance, to describe the position in which it is to be observed, in order to give the student a clearly defined notion of what is intended, when terms expressive of height, depth, length, breadth, &c. are used, as well as when the anterior and posterior extremities are spoken. For this purpose, we must suppose the animal to be living and creeping along the bed of the sea by means of its foot; where this foot protrudes, will be the *ventral margin*, and the opposite part the *dorsal margin* of the shell. There will then be a valve on each side; and if we further suppose the animal to be walking forward with its back to the observer, the *right* and *left* valves will correspond with his right and left sides.

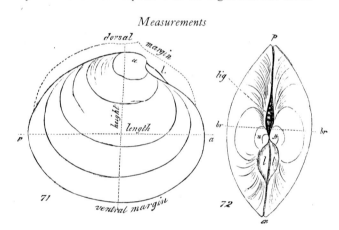

Measurements

The *length* will be measured from *anterior* (*a*) to *posterior* (*p*), and the lines of growth running in the same direction will consequently be *longitudinal* or *concentric*; *transverse* of some authors. The height will be from the umbones (*u*), to the *ventral margin*, and lines or bands in that direction are termed *radiating*; longitudinal, according to some authors.

The points from which the growth of the shell commences, are called the *umbones*; these usually turn towards the anterior part of the shell: if this circumstance fails to point out the *anterior*, the opposite may in many cases be distinguished by the muscular impressions of the mantle, the sinus or winding of which, if any, is always near the *posterior* muscular impression; and in all cases where there is an external ligament, it is on the posterior side.

There is sometimes an external impression near the front of the umbones, which forms a semicircle on each valve; the space within this semicircle is called the *lunule* (wood-cut, fig. 71); a corresponding depression, when it exists on the posterior margin near the umbones, is named the *escutcheon* or *posterior area*.

Hinge

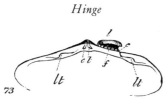

Fig. 73, *l t*, *lateral teeth; c t, cardinal teeth; c, cartilage under the*
ligament; l, ligament; f, fulcrum of the ligament.

The *hinge* of the shell is on the *dorsal* margin, and is composed of the various apparatus by which the two valves act upon each other in opening and shutting. It consists of a *ligament*, which is placed on the dorsal margin, just at the back of the umbones, and unites the two valves together; and the *cartilage* or thick gristly elastic substance, sometimes found close to the *ligament*, to which it then forms an inner coating, and sometimes received into a pit within the shell. It serves the purpose of keeping the shell open when not forcibly closed by the adductor muscles. An inner layer of shelly matter upon which are placed teeth, and pits to receive them on the two valves reciprocally. Each of these it will be necessary to explain more fully; observing, at the same time, that in some species of Bivalves these parts may be wholly or partially wanting. Thus we meet with some shells, such as the Muscle, without teeth; and in the group containing Pholas, &c. the hinge is destitute of teeth and ligament, the two valves being kept together by loose cartilages, and by the stone in the hollow of which they are confined.

Ligament and Ligamentary Cartilage of the Hinge

These two distinct substances have been described by many writers, as though, composing the same mass, they were of one substance; but the difference may very easily be explained. The *true ligament* is external, being fixed on the edge of one valve behind the umbones, and passing over in an arch to the corresponding edge of the other, very correctly retaining the name of *ligament*, because it serves the purpose of binding the two together. The thick, elastic substance, which Mr. Gray names the *cartilage*, is sometimes found in connexion with the ligament, so as to form one mass with it, although it is always separable and placed within it: it is sometimes placed quite within the shell, and separated from the ligament, in a pit or hollow formed for its reception in the hinge lamina, near the centre. It is found in both valves, and being elastic, the portion in one valve presses against that in the other, so as to keep the valves apart, unless voluntarily closed by the adductor muscles of the animal. The ligament is sometimes spread over an external area, as in Arca, while the cartilage is placed in several grooves of the same area, beneath the outer covering.

Hinge lamina, Teeth and Fulcrum of the Ligament

In a great variety of cases, there is a thickening of the substance of the shell within, under the dorsal margin; this is named the hinge lamina. It is sometimes merely callous; but in many cases it has raised *teeth* in both valves, those in one valve entering into

corresponding cavities in the other. Those which are placed immediately below the umbones, and seem to take their rise from beneath them, are called *cardinal teeth*; those at a distance from the umbones, which are seen to lie along the upper margin of the shell are named *lateral teeth*.

When the cardinal teeth terminate in a double point, which is not unfrequently the case, they are said to be *bifid*. The lateral teeth, in various species, are distinguished as terminating *near* to, or at a *distance* from the umbones. In the Nuculæ and Arcæ there is a row of teeth placed across the hinge lamina. In which case, the lateral cannot be distinguished from the cardinal teeth.

Muscular Impression

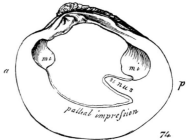

Fig. 74. *a, anterior; p, posterior; m i, muscular impressions.*

Lamarck divides the Bivalve shells into two general orders; the first is named "Dimyaria," having two adductor muscles; and the second, "Monomyaria," having but one. These adductor muscles are used for the purpose of drawing the valves together, being composed of contractile fibrous gristle, fastened firmly to the inner surface of each valve. The place where they are thus fixed may be seen when the animal is removed by depressed areas, which are generally pretty well defined and are named *muscular impressions*. Where there is but one adductor muscle, there will be but one of these impressions near the centre of each valve, but in the Dimyaria, where there are two, the impressions are seen, one on the anterior, and one on the posterior of each valve, just below the *hinge* lamina. They are sometimes *complex*, that is, composed of several portions in a group; but in general, they are simple and well defined.

They are also described as large or small, in proportion to the size of the shell; regular or irregular in form. The animal is attached to the inner surface by the fibrous portions of the mantle, which creates a linear impression or *cicatrix*, commonly described as the *palleal impression*, or muscular impression of the mantle. It runs near the ventral margin from one muscular impression to the other, sometimes in a smooth *continuous* line or band, and sometimes in an interrupted series of small impressions. Near the point of union with the posterior muscular impression, there is sometimes a more or less considerable winding inwards towards the centre of the shell, and back again towards the point of union. This is named the *sinus*, and is distinguished as being *angular* or *rounded*, large or small, according to the species. When it enters towards the centre of the shell in a tongue-shaped outline it is said to be *ligulate*. Where it exists it affords a certain index to the posterior side of the shell; as it is the region through which the excretory tubes pass.

Umbones

These are the prominent points of the dorsal edge, where the growth of the shell commenced, and are called beaks, by some English writers. In some instances they are close to each other; in others they are rendered distant from each other by the intervention of areas in the hinge, as in Spondyli, &c. In Pectunculus they are *straight*; in Venus *curved* towards the anterior margin; in Isocardia, *spiral*; in Chama, spirally *decumbent*; in Diceras, *free*. In shells subject to external corrosion, the process commences at the umbones.

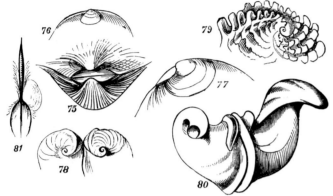

Fig. 75, distant; 76, straight; 77, curved; 78, spiral; 79, decumbent; 80, free; 81, close.

GENERAL CHARACTER OF BIVALVES

When the *breadth* is spoken of, the distance between the most convex parts of both valves, when closed, is intended; but when an expression implying *thickness* is used, it refers to the substance of each valve: it is important to bear this in mind, as many persons have been misled by descriptions in which the distinction has not been attended to. Glycimeris (fig. 67 in the plates) is a *thick* shell, but Anatina (fig. 69 in the plates) is a *broad* one.

Regularity

A great number of Bivalves are extremely regular in their form. Their animals are generally locomotive, and the shells consequently free from those obstructions in growth which occur to stationary shells. The latter, being confined to a particular position, or particular spot, modify their shape according to the substance with which they come in contact, and thus become irregular. This is generally the case with shells which are attached to submarine substances, such as Spondyli, Oysters, &c.; and the degree of irregularity will depend upon the extent of surface involved in the attachment. In the case of fixed shells, the attached valve is usually termed the under valve, and the other which moves freely upon the hinge, is termed the upper valve.

Form and Proportions

Bivalves are said to be *equivalve* when the two valves correspond in extent, breadth, and thickness; and of course *inequivalve* in the contrary case. They are *equilateral* when a line drawn from the umbones to the ventral margin would divide the shell into two nearly equal parts; and of course *inequilateral* in the opposite case, which occurs in the great majority of instances.

A Bivalve is said to be *compressed*, when the distance is small from the most prominent part of one valve to that of the other. It is *cylindrical* when lengthened, and more or less rounded in its breadth, as in Lithodomus (fig. 161 in the plates.) It is *cordiform* when the shape presents a resemblance to an imaginary heart, as in Cardium cardissa (fig. 122 in the plates), and in the Isocardia (fig. 126 in the plates). It is *linguiform* when it resembles a tongue in shape, as in Vulsella (fig. 185 in the plates); *rostrated* when it protrudes at either extremity, and terminates in a kind of point, as in Sanguinolaria Diphos (fig. 99 in the plates); *truncated* when it ends in a square or angle, as if cut off; an example of which may be seen in Solen (fig. 60 in the plates).

Other Bivalves are distinguished as being *auriculated*, or having processes flattened and expanded on either side of the umbones, as in Pecten (cut, fig. 82). When there is one of these on each side of the umbones, it is *bi-auriculated*; when only on one side, it is *uni-auriculated*. When the expansion is very broad, as in Unio alatus (fig. 142 in the plates), and in the Hammer Oyster (cut, fig. 83), the term *alated* is used.

Fig. 82, auriculated; 83, auriculated, alated.

With regard to these alated species of *Uniones*, it is necessary to observe that they are also "*adnate*," as it is termed; the two valves being joined to each other by the dorsal edge of the expanded parts, and united so completely in substance with each other, that they cannot be separated without being broken. Many other terms are used to express differences in Bivalves, but being equally applicable to Univalves and Multivalves, as well as to them, they will be explained at large in the alphabetical part of the work.

MULTIVALVE SHELLS

These are of three different kinds; the first, the "*dorsal*" as they are termed by Linnæus, because they form a ridge in the back of the animal. They are composed of eight pieces, or separate valves, placed in a longitudinal series, being joined to each other by inserted lamina, and named *Articulata* by De Blainville, on that account. The genus Chiton is the only example of this kind of Multivalve.

The second kind, not shells of true Mollusca, M. De Blainville terms the *lateral* bivalves, the pieces being placed in pairs on each side of the animal; these compose the "Pedunculated Cirripedes," or Lepadæ.

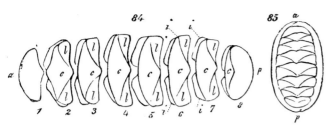

Fig. 84, 85, Chiton. a, anterior; p, posterior; d, dorsal ridge; l l, lateral areas of the valves; c c, central areas; i i, inserted lamina; m, margin.

They differ considerably in the number and arrangement of the valves; the small ones, which are found near the peduncle in some species, are sometimes termed accessary valves; those which form the edge through which the bunch of Cilia protrude, are termed *ventral*, and those on the opposite side *dorsal*. The extremity joining the peduncle is the basal, or anterior; and the upper extremity is the apicial, or posterior.

Fig. 86, Lepas. a, peduncle; b, cavina; c, scutum; d, tergam; e, cirri.

The third kind are termed *coronular* by De Blainville, and compose the order Sessile Cirripedes of Lamarck; they consist of a number of valves placed against each other side by side in a circle, supported on a plate, or tube, or cup, and closed by an operculum composed of two or more valves.

The *basal support* is sometimes thick and flat, sometimes forming an elongated tube, and sometimes hollowed out into a cup. In other species it is altogether wanting. The operculum always consists of more than one piece, generally of two pairs: they are either articulated to each other by serrated edges, and placed against each other conically, as in Balanus, or they lie flat in two pairs against each other. Through the ventral pair the *cirri* protrude.

The *parietal* valves, composing the principal part of the shell, vary in number, form and position. The *anterior* valves are placed on the same side with the cirri; the *posterior*, those on the opposite side; and those which remain between on each side are the lateral valves. In many cases, particularly in Balanus, each valve is separated into the *prominent* and *depressed* areas, and the inserted

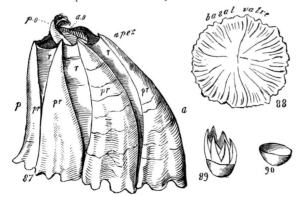

lamina. In some instances, the parietal portion is formed by a single rounded piece.

In the accompanying cut (87), the prominent areas are distinguished by the letters *pr*, and the depressed areas by *r*; the posterior valves of the operculum are marked *p. o.*, and the anterior *a. o.* The basal valve (fig. 88) belongs to a Balanus. Fig. 89 is an Acasta, the cup-shaped base of which is represented at fig. 90.

In the foregoing explanations we have omitted many of those general terms which, relating to external characters, are applicable to shells in almost every division of the system. It may be as well, however, to enumerate a few of them in this place, although they are explained under their respective letters in the alphabetical part of the work.

When bars or ribs, or large striæ are crossed by others radiating from the umbones, shells are said to be *cancellated*, as represented in cut, fig. 91. When there is a series of nodules or spines on the upper part of the whorls, they are *coronated*, as shewn in cut, fig. 92. When a series of projecting parts overlay each other, in the manner of tiles, as in the cut, fig. 93, the word *imbricated* is applied. When characterized by a regular series of ridges, radiating from the apex, they are *pectinated*; the species of Chiton, a single valve of which is represented in cut, fig. 94, has received the specific name of *pectinatus*, in consequence of this character. Shells are said to be *plicated* when characterized by angular bendings or foldings in their surface, as shewn in cut, fig. 95. A remarkable instance of this is seen in the Ostræa Crista-Galli. When the margin of any shell has a series of minute notches, resembling the teeth of a saw, it is said to be *serrated*; when covered with raised points or spines it is *aculeated*; and when striated in both directions, it is *decussated*; when covered with a number of raised rounded points, it is *granulated*; and having a series of these points placed in a row, near or upon the edge, it is *denticulated*, as already explained in reference to the outer lips of

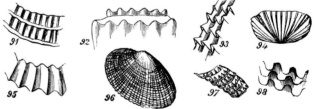

External surface. Fig. 91, cancellated; 92, coronated; 93, imbricated; 94, pectinated; 95, plicated; 96, decussated; 97, muricated; 98, foliated.

Spiral Univalves. When the external surface is rendered uneven by raised knobs, it is said to be *tuberculated*; and if rendered rough and prickly by sharp points it is *muricated*, as in the cut, fig. 97. The term *reticulated* is applied to fine raised lines, crossing each other, and resembling fine net work.

By the foregoing general observations and explanations, it is trusted that the reader will be prepared for the following exposition of the general arrangement of Lamarck, and the principles upon which it is founded.

GENERAL ARRANGEMENT ACCORDING TO LAMARCK

In Lamarck's "Histoire Naturelle des Animaux sans Vertebres," he divides the invertebrata into classes, the 9th, 10th and 11th of which include animals possessed of shells properly so called. These are the Annelides, the Cirripedes, the Conchifera, and the Mollusca.

The class Annelides constitutes the 9th, and is divided into three orders, namely, the "Apodes," "Antennees," and "Sedentaires;" the last of which, the *Sedentaria*, alone contains testaceous animals. This order includes tubular shells, which with the exception of Dentalium, are irregularly twisted, and attached to each other, or to extraneous substances. The first family, *Dorsalia*, contains the genus Siliquaria (plates, fig. 1), known from the Serpulæ, by the slit which passes through the whole length of the shell on the upper surface of the tube. The second family, *Maldania*, has the genus Dentalium (plates, fig. 2), a species of which are commonly known by the name of "tooth shells;" these are regularly formed, curved, conical tubes, open at both extremities. The third family, *Serpulacea*, includes the genera Serpula, Spirorbis, Galeolaria, Vermilia, Spiroglyphus, and Magilus. The only shell that a learner would be likely to place among these incorrectly, according to the system, is the Vermetus (plates, fig. 345), which being regularly spiral at the apicial extremity, has been placed among the Mollusca; to which situation the whole of the shells under consideration have a better title than is generally supposed. It may here be mentioned that the Serpulacea are provided with opercula.

Class Cirripedes

This class constitutes the tenth of invertebrated animals and receives its name from the jointed and ciliated branchia which protrude between the opercular valves. They are Multivalve shells, and were all included in the single genus Lepas in the system of Linnæus, and are commonly known by the name "Barnacles." Lamarck has, however, divided them into two distinct orders. First, the *Sessile* Cirripedes, or those which being composed of several valves, joined to each other, side by side in a circle, are attached to each other, or to submarine bodies by the basal portion of their own substance, and form a hollow, irregular cone, with the aperture above closed by an operculum consisting of two or more valves. Secondly, the *Pedunculated Cirripedes*, which are composed of valves placed in pairs against each other, so as to form a flattened disc attached by means of a tendinous tube called a peduncle. The first of these orders includes the genera Tubicinella, Coronula, Platylepas, Clitia, Conia, Elmineus, Catophragmus, Octomeris, Balanus, Creusia, Nobia, Savignium, Pyrgoma, Adna, Megatréma. The second contains the genera Sepas, Scalpellum, Alepas, Pollicipes, Anelepas, Lithotrya, Ibla, Conchoderma, Dichelaspis.

The study of this class is not properly connected with Conchology. It is now regarded as a sub-class of Crustacea.

Class Conchifera

The shell of a conchiferous animal is always bivalve, composed of two pieces placed opposite to each other, joined at the dorsal margins by an elastic hinge. All true bivalve shells belong to animals of this class; and the correspondence between the shell and the animal is so true that on examining an empty bivalve shell we can not only determine that its inhabitant belonged to this class, but also decide on the particular order and family in which it should be placed, without seeing the soft parts.

The first general division of Conchifera is that which results from observing the muscular impressions, or marks made on the inner surface of the valve by the insertion of the adductor muscles. All Conchifera are divided into two orders, as follows:

First Order, *Conchifera Dimyaria*

Having two adductor muscles, and consequently two impressions in each valve. They are separated into the following families:

1. *Tubicolæ* (plates, fig. 44 to 54), having shelly tubes besides the valves. This family contains the genera Aspergillum, Clavagella, Teredina, Teredo, Xylophaga, Fistulana, and Gastrochæna.

2. *Pholadaria* (plates, fig. 55 to 59), cylindrical, living in holes in rocks pierced by animals. Lamarck places in this family the genera Pholas and Gastrochæna, the last of which belongs more properly to the family Tubicolæ, as placed above.

3. *Solenaceæ* (plates, fig. 60 to 68), longitudinally (transversely, Lam.) elongated, open at the anterior and posterior extremities. This family contains the genera Solen, Pholadomya, Panopæa, Glycimeris, (Solecurtus) and Solenimya.

4. *Myaria* (plates, fig. 69 to 76), ligament internal. A spoon-shaped ligamentary pit in one or both valves. Shell generally gaping at one or both extremities. This family includes the genera Anatina, Mya, Anatinella, Kelladiæ, Lyonsia, Myochama, Cleidotherus.

5. *Matracea* (plates, fig. 77 to 88), the cartilage placed in a trigonal pit, with a small external ligament. The genera Lutraria, Mactra, Crassatella, Erycina, Ungulina, Amphidesma, and Solenimya belong to this family, the last of which ought to have been placed among the Solenacea, as above.

6. *Corbulacea* (plates, fig. 89, 90), inequivalve, with an internal ligament resembling the Mactracea, but differing in having one valve deeper than the other, although regular shells. This small family contains only the genera Corbula and Pandora.

7. *Lithophagidæ* (plates, fig. 91 to 97), irregular, terebrating, living in holes of rocks. The genera are Saxicava, Petricola, and Vencrirupis.

8. *Nymphacea* (plates, fig. 98 to 110), ligament external, generally placed upon a prominent fulcrum, which passes from the inside to the outside of the hinge; valves generally gaping at the extremities. This family contains the genera Sanguinolaria, Psammobia, Psammotæa, Tellinides, Corbis, Lucina, Donax, Capsa, and Crassina.

9. *Conchacea* (plates, fig. 111 to 121), regular, having several cardinal teeth and sometimes lateral teeth. The Conchacea constitute one of the most beautiful and numerous families of the class; they present equivalve shells, which are always regular, unattached, and in general closed, especially at the sides; they are always more or less inequilateral. They are divided into the *fluviatile* and *marine Conchacea*, the first containing the genera Cyclas, Cyrena, and Galathæa, found in rivers; and the second, Cyprina, Cytherea, Venus, and Venericardia.

10. *Cardiacea* (plates, fig. 122 to 130). This family, which resembles the last in some general characters, are also regular and equivalve, and are generally provided with radiating ribs, which are seldom seen in the Conchacea. The genera enumerated in this family are Cardium, Cardita, Cypricardia, Hiatella, and Isocardia.

11. *Arcacea* (plates, fig. 131 to 138). These are known by having a row of numerous small teeth on the cardinal hinge in each valve. The genera included are, Cucullæa, Arca, Pectunculus, Nucula.

12. *Trigonacea* (plates, fig. 139 and 140). It is doubtful whether this family should remain distinct. As of the two genera placed in it, the first Trigonia, is thought by some naturalists to have strong affinities with Nucula, in the family of Arcacea; and the latter, Castalia, certainly belongs to the Nayades.

13. *Nayades* (plates, fig. 141 to 152). These are fresh water shells, covered on the outside by a thick horny epidermis, and pearly within. They include the genera Unio, Hyria, Anodon, Iridina.

14. *Chamacea* (plates, fig. 153 to 155), inequivalve, irregular, foliaceous, attached; containing the genera Diceras, Chama and Etheria.

Second Order, *Conchiferra Monomyaria*

Having one adductor muscle, and therefore only one impression in each valve. They are separated into the following families:

1. *Tridacnacea* (plates, fig. 156 & 157), transverse, equivalve, with an elongated muscular impression, near the centre of the ventral margin; margin undulated at the termination of the radiated large ribs. The genera Tridacna and Hippopus are included.

2. *Mytilacea* (plates, fig. 158 to 162), generally regular, with the hinge linear, without teeth, occupying the greater part of the dorsal margin. This family includes the genera Modiola, Mytilus, Pinna.

3. *Malleacea* (plates, fig. 163 to 170), shell generally thin, inequivalve, irregular, foliaceous, with the hinge linear. This family contains the genera Crenatula, Perna, Malleus, Avicula, Meleagrina.

4. *Pectinides* (plates, fig. 171 to 178). The pectinides are generally regular or nearly so, with the shell solid; the greater part of them are auriculated at the dorsal margin, and generally characterized by ribs radiating from the umbones. The genera are Pedum, Lima, Plagiostoma, Pecten, Plicatula, Spondylus, Podopsis.

5. *Ostracea* (plates, fig. 180 to 192). The shells of this family are irregular, generally attached and foliaceous. They compose the genera Gryphæa, Ostræa, Vulsella, Placuna, Anomia.

6. *Rudistes* (plates 193 to 200). This family is composed of a particular association of shells, which appear on one side to be connected with the Ostracea; and on the other to approach the Brachiopoda. They differ from Ostracea in having no hinge or ligament, and only resemble them in their irregularity and foliaceous structure. The following six genera are placed by Lamarck in this family:—Sphærulites, Radiolites, Calceola, Birostrites, Discina, Crania. Of these, Calceola, Discina, and Crania are shewn to belong to the Brachiopoda.

7. *Brachiopoda* (plates, fig. 201 to 219). The shells of this family are inequivalve, equilateral, and attached to marine bodies by a tendon passing through one of the valves. The animals have, near their mouth, two elongated, ciliated arms, which are spirally rolled when at rest. The following genera are enumerated by Lamarck, Orbicula, Terebratula, Lingula.

MOLLUSCA

Lamarck applies, or rather restricts, this name to those invertebrated animals, which while they are inarticulate in all their parts, have the head sufficiently advanced at the anterior part of the body to be distinguished; which is not the case with the Conchifera. All the shells are univalve, and are divided into six orders, namely, the PTEROPODA, which have wing-shaped natatory organs or fins, and have *light, thin transparent, nearly symmetrical* shells; the GASTEROPODA, with the foot not distinguishable from the rest of the body, have *patelliform, open* and *scarcely spiral* shells; the TRACHELIPODA with the foot distinct and attached to the neck of the animal, have *spiral, non-symmetrical* shells. The CEPHALOPODA, with arms covered by suckers, surrounding the head of the animal, have generally *symmetrical convolute* shells. The Cephalopoda are divided into C. *polythalamia*, which have the internal cavity divided into chambers by septa, as in the Nautilus; and the C. *Monothalamia*, which are not so divided, as the Argonauta. The order *Heteropoda* contains the genus Carinaria alone.

Order *Pteropoda*

This order, containing hyaline, symmetrical, non-spiral shells, as above described, is not divided into families, but contains the following genera, Hyalæa, Cleodora, Limacina, Cymbulia; the first of which, although composed of a single piece, resembles a bivalve so nearly, that Linnæus actually placed it in his genus Anomia.

Order *Gasteropoda*

With the exception of the genus Bulla and Vitrina, the last of which forms a passage into the next order, the shells contained in this order are *patelliform, open, and scarcely spiral.* They are divided into the following families:

1. *Phyllidiana* (plates, fig. 227 to 231), containing the genera Chiton, Chitonellus, and Patella, the two former of which present the only exception to the statement above made, that all the shells of Mollusca were univalve.

2. *Semiphyllidiana* (plates, fig. 232 and 233). Of the two genera contained in this family, Pleurobranchus is broad, thin, and slightly spiral at the apex, and Umbrella is flat, circular, with a central apex.

3. *Calyptracea* (plates, fig. 234 to 246). The patelliform shells of this family, although united by no other general characters, are brought together by the characters of the animals which produce them. The genera are Parmophorus, Emarginula, Siphonaria, Fissurella, Pileopsis, Calyptræa, Crepidula, Ancylus.

4. *Bulleana* (plates, fig. 247 to 258), contains the genera Bulla and Bullæa.

5. *Aplysiacea* (plates, fig. 254 and 255). The genera Aplysia and Dolabella are both expanded, somewhat flattened shells, with the apex placed at one extremity, and slightly spiral.

6. *Limacinea* (fig. 256 to 263). Many of the animals (slugs) are without shells; some, as the Limax, or common garden slug, have a slightly developed calcareous piece, hidden beneath the mantle, and of others the shells are scarcely spiral. The genera included in this family are, Parmacella, Limax, Testacella, Vitrina.

Order *Trachelipoda*

All the remaining spiral non-symmetrical shells are arranged in this order, which is divided into the following families:

1. *Colimacea* (plates, fig. 264 to 307). With the exception of the few contained in the family of Limacina, which ought not to be separated from this order, the whole of the land-shells are contained in this family, and although it is difficult to notice any one character by which terrestrial shells may be distinguished from others, few at all conversant with the subject are liable to mistake them. There is a general lightness and simplicity of form, which, though not clearly definable, is generally understood. The following distribution of genera by Lamarck, is generally acknowledged to require numerous modifications; the genera are Helix, Carocolla, Anostoma, Helicina, Pupa, Clausilia, Bulinus, Achatina, Succinea, Auricula, Cyclostoma.

2. *Lymneana* (plates, fig. 308 to 312). The shells of this family are found in fresh water, wells, ditches, and ponds. They are of a light horny structure, and simple form. The genera Planorbis, Physa, and Lymnea are placed in this family by Lamarck.

3. *Melaniana* (plates, fig. 313 to 317). These are also found in fresh water, principally in rivers; they are thicker than those of the last family; and the greater part of them have elevated spires composed of numerous whorls. This family contains the genera Melania, Melanopsis, Pirena.

4. *Peristomata* (plates, fig. 318 to 322). These are also fresh-water shells, having opercula, and covered by a smooth green, or greenish-brown epidermis. They differ from the last family in having the peritreme entire. The genera are Valvata, Paludina, and Ampullaria.

5. *Neritacea* (plates, fig. 323 to 333). The peculiarity of the shells of this family consist in the inner lip being flattened and rather straight at the inner edge. The genera are Navicella, Neritina, Nerita, Natica, and Janthina, the last of which forms an exception to the general character, and is placed by De Blainville in a family by itself.

6. *Macrostomata* (plates, fig. 334 to 341), so named, on account of the large open aperture which they present in comparison to the spire. The shells of this family, which contains the genera Stomatia, Stomatella, and Haliotis, are pearly within.

7. *Plicacea* (plates, fig. 342 to 344), contains the genera Tornatella and Pyramidella.

8. *Scalariana* (plates, fig. 345 to 352). The genera Vermetus, Scalaria and Delphinula, seem to have been placed in this family, by Lamarck, on account of the whorls being distinct from each other.

9. *Turbinacea* (plates, 353 to 371). The shells contained in this family are all more or less globose, or angular, thickened and pearly within. The following genera are included in this division by Lamarck, Solarium, Rotella, Trochus, Monodonta, Turbo, Planaxis, Phasianella, and Turritella.

10. *Canalifera* (plates, fig. 372 to 401). The numerous genera of which this family is formed, namely, Cerithium, Pleurotoma, Turbinella, Cancellaria, Fasciolaria, Fusus, Pyrula, Ranella, Murex, Triton, are distinguished by having at the anterior termination of the aperture, a more or less elongated canal.

11. *Alatæ* (plates, fig. 402 to 406). These are known by having the outer lip more or less expanded and generally a posterior canal leaning towards the spire. The genera are Rostellaria, Strombus, and Pteroceras.

12. *Purpurifera* (plates, fig. 407 to 429). In these, the canal, if such it may be called, is extremely short, and turning abruptly backwards, produces a kind of varix at the lower part of the whorl. The genera enumerated in this family are Cassidaria,

Cassis, Ricinula, Purpura, Monoceras, Concholepas, Harpa, Dolium, Buccinum, Eburna, Terebra.

13. *Columellata* (plates, fig. 430 to 433). The shells of this family are emarginated at the anterior extremity of the aperture, and the inner lip is characterized by plates or folds, which with the exception of those on Columbella are distinct. The genera are Mitra, Voluta, Marginella, Volvaria, Columbella, the latter of which would be better placed among the Purpurifera.

14. *Convolutæ* (plates, fig. 444 to 462). The well-known shells contained in this family are distinguished for the small proportion of the spire, if any, which remains uncovered by the last whorl. They might be well divided into two groups, the first containing the genera Ovulum and Cypræa, under the name of Cypræadæ, which are truly convolute, having the spire entirely hidden; and the second containing the genera Oliva, Ancillaria, and Conus.

Order *Polythalamous, or Chambered Cephalopoda*

The greater part of the shells belonging to this order are symmetrical, and the internal cavity is divided into separate compartments, by plates called *Septa*. It is divided into the following families:

1. *Orthocerata* (plates, fig. 463 to 470), containing the genera Belemnites, Orthoceras, Nodosaria, Hippurites, And Conilites. Hippurites certainly has no affinity with the Cephalopoda, but is ascertained to be a bivalve shell, properly belonging to the family Rudistes; the other genera are straight, elongated, and conical.

2. *Lituacea* (plates, fig. 471), containing the genera Spirula, Spirulina, and Lituola, the two latter of which are microscopic.

3. *Cristacea, containing the microscopic genera Renulina, Orbiculina, and Cristellaria.*

4. *Spherulacea*, containing the microscopic genera Miliola, Gyrogona, and Melonia.

5. *Radiolacea*, containing the microscopic genera Rotalites, Lenticulina, Placentula.

6. *Nautilacea* (plates, fig. 472 to 476). This family contains the following genera—Discorbites, Siderolites, Polystomella, Vorticialis, Nummulites, and Nautilus; the two latter of which alone are now received in cabinets of shells, the four former belonging to that class of microscopic fossils, now termed Foraminifera; the genus Nummulites, although large, may probably belong to the same class, and perhaps it would have been better to have included the remaining genus, Nautilus, in the next family, from which it differs in having the septa which divided the chambers simple at their edges.

7. *Ammonacea* (plates, fig. 477 to 484). The edges of the septa of these are all more or less sinuous and complicated. This family contains the following genera, Ammonites, Ammonoceras, Baculites, and Turrilites, the latter of which presents a singular anomaly in having an oblique spire, like that of the order Trachelipoda, while it is divided into chambers by sinuous septa.

Order *Monothalamous Cephalopoda*

The only shells included in this order belong to the genera Argonauta (plates, fig. 485), placed here by Lamarck, and Bellerophon (plates, fig. 486 and 487), a fossil genus subsequently added.

Order *Heteropoda*

The singular and beautiful transparent shell contained in this order, under the generic name Carinaria, forms a covering to a small portion of an animal, equally remarkable and equally distinct from those of all other orders.

The above arrangement, although far from perfect and requiring numerous modifications, is perhaps liable to as few objections as any other yet proposed, and will certainly be more easily understood by those who have not the opportunity of studying the soft parts of the animal.

CONCHOLOGICAL MANUAL

ABIDA. Leach, 1819. A genus founded on a species of PUPA, which has the peristome slightly reflected, and numerous plaits in the aperture. Pupa Juniperi, Pupa secale, *Draparnaud*. Great Britain; also Central and Southern Europe.

ABRA. Leach, 1817. *Fam.* Mactracea. A genus composed of AMPHI-DESMA tenue, *Lamarck*, prismaticum, and other small thin species. British Channel and Mediterranean. Pl. xxiv. f. 496.

ABSIA. Leach. LITHOTRYA, Sowerby. *Fam.* Pedunculated Cirripedes.

ACAMAS. Montfort. BELEMNITES multiforatus, Blainville. A species described as being perforated at the apex, by a stellated perforation. No species of Belemnite at present known agreeing with the description; it is supposed to have been taken from a broken specimen.

ACANTHIZA. Fischer. Monoceras, *Lamarck*.

ACANTHOCHETES. Leach, 1819. A name given to Chitones, having bunches of bristles at the sides of the valves. Ex. Ch. fascicularis, Pl. xxiv. fig. 506.

ACANTHOPLEURA. Guilding, 1835. A generic name given to species of Chiton having bristles on the margin. Ex. Ch. spinosus, f. 227.

ACARDO. Lam. 1801. Umbrella. Lam. 1812.

ACARDO. Commerçon. Described from a pair of bony plates, taken from the vertebræ of the Whale, and mistaken for a bivalve shell, destitute of a hinge.

ACARDO. Swainson. See APHRODITE, Lea. C. Greenlandicum, Pl. vi, fig. 123*.

ACASTA. Leach. *Order*, Sessile Cirripedes, *Lamarck*. BALANUS *Monta-gui*, Sowerby. A small genus separated from Balanus, on account of the cup-shaped base, but re-united by Sowerby, who shews, in his Genera of Shells, that this is a merely accidental circumstance, resulting from the situations in which the shells acquire their growth. If, for instance, the Balanus be attached to a flat surface, in an open situation, the base will be short and flat; if it be placed in a hollow among other growing substances, it will be lengthened out in order that the aperture of the shell may be even with the outer surface of the surrounding mass; and if, as in the Acastæ, it be imbedded in a soft and loose substance, the base, being left to itself, will take a regular form. The Acastæ are found imbedded in sponges. Also found in the Pacific ocean and Philippines. *Ex.* Balanus Montagui, of Great Britain, Pl. i. fig. 26.

ACAVUS. Montfort, 1810. *Fam.* Limacinea, Blainville; Colimacea, Lamarck. A division of the genus Helix, which may be considered synonymous with De Ferrusac's sub-genus Helicogena. De Montfort has given H. Hæmastoma, as an example. Plate xiii. fig. 267.

ACCESSARY VALVES, are the smaller or less important testaceous plates, found on the hinge or dorsal margins of the true valves of some shells. Example, the small plates on the hinge of Pholas, fig. 55, *a*. The Pholades were placed by Linnæus and Bruguière among multivalve shells.

ACEPHALOPHORA. Blainville (*a*, without; κεφαλε, head.) The third class of the type Malacozoaria, Bl. including all bivalve shells, the animals of which have no distinct head. This class corresponds with the Conchifera of Lamarck, and is divided into the orders Palliobranchiata, Rudistes, Lamellibranchiata, and Heterobranchiata, the last of which contains no genera of testaceous Mollusca.

ACHATINA. Auctorum. *Fam.* Colimacea, Lam. (from Achates, an agate.) *Fam.* Limacineæ, Bl. *Gen.* POLYPHEMUS, Montf.—*Descr.* Shell oval or oblong, sub-turrited, light, thin; aperture oval, or pyriform; outer lip sharp; columella smooth, tortuous, truncated, so as to form a notch at its union with the outer lip.—*Obs.* It is from this notch that we are enabled to distinguish Achatinæ from Bulini, which, moreover, generally have a reflected outer lip. The Polyphemi of Montfort have an undulation in the centre of the outer lip. Achatina Virginea, fig. 286. Polyphemus Glans, fig. 288. These land shells are found in various parts of the globe, but attain the greatest size and richness of colouring in tropical climates; particularly in the West India Islands. Mr. Reeve's monograph contains 129 species. Subulina, f. 514, has an elongated spire, it is otherwise an Achatina. Pl.

ACHATINELLA. Swainson, 1828. A genus of shells, differing from Achatina in having the inner edge of the outer lip thickened, and a slight groove near the suture of the spire. Reeve's monograph contains 45 species. Fig. 287.

ACHELOIS. Montf. CONILITES Achelois. Knorr. Supp. T.4. fig. 1.

ACICULA. Risso, 1826. ACHATINA Acicula, Auct. CIONELLA, Jeffreys.

ACIONA. Leach, 1815. SCALARIA, Lamarck, 1801.

ACMÆA. Pattelloidea, Gray. Lottia, Gray.

ACME. Hartmann. A genus formed of TURBO fuscus, Walker. AURICU-LA lineata, Drap. thus described—"Shell sub-cylindrical, with a blunt tip; mouth ovate, simple, thin, slightly reflected over the pillar, forming a slight perforation." The animal is said to resemble a Cyclostoma, but has no operculum. Auricula lineata, Drap. Hist. 57, t.3, fig. 20, 21. Southern Europe.

ACTEON. Montf. TORNATELLA, Lam.

ACTINOCAMAX. Stokes. A genus of Belemnitiform Fossils.

ACULEATED. Beset with sharp spines, as the margin of Chiton aculeatus, fig. 227.

ACUMINATED. Terminating in a point, as the apex of Melania subulata, fig. 313.

ACUS. Humphrey. TEREBRA of Lamarck.

ACUTE. Sharp, pointed, or sharp-edged.

ADDUCTOR MUSCLE. That which draws the two valves of a shell together, and leaves a mark on the inner surface of each, called the MUSCULAR IMPRESSION.

ADELOSINA. D'Orb. A genus of microscopic Foraminifera.

ADEORBIS. Wood. A genus of Trochæform shells, approaching Delphinula, and represented by Ad. subcarinata. Pl. xxviii. f. 588.

ADESMACEA. Bl. (*a*, without; Δεσμα, *desma*, ligament.) The 10th family of the order *Lamellibranchiata*, Bl. composed of Mollusca which either bore tubular dwellings in rocks, wood, &c. or live in testaceous tubes, their shells being consequently destitute of the hinge ligament. The action of opening and shutting the valves being limited to the narrow space to which they are confined, or else the valves themselves being soldered into the tube, renders it unnecessary for them to have a ligament to keep them in their places. The genera Pholas, Teredina, Fistulana, and Septaria, belong to this family, which corresponds in part with the families Tubicolaria and Pholadaria, of Lamarck.

ADNA. Leach. One of the genera separated by Leach from *Pyrgoma*, and characterized as consisting of an upper valve, supported on a funnel-shaped base, which is not buried in the coral to which it is attached, Like Pyrgoma, but is seen externally. The operculum consists of four valves. British Channel and Mediterranean. Adna Anglicum, Pl. i. fig. 2.

ADNATE. A term applied by some authors to those shells belonging to the family of Unionidæ, which have the valves joined together at the dorsal margin, not like other bivalves, by a distinct ligament, but by the substance of the shell itself, the valves appearing to grow together in such a manner that they cannot be separated without one of them being broken, as will be seen in our figure of Dipsas plicatus, fig. 142. This circumstance has been made the foundation of specific and even generic distinctions, for which however it is insufficient, because many species which when young are "adnate," when fully grown have their valves joined together only by a ligament.

ÆGLIA. Say. A division of "Unionidæ," described as having the "shell cuneate; bosses prominent; cardinal teeth much compressed, placed on one side of the bosses. Æglia ovata, *Say.* Occidens *Lea.* Am. Tr. iii. pl. 10." Lardner's Encyclopedia of Malacology.

AGANIDES. Montf. ORBULITES. Lam. Pl. xxiii. f. 479*.

AGAROMA. Gray, 1839. A genus of shells, of which Voluta hiatula is the type.

AGATHIRSES. Montf. SILIQUARIA, Auct.

AGINA. Turton, 1822. Corbula, Brug. 1792.

AKERA. Bl. The fourth family of the order Monopleurobranchiata, Bl. containing the genera Bulla, Bullæa and Bellerophon, which, excepting the last, constitutes the family Bullæana, Lam.

AKERA. Müller. A genus of extremely light horny shells, belonging to the family of Bullidæ. Six species are described in Mr. Adams' Monongraph, No. 11. Sowerby's Thesaurus. *Ex.* Bulla Hanleyi, f. 247.

ALÆA. Jeffreys. A genus of minute land shells, resembling *Vertigo*, but separated because they are dextral, while Vertigo is sinistral. A. marginata, Pupa marginata, Drap. found in marshy ground, roots of trees, moss &c. Britain and Southern and Central Europe. Pl. xiv. f. 292.

ALASMODON. Say. MARGARITUM. *Ex.* A. complanatus, pl. vii. fig. 141. Schum.

ALATÆ. Lam. A family of the order Trachelipoda, Lam. containing the following genera, which may be thus distinguished:

1. ROSTELLARIA. Sinus close to the canal; including *Hippochrenes, and Aporrhais*. Fig. 402 to 404.

2. STROMBUS. Sinus not close to the canal. Fig. 406.

3. PTEROCERAS. Same, digitated. Fig. 405.

ALATED. (From Ala, a wing.) Winged, a term applied to shells when any portion of them is spread out in any direction, as in fig. 403. Hippochrenes, Montf. and fig. 147, Unio Alatus.

ALATUS. Humphrey. STROMBUS, Auct.

ALCADIA. Gray? (B. M. Syn. p. 134.) Helicinæ which have a notch in the aperture. A distinction which it is impossible to maintain. See HELICINA.

ALCADIA. Gray. Helicina major, &c. Species with a notch, Pl. xiv. fig. 306, 307.

ALECTRION. Montf. BUCCINUM Papillosum, Auct. fig. 422.

ALEPAS. Rang. A genus of Pedunculated Cirripedes, either without any shell, or with a scarcely visible valve on each side near the orifice.

ALVANIA. Leach, M.S. Risso, 1818. A very imperfectly described genus, founded on a single species in the British Museum collection, labelled by Leach, A. globella. We figure the Cray fossil, A. ascaris. Pl. xxviii. fig. 586.

ALVEOLINA. D'Orbigny. A genus of microscopic Foraminifera.

AMALTHŒA. Schumacher, 1817. A generic name given to the small flattish species of Capulus.

AMALTHUS. Montf. A. margaritaceus, Montf. is a species of AMMONITES, described as a very flat, keeled, with an angular aperture. It belongs to the family Ammonacea, Lam.

AMATHINA. Gray, Syn. 1840. Pileopsis, or Capulus tricarinatus.

AMARULA————? A genus composed of MELANIA Amarula, Auct. and similar species.

AMBIGUÆ. Lam. The fourth section of the order Conchifera Dimyaria, containing the family Chamacea, fig. 153 to 155.

AMICULA. Gray, 1842. A genus formed for the reception of CHITON vestitus, the valves of which are covered by an integument; so as to be almost hidden externally. Pl. xxiv. fig. 507.

AMIMONUS. Montf. CONILITES ungulatus, Knorr. A species distinguished only by being slightly curved; *Fam.* Orthocerata, Lam.

AMMONACEA. Bl. The fourth family of the order Polythalamia, Bl. or chambered shells, described as thin, chambered, discoidal, convolute, symmetrical, generally compressed, with visible whorls. This last character is used in De Blainville' System to distinguish the Ammonacea from the Nautilacea. This family contains the genera Discorbites, Scaphites, Ammonites, and Simplegas.

AMMONACEA. Lam. The seventh family of Polythalamous Cephalopoda. Lam. containing the genera Ammonites, Orbulites, Ammonoceras, Turrilites, and Baculites, to which may be added Amalthus, Simplegas, Ellipsolites, Nautellipsites, Hamites, Icthyosarcolites, and other genera mentioned in the list of figures 477 to 484.

AMMONITES. Auct. (from Jupiter Ammon.) *Fam.* Ammonacea, Lam. and Bl.—*Descr.* Symmetrical, convolute, discoidal, orbicular; chambers numerous, divided by lobated, branched, or sinuous septa, perforated by a siphon; aperture generally more or less modified by the last whorl. The fossils of the secondary strata which compose this genus are numerous and well known: they are vulgarly termed "snake-stones", and some of them are extremely beautiful, particularly when the external structure is exhibited by a section. There is some difficulty in distinguishing them from the Fossil Nautili, for although the whorls, being visible, and the septa *sinuous*, may be taken as the characteristics of the Ammonites, yet there are several species which partake the characters of both. The Orbulites of Lamarck (fig. 479) for instance, have sinuous septa like Ammonites, but the last whorl covers those which precede it as in Nautilus. Simplegas Montf. and Bl. (fig. 475) has the whorls visible externally, and the septa simple. Ammonites is figured in the plates—Pl. xxii. fig. 478.

AMMONOCERAS, or AMMONOCERATITES. } Lam. (from *Ammon* & Κερας, ceras, horn.) The shells described under this Lamarckian genus present an anomaly which is considered by Mr. G. B. Sowerby, sen., as merely accidental. They resemble the Ammonites in internal structure, but instead of being spirally convolute, they are merely curved like a horn. *Ex.* (copied from De Blainville) Pl. xxii. fig. 477.

AMPHIBOLA. Schum. 1817? A genus formed for the shell usually named Ampullaria avellana, fig. 538.

AMPHIBULIMA. Lam. 1812. Succinea Patula, Auct. (fig. 266) was first published in the Ann. du Mus. D'Hist. Nat. under the name Amphibulima cucullata. The generic name was afterwards abandoned by its author, and the species stands in his system as Succinea cucullata. West Indies. Pl. xiii. fig. 266.

AMPHICERAS. Gronovius, 1781. Ovula, Bruguière; Ovulum, Sowerby.

AMPHIDESMA. Lam. (from Αμφω, *ampho, ambo,* Δεσμος, *desmos, ligamentum*). *Fam* Mactracea, Lam.—*Descr.* Equivalve, oval or rounded, sub-equilateral, sometimes rather gaping at the sides, with slight posterior fold; hinge with one or two cardinal teeth in each valve, and two elongated lateral teeth, distinct in one valve, nearly obsolete in the other; ligament short, separated from the cartilage, which is elongated and couched obliquely in an excavation of the hinge.—*Obs.* In most bivalve shells, the cartilage and ligament are united in one mass, or placed close to each other; the contrary in this case gives rise to the name, which signifies *double ligament*. This circumstance distinguishes the genus Amphidesma from Tellina, which in other respects it greatly resembles. From Lutraria it may be known by its distinct lateral teeth, and also by its valves being nearly close all round, while the Lutrariæ gape anteriorly. The species do not appear to be numerous; no fossil species are known. A. *Reticulatum*, fig. 85. West India Islands, Brazil, Coast of the Pacific, &c. Pl. iv. fig. 85; Pl. xxiv. fig. 495.

AMPHIPEPLEA. Nilson, 1822. The type of this proposed genus is Limnea glutinosa, Auct. Gray's edition of Turton, page 243, Pl. ix. fig. 103. The shell is polished, and the inner lip expanded.

AMPHISTEGINA. D'Orb. A genus of microscopic Foraminifera.

AMPLEXUS. J. Sowerby. A. *Corralloides*, fig. 463. A singularly formed fossil, described as nearly cylindrical, divided into chambers by numerous transverse septa, which embrace each other with reflected margins. It occurs in the Dublin limestone, and resembles a coral or madrepore. Pl. xxi. fig. 463.

AMPLEXUS. A generic name proposed by Captain Brown for Helix pulchella. Drap. 112, tab. 107–134; and other similar species. Zurama, Leach.

AMPULLARIA. Lamarck, 1801. (*Ampulla*, a rounded vessel.) *Fam.* "Peristomiens," Lam. Ellipsostomata, Bl.—*Descr.* Spiral, globular, sometimes discoidal, frequently umbilicated, covered with a rounded, horny epidermis; spire short; whorls rapidly enlarging; aperture elliptical, rounded anteriorly; peristome nearly or quite entire, thickened, and slightly reflected; operculum, testaceous, annular, with a sub-central nucleus.—*Obs.* This genus of fresh-water shells of which a few fossil species occur, is easily distinguished from other genera by obvious characters, particularly by a thick, horny, greenish-brown

epidermis, and the rotundity in form. One species (fig. 320) the A. Cornu-arietis, (*Genus*, Marisa, Gray), which forms the type of Lamarck's genus Planorbis, requires notice on account of its flatness, but may be known by the aperture which in the Ampullaria is longer than wide, and in Planorbis the contrary. Lanistes, Montf. is described from a *reversed* species of Ampullaria, fig. 319. The Ampullaria is vulgarly called the Idol Shell, and is said to be held in high veneration by the South American savages. The animal has a large bag, opening beneath, placed on the side of the respiratory cavity. It is supposed that the animal has the power of filling this bag with water, and that it is thus enabled to live a long time out of water. Ampullariæ have been brought as far as from Egypt to Paris *alive*, packed in sawdust. East and West Indies, North Africa, South America, &c. Pl. xiv. fig. 318.

AMPULLINA. Blainville, 1825. Part of the genus Helicina, Auct.

AMUSIUM. Megerle, 1811. A generic name for species of Pecten, which are flat and smooth outside. Pecten Pleuronectes.

ANALOGOUS. A term applied to certain species of fossil shells, which present a certain degree of resemblance to recent species; but which are not sufficiently similar to warrant the use of the term "identical," or any other implying that they are of the same species.

ANASTOMA or ANOSTOMA. Fischer. (from Ανα, *ana,* backwards; Στομα, *stoma,* mouth) *Fam.* Colimacea, Lamarck. A genus of land shells so named from the singular circumstance of the last whorl taking a sudden turn and throwing the mouth upwards; so as to present it on the same plane with the spire; the animal walking with the spire of the shell downwards resting on the foot. In other respects, these shells resemble other Helices; and belong to De Ferrusac's division "Helicodonta." *Tomogerus* is the earlier, and therefore, correct name for this genus. *T. depressum* is represented in figs. 271, 272. The nearest approach to this genus will be found in the fossil shell named Ferrusina by Grateloup, Strophostoma by Deshayes, which however, has no teeth in the aperture and is provided with an operculum like Cyclostoma. South America. Pl. xiii. figs. 271, 272.

ANATIFER. Brug. Anatifa, Lam. This name, which signifies Duck-bearing, has been given to the shells commonly called Barnacles, on account of an absurd notion entertained among the ancients, that they inclose the young of the Barnacle duck, in an embryo state. The beautiful bunch of jointed arms, the ciliæ of which serve the purpose of agitating the water, so as to draw in food by the current, were supposed to be the feathers of the future bird. For a description of these shells, see Pentelasmis; and fig. 34.

ANATINA. Lam. (*That which belongs to a duck*) *Fam.* Myaria, Lam. Pyloridea, Bl.—*Descr.* Thin, transparent, generally equivalve, inequilateral, transverse, marine; hinge with a spoon-shaped process in each valve, containing the cartilage.—*Obs.* Some species included in the genus Anatina of authors, A. striata, for instance, have not the spoon-shaped prominence, but in its place a small, testaceous, moving appendage, connected with the interior of the hinge. These are now separated, and form the genus Lyonsia. The genus Næara, Gray, is composed of Anatina longirostrum, and similar species, which have not the bony appendage, while the spoon-shaped prominence is small, and only found in one valve. Mya is distinguished from Anatina, by the thickness of the shell, and also by having the prominence only in the hinge of one valve. Pl. iii. fig. 69.

ANATINELLA. G. B. Sowerby. (1835). (Diminution of *Anatina*.) A genus so named from its resemblance to Anatina, from which it differs in being destitute of the internal appendage, and having no sinus in the palleal impression. *Ex.* Anatinella Sibbaldii, fig. 70.

ANATOMUS. Montf. Tom. 2, plate 279. A microscopic shell, apearing, from the figure, to resemble SCISSURELLA.

ANAULAX. Roissy? ANCILLA, Lamarck.

ANCILLA. Lam. (1801.) ANCILLARIA. Lam (1822.) (*A handmaid.*) *Fam.* convolutæ, Lam. Angyostomata, Bl.—*Descr.* Smooth, oblong, subcylindrical. Spire short, sutures hidden by enamel. Aperture long, anteriorly emarginated and somewhat effuse. Columella tortuous, oblique, tumid, truncated.—*Obs.* The Ancillariæ are pretty shining shells, enveloped almost entirely by the soft parts of the animal. They resemble Oliva, from which they are distinguished by the suture of the spire being filled up with shelly enamel, nearly covering the surface. The whorls in Oliva being separated by a distinct canal. Ancillaria may be known from Terebellum by the tumid varix at the base of the columella. The well known Ivory shell, Eburna glabrata, *Lam.* must retain its name, and be removed, with several congeners from this genus. The recent species are found in the Islands of the Indian Ocean and Australian Seas. Eburna glabrata is represented in the plates fig. 455; Ancillaria cinnamonea, fig. 456.

ANCULOTUS. Say, 1825. *Fam.* Melaniana, Lam. Ellipsostomata, Bl. A genus proposed to include some fresh-water shells resembling those of the genus Melania, the differences between them being that the spire of Anculosa is more depressed, and the anterior of the outer lip more angulated than in Melania. On an examination of the different species, however, it will be found that this is quite unsatisfactory, as a generic distinction; because the same species which have short flattened spires, do not always have angulated apertures. An example of each from N. America is represented, Pl. xiv. fig. 314.

ANCYLUS. Geoffroy, 1767. *Fam.* Calyptracea, Lam. Otides, Bl.—*Descr.* Thin, obliquely conical, patelliform; apex acute, turned sidewise and backwards; aperture oval; margin simple.—*Obs.* Although the little fresh-water shells described under this name, resemble those of the genus Patella, the animals which produce them are nearly allied to Lymnea. And, it may also be observed, that the shells themselves differ from Patella in not being quite symmetrical, having the apex turned on one side. A. fluviatilis, Pl. xiii. fig. 246. Pl. xxiv. figs. 510, 511.

ANDROMEDES. Montf. VORTICIALIS, Dam. *Fam.* Nautilacea, Lam. A genus of microscopic Foraminifera.

ANELASMA. Darwin. Cirrip. P. 169. A genus of pedunculated Cirripedes distinguished from ALEPAS in important respects, but like in having no shell.

ANGULITES. Montf. A genus composed of species of fossil NAUTILI, described by De Blainville as not umbilicated, with a dorsal keel and angular aperture. NAUTILUS triangularis, Buffon.

ANGIOSTOMATA. Bl. The third family of Siphonobranchiata, Bl. described as differing little from the family of Entomostomata, but having long, narrow, straight apertures, and the columellar lips straight or nearly so. Were it not for the admission of the genus Strombus into this family, it would correspond with COLUMELLARIA and CONVOLUTÆ of Lamarck.

ANNELIDES. The ninth class of invertebrated animals, divided into three orders, namely, A. Apodes, A. Antennés, and A. Sedentaires. The last only contains families of testaceous Mollusca. The animals are vermicular, some naked, others inhabiting shelly tubes. See SEDENTARY ANNELIDES.

ANNULAR OPERCULUM is one which has the nucleus central, or nearly so, the other layers surrounding it in flattened rings. The term concentric is also applied. See Introduction.

ANNULATED. (Annus, a ring.) Composed of, or surrounded by rings, as in the case of Tubicinella, fig. 14.

ANODONTA. Cuvier, 1798. *Fam.* Submytilacea, Bl. Nayades, Lam. A genus composed of such species of NAYADES as have no teeth on the hinge. Europe, North America, &c. The example given is A. Cataractus, Pl. viii. fig. 152.

ANOMALINA. D'Orb. A genus of microscopic Foraminifera.

ANOMALOCARDIA. Schum. 1817. Venus flexuosa, and similar species. See THESAURUS Conchyliorum, Pl. xiii.

ANOMIA. *Fam.* Ostracea, Lam. and Bl.—*Descr.* Irregular, inequivalve, sub-equilaternal, foliaceous, pearly within; adhering to marine substances by means of a bony appendage, which passes through a large circular opening in the lower valve; muscular impression divided into three irregular portions; hinge destitute of teeth with a short cartilage.—*Obs.* The Linnæan genus included not only the shells to which the description above given would apply, but also many other genera, such as Crania, Orbicula, Terebratula, &c. which belong to the Brachiopoda, and are perfectly distinct. The Anomiæ are found in Europe, N. America, Moluccas, Philippine Islands, &c. Fig. 186, in the plates, is a somewhat reduced representation of a full grown specimen of A. Ephippium. Fig. 187, the hinge of the under valve, with the bony process. Fig. 188, the hinge showing the opening through which it passes, Pl. xi. figs. 186, 187, 188.

ANOSTOMA. See ANASTOMA, and TOMOGERUS.

ANASTES. Klein. A genus formed of those species of Patella which have a produced, recurved beak. Helcion, Montf. *Ex.* Patella pellucida, fig. 230.

ANSULUS or ANSYLUS. See ANCYLUS.

ANTENOR. Montf. A genus of microscopic Foraminifera.

ANTERIOR. In Bivalves is the side on which the head, or part analogous to the head of the animal lies; it is known in the shell by the umbones, which if turned at all, are turned towards that part. If there be a sinus in the impression of the mantle, it is always on the posterior part of the shell. If the ligament be placed only on one side of the umbones, it is only on the posterior side. The anterior of a *spiral univalve* is that part of the outer lip which is at the greatest distance from the apex. Of a *symmetrical conical univalve* such as Patella, it is that part where the head of the animal lies, indicated by the interruption of the muscular impression. Of *Brachiopoda*, that part which is farthest from the umbones and which corresponds with the ventral margin in other Bivalves. The anterior of *symmetrical, convolute univalves*, is the outer or dorsal part of the aperture, or that part which is farthest from the spire. Lamarck and other Conchological writers have occasioned much confusion by their errors on this subject; describing the same part of a shell at one time anterior, at another posterior; but generally the reverse of the above arrangement, which is founded upon the natural position of the animal, and generally adopted. The anterior will be indicated by the letter *a*, in figs. 119, 421, 229, 34, 202.

ANTIGONA. Schum. 1817. A genus composed of VENUS cancellata, Lam. (fig. 119.) and similar species.

ANTIQUATED. This word, signifying *out of date*, is occasionally used to express that species of composition which constantly occurs in shells, by each fresh deposit or layer of calcareous matter, forming a new margin, which being replaced by its successor, is no longer used as the margin, and is consequently said to be out of date.

APEX. This term does not apply to the natural position of a shell, but is used in a mathematical sense, to indicate the nucleus or first formed part; which may be considered as the point of the spiral cone. From this point, the shell enlarging rapidly or slowly as it descends, takes a spiral, arched, straight, oblique, convolute, or irregularly spiral course. The apex is indicated by the letter *a*, in fig. 282 and 466.

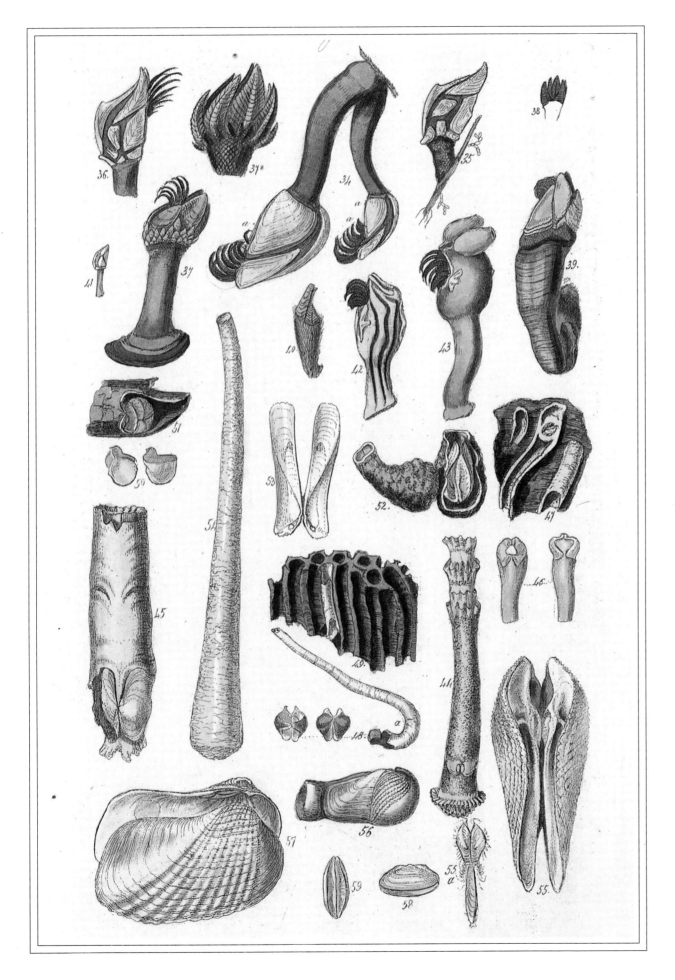

APERTURE or MOUTH. The entrance to the spiral cavity of univalve shells. The parts of the aperture are separately described, as follows: The *inner lip* or *labium* is that part which lies over the preceding whorl of the shell. It terminates anteriorly, or towards the lower part in what is termed the *columella*, so called because it forms a kind of axis on which the volutions turn. The outer lip, sometimes called the labrum, is on the opposite side, or the farthest from the axis. If the edges of the inner and outer lips unite all round, they are described as composing the *peritreme*. In fig. 318, the aperture is marked by the letter *a*.

APHRODITE. Lea. (from Αφροδιτη, Greek name of Venus.) ACARDO, Swains. A genus composed of CARDIUM Grœnlandicum, Auct. fig. 123,* and other similar species of Cardium, the teeth of which are either wholly wanting, or very indistinct. Northern Ocean. Pl. vi. fig. 123.*

APICIAL. Belonging to the apex. The apicial extremity of the aperture of a univalve shell, is that which is nearest to the apex of the spire.

APLEXA. Fleming. 1824. A genus composed of PHYSA Hypnorum, Drap. &c. and described as having the inner lip simple, and not spread over the body whorl.

APLODON. Rafinesque. A genus proposed to be established at the expense of the genus HELIX, but upon what grounds does not appear from the imperfect description, which is unaccompanied by a figure.

APLUSTRUM. Schum. A genus formed for the reception of some species of BULLA which have the spire uncovered. *Ex.* Bulla Thalassiarchi, fig. 289. Three species are enumerated by Mr. Adams in his Monograph of the Bullidæ in Sowerby's Thesaurus, Pl. xi.

APLYSIA. Gmel. 1790. (*a*, without; Πλυω, to wash.) *Fam.* Laplysiens, Lam. Aplysiana, Bl.—*Descr.* Horny, transparent, clypeiform, or shield-shaped, placed horizontally on the back of the animal, with its convex side uppermost: apex slightly in-curved.—*Obs.* The animal producing this shell has derived its name from the purplish liquor which it exudes, when disturbed. In contour, it has been fancied to present a certain likeness to a hare crouching, and on this account was called *Lepus marinus*, or sea hare, by the ancients. The shell bears a strong resemblance to Dolabella, which, however, is much thicker, and more testaceous. The species are found in the Mediterranean, European, and West Indian Seas. A. Petersoni. Pl. xiii. fig. 254.

APLYSIACEA. Bl. The second family of the order Monopleurobranchiata, Bl. The animals composing this family are either destitute of shells, or are provided with internal ones, which are flat, open, oblique, with the apex or nucleus slightly incurved, not distinctly spiral. This family contains the genera Aplysia and Dolabella. The first sub-spiral, with the apex terminal; shell thin, horny. Fig. 254. The second the same, but thick and shelly. Fig. 255.

APOLLON. Monft. RANELLA. Lamarck.

APOROBRANCHIATA. Bl. The first order of the second section of Paracephalophora Monoica, Bl. The Thecosmata is the only family of this order containing any approach to shells, these are Hyalæa and Cymbulia.

APORRHAIS. Da Costa, 1778. A genus formed of ROSTELLARIA Pespelicani, *Auct.* and similar species. Although the shell presents no characters to distinguish it generically from Rostellaria, those who have examined the soft parts are convinced that it is distinct. Of the three species now known and figures in part I. of Thesaurus Conchyliorum, by the Author, one is common on our own coast, and in the Mediterranean. See ROSTELLARIA; and our plates: Pl. xviii. fig. 404.

AQUATIC. A term applied by some authors to those species of Molluscous animals, which inhabit fresh water, either in rivers or salt water standing pools, as distinguished from the marine or Mollusca. See Fresh-water.

AQUILLUS. Montf. TRITON Lampas, Cutaceus, &c. Auct. Placed by De Blainville in the division of the genus Triton, which is described as having a short spire, being covered with tubercles and umbilicated. Triton Cutaceus. Pl. xviii. fig. 309.

ARCA. Linn. (Anglicè, a boat.) *Fam.* Arcacea, Lam.—*Descr.* Obliquely transverse, subquadrate, equivalve, or nearly so, inequilateral, thick, ventricose, longitudinally ribbed, dentated near the inner margins; hinge rectilinear, forming a flat, external area, upon which the ligament is spread in cross rows, and having a series of small, regular teeth, extending on both sides of the umbones in each valve; muscular impressions distant.—*Obs.* The shells composing this genus are easily distinguished from those of all other bivalve shells, by the straight, linear row of small notched teeth, and by the area between the umbones. The genus *Cucullæa* makes the nearest approach to it in this respect, but it may easily be known from it by the outermost teeth on each side of the row being oblique, and lengthened out; and also by the prominent edge of the muscular impression. These shells are recent, found in various marine localities; fossil, in the tertiary deposits. The Arca Noæ, formerly regarded as the type of this genus, has, with several other species, been separated from it under the name of Bysso-area, by Swainson, on account of an hiatus in the ventral margin, to admit the passage of a byssus; this is not found in the true Arcæ. The true Arcæ are mostly tropical. Mr. Reeve's Monograph contains 122 species. Arca Antiquata, fig. 121. Byssoarca Noæ, 132. Pl. vii.

ARCACEA. Lam. A family of the order Conchifera Dimyaria, characterized by a series of teeth placed on the hinge in a line. The genera may be distinguished as follows,

1. ARCA. Hinge straight; valves close. Fig. 131.
2. BYSSO-ARCA. Valves gaping. Fig. 132.
3. CUCULLÆA. Distant teeth oblique; posterior muscular impression prominent. Fig. 133.
4. PECTUNCULUS. Hinge curved. Fig. 134.
5. NUCULA. The same, with a pit in the centre of the hinge, including Myopara and Crenella. Figs. 135 to 137.
6. SOLENELLA. Fresh water, oval; a series of teeth on one side of the hinge, only two or three on the other. Fig. 138.

ARCHAIAS. Montf. A genus of microscopic Foraminifera.

ARCHONTE. Montf. HYALÆA, Auct.?

ARCINELLA. Schum. 1817. ACANTHIZA, Fischer. 1807. Claimed as a prior name for MONOCEROS, Lamarck. CHAMA Arcinella, Auct.

ARCTICA. Schum. CYPRINA. Lamarck.

AREA. A flat space or disc, on any part of a shell. *Ex.* the triangular space on the hinge of Arca, fig. 132, and Spondylus.

ARENACEOUS. (Arena, sand.) Of a sandy texture, as the sand tubes surrounding the bodies of some of the Annellides, named Arenaria on this account. But the word is more commonly used to intimate the habits of the animal, burrowing with its shell in the sand.

ARETHUSA. Montf. A genus of microscopic Foraminifera.

ARGONAUTA. Lamarck. Commonly called the "Paper Sailor." *Fam.* Pteropoda, Bl. *Order* Cepholopoda Monotholamia, Lam.—*Descr.* Light, thin, transparent, or nearly so, symmetrically convolute, carinated by a double row of tubercles, terminating smooth or tuberculated ribs radiating towards the centre; aperture large, elongated; peritrême acute, interrupted by the body whorl.—*Obs.* The exquisitely beautiful, light and delicate fabrics included under the above name are inhabited by a molluscous animal named the *Ocythöe*,

which is provided with tuberculated arms. These, hanging over the sides of the aperture, give to the whole the appearance of a vessel propelled by oars: a poetical illusion further heightened by the broad, flat membranes of the two arms, which, when vertically expanded, present an idea of sails. Pliny has described the Nautilus (the name has been changed by the moderns) as sailing gracefully on the Mediterranean waters; and Pope has versified the idea in the well known lines—

> "Learn of the little Nautilus to sail,
> Spread the thin oar and catch the driving gale."

Scientific men have long been engaged in the interesting discussion, whether the animal really belongs to the shell in which it is found, or whether, having destroyed the rightful owner, it has possessed itself of the "frail bark." It is now, however, proved beyond the shadow of a doubt that the Argonaut is the testaceous part of the Ocythöe, and that the broad membranes which in some representations have been artificially placed as sails, are naturally bent backwards over the shell like the mantle of some other molluscs. The interesting experiments of Madame Power, in the Mediterranean, have contributed very materially to lead the investigations of naturalists to a satisfactory conclusion. This lady kept a cage under water, in which Argonautæ were bred in great numbers, giving her an opportunity of tracing the gradual development of the shell in all its stages, from the elastic and transparent nucleus to the full grown "Paper Sailor." Pl. xxiii. fig. 485.

ARGUS. Poli, 1795. Equivalve pectens, like P. opercularis.

ARIANTA. Leach, 1819. A sub-genus of land shells, containing HELIX arbustorum, Auct. (Gray, Turton, p. 137.)

ARION. Ferrussac, 1817. A genus of slugs, originally described as having no shells, but the shell of which is now ascertained to be a Limarella.

ARROW-HEADS. One of the names by which fossils of the genus Belennites were formerly known.

ARTEMIS, or ARTHEMIS. Poli: DOSINIA? Scopoli. A genus of bivalve shells, distinguished from those of the genus Cytheræa by having a rounded, denticular form, and a deep, angular sinus in the palleal impression; although palleal impressions of the Veneres are subject to great variations, this may be considered a pretty well defined genus. The author is preparing a Monograph in the Thesaurus Conchyliorum, containing 60 species. A. lincta, Pl. vi. fig. 118.

ARTICULATED. (Jointed.) Applied to distinct parts of shells, which are fitted or jointed into each other, as the valves of Chitones and those of Balani. The operculum of Nerita is said to be *articulated* to the columella, having a small process by which it is as it were locked under the edge. See *Introduction*. The word is also applied to the Cirri, which protrude from the oral openings of Cirripides.

ARTICULINA. D'Orb. A genus of microscopic Foraminifera.

ASIPHONIBRANCHIATA. Bl. The second order of Paracephalophora Dioica, Bl. Consisting of spiral univalves, which have no notch or canal at the anterior part of the aperture. This order is divided into the families Goniosomata, Cricosomata, Ellipsostomata, Hemicyclostomata, and Oxystomata.

ASPERGILLUM. Lam. (From *Aspergo*, to sprinkle.) *Fam.* Tubicolæ, Lam. Pyloridea, Bl.—*Descr.* The small, equal equilateral valves are cemented into, so as to form part of, a large tube; the umbones are slightly prominent outside. The tube is elongated, rather irregular, granulated with sandy particles, and terminated at the base by a convex disc, which is perforated by small pores, elongated into tubes round the edge, presenting a resemblance to the spout of a watering pot, whence the name is derived. *Loc.* New Holland, Java, New Zealand, Red Sea. Aspergillum Vaginiferum. Pl. ii. fig. 44.

ASSIMINEA. Leach, 1819. *Fam.* Turbinacea, Lam.—*Descr.* Inclining to oval, light, thin, covered with a horny epidermis, spire produced into an acute pyramid; whorls slightly angulated in the centre, rounded beneath; aperture elliptical, slightly modified by the last whorl; inner lip planed; outer lip thin; operculum horny, subspiral. Found in brackish water; one species may be procured abundantly on the muddy shores of the Thames, in Kent. There are also species from Calcutta, China, Tahiti, and Australia. Without comparing the animals, it is difficult to distinguish this genus from some species of Littorina. A. Grayana. Pl. xvi. fig. 363.

ASTACOLUS. Montf. A genus of microscopic Foraminifera. CRISTELLARIA Crepidula, Lam.

ASTARTE. J. Sowerby, 1816. (Name of a Sidonian goddess, *Ashtaroth* in Scripture.) *Fam.* Nymphacea, Lam. Genus Crassina, Lam.—*Descr.* Suborbicular, equivalve, inequilateral, thick, compressed; hinge with two solid diverging teeth in the right valve, one tooth and a slight posterior elevation in the left; muscular impressions, two in each valve, uniform, united by a simple palleal impression; ligament external.—*Obs.* This genus differs from Venus, Cytheræa, &c. in not having a posterior sinus in the impression of the mantle. The hinge also differs in having but two cardinal teeth. Astarte differs from Crassatella in having no internal cartilage in the hinge. Some of the species are British, others are from America, and one from Sicily. The fossils occur in Crag, Lower Oolite, &c. A. Danmoniensis. Pl. v. fig. 110.

ASTROLEPAS. Klein. CORONULA Testudinaria, Auct. CHELONOBIA, Leach. Fig. 15.

ATLANTA. Lesueur. *Fam.* Pteropoda, Lam. and Bl.—*Descr.* Spiral, convolute, transparent, fragile, compressed, with a broad, fimbriated, dorsal keel, and a narrow aperture. This shell, which is called "*corne d'ammon vivant*," is found in the Atlantic. The small Pteropod, figured in Sowerby's Genera as Limacina, belongs to this genus. Atlanta Helicialis, Pl. xii. fig. 220.

ATLAS. Lesueur. A genus of Bullidæ without any shell.

ATRACTODON. Charlesworth. (Mag. Nat. Hist. 2nd series, vol. 8. p. 218.) A genus proposed for the admission of a singular fossil-shell, found on the beach at Felix-stone, of which the following are the characters:—fusiform, aperture equalling the spire in length, terminating anteriorly in a slightly recurved canal; columellar lip smooth, curved, thickened posteriorly into a blunt tooth; spire obtuse.—*Obs.* This shell would be a Fusus were it not for the tooth on the posterior extremity of the columellar lip. The only species known is regularly striated in a spiral direction, and named A. elegans.

ATRYPA. Dalman. A genus of brachipodous bivalves, distinguished by the valves being nearly equal, and the umbones not separated by an intermediate area. A. reticulata, Pl. xi. fig. 302.

ATTACHED. Shells are attached to marine substances by various means; in some cases by a *byssus*, or a bunch of tendinous fibres passing through an opening between the valves, which gape at their margins to admit a free passage, as in the genera Byssoarca and Mytilus. In other cases the byssus is of a more compact substance, and passes through a perforation in the shell itself. This is the case with many of the brachiopodous shells, in some species of which the perforation is in the point of the umbones, a specimen of which is represented in the Introduction. This species of attachment does not keep the animal motionless, although it is confined to a particular spot. Other shells are attached by a portion of their own substance, as in Chama, Spondylus, Serupla, &c. in which instances, the attached valve is motionless, and is termed the under valve. The pedunculated Cirripedes are attached by a tubular tendinous process, called a peduncle.

ATURIA. Bronn. A genus typified by Nautilus zigzag, having an angularly lobed septum. Edwards. Cephalopoda of London clay. P. 54.

ATYS. Montf. 1810. A generic name including those species of Bulla, which are described as "convolute, with the last whorl covering the rest and hiding the spire, the apex rounded at both ends." In Sowerby's Thesaurus Mr. Adams enumerates 22 species. Bulla Naucum, Auct. fig. 250.

AURICLE. (A little ear.) See Auriculated.

AURICULA. Lam. 1801. (Dim. from *Auris*, an ear.) *Fam.* Auriculacea; Bl. Colimacea, Lam.—*Descr.* Oval or oblong, cylindrical or conical; aperture long, narrow, generally narrowest in the centre; rounded anteriorly, with two or three strong folds on the inner lip, and the outer lip thickened, reflected, or denticulated; spire short, obtuse, epidermis horny, brown.—*Obs.* The above description includes the A. coniformis, f. 298. and several other conical species with narrow apertures, which formed the genus *Melampus*, Montf. and *Conovulus*, Lam. The latter author suppressed his genus on ascertaining the Conovuli to be land shells. We exclude, however, the A. Dombeyana, Lam. f. 300. and several similar species, which being more rounded, having thin outer lips and but one fold on the columella, are described under the generic name *Chilina*, Gray. It appears rather more doubtful whether the Auriculæ are marine or fluviatile, but the animals appear to be amphibious. The Auriculæ are principally found in salt marshes of tropical climates, some small species are found on the southern European coasts, as far north as Britain and south as Tierra del Fuego. The Auriculæ formed a part of the genus Voluta of Linnæus, f. 297. A. Judæ, f. 298. A. Coniformis, Pl. xiv.

AURICULATED. Some bivalve shells, such as *Pecten*, fig. 171, 172, have a flat, broad, somewhat triangular appendage on one or both sides of the umbones, called an *auricle*, or little *ear*. If on one side only, they are said to be *uni-auriculated*; if on both, they are said to be *bi-auriculated*.

AURICULACEA. Bl. The second family of the order Pulmobranchiata, thus described: "shell thick, solid; aperture more or less oval, always large, rounded anteriorly, and contracted by teeth or folds on the columella." This family is included in the genus Voluta of Linnæus, on account of the plaited columellar lip, a character by which that heterogenous assemblage of shells is distinguished. It forms part of the family of *Colimacea*, Lam. from which they differ not only in general form, but also in the fact of the animals being partly amphibious, always living (according to De Blainville) on the sea shore, and being occasionally covered with water for a short time. It contains the genera Pedipes, Auricula, Pyramidella.

AURIFERA. Blainville, Otion, Auct.

AURIFORM. (From *Auris*, an ear; *forma*, shape.) Ex. *Haliotis*, fig. 338.

AURISCALPIUM. Megerle, 1811. Anatina, Lam. 1812. Laternula, Bolton, 1798.

AVICULA. Lam. (From *Avis*, a bird.) *Fam.* Mallacea, Lam. Margaritacea, Bl.—*Descr.* Inequivalve, inequilateral, foliaceous, subquadrate, oblique, pearly; hinge rectilinear, lengthened into auricular appendages, with a small indistinct tooth in each valve, an elongated, marginal, ligamentiferous area, and an hiatus in the left valve, for the passage of a byssus; one circular muscular impression, near the centre of each valve, with a series of smaller ones arranged in a line towards the umbones.—*Obs.* The Meleagrinæ of Lamarck, Margaritiferæ, Schum. included in this description, consist of the more rounded species, and do not present the elegant obliquity of form, nor the wing-like auricles from which the genus Avicula receives its name. The

Aviculæ are pearly within. From A. margaritiferæ, a young specimen of which is figured in the plates, fig. 164, is obtained oriental pearls. This is an example of Meleagrina. A. Hirundo, fig. 163, belongs to the genus Avicula of Lamarck. It is, however, needless to continue the separation. Avicula are from E. and W. Indies, Mexico, Coasts of the Pacific, Mediterranean, British Islands, &c. Fossil species occur in the London clay, &c. Pl. ix. fig. 163, 164.

AXINEA. Poli, 1795. A generic name used by some authors in preference to Pectunculus of Lamarck, as claiming the priority.

AXINUS. J. Sowerby.—*Descr.* Equivalve, transverse; posterior side very short, rounded, with a long ligament, placed in a furrow, extending along the whole edge; anterior side produced, angulated, truncated, with a flattish *lunule* near the beaks. The late Mr. James Sowerby, who described this shell in the Mineral Conchology, did not consider his genus as established, not having seen the hinge. It is stated to have been previously named Thyassira; but Cryptodon, Turton, is the first name accompanied by true character.

AXIS. The imaginary line, round which the whorls of a spiral shell revolve. The extremities of the axis are pointed out in fig. 379, by the letters, a. a. See "Columella."

AZECA. Leach. Gray, 1840. *Fam.* Colinacea, Lam.—*Descr.* "Animal like Bulinus, with subcylindrical, rather obtuse shell, covered with a polished periostraca (epidermis); aperture pear-shaped, curved and pointed at the top; the margin thick, obtuse, united all round and toothed; the axis imperforated." Gray's edition of Turton's British Shells, page 189.—*Obs.* The Turbo Tridens of Montagu, upon which this genus is founded, resembles Bulinus lubricus in general form and character. Both these shells differ from the true Bulini in having the peritreme entire, and in being pellucid and glossy. Azeca differs from Bulinus lubricus in having three teeth in the aperture, two on the inner lip and one on the outer. Not seeing the necessity for creating a genus on grounds so slight, I have simply transcribed the description given above, leaving others to form their own conclusions as to the propriety of separating this shell from the genus Bulinus. Britain, Central and Southern Europe. Azeca Tridens, Pl. xiv. fig. 290.

AZEMUS. Ranzani. Conia, Leach.

BACULITES. Lam. *Fam.* Orthocerata, Bl. Ammonacea, Lam.—*Descr.* Straight, conical, tubular, laterally compressed; chambers divided by very sinuous lobed septa, the last elongated; aperture elliptical; siphon dorsal.—*Obs.* This genus differs from Orthoceras in the same manner in which Ammonites differs from Nautilus, having its septa sinuated and branched. A Baculite might be described as a straight Ammonite. This genus is known only in a fossil state. It is found in the Cretaceous Limestone of Maëstricht and Valognes. B. Faujasii. Pl. xxiii. fig. 484.

BALANUS Brug. (an Acorn; "gland de mer." Fr.) *Order* Sessile Cirripedes, Lam. *Fam.* Balanidea, Bl.—*Descr.* Shell composed of six valves articulated to each other side by side in a circle, by the insertion of lamina; closed at the base by a flat, cylindrical or cup-shaped valve, by which it is generally attached; and at the apex by a conical operculum, consisting of four valves in anterior and posterior pairs. Each valve of the shell is divided into a rough triangular portion pointed towards the apex, and a flat area on each side.—*Obs.* This description includes the *Acasta* of Leach, which growing in sponges, has the base cup-shaped; *Conoplœa* of Say, which being attached to the stems of Gorgonia and sea-weeds has the base elongated and lanceolate, and *Chirona*, Gray. Balanus is the only genus of Sessile Cirripedes the shells of which consist of six parietal valves, except *coronula*, which has no shelly base, is flatter, and has the valves of the operculum placed horizontally. The Balani are common in all seas, adhering to rocks, corals, floating timber, and to each other. The fossil species are found in the newest strata, at Bordeaux, Paris, &c. Fig. 25. B. Tintinnabulum; 26. *Acasta* Montagui; 27. Balanus galeatus, *Conoplœa*, Say. Pl. i. figs. 25 to 27.

BALANIDEA. Bl. The second family of the class Nematopoda, Bl. corresponding with Sessile Cirripedes, Lam., and consisting of Coronular Multivalves, which are fixed, and in a manner soldered to submarine substances, by the base of the shell; as distinguished from the Lepadicea, Bl., Pedunculated Cirripedes, Lam., which are attached by a fleshy stalk. The Balanidea are composed of two sets of valves, besides the shelly plate or base on which they rest. The first, called the Parietal valves, are arranged so as to surround the body of the animal; the second, called the Opercular valves, are placed horizontally, so as to cover the aperture.

BALEA. Prideaux. Gray. 1824. *Fam*. Colimacea, Lam.—*Descr*. Spiral, turrited, concentrically striated, sinistral, and covered with a thin brown epidermis; spire composed of numerous whorls, gradually increasing in size; aperture small, sub-quadrate; peritreme entire, slightly thickened, with a very slight fold on the columella; axis perforated.—*Obs*. A genus of small land shells, found in moss at the roots of trees in Britain, not very nearly resembling any other land shells, except Clausilia, from which they differ in not having the clausium. They have been placed in Helix by De Ferrusac, and in Pupa by Draparnaud. *Helix perversa*, Fer. *Pupa perversa*, Drap. B. fragilis, Pl. xiv. fig. 296.

BARBATA. Humphrey. 1797. Dipsas. Leach. 1817.

BARNACLES. Pentelasmis, Auct. (fig. 34.) Called Anatifa, by Linnæus and Lamarck, from the ancient notion that they were the eggs or embryo of the Barnacle Duck. See Anatifer.

BASE. In all shells which are attached to sub-marine substances the base is that part of the shell which forms the point of attachment—as for instance, the attached valve of Spondylus, the basal plate of Balanus, the lower part of the peduncle of Pentelasmis: in unattached Bivalves, the margin opposite to the umbones, where the foot of the animal, or the part analogous to it, protrudes; in spinal univalves, the aperture, which rests on the back of the animal when walking. Lamarck and some other authors have used the term *base* as simply opposed to apex, and apply it to the anterior of the aperture.

BATOLITES. Montf. Hippurites, Auct.

BEAK. The Apices, or points of the valves of a bivalve shell, generally termed Umbones, in descriptions. Also any part which is rostrated or drawn out like a beak.

BEAKED. See Beak and Rostrated.

BEAR'S PAW-CLAM. The common name for Hippopus maculatus, a representation of which is given in the plates, fig. 156.

BELEMNITES. Lamarck. 1801. (Βελεμνον, *belemnon*, a dart, or arrow.) *Fam*. Orthocerata, Bl. and Lam.—*Descr*. Straight, conical, consisting of two parts; the *external* portion forming a thick solid sheath, with a cavity at the base to admit the internal portion or nucleus, which is mathematically conical, and is divided into chambers by smooth simple septa perforated by a lateral siphon—*Obs*. These singular fossils, which are found in most secondary beds, have long attracted the attention of philosophers as well as the ignorant, from whom they have received the various appellations of Thunder-Stones, Petrified Arrows, Petrified Fingers, Devil's Fingers, Spectre Candles, &c. The above description is framed to include the genera Hibolithes, Porodragus, Cetocis, Acamas, and Paclites of De Montfort, and Actinocamax, Stokes. Pl. xxii. fig. 466 to 468.

BELLEROPHON. Montf. 1810. (or Bellerophus).—*Descr*. Convolute, symmetrical, umbilicated with a double dorsal ridge; aperture wide, semilunar.—*Obs*. The fossils composing this genus resemble Nautilus in general appearance, but not being chambered shells they approach very near to Argonauta, from which they differ in the thickness of their shell and in roundness of their external form. This genus is erroneously placed by De Montfort among chambered shells, and by De Blainville next to Bulla. It belongs to the Monothalamous Cephalopoda of Lamarck. This fossil is found principally in the Carboniferous Limestone. B. tenuifasciata. Pl. xxiii. fig. 486, 487.

BELOPTERA. The bony support of a species of Cuttlefish, partly resembling Sepia.

BEZOARDICA. Schum. part of the genus Cassidea, Swainson. Cassis glauca, &c.

BIAPHOLIUS. Leach. A genus believed to be identical with Hiatella.

BI-AURICULATED. Having two auricles placed at the sides of the umbones, as in Pecten, fig. 171. See Auriculated.

BIFID. Divided, double.

BIFRONTIA. Deshayes. 1833. Also Omalaxis. Desh. 1830. *Fam*. Turbinacea, Lam.—*Descr*. Discoidal, planorbicular, with whorls sometimes not contiguous; umbilicus deep, keeled at the margin; aperture subtriangular, somewhat dilated; outer lip acute, separated by a deep notch at both extremities.—*Obs*. We do not see any reason for separating this genus from Solarium, except the last mentioned character. The few fossil species which this genus contains (Solarium disjunctum, Bifrons, &c.) are found principally in the Paris basin. Solarium Bifrons. Pl. xvi. fig. 354.

BI-FURCATE. Double pronged, or having two points. *Ex*. the internal appendage of Calyptræa Equestris, fig. 234.

BIGENERINA. D'Orb. A genus of microscopic Foraminifera.

BILABIATED. Having the edge of the outer lip as it were doubled, by one part of the lip being more thickened and reflected than the other, so as to form a ledge, or second lip.

BILOBATE. Having two prominent parts, as the outer lip of Rostellaria Pes-Pelecani, fig. 404.

BIPARTITE. Composed of or divided into two parts; as the valves of Platylepas, fig. 19, each of which has a septiform division in the centre; also the area on the hinge of the Spondylus. See Frontispiece.

BIROSTRA. Sw. A genus composed of species of Ovulum, which have elongated extremities, as for instance, Ovulum Volva, fig. 442.

BIROSTRITES. Lam. (Double Beak.) A fossil formerly considered as a distinct bivalve shell, with conical umbones, and placed in the family of Rudistes by Lamarck, but now known to be an internal cast of Sphærulites. Pl. xi. fig. 196.

BITHINIA. Gray. 1824. A genus described as differing from Paludina, in having the operculum shelly, and the mouth of the shell thickened internally. Paludina impura, Auct. Pl. xxv. fig. 537.

BITOMUS. Montf. A microscopic shell, deriving this general appellation, from the appearance of a double aperture.

BIVALVE. A shell composed of two equal, or nearly equal principal parts, each part having a separate nucleus, turning upon each other by means of a hinge. The class Conchifera of Lamarck, and Acephalophora of De Blainville severally include the whole of the bivalve shells; the latter name being derived from the fact that the animals have not distinct heads, and neither eyes nor tentacula. All bivalve shells are marine or fresh-water. They form the class Dithyra of Aristotle. It may be observed that some of the Acephalophora, the Pholades, for example, have small testaceous pieces fixed on the hinge, which are called accessory valves. These are still fairly bivalve shells, although the genus Pholas has been placed by some writers among the multivalves.

79. Mactra Stultorum.
80. ——plicataria. Spisula? Gray.
81. ——Spengleri. Schizodesma,
    Gray.
82. ——bicolor. Mulinia, Gray.
83. Gnathodon cuneatus. Clathodon,
    Conrad.
84. Crassatella rostrata.
85. Amphidesma reticulatum.
86. Erycina plebeja. mesodesma,
    Desh.
87. Cumingia mutica.
88. Ungulina transversa, (from
    Sowerby's genera.)
    Abra, fig. 495.   ⎱ To be added
    Ervilia, fig. 497. ⎰ to this family.

    Fam. Corbulacea

89. Corbula nucleus.
90. Pandora rostrata. Potamomya,
    fig. 498, 499. To be added to
    this family.

    Fam. Lithophagidæ

91. Petricola Roccellaria.
92. ——Carditoidea.
    Coralliophaga, Bl.
93. Thracia corbuloides.
94. Saxicava rugosa.
95. Hiatella biaperta.
96. Sphænia Binghamii.
97. Venerirupis vulgaris.

    Fam. Nymphacea.

98. Sanguinolaria rosea. Lobaria,
    Schum.
99. ——Diphos. Soletellina, Bl.
100. Psammobia Ferroensis. Gari,
    Schum.

BIVONIA. Gray. VERMETUS glomeratus, Brown.

BOAR'S TUSK. A common name given to shells of the genus Dentalium. One particular species has received a specific name in accordance with a supposed resemblance, namely, Dentalium Aprinum, (of a Boar.)

BONELLIA. Desh. NISSO, Risso, ante. A genus formed, in the first instance, for the reception of BULINUS terebellatus, Lam. which Mr. G.B. Sowerby, in his Genera of Shells, united with the genus PYRAMIDELLA. M. Deshayes, however, in his new edition of Lamarck, makes the genus Bonellia include several species which I have arranged in the genus Eulima. From the remarks of M. Deshayes, tom. 8, p. 286, 287, we are led to suppose that the estimated difference between Eulima and Bonellia consists in the latter having the axis perforated; or in other words, umbilicated. After remarking "que Mr. Sowerby, junr. confond deux choses bien distinctes, sous le nomme d'Eulima," M. Deshayes gives the following description of his genus, (translated) "shell turriculated, smooth, polished, with the apex acute and laterally inclined; axis perforated throughout its length; aperture small, entire, angular at the extremities; columella simple and without folds; outer lip thin, simple, nearly parallel with the longitudinal axis." That author further remarks, "Mr. Sowerby, junr. à signalé cinqu espèces vivant, que nous rapportons à notre genre." (Sowerby, junr. Conchological Illustrations, parts 52 and 53; Bohn, York Street, Covent Garden.) The species thus selected are E. splendidula, E. marmorata, E. interrupta, E. imbricata, E. brunnea; the two last of which have the umbilicus so inconsiderable, as to be scarcely distinguishable from other species, which M. Deshayes has left in the genus Eulima, and which have a slight hollow, almost approaching to a perforation, behind the columella. Eulima marmorata, (Bonellia, Desh.) is figured in the plates. Pl. xv. fig. 348.

BODY WHORL. The last whorl, constituting the bulk of the shell.

BORELIS. Montf. MELONIA, Bl. A genus of microscopic Foraminifera.

BORER or PIERCER. A term applied to those species of Acephalopodous Mollusca, which bore holes as dwellings in the rocks, as the Pholades, and some others.

BRACHIOPODA. Lam. A family of symmetrical bivalves belonging to the third section of Lamarck's *order* "Conchifera Monomyaria," described as bivalve (generally symmetrical) adhering to marine bodies, by a tendon passing through the shell, having no true ligament. What most distinguishes this family and renders it remarkable is the structure of the animal. It has two elongated, tendril-shaped arms. When the animal is in a state of repose these arms are coiled up spirally and enclosed in the shell, but when required for use, are unfolded and extended. This family contains the genera Orbicula, Terebratula and Lingula, in the system of Lamarck, to which may be added Thecidium, Productus, Spirifer, Magas, Pentamerus, Crania, Strigocephalus, Strophomena, and some others enumerated in the explanation of figures 201 to 219. The above genera may be thus distinguished.

    1. ORBICULA. Umbones central; byssus passing through a hole in the flat valve. Fig. 201.

    2. ATRYPA. Without foramen or space between the valves. Fig. 203.

    3. PRODUCTA. The same, valves produced, overwrapping: including Leptæna. Fig. 206, 206*.

    4. TEREBRATULA. Hinge of the upper valve produced beyond that of the other, with a pit or foramen; including *Delthyris, Orthis, Trigonosemus, Magas, Strophomena.* Fig. 202, 205, 207, 208, 209.

    5. SPIRIFER. The same, with deep triangular area; spiral folds in

the interior; including *Trigonotreta* and *Cyrtia.* Fig. 204, 214, 215.

    6. THECIDIUM. Large valve attached; curved ridges in the inner surface; two jutting points or teeth on the hinge. Fig. 216.

    7. CRANIA. Attached by the surface of the valve; muscular impressions four, forming a face. Fig. 197, *a*, *b*.

    8. PYCNODONTA. Irregular; hinge with raised pointed teeth. Fig. 217, 218.

    9. PENTAMERUS. Valves divided by septa; including *Gypidia.* Fig. 210 to 213.

    10. LINGULA. Valves equal, gaping, with a peduncle. Fig. 219.

BRACHISTOMA. Swainson. 1840. Clavatula, Lamarck. 1801.

BRANCHIFERA. Bl. The second family of the order Cervicobranchiata, containing the following genera of symmetrical univalves:—Fissurella, Emarginula, and Parmophorous.

BRISNÆUS. Leach. *Order.* Pedunculated Cirripedes. Lam. B. Rhodiopus. Part of the genus LITHOTOYA. Pl. ii. fig. 37.

BROCCHIA. Brown. Patella sinuata?

BRODERIPIA. Gray, 1847. Part of the genus Scutella, Broderip-type, Scutella rosea. Pl. xxiv. gigs. 508, 509.

BRONTES. Montf. 1810. This generic name is given to such species of MUREX as have a very long, closed canal; with a short spire, circular aperture, and are destitute of spires and ramifications. Brontes (Murex) Haustellum, Pl. xvii. fig. 396.

BRYOPA. Gray, 1840. CLAVAGELLA aperta, &c.

BUCARDIA. Schum. ISOCARDIA, Auct.

BUCCINUM. Linn. *Fam.* Purpurifera, Lam. Entomostomata, Bl.—*Descr.* Subovate or oblong, covered with an epidermis; spire turrited, consisting of few whorls; aperture wide, subovate, terminating anteriorly in a very short canal, reflected over the back; outer lip simple, slightly reflected; inner lip spread over a portion of the body whorl, terminating in a thick, smooth columella; operculum horny. *Hab.* British Seas, Northern Ocean, and Coast of Africa. Most of the fossil species occur in Crag, some in upper marine formation and London clay.—*Obs.* There are considerable difficulties in keeping this genus distinct from others nearly related to it, into which many of the species run by imperceptible gradations. The genus *Nassa* has been separated on account of the little notch, which terminates the columella. Some species of Terebra so nearly resemble the Buccina, that it is difficult to say where one genus ends and the other begins. Mr. Reeve's Monograph contains 118 species. T. Buccinoides, fig. 427. Buccinum Undatum, the common Whelk, Pl. xix. fig. 421.

BUFO. Montf. A generic division of the species composing Ranella, characterized as having the shell not umbilicated. The above character is scarcely sufficient in some cases, even as a specific distinction. Ranella Ranina, Pl. xvii. fig. 394.

BULBUS. Humph. RAPELLA, Swainson. A genus formed for the reception of PYRULA papyracea, Auct. (fig. 389), and similar species. RAPANUS, Montf.

BULIMIMA. Montf. A genus of microscopic Foraminifera.

BULIMULUS. Leach. 1826. *Fam.* Colimacea, Lam. The author is unacquainted with the characters by which the two or three species included in this genus are to be distinguished from Bulinus. We have represented, (fig. 283), Bulimulus trifasciatus, Leach, (Bulinus Guadaloupensis, Auct.) This occurs in the same limestone which encloses the half fossilized human remains from the Grand Terre of Guadaloup. Several species are described by the Rev. L. Guilding in the Zoological Journal, namely, the B. Undulatus, Antiguensis, and

101. Corbis fimbriata. Fimbria, Megerle.
102. Grateloupia Moulinsii, (from Lea.)
103. Egeria triangulata, (from Lea.)
104. Lucina tigerina.
105. Tellina radiata.
106. ——lingua-felis; *a*, showing the fold in the ventral margin.
107. Tellinides rosea.
108. Donax cuneatus.
109. Capsa Braziliensis, young.
110. Astarte Danmoniensis. Crassina, Lam.

| Diplodonta, fig. 576. | To be added to this family. |
| Cryptodon, fig. 575. | |

Fluviatile Conchacea

111. Cyclas rivicola. Cornea, Megerle.
112. Pisidium amnicum. Pisum, Megerle.
113. Cyrena fuscata. Corbicula, Megerle.
114. Cyrenoides Dupontia.
115. Potamophila radiata. Galathæa, Lam. *v.* ventral margin. Pera, fig. 500. To be added to this family.

Marine Conchacea

116. Cyprina vulgaris. Arctica, Schum.

Proteus; but neither from the shells themselves, nor from the figures of the animal, can we draw any information as to the generic character; the difference alleged by Mr. Swainson and Mr. Gray being a comparative thinness in the outer lip. Pl. xiv. fig. 283.

BULINUS. Brug. (Bulinus, Lam.) *Fam.* Colimacea, Lam. Limacinea, Bl.—*Descr.* Oval or oblong, light, covered with a thin epidermis; spire obtuse, variable in length and in the number of whorls, which are generally few; aperture wide, oval, rounded anteriorly; outer lip simple, usually reflected, joining the columella without a sinus; inner lip reflected over part of the body-whorl. The Bulini are land shells, found in many parts of the world.—*Obs.* The genus Bulinus can only be distinguished from Helix by its oval form; it forms part of the genus Helix of De Ferrusac, under the sub-generic designation of Cochlostyla. It is known from Achatina by the absence of the notch at the point of union between the inner and the outer lips. The young are produced from eggs, which are as firm and opaque as those of birds. (See Introduction.) Bulinus rosaceus, fig. 282. B. Guadaloupensis, fig. 283. B. Lionetianus, fig. 284. B. lubricus, fig. 285. Many new species were brought to this country by Mr. Cuming, and are represented in the Conchological Illustrations, published by the Author at 50, Great Russell Street, Bloomsbury, (in parts 21, 22, 23, 26, 27, 30, 31, 34, 35, 137 to 146, 185, 186.) Species occur in Europe, West Indies, Brazil, and South America generally. Reeve's Monograph contains 662 species. Some small species are British. Pl. xiv. fig. 282.

BULLA. Auct. *Fam.* "Bulléens," Lam. Akera, Bl.—*Descr.* Generally thin, smooth, oval, oblong or cylindrical, more or less convolute; spire short, depressed, or hidden by the last whorl; aperture long, wide in front, gradually narrowing towards the spire; outer lip thin; inner lip spread over a part of the last whorl.—*Obs.* The shells composing this genus are very variable in form. The light horny species with an elastic lip is called Akera, fig. 247. The more decidedly convolute species with hidden spires are the Atys, Montf. B. Naueum, fig. 250. B. Lignaria, fig. 251, is Scaphander of Leach. The light, thin species, with extremely wide aperture, fig. 248, is Bullæa aperta, Lam. The genus Bullinula of Dr. Beck, consists of those species which have more produced spines, fig. 253. The Bullæ are marine, and inhabit all climates. The fossil species occur in tertiary beds. Since the first edition of this work was published, a very valuable monograph of the family by Mr. Adams has appeared in Sowerby's Thesaurus, part 11, in which the animals and their shells are arranged in the following genera or subgenera, Bullina, Aplustrum, Hydatina, Cornatina, Utriculus, Akera, Scaphander, Bulla, Haminea, Atys, Cylichna, Volvula, Linteria, Cryptopthalmus, Phaneropthalinus, Sormetus, Philine, Doridium, Chelidonura, Gasteropteron, and Atlas. Fig. 247 to 253.

BULLÆA. Lam. BULLA aperta, Auct. fig. 248.

BULLÆANA. ("Bulléens, Lam.") A family belonging to the first section of Lamarck's order, Gasteropoda, containing the genus Bulla. The genera Bullæa, Akera, Aplustra, Atys, Scaphander, Bullinula, into which it has been divided, may all be fairly included under the name BULLA.

BULLIA. Gray. 1834. A genus of shells partly resembling Buccinum, and Terebra in general form, being more elongated than the former and more ventricose than the latter. Mr. Gray remarks in the Synopsis of the British Museum, page 114, that the Bulliæ resemble the Nassæ in most characters, "but they have a very large, broad foot, and the hinder part of the inner lip of the shell being extended beyond the mouth, forms a raised enamelled band round the suture of the whorls, as is also the case with the Ancillariæ and some Volutes." Bullia vittata,

fig. 427, is an example of the genus. The name Subula is given by De Blainville to the other species of Terebra, so that if both these genera were admitted, the old genus Terebra must be expunged. Pl. xx. fig. 427.

BULLIDÆ. See BULLA.

BULLINA, Fer. BULLINULA. Beck. Species of BULLA, with produced conical spires, fig. 253. Three species are enumerated by Mr. Adams in his Monograph in Sowerby's Thesaurus Conchyliorum.

BYSSOARCA. Sw. 1835. (*Byssus* and *Arca*.) *Fam.* Aracea. Lam. A genus of bivalve shells, composed of the Arca *Noœ*, and several other species, separated from the genus Arca on account of their shells being attached by means of a byssus passing through an hiatus in the ventral margins. B. *Noœ*, fig. 132. The species occur in Southern Europe, East and West Indies, China; also, on the coasts of Great Britain. Pl. vii. fig. 132.

BYSSOMYA. Payr. 1826. (*Byssus* and *Mya*.) De Blainville states that, although the shell of this proposed genus resembles Saxicava, the animal is sufficiently different to justify the separation.

BYSSUS. (Βυσσος, byssus, ancient name for linen.) The tendinous fibres by which some Bivalves are as it were anchored or moored to submarine substances. A fine example of this is to be seen in the Pinnæ, which bear some resemblance to large Mussel Shells, and have an hiatus in the margin of the valves, through which a bunch of silken fibres passes. In the British Museum there is preserved a pair of gloves, which have been woven of these fibres. The Byssus is peculiar to some bivalve shells, such as Mussels, Hammer Oysters, Arca Noæ, &c.

CÆCUM. Fleming. A genus of minute shells resembling Dentalia, as if truncated, &c. the opening filled by a kind of septum. The position of this genus in the system is not yet accurately ascertained. Cæcum trachea, British Mollusca, Pl. lxix. fig. 4; our figure, Pl. xxvii. fig. 565.

CALCAR. Montf. 1817. (a spur.) A genus composed of TROCHUS STELLARIS, Lam. and other depressed species of Trochus which are characterized by a stellated keel round the angle of the last whorl; but not including T. Imperialis, which is the genus Imperator, Montf. The difference consists in the latter being umbilicated, and the former not. T. stellaris, fig. 358.

CALCAREOUS. (*calx*, lime.) A term applied to a shell, or to its operculum, which is composed principally of lime or shelly matter, as is usually the case, in distinction from one which is of a horny, membranaceous texture. The greater number of shells are calcareous, but it forms an important point of distinction with regard to the operculum. The only difference between the genera Trochus and Turbo, as at present established, depends upon the calcareous or shelly, and the corneous or horny, texture of the operculum.

CALCEOLA. *Fam.* Rudistes, Lam. and Bl.—*Descr.* Equilateral, inequivalve, triangular; umbones separated by a large triangular disc in the lower valve; cardinal margin straight, linear, dentated, lower valve large, deep; upper valve flat, semi-orbicular, forming a kind of operculum to the lower.—*Obs.* This singular shell, known only in a fossil state, in the Palæozöic beds, is placed by Linnæus in the genus Anonia. Lamarck places it among his Rudistes, but Mr. Sowerby, in his genera of shells, states that it should be added to the family of Brachiopoda. C. Sandalina, Pl. xi. fig. 194, 195.

CALANTICA. Gray. Part of Scalpellum.

CALLIA. Gray, 1840? A genus described as having a peculiarly polished shell like Pupina, but wanting the notch, Pl. xxv. fig. 528.

CALLIPARA. Swainson. VOLUTA bullata; Sowerby's Thesaurus Conchy-

117. Cythera Meretrix; *e.* escutcheon.
117. *a.* C. Meroe; *Gen.* Meroe.
117. *b.* C. Tripla; *Gen.* Trigona.
117. *c.* C. Maculata; *Gen.* Chione.
117. *d.* C. Castrensis.
118. Artemis lincta; *s*, sinus in the palleal impression.
119. Venus cancellata. Antigona, Schum. *a.* anterior; *p.* posterior; *c.* cardinal teeth.
119. *a.* V. Verrucosa. Dosina, Schum.
120. Pullastra Textile.

Fam. Cardiacea

121. Venericardia, recent species, resembling V. planicostata, Lam.
122. Cardium Dionæum. Cardissa, Sw. Hemicardium. Nonnull.
123. ——angulatum.
123*.——Greenlandicum. Aphrodita, Lea, Acardo, Sw.
123**.——hemicardium. *Gen.* Hemicardum.
124. Cardita calyculata.
125. Cypricardia angulata.
126. Isocardia Moltkiana.
128. Hippagus Isocardioides, (from Lea.)

liorum, Pl. liii. fig. 88.

CALLISOSTOMA. Sw. A genus of shells separated from Trochus, and thus described: "Imperforate; spire elevated, acute; aperture broader than high, transversely ovate, hardly sinuated at the base, and slightly oblique; shell always smooth, and often polished." C. zixyphina is mentioned as an example.

CALLISCAPHA. Gray? Iridina Nilotica, Sow. Zool. Journ. 1. pl. 2. Separated from Iridina on account of the hinge margin being smooth.

CALLITHEA. Sw. A sub-genus of Mitræ, consisting of those species, which like M. sanguisuga, have the "spire and aperture of nearly equal length: internal channel nearly obsolete; shell with longitudinal linear ribs, crossed by transverse striæ and bands; base contracted." Swanson, Mallac. Lard. Cyclop.

CALLOCHITON. Gray, 1847. Chiton lævis, &c.

CALLOSITY. A term used in general zoology to express those hard horny tumidities formed in the skin of some animals (such as the Dromedary, for instance) in those parts which are most frequently used. It is not used in this sense by Conchologists, who apply it to those undefined tumidities or bumps which appear on the inner surface and hinge of some bivalve shells, and to the thickening over the umbilicus of Natidæ. Glycimeris, fig. 97; Natica, fig. 327, 328.

CALPURNUS. Montf. 1810. Ovulum verrucosum, Auct. Distinguished by the small circular tubercle at the back of each extremity of the shell. Pl. xx. fig. 441.

CALYPTRACEA. Lam. A family belonging to the first section of the order Gasteropoda, Lam. the shells of which are described as always external, covering the animal, and having no operculum. The genera contained in this family may be thus distinguished:

1. Calyptræa. Conical; apex central, septum spiral, cup-shaped, or forked; including Infundibulum, fig. 234 to 238.
2. Crepidula. Apex terminal; septum flat, reaching half way across the aperture. Fig. 239.
3. Capulus. Conical; apex obliquely curved, no septum. Fig. 240.
4. Emarginula. Apex curved backwards; a notch in the anterior margin; including Parmophorus. Fig. 241, 242.
5. Cemoria. A slit near the apex. Fig. 244.
6. Fissurella. A slit upon the apex. Fig. 245.
7. Rimula. A slit near the margin. Fig. 243.
8. Ancylus. Apex curved sidewise. Fig. 246.

CALYPTRACEA. Bl. The second family of the order Scutibranchiata. Bl. thus described: "Shell more or less conical, not spiral, or very slightly so; aperture large and entire." The genera included in this family are Crepidula, Calyptræa, Capulus, Hipponyx, and Notrêma.

CALYPTRÆA. Lamarck. Fam. Calyptracea. Lam. and Bl.—Descr. Conical, patelliform, irregular, with an internal, lateral, salient plate or septum, varying in form.—Obs. The species of this genus or family are divided very properly in the British Museum Synopsis according to the character of the septum, reserving the name (Calyptræa (or Calyptra) for species with a forked septum, C. equestris, fig. 234. The name Crucibulum is applied to the "cup and saucer" division; Galerus to the species with a half-spiral septum, fig. 236; Trochita to the trochæform, spiral species (Infundibum, Montf.) fig. 237; and Crypta to Crepidula, Lamarck, with a septum across the shell, fig. 239, Pl. xii.

CAMERIMA. Brug. Nummulites, Auct.

CAMILLUS. Montf. A genus founded upon a minute, spiral, shell, with a triangular aperture, turned over the back of the last whorl. It is figured in Soldani's Testacea Microscopica.

CAMITIA. Gray, described——? (adopted from his Synopsis.) A genus founded on a very interesting shell brought by Mr. Cuming from the Isle of Luzon, Philippines. It is round and flat, and in general appearance like a Rotella; but the Columella presents very singular characters, being quite separated from the body whorl by a spiral slit, and from the outer lip by a deep notch under a strong tooth. Behind the Columella is a spiral canal. Ex. C. pulcherrima, Pl. xxviii. fig. 590.

CAMOSTRÆA. Roissy? Cleidotherus, Stutchbury.

CAMPULOTUS. Guettard, 1759. Magilus, Montfort, 1810. The former is therefore used by some authors on the ground of priority.

CANALICULATED. Applied generally to any distinct groove or canal.

CANAL. A groove which characterizes some spiral univalves, where the inner and outer lips unite at the front part of the aperture. This canal is drawn out in some shells to a considerable length, in others it is turned abruptly over the back. The family Canaliferæ, Lam. (fig. 372 to 401) are all provided with this canal.

CANALIFERA. Canalifères, Lam. A family belonging to the order Trachelipoda. Lam. nearly corresponding with the family Entomostrata in De Blainville's system, and described as having a canal of greater or less extent at the anterior part of the aperture. This canal is sometimes straight, sometimes tortuous, and in some genera it is recurved over the back of the shell. All the shells have an operculum, and the thickness of the perfectly formed outer lip does not increase with age. The Canalifera are characterized by having a canal, in distinction from the Purpurifera, which have only a notch. This family contains the following genera:

1. Cerithium. Club-shaped. Fig. 372.
2. Potamis. The same, fresh water. Fig. 377.
3. Nerinea. The same, with internal folds. Fig. 374.
4. Triphora. Anterior and posterior canals closed, so as to present three openings. Fig. 375, 376.
5. Telescopium. Pyramidal, trochiform. Fig. 378.
6. Pleurotoma. A slit on the outer part of the outer lip; including Clavatula. Fig. 379, 381.
7. Turbinella. Three horizontal folds on the columella. Fig. 382, 383.
8. Spirillus. Spire papillary; one fold on the columella. Fig. 384.
9. Cancellaria. Three folds, and internal costæ. Fig. 385.
10. Fasciolaria. Oblique folds, the lowest the largest. Fig. 386.
11. Fusus. Fusiform; no folds on the columella. Fig. 317.
12. Pyrula. Pear-shaped. Fig. 388 to 390.
13. Struthiolaria. Outer lip thickened; sinuated. Fig. 391.
14. Ranella. Two rows of varices; a canal at each extremity of the aperture. Fig. 393, 394.
15. Murex. Three or more rows of varices; only one distinct canal. Fig. 395, 396.
16. Typhis. A tubular perforation between each varix. Fig. 307.
17. Triton. Varices not in rows. Fig. 398 to 401.

CANCELLARIA. Lamarck, 1801. (From Cancellatus, cross-barred, like window-frames or net work.) Fam. Canalifera, Lam. Entomostomata, Bl.—Descr. Oval, thick, cancellated; spire generally short, pointed; aperture sub-ovate, emarginated anteriorly, pointed at the posterior extremity: outer lip marked within by transverse ridges; inner lip spread over part of the body whorl, terminating in a straight, thick obtuse columella, with several strong oblique folds. Hab. Indian Ocean, Coast of Africa, America, and West Indies. Fossils found in London Clay and Calc-grossier of Paris. Differing from Turbinellus in

127. Megalodon cucullatus, (from
Sow. Min. Con.)
129. Hippopodium ponderosum,
(from Sow. Min. Con.)
130. Pachymya gigas, (from Sow.
Min. Con.)
Cardilia, fig. 581,
582.
Papyridea, fig. 503,
504.
Pleurorynchius, fig.
505.
} To be
added
to this
family.

Fam. Arcacea

131. Arca antiquata.
132. Bysso-arca Noæ.
133. Cucullæa auriculifera, (from
Sowerby's Genera.)
134. Pectunculus pilosus.
135. Myopara costata, (from Lea.)
136. Crenella.
137. Nucula margaritacea, three
views.
138. Solenello Norrissii.
Leda, fig. 578.
Nucinella, fig.
579.
} To be
added to
this family.

Fam. Trigonacea

139. Trigonia pectinata.
140. Castalia ambigua. Tetraplodon
pectinatus, Spix.

Fam. Nayades

141. Alasmodon complanatus, Say.
Margaritana, Schum.

45

form and in the transversely ribbed inside of the outer lip. Fig. 315. C. reticulata.—*Obs.* The latest enumeration of the species of this genus is contained in a catalogue published by Mr. G. B. Sowerby, senior, accompanying the author's figures of the new species, amounting to 38 in parts 9 to 13 of the Conchological Illustrations. The greater part of these new species were brought to this country by Mr. Cuming. The monograph subsequently published by the author in pl. ix. of the Thesaurus Conchyliorum, contains 68 species. See our plate xviii. fig. 385.

CANCELLATED. (From *Cancellatus*, cross-barred.) Applied generally to any shells which are marked by ridges crossing each other as Cancellaria, fig. 385.

CANCILLA. Sw. A sub-genus of Mitræa, described as having "the whorls crossed by transverse linear ribs; inner canal wanting, plates very oblique; form slender; outer lip thin." *Ex.* M. Isabella, M. sulcata.

CANCRIS. Montf. CREPIDULINA, Bl. A genus of microscopic Foraminifera.

CANOPUS. Montf. A genus of microscopic Foraminifera.

CANTHAPLEURA. Swainson, 1840. ACANTHOPLEURA, Guilding, 1835. C. spinosus. fig. 227, and similar species of Chiton.

CANTHARIDUS. Montf. 1810. TROCHUS IRIS, Auct. and analogous species. ELENCHUS, Humph. Pl. xxv. fig. 543.

CANTHARUS. Montf. A genus of microscopic Foraminifera.

CANTHIDOMUS. Swainson, 1840. A sub-genus of Melanopsis, thus described: "spire generally short; whorls coronated with spines, or marked with longitudinal ribs; base obtuse. C. costata, Sow. Gen. f. 3." Melanopsis costata. Pl. xiv. fig. 315.

CANTHORBIS. Sw. A sub-genus of the sub-family Trochinæ, Sw. Described as being "nearly disc-shaped: spire but slightly raised; the margin of the body-whorl flattened, and serrated with flat spines; inner lip united to the outer; pillar and aperture as in the last. (Tubicanthus) C. imperialis. Mart. 173. f. 1714," This sub-genus appears to include those species of which De Montfort's genera Imperator and Calcar are formed.

CAPITULUM. Klein. POLLICIPES Mitellus, Lam. Pl. ii. fig. 37*.

CAPRELLA. Guilding, 1825. PLEKOCHEILUS. Also of Guilding, AURICULA Caprella, Lam. Pl. xxv. fig. 522, 523.

CAPRINA. D'Orb. DICERAS. Auct.?

CAPRINUS. Montf. (Conch. Syst. t. 2, p. 143.) The figure appears to be intended to represent Helix Nux-denticulata.

CAPSA. Lamarck. *Fam.* Nymphacea, Lam.—*Descr.* Equivalve, transverse, subequilateral, subtrigonal; cardinal teeth, two in one valve, a notched one in the other; lateral teeth remote, obsolete; an external ligament; two muscular impressions in each valve; a large sinus in the muscular impression of the mantle.—*Obs.* This genus is so nearly related to Donax, that it is difficult to distinguish it at first sight. The Capsæ, however, have not the short, plain, straight, posterior side, the distinct lateral teeth, nor the crenulated margins which characterize nearly all the Donaces. They are found in the British Channel, Brazil and coast of Pacific Ocean. They are known from Eyrcina by not having the pit in the hinge for the ligament. C. Braziliensis. Pl. v. fig. 109.

CAPULUS. Montf. 1810. *Fam.* Calyptracea, Lam.—*Descr.* Obliquely conical, posteriorly recurved; apex pointed, sub-spiral; aperture large, rounded, oval; with two muscular impressions, lateral, meeting behind; epidermis horny, rather velvety. Britain, Mediterranean, West Indies, California, Australia. *Ex.* C. ungaricus. Pl. xii. fig. 240.

CARDIACEA. (Cardiacées, Lam.) A family of the order Conchifera Dimyaria, Lam. Most of the genera of shells contained in this family are included in the very extensive family of Conchacea, in the system of De Blainville. They are described as having irregularly formed cardinal teeth. Most of the species are ventricose, and have regular radiating ribs. The family contains the genera Cardium, Cardita, Cypricardia, Hiatella, Isocardia, and others enumerated in the explanation of figures 122 to 130. Their characters may be thus explained.

1. CARDIUM. Two cardinal and two lateral teeth in each valve, including *Hemicardium*, *Papyridea* and *Aphrodita*, in the last of which the teeth are nearly obsolete. Fig. 122, 123, 123*, 123**.

2. VENERICARDIA. Two oblique cardinal teeth, one elongated; including *Cardita*, which has the umbones nearly terminal. *Pachymya* may probably be included, but the hinge is not known. Fig. 121, 124, and 130.

3. HIPPOPODIUM. One elongated cardinal tooth. Fig. 129.

4. MEGALODON. Hinge broad, septiform, with a large tooth in the centre of one valve. Fig. 127.

5. ISOCARDIA. Teeth laminar; umbones spiral. Fig. 126.

6. CARDILIA. The same with a septiform posterior laminar tooth.

7. HIPPAGUS. Shaped like Isocardia, without teeth. Fig. 128.

CARDILIA. Desh. 1837. HEMICYCLONOSTA. *Fam.* Cardiacea, Lam. A genus formed for the reception of Isocardia semi-sulcata, Lam. and a small fossil shell, which Deshayes had formerly named Hemicyclonosta Michelini; thus described, (translation) "shell oval, oblong, longitudinal, white, heart-shaped, ventricose, with large prominent umbones; hinge with a small cardinal tooth and a pit at the side; a spoon-shaped projection for the reception of the internal ligament; anterior muscular impression rounded, not deep; the posterior being upon a thin, horizontal lamina, projecting in the anterior." Deshayes further remarks that although the animal is unknown, the relations of the genus may be established by means of the shell alone. Two families contain all the shells which have the internal ligament inserted in a spoon-shaded projection; in the one, that of the Anatinæ, the ligament is supported upon a little bone, which is not soldered to the hinge; in the other, that of the Mactraceæ, this little bone has no existence. In the former, all the shells are inequivalve; in the latter equivalve. And M. Deshayes, considering that the valves are equal, and that there is no separate bone to the hinge, is of opinion that the genus ought to be placed near the Lutrariæ, and not far from the Anatinæ. C. semisulcata, pl. xxiv. fig. 501, 2.

CARDINAL MARGIN. The edge of a bivalve shell on which the teeth is placed.

CARDINAL TEETH. The teeth upon the hinge directly beneath the umbones of a bivalve shell, as distinguished from the lateral teeth, which are placed at a distance on each side. In Venus, fig. 119, the cardinal teeth are marked by the letter *c*.

CARDIOCARDITES. Bl. A genus separated from CARDITA, Auct. Thus described, (translation) "oval species, with the inferior margin nearly straight, or a very little inflated, crenulated and completely closed. *Ex.* La C. Ajar, Adans. Seneg. pl. xvi. fig. 2."

CARDISSA. Megerle, 1811. A genus composed of those species of CARDIUM *Auct.* which are heart-shaped. *Ex.* C. dionæum, fig. 122. and C. Cardissa.

CARDITA. Brug. 1789. *Fam.* Cardiacea, Lam. Submytilacea, Bl.—*Descr.* Equivalve, inequilateral, ovate, subquadrate or oblong, marked externally by ribs radiating from the umbones and terminating in a

142. Dipsas plicatus, Leach.
     Cristaria, Schum.
143. Hyria corrugata, Lam.
     Paxyodon, Schum. Triplodon.
144. Syrmatophora, Sow. Prisodon,
     Schum. Diplodon, Spix.
145. Unio littoralis, Lam. Mysca.
     ovata, Turton.
147. —— Alatus. Symphynota, Lea.
148. —— Atratus, Lam. Naia, Sw.
149. Monocondylæa Paraguayana.
150. Iridina elongata.
     Pleiodon, Conrad.   ⎫
151. Mycetopus   ⎬ Platiris
     solenoides, D'Orb.   ⎟ Lea.
     Spatha, Lea.   ⎭
152. Anodon Cataractus.

crenulated margin on the inner surface; cardinal teeth in one valve, one long, thick, oblique; another short, more straight; in the other valve one long, oblique, thick. Muscular impressions two in each valve, rather oval; palleal impression not sinuated.—*Obs.* This description includes Lamarck's genus Venericardia, which, although consisting of the more oblong species, is not considered sufficiently distinct to justify the separation. Cypricardia is distinguished from this genus by a remote lateral tooth. Mediterranean, Africa, East Indies, &c. Cardita calyculata, fig. 124.

CARDIUM. Linn. *Fam.* Cardiacea, Lam. Conchacea. Bl.—*Descr.* Equivalve, sub-equilateral, sometimes gaping posteriorly, ornamented on the outside by ribs radiating from the umbones; cardinal teeth, two in each valve, locked into each other cross-wise, lateral teeth, two in each valve, remote; muscular impressions, two in each valve; palleal impression entire. Ligament external, inflated.—*Obs.* Although this genus includes many remarkable forms, the characters are so easily defined that there is no difficulty in distinguishing it from any other genus. The principal forms are Cardium Angulatum, fig. 123, and C. Hemicardium, fig. 123**; Cardium Grœnlandicum, fig. 123*. (APHRODITE) Cardium Dionæum, fig. 122, (CARDISSA) and Apertum, fig. 503, 4. (Papyridea.) Pl. vi. It is somewhat surprising that this genus, which contains some of the most beautiful forms of bivalve Testacea, should have been left till quite lately without any attempt to revise the species and settle the synonyms. The monograph in the Author's Conchological Illustrations contains sixty species from all climates. Pl. vi. fig. 122, 123, 123*, 123**. Pl. xxiv. fig. 503, 504.

CARINARIA. Lamarck, 1801, *Class,* Cephalopoda. *Division,* Monothalamia, Lam. *Fam.* Nectopoda, B.—*Descr.* Symmetrical or nearly so, conical, thin, glassy, fragile, patelliform; with a fimbriated dorsal keel; apex convolute, bent forwards; aperture oval, pointed at the dorsal extremity. *Hab.* Amboyna, Indian Ocean, and Mediterranean Sea.—*Obs.* A most singular and beautiful shell, remarkable for its transparency, its fragile structure, and the dorsal keel, whence it derives its name. It was once so rare that a single specimen of the large species realized a hundred guineas. C. Mediterranea. Pl. xxiii. fig. 488.

CARINATED. (From *Carina,* a keel.) Applied to any shell having a raised, thin ledge, passing round a whorl or any other part of a shell, as in Carinaria, fig. 488.

CARINEA. Swainson, 1840. ULTIMUS, Montf. 1810. OVULUM gibbosum, Auct. fig. 343, and similar species.

CARINELLA. Adanson. LUTRARIA papyracea, Lam. *Fam.* Mactracea, Lam. Fig. 77.

CARINIDEA. Swainson, 1840. INFUNDIBULUM. Montf. 1810.

CAROCOLLUS. Montf. *Fam.* Colimacea, Lam.—*Descr.* Orbicular, depressed, with the outer side of the whorls angulated or keeled, whorls few; peritreme reflected; columella contiguous to the axis; epidermis thin.—*Obs.* This genus differing from Helix only in the whorls being angulated, is hardly distinct enough from the latter to justify the separation. In De Ferrusac's system these species constitute the division Helicigona, of the genus Helix. C. Lamarckii, fig. 277. East and West Indies, Philippines, South America and Europe. Pl. xiii. fig. 277.

CARTILAGE. See LIGAMENT.

CARYCHIUM. Müller, 1774. *Fam.* Auriculacea, Bl. Colimacea, Lam.—*Descr.* Oblong or cylindrical, with gradually increasing whorls, few in number; aperture straight, short, with a fold on the columella.—*Obs.* This genus of minute land shells differs from Auricula chiefly in the soft parts. De Ferrusac enumerates three species,

C. Lineatum, C. Corticaria, (*Odostomia,* Flem.) and C. Minimum, fig. 301. De Blainville places it in his genus Auricula, as "species with two folds and a posterior tooth on the columella," giving a figure of A. Mysotis as his example, and quoting the name Phitia, Gray. Europe. Pl. xiv. fig. 301.

CASSIDARIA. Lam. 1812. Should be MORIO. Montf. 1810, on the ground of priority. (From Cassis.) *Fam.* Purpurifera, Lam. Entomostomata, Bl.—*Descr.* Oval, ventricose, spirally grooved and tuberculated, with a short turrited spire and a large aperture, terminating anteriorly in a recurved canal; outer lip thickened, reflected, undulated or denticulated; inner lip expanded over a part of the body whorl and the columella, with part of its lower edge free.—*Obs.* The recent species of this genus are not numerous; the few fossil species occur in the tertiary strata. C. carinata is found in "Calc-grossier" and London Clay. In general form this resembles CASSIS, but is at once distinguished by the canal, which does not turn abruptly back, but is slightly curved upwards. ONISCIA (C. Oniscus, &c. Lam.) is distinguished by the shortness of the canal, and the granulated surface of the inner lip. C. Echinophora. Mediterranean. Pl. xix. fig. 407, 408.

CASSIDEA. Sw. (From Cassis.) A genus composed of those species of the genus CASSIS, Auct. which have the "aperture wide; outer lip never broad or flattened, but sometimes slightly inflected; inner lip spreading, but never dilated or detached beyond the base into a prominent rim." East Indies. *Ex.* C. Glauca. C. Bezoardica. Schum. 1837. Pl. xix. fig. 411.

CASSIDULUS. Humph. The genus Pyrula being restricted to the fig-shaped species, this name is used for the turrited and turbinated species that remain. C. melongena, &c. but not including P. perversa. Fulgur. Montf.

CASSIDULINA. D'Orbigny. A genus of microscopic Foraminifera.

CASSIS. Browne, 1756. (A helmet.) *Fam.* Purpurifera, Lam. Entomostomata, Bl.—*Descr.* Oval or triangular, ventricose, thick, generally tuberculated, with a short varicose spire; aperture long, sometimes narrow, with the outer lip thickened and reflected, generally denticulated; the inner lip spread over the surface of the body whorl, indented and incrassated at its inner edge; canal turned suddenly over the back of the shell.—*Hab.* Seas of tropical climates. The fossil species are rare, occurring in the tertiary strata.—*Obs.* The large, common species of this well known genus are used for shell cameos and as ornaments on chimney pieces, grottos, &c. and are remarkable for the triangular disc, presented by the inner lip, which, in many species, is thickened and spread over the front of the body whorl and the angulated outer lip. The smaller, more rounded species, which have widened apertures, have been separated by Swainson, under the generic name CASSIDEA. The C. rufa, coarctata, &c. are formed by Mr. Stutchbury into a new genus under the name CYPRÆCASSIS, for reasons which will be stated under the word. Cassidaria is distinguished by the gradual curve of the canal. Mr. Reeve's monograph contains 43 species. C. tuberosa (diminished.) Pl. xix. fig. 410.

CASTALIA. Lamarck, 1819. *Fam.* Trigonées, Lam.—*Descr.* Fluviatile, equivalve, inequilateral, trigonal, with corroded umbones; hinge with two laminar, transversely striated teeth, one of which is posterior, remote from the umbones, short, divided, the other anterior, elongated; epidermis thick; internal surface pearly. Lamarck, in describing this shell, states that he regards it as intermediate between Trigonia and Unio. It should, however, certainly have been placed in the family of "Nayades," and perhaps should form a part of the genus UNIO itself. C. ambigua, Lam. Pl. vii. fig. 140.

CATILLUS. Brong. Inoceramus, Sowerby. Catillus. Humph. 1797. Cimber. Montf. 1810. Navicella. Lamarck, 1822. Pl. x. fig. 158.

CATOPHRAGMUS. Sow. (From Κατω, *beneath*; φραγμος, *a place paled in.*) *Order*, Sessile Cirripedes, Lam.—*Descr.* Eight principal valves, cemented side by side in a circle; eight small pointed valves beneath, covering the joints of the upper circle, and numerous still smaller valves forming the base of the shell; operculum, four valves.—*Obs.* Catophragmus is the only genus of Sessile Cirripedes, which consists of eight principal valves, excepting Octomeris. The latter genus has not the accessary pieces from which the former derives its name. C. imbricatus. Pl. i. fig. 23.

CAUDAL CANAL. The elongated hollow process which terminates the aperture anteriorly of some univalve shells. For instance, Murex Haustellum, fig. 396, has an elongated caudal canal.

CELLANTHUS. Montf. Vorticialis, Bl. A genus of microscopic Foraminifera.

CELLULACEA. Bl. The second order of Cephalophora, Bl. consisting of doubtful microscopic bodies, with a number of variously arranged shells, as distinguished from the true Polythalamia, Bl. or chambered shells. See Foraminifera.

CEMORIA. Leach. 1819. A small patelliform shell, differing from Fissurella, in having the fissure placed behind the apex, which is produced, pointed and incurved. It is the Patella Fissurella, Müll. Patella Noachina, Chemn. F. Noachina, Sow. Puncturella, Lowe. Scotland and Tierra del Fuego. Cemoria Flemingii. Pl. xiii. fig. 244.

CENTRAL. A term used to indicate the position of the muscular impression of a bivalve shell when it is near the centre of the inner surface. It is also applied to the siphon perforating the septum of a chambered shell when it is placed near the centre of the plate. *Sub*-central is also used as a comparative term, to indicate the position of the siphon, or of the muscular impression, is *near* the centre. Thus in Placuna (fig. 184), the muscular impression is central: in Exogyra (fig. 183), it is *sub*-central.

CEPA. Humph. 1797. Anomia, Linn. Müller. 1776.

CEPHALOPHORA. Bl. The first class of Malacozoæ, Bl. Divided into: *Order* 1. Cryptodibranchiata; 2. Cellulacea; 3. Polythalamacea. The first consisting of Cuttle-fish, &c. which are destitute of shells; the second composed of those microscopic cellular bodies, which are regarded as shells by some authors; and the third containing the true chambered shells.

CEPHALOPODA. Lam. (Cephalopodes.) (Κεφαλη, *kephale*, head; πους, ποδος, *podos*, foot.) The fourth order of the *class* Mollusca, Lam. containing molluscs, which are characterized by having a series of arms surrounding the head, which is placed above a sack-shaped body. This order is divided into Polythalamia, or many-chambered shells) Monothalamia, or single-chambered Cephalopoda: and Sepiaria, or cuttle-fish. Fig. 463 to 488.

CERATISOLEN. Forbes. Pharus, Leach. Ms. Gray. Syn. Brit. mus. A genus formed for the reception of Solen legumen, which differs from the true Solens, or razor shells, in having the umbones nearly central, &c.

CERATODES. Guild. 1828. Marisa, Gray. 1824. (Κερατώδης, like a horn.) A genus composed of the flat, orbicular species of Ampullaria, Auct. which present so near a resemblance to the Planorbes, as to have been considered as belonging to them. Planorbis has, however, a horny texture, and no operculum, and it is always *reversed*. Pl. xv. fig. 320, represents Ampullaria (Ceratodes) Cornu-arietis.

CERIPHASIA. Swainson, 1840. A sub-genus of Melanianæ, thus described, "Cerithiform; outer lip thin, dilated at the base; aperture small, slightly emarginate, without any internal groove; inner lip thin. C. sulcata, Sw. fig. 38. p. 204." (Sw. Lard. Cyclop. Malac. p. 342.)

CERITHIDEA. Swainson. Part of Potamis, sp. decollatus, with rounded whorls, and spread outer lip sinuous at the base.

CERITHIOPSIS. Forbes and Hanley, 1851. A genus of shells distinguished from Cerithium on purely anatomical grounds. Ex. C. tuberculare. British Moll. Pl. xci. figs. 7, 8. p. 365.

CERITHIUM. Adanson, 1757. *Fam.* Canalifera, Lam. Entomostomata, Bl.—*Descr.* Elongated, ribbed, tuberculated, or rarely smooth, with a lengthened, turrited, pointed, pyramidal spire, consisting of numerous whorls; aperture sub-quadrate, terminated anteriorly by a tortuous canal; outer lip thickened, sometimes reflected, expanded; inner lip thickened posteriorly; operculum horny, spiral, with numerous whorls.—*Obs.* The fresh-water shells described as Cerithia by Lamarck, are separated under the name Potamis, and may be known by the thick, horny epidermis. Triphora, Desh. has the canal closed, except at the extremities. Cerithium Telescopium, does not appear to present the same characters as the other Cerithia, and has been separated by some writers under the generic name Telescopium. Cerithium Aluco, fig. 372. Mediterranean, East and West Indies, Coasts of the Pacific, Gallapagos, Australia, &c. Some small species are British. Fossils are numerous in the tertiary beds. Pl. xvii. fig. 372.

CERVICOBRANCHIATA. Bl. The second order of Paracephalophora Hermaphrodita, Bl. containing symmetrical patelliform shells, divided into the families Retifera and Branchifera.

CETOCIS. Montf. *Fam.* Orthocerata, Lam. and Bl. Placed by De Blainville in his section of Belemnites, characterized as having small folds at the apex. *Ex.* B. Penicillatus.

CETOPIRUS. Ranz. Coronula Balenaris, Auct. Pl. i. fig. 16.

CHÆNA. Gray. Fistulana, Lamarck.

CHAMA. Linnæus. *Fam.* Chamacea, Lam. and Bl.—*Descr.* Inequivalve, irregular, thick, foliaceous, attached by the umbone of the lower and larger valve. External ligament placed in a groove, following the curve of the umbones. Umbones spiral, coiled round on the back of the valves; hinge with a thick, crenated, lengthened tooth, in one valve, entering a corresponding cavity in the hinge margin of the other; muscular impressions, two in each valve, distinct, lateral.—*Obs.* The Linnæan genus Chama, included the beautiful shells now called Tridacna. These are exceedingly different from the true Chamæ, being regular and unattached. The Chama (Tridacna) gigas, when at its full age and development, is the largest shell known. Specimens have occurred weighing upwards of 500 lbs., and measuring two feet across. Diceras may be known from Chama by the spiral horns into which the umbones are produced; Isocardia, by the regularity of the shells, and it is hardly necessary to mention Spondylus, which may be known by the triangular disc between the umbones; Cleidothærus, Stutch. which resembles Chama in general form, has a separate bony appendage attached to the hinge, and may, moreover, be distinguished by its elongated muscular impression. 55 species are contained in Mr. Reeve's Monograph. E. and W. Indies. Ch. Lazarus, Pl. ix. fig. 153.

CHAMACEA. Bl. The seventh family of the order Lamellibranchiata, Bl. containing the genera Chama, Diceras, Etheria, Tridacna, Isocardia and Trigonia.

CHAMACEA. Lam. A family belonging to the order Conchifera Dimyaria, Lam. described as inequivalve, attached, irregular; with or without a single rough tooth on the hinge; with two lateral muscular impressions in each valve. This family contains the genera:

1. CHAMA. Leafy; umbones spiral. Fig. 153.
2. ETHERIA. Very irregular, pearly, without teeth. Fig. 155.
3. DICERAS. Like Chama, but with the umbones free, produced. Fig. 154.

CHAMBERED. When the cavity of a shell is not continuous, but is divided by shelly diaphragms or septa, it is said to be chambered. This is the case with the shells of the Polythalamous Cephalopoda, as in the Nautilus (see Introduction). The character is not confined to these, as it occurs in some species of Spondyli, and in several turrited univalves.

CHAMOSTRÆA. De Roissy. CLEIDOTHÆRUS. Stutch.

CHARYBS. Montf. A genus of microscopic Foraminifera.

CHELIBS. Montf. A genus of microscopic Foraminifera.

CHELIDONURA. Adans. Sowerby's Thesaurus, 1850. A sub-genus of Bullidæ, the shell of which is thus described, "hid in the thickness of the mantle, thin, very open, scarcely spiral, with the right border ending in a point."

CHELINOTUS. Swainson. A genus of "HALIOTIDÆ," Sw. including Velutina, Lam. a species of Sigarctus from Tonga, and Coriocella, Bl. Thus described, "Animal cheloniform, broad; depressed; the mantle larger than the shell, lobed in front; tentacula two, short, obtuse; eyes basal; mouth circular; shell ear-shaped, thin, fragile, imperforate; pillar none."

CHELONOBIA. Leach. CORONULA Testudinaria, Auct. Pl. i. fig. 15.

CHEMNITZIA. D'Orbigny. A genus of small transparent shells, resembling Scalariæ in some respects, but without varices. C. varicula. Pl. xxviii. fig. 585.

CHERSINA. Humph. Part of ACHATINA, Lam.

CHICOREUS. Montf. 1810. A generic division of the genus MUREX, consisting of such species as have three ramified varices. Ex. M. inflatus, fig. 395.

CHILINA. Gray. Fam. Auriculacea, Bl. Colimacea, Lam.—Descr. Oval, thin, covered with an olive green epidermis; spire rather short, consisting of few whorls; aperture large, oval, rounded anteriorly; outer lip thin, joining the inner lip without a sinus; inner lip spread over part of the body whorl, terminating in a thick columella with one or two folds.—Obs. These shells differ from the true Auriculæ in the thinness of the outer lip. C. Dombeyana (Auricula Dombeyana, Auct.) Fig. 300. The illustrated catalogue published by the author (Sow. Conch. illustr. parts 135, 136) contains 13 species. Rivers of South America. Pl. xiv. fig. 300.

CHILOTREMA. Leach, 1819. A sub-genus of HELIX, containing Helix lapicida. Auct. Gray, Turton, p. 440.

CHIMOTREMA.——? Belongs to HELIX.

CHIONE. Megerle. CYTHERÆA maculosa, (fig. 117, c.) sulcata, circinata, &c. Auct. and other similar species. See Thesaurus Conchylium, No. 12, and our figure. Pl. vi. fig. 117, c.

CHISMOBRANCHIATA. Bl. The second order of the first section of Paracephalophora Monoica, Bl. Those Mollusca belonging to this order which have shells, have them either internal or external, but always scutiform, with depressed spires and wide, haliotoid, oblique apertures, without a columellar lip properly so called. This order partly answers to the family MACROSTOMATA, in the system of Lamarck. It contains the genera Coriocella, Sigaretus, Cryptostoma, Oxinoe, Stomatella, and Velutina.

CHITON. Lamarck. (χιτον, an integument), Fam. Phyllidiana, Lam. Class, Polyplaniphora, Bl.—Descr. Oval, consisting of eight arched valves arranged in a series across the body of the animal and fixed in the skin which forms a rim around them, sometimes scaly, spinose, or rugose, sometimes smooth.—Obs. The genus Chiton, commonly called "Coat of Mail," from its resemblance to jointed armour, remains to the present day in exactly the same state with regard to its boundaries as that in which Linnæus found it, and in which he left it. That illustrious Naturalist placed it among the multivalves in his purely Conchological system, although the animal is totally different from the Cirripedes. The shells are prettily marked, and are found attached to the rocks in all seas of Tropical and Southern climates, but fossil species are almost unknown. Fig. 227, C. Spinosus. The genus is divided in the British Museum Synopsis, according to the character of the marginal integument into the genera LOPHUNS, Ex. Chiton squamosus; RADSIA, Ex. Chiton Barnesii; CALLOCHITON, Ex. Ch. lævis; ISCHNOCHILON, Ex. Ch Textile; LEPTOCHITON, Ex. Ch. cinereus; CONICIA, Ex. Ch. elegans; ACANTHAPLEUSA, Ex. Ch. spinosa; CHITON, Ex. Ch. gigas; SCHIZOCHITON, Ex. Ch. inscisus; COREPHEUM, Ex. Ch. Echinalus; PLANIPHORA, ORNITHOCHITON, ENOPLOCHITON, MOPALIA, KATHARINA, CRYPTOCHITON, CRYPTOCONCHUS, AMICULA, ACANTHOCHETES, CHITONELLUS, ERYPHOCHITON, METOPOMA. Our Plate xii. fig. 227, 228. Pl. xxiv. fig. 506, 507.

CHITONELLUS. Lam. (From Chiton.) Separated by Lamarck from Chiton, on account of the valves being placed at a greater distance from each other, the soft integument of the animal intervening. C. striatus. Philippines. Pl. xxii. fig. 228.

CHLOROSTOMA. Swainson. A sub-genus of "Trochinæ." Sw. (Trochus) of which C. argyrostoma is given as an example. Sw. Lard. Cyclop. p. 350.

CHORUS. Gray, 1850. Monocerous Giganteus. Lesson.

CHRYSOAR. Montf. Probably a species of ORTHOCERAS.

CHRYSODOMUS. Swainson, 1840. "Distinguished from Fusus, by the comparative shortness of the basal channel, and the ventricose or enlarged shape of the body whorl. The beautiful orange-mouthed Whelk of England is a typical example; and the few others known are of a very large size, and chiefly found in Northern Seas, where they represent the more elegant Fusi of tropical latitudes; the outer lip is always thin and smooth." Sw. p. 90, paragraph 78, described at page 308.

CHRYSOLUS. Montf. POLYSTOMELLA, Bl. A genus of microscopic Foraminifera.

CHRYSOSTOMA. Swainson, 1840. A genus of the family "Rotellinæ," Sw. Thus described, "Shell turbinate; the whorls few and convex; aperture effuse, round; inner lip thickened just over, and almost concealing the umbilicus. Nicobaricus, Martini, 182 fig. 1822–5." Sw. Lard. Cyclop. Malac. p. 327. Pl. xxv. fig. 542.

CHTHALAMUS. Ranz. Fam. Balanidea, Bl. Order, Sessile Cirripedes, Lam.—Descr. "Shell much depressed, valves thick, thickened at the base, with prominent areas; operculum nearly horizontal, composed of four valves."—Obs. This description would apply generically to the shell called Platylepas in the British Museum, only nothing is said about the prominent plates jutting from the internal surface of the valves. The difference between this genus and BALANUS consists principally in the horizontal position of the operculum, and general flatness of the shell. C. stellatus. Pl. i. fig. 18.

CIBICIDES. Montf. A genus of microscopic Foraminifera.

CIDARIS. Swains. 1840. A genus composed of TURBO Smaragdus, petholatus, and other similar species. The word Cidaris is, however, already in use for a genus of Echinæ.

CIDAROLLUS. Montf. A genus of microscopic Foraminifera.

CILIATED. (Ciliæ, hairs.) Having minute hairs as in Orbicula, Lingula, &c. and the jointed feelers of the Cirripedes.

CIMBER. Montf. 1810. NAVICELLA. Lamarck, 1822. "Cimber" claims priority.

CINERAS. Leach (*Cinereus*, ash-coloured.) Included by Darius with Otion, under the name CONCHODERMA. Olfus, 1814. *Order*, Pedunculated Cirripedes, Lam.—*Descr*. Animal with a quadrilateral body, supported on a fleshy peduncle, with an opening in front of the upper part for the passage of a bunch of ciliated tentacula. Immediately above this aperture is a pair of small elongated valves, placed in a nearly horizontal position; at the lower part is another tripartite pair placed perpendicularly, one on each side, and a narrow, angulated, keel-shaped piece placed at the back.—*Obs*. The nearest approach to this genus is Otion. (C. Vittatus.) Found upon substances floating in the sea. Pl. ii. fig. 42.

CINEREOUS. (*Cinereus*.) Ash-coloured.

CINGULA. Fleming, 1828. RISSOA, Freminville, 1814.

CIONELLA. Jeffreys. ZUA, Leach, MS. Gray, 1840. *Fam*. Colimacea, Lam.—*Descr*. Oblong or elongated; last whorl large; apex rather acute; columella, sub-interrupted; aperture canaliculated, sub-effuse at the base; margins very unequal; no umbilicus. BULINUS octonus, lubricus, acicula, &c. Auct. C. lubrica. Pl. xiv. fig. 285.

CIRCE. Schum. Distinguished from CYTHERÆA by the total want of Pallæal sinus, and by a peculiar flatness near the umbones. The monograph in Thesaurus Conchyliorum, by the Author (No. 12) contains sixteen pieces. Circe pectinata and C. scripta, represent the two groups. Circe scripta, Pl. xxvii. fig. 577.

CIRRIPEDES. Lam. The tenth class of invertebrated animals, so named from the curled and ciliated branchia which protrude from the oval aperture of the shells. The class Cirripedes of Lamarck constitutes the entire genus *Lepas* of Linnæus. They are divided into two sections; first, Sessile Cirr. attached by the basal portion of the shell; second, Pedunculated Cirr. supported upon a peduncle. Figs. 14 to 45.

CIRROBRANCHIATA. Bl. The first order of Paracephalophora Hermaphrodita, Bl. This order has been formed for the purpose of giving a place in the system to the genus Dentalium. The animal of which has lungs, consisting of numerous filaments, having their basal origin in two radical lobes under the dock.

CIRRUS. J. Sowerby (cirrus, a tendril.) *Fam*. Turbinacea, Bl. and Lam.—*Descr*. Spiral, conical, with a hollow axis; whorls contiguous, numerous, rounded, or slightly angulated.—*Obs*. This fossil genus resembles Trochus, from which it is known by the deep funnel-shaped umbilicus. C. nodosus. Pl. xvi. fig. 349.

CISTULA. Humph. Part of CYCLOSTOMA, Lam. C. fimbriata. See Thesaurus Conchyliorum.

CLANCULUS. Montf. 1810. TROCHUS *Pharaonis*, Lam.—*Obs*. This, with several other species, belong more properly to MONODONTA, Lam. ODONTIS, Sow. Pl. xvi. fig. 361.

CLATHODON. Conrad. GNATHODON, Gray.

CLATHRUS. Oken, 1815. The species of Scalaria, which have the whorls contingent. *Ex*. Scalaria Clathrata.

CLAUSILIA. Drap. 1805. (*Clausium*, a valve or folding door.) Colimacea, Lam. Limacinea, Bl.—*Descr*. Spire elongated, consisting of many volutions; aperture small, sub-quadrate, having several tooth-shaped folds in the columella. A small, elastic shelly plate, attached to the columella within, called the Clausium, its office being to enclose the aperture when the animal has retired within the shell.—*Obs*. This last character distinguishes it from the Pupæ, to some of which it bears a very near resemblance.—*Hab*. Land, in the central and southern parts of Europe, several British species. C. Macascarensis. Pl. xiv. fig. 295.

CLAUSIUM. A name applied to the beautiful contrivance whence the genus Clausilia derives its name, consisting of a little bony tortuous plate, placed in a groove in the columella. Here it serves the purpose of a door, which, when not prevented by counteracting pressure, springs forward on its elastic ligament, and encloses the animal in his retirement. The aperture is opened by pushing back the clausium into the groove.

CLAUSULUS. Montf. Conch. Syst. 1, 179. A genus of microscopic Foraminifera.

CLAVA. Humph. CERITHIUM, Lam.

CLAVAGELLA. Lamarck, 1818. (*Clava*, a club.) *Fam*. Tubicolæ, Lam. Pyloridea, Bl.—*Descr*. Two irregular flattish valves, one fixed or soldered, so as to form part of the side of an irregular shelly tube; the other free within the tube near the base.—*Obs*. The shells composing this genus are found in stones, madrepores, &c. and appear to form the connecting link between Aspergillum, which has both valves cemented into the tube; and Fistulana, in which both are free. Found recent on the coast of Malta and New South Wales. A fossil species. Pl. ii. fig. 45.

CLAVALITHES. Swainson, 1840. A genus composed of some fossil shells, separated from the genus Fusus, which, having the general form of Turbinella Rapa, &c. are considered by Swainson, as holding an intermediate station between Fusus and the Turbinellidæ.—*Descr*. "Unequally sub-fusiform; the body whorl, and spire, being conic; and the canal suddenly contracted and attenuated; terminal whorls papillary; inner lip thick; pillar smooth, C. longævus, clavellatus, Noæ, ponderosus, Sw."—*Obs*. The papillary spire may form a sufficient reason for separating this genus from Fusus, while the absence of plates on the columella places them at a still greater distance from Turbinella. Pl. xxvi. fig. 548.

CLAVATE. When one extremity of the shell is attenuated, and the other becomes suddenly ventricose or globular, it is said to be Clavate. *Ex*. Murex Haustellum, fig. 396.

CLAVATULA. Lamarck, 1801. The generic name by which Lamarck originally distinguished those species of Pleurotoma which were remarkable for the shortness of their canals. In his system, however, they are re-united to Pleurotoma. P. Strombiformis. BRACHISTOMA, Swainson. Pl. xvi. fig. 381.

CLAVICANTHA. Swainson, 1840. CLAVATUTA, Lamarck, 1801. A genus separated from Pleurotoma, Lam. consisting of species, which are described as "thick, sub-fusiform; the surface rugose, and the whorls sub-coronated; channel short; slit assuming the form of a short, broad sinus. C. imperialis, E. M. 440, spirata, E. M. 440, fig. 5, conica, E. M. 439, fig. 9, echinata, E. M. 439, fig. 8, Auriculifera, E. M. 439, fig. 10."

CLAVICLE. (*clavis*, a key.) A little key. This term is applied to the bony appendage in the hinge of some species of Anatina, (those included in the generic term Lyonsia) Cleidothærus, Myochama, &c.

CLAVULINA. D'Orb. A genus of microscopic Foraminifera.

CLEIDOTHÆRUS. Stutchbury, 1835. (Θαιρος, hinge, Κλεις, clavicle.) *Fam*. Chamaceæ or Myariæ, Lam.—*Descr*. Inequivalve, irregular, solid, attached; with one cardinal, conical tooth in the free valve, entering a corresponding indenture in the other; and an oblong shelly appendage, fixed by an internal cartilage in a groove under the umbones; muscular impressions, two in each valve, one elongated, the other uniform.—*Obs*. This shell is like Chama in general form, but is distinguished by the clavicle or shelly appendage from which its name is derived. Pl. iii. figs. 75, 76.

CLEMENTIA. Gray, 1840. Venus Papyracea. Wood's Supplement, fig. 8. See Monograph of Veneridæ, forthcoming in Pt. xiii. xiv. Thesaurus Conchyliorum, by the Author.

CLEODORA. *Per. et Les. Fam.* Pteropoda, Lam. Thecosomata, Bl.—*Descr.* Thin, transparent, pyramidal, with flat alate sides, and oval aperture. Pl. xii. fig. 221, C. cuspidata.

CLISIPHONITES. Montf. Microscopic. LENTICULINA, Bl.

CLITHON. Montf. 1810. NERITINA Corona, spinosa, &c. Auct. fig. 325.

CLITIA. Leach. *Fam.* Balanidea, Bl. *Order*, Sessile Cirripedes, Lam.—*Descr.* Sub-conical, compressed, consisting of four unequal valves, two larger and two smaller, joined together side by side, by the interlocking of their dentated edges, a process somewhat like that which joiners call dove-tailing. Operculum, consisting of two unequal pointed valves.—*Obs.* Clitia is known from Creusia, by the articulations of the valves, and by the operculum, which in Creusia consists of four valves. C. Verruca, (Lepas Verruca, Gmelin.) Britain and Peru. Pl. i. fig. 20.

CLOSE. The margins of a bivalve shell are described as being close, when there is no hiatus between them in any part, otherwise they are described as *gaping*.

CLOTHO. Faujas. *Fam.* Conchacea, Bl. More properly belonging to the Pyloridea, Bl.; and the Lithophagidæ, Lam.—*Descr.* "Oval, nearly regular, longitudinally striated, equivalve, sub-equilateral; hinge consisting of a bifid tooth, curved like a crochet, larger in one valve than in the other." This description is translated from Blainville, who states that he has never seen the shell. Annales du Museum D'Histoire Naturelle, tom. 9, pl. 17, fig. 4—6.

CLYPEIFORM. (*Clypeus*, a shield.) Open, flat, shaped like a shield or buckler, as Umbrella, fig. 233, and Parmaphorus, fig. 242.

CLYPIDELLA. Sw. A sub-genus of Fissurella, described as having one extremity of the shell slightly raised. C. pustula, Sow. Gen. fig. 3.

COAT OF MAIL. A common name given to shells of the genus CHITON, on account of their resemblance to jointed armour.

COBRESIA. Hübner. VITRINA, Draparnaud.

COCHLEATE. (*Cochleare*, a spoon.) Applied to any shell or part which is hollow and oval, as Patellæ, &c. The cavity containing the cartilage in Mya, fig. 71, is Cochleate.

COCHLICELLA. One of the sub-genera into which De Ferrusac has divided the genus Helix, consisting of Bulinus decollatus, fig. 279, and similar species. See Helix.

COCHLICOPA. Fer. A sub-genus of Helix, partly corresponding with Polyphemus of De Montfort, and consisting of species of Achatina, which have the outer lip undulated.

COCHLITOMA. Fer. A sub-genus of Helix, corresponding with the genus Achatina, Auct. not including those with undulated outer lips.

COCHLODESMA. Couthoy. Boston Journal. Forbes and Hanley. British Mollusca. *Fam.* Myaria. Thin, inequivalve; muscular impressions connected by a deeply sinuated palleal impression; hinge with spoon-shaped process in each valve, with a cartilage; external ligament slight; beaks fissured. Distinguished from Thracia by the character of the hinge. *Ex.* C. præternis. Pl. xxvii. fig. 573.

COCHLODINA. Fer. A sub-genus of Helix, including the genus Clausilia, Auct.

COCHLODONTA. Fer. A sub-genus of Helix, containing Pupa Uva, Auct. &c.

COCHLOGENA. Fer. A sub-genus of Helix, containing pupiform shells, such as Azeca tridens, fig. 290.

COCHLOHYDRA. Fer. A sub-genus of Helix, composed of the genus Succinea, Auct.

COCHLOSTYLA. Fer. A sub-genus of Helix, composed of the genus Bulinus, Auct.

COLIMACEA. Lam. This Family, of the order Trachelipoda, Lam. includes all land shells, which might with propriety be divided into three sections, the first of which contain the following well known genera:—

1. SUCCINEA. Oval, transparent, oblique; animal amphibious. Fig. 265, 266.
2. HELIX. The type of which is the common snail shell. The separation of *Carocolla*, on account of the angulated whorls, or that of *Geotrochus*, on account of the turbinated shape, cannot be well maintained. Fig. 264, 267, 268, 273 to 276, 278 to 281, 294.
3. ANOSTOMA. The aperture turned up towards the spire. Fig. 271, 272.
4. STREPTAXIS. Whorls excentric. Fig. 269, 270.
5. BULINUS. Oval; aperture entire, including *Bulimulus, Balea, Cionella, Azeca*. Fig. 282 to 285, 289, 290, 296.
6. ACHATINA. A notch terminating the columella. Fig. 286 to 288.
7. PUPA. Cylindrical; including *Vertigo, Alæa*, &c. Fig. 291 to 293.
8. CLAUSILIA. Cylindrical, with a clausium. Fig. 295.

Obs. The above are united in the system of De Ferrusac under the generic name Helix, and divided into sub-genera as explained under that word.

The next section, included in the family Auriculacea, Bl., contains the genera Auricula, Chilina, Carychium, Marinula, Scarabæus, and Partula. Fig. 297 to 302.

The third section contains the following genera of land shells with opercula.

1. CYCLOSTOMA. Aperture round; operculum spiral. Fig. 303, 304.
2. NEMATURA. Last whorl contracted; operculum spiral. Fig. 305.
3. HELICINA. Aperture semi-lunar or angulated; operculum concentric. Fig. 306, 307.
4. PUPINA. Shell polished; operculum concentric; aperture round. Fig.
5. STROPHOSTOMA. Aperture turned up towards the spire, like Anostoma, but said to have an operculum. Only known fossil. Fig. 97.

COLUMBELLA. Lamarck, 1801. (Columba, a dove.) *Fam.* Columellata, Lam.—*Descr.* Thick, oval, or angular; with short spire, and long narrow aperture, contracted in the centre, and terminating in a short canal; outer lip thickened and dentated; inner lip irregularly crenated. Epidermis thin, brown. Operculum very small, horny.—*Obs.* Those species of Mitra, which resemble Columbella in shape, may easily be distinguished by the plaits on the columella. The Columbellæ are marine, and few fossil species are known. Fig. 430, C. Mercatoria. Swainson has divided this genus into the following: *Columbella*, consisting of C. Mercatoria, &c.; *Pusiostoma*, consisting of the Strombiform species; *Crassispira*, which is most probably a Cerithium; *Nitidella*, consisting of the smooth species; *Conidea*, consisting of the more conical species; another set of the more conical species has been removed from this family, and placed in that of the "Coninæ," but as they are separated by no essential character, we suppose this has merely been done for the purpose of completing the "circle" of the last mentioned family, which otherwise would not have reached the required number of five. Mediterranean, East and West Indies, South America, Coast of California, Gallapagos, &c. The Monograph of this genus in the Author's Thesaurus Conchyliorum, contains 102 species. Plates 36 to 40. Our figure, Pl. xx. fig. 430.

COLUMELLA. The column formed by the inner sides of the volutions of a spiral univalve. It is sometimes described as the inner lip of the aperture, of which it forms a part; but the term would be more properly confined to that portion of the inner lip which is seen below the body whorl, over which the remainder of the lip is frequently spread. All the inner edge of the aperture, including that part of it which covers the body whorl, is called the columellar lip. In fig. 431, the anterior termination of the columella is indicated by the letter *c*. The axis, is an imaginary line drawn strictly through the centre of the whorls, whether their inner edges form a solid column or not.

COLUMELLAR LIP. The inner lip. See COLUMELLA.

COLUMELLATA. Lam. A family of the order Trachelipoda, Lam. containing the following genera:—

    1. MITRA. Elongated; aperture narrow; strong folds on the columella; including *Mitrella, Mitreola, Tiara,* and *Conohelix.* Fig. 431, 432.

    2. MARGINELLA. Outer lip reflected; including *Volutella, Persicula, Gibberula,* and *Glabella.* Fig. 437.

    3. COLUMBELLA. Outer and inner lips denticulated or granulated. Fig. 430.

    4. VOLUTA. Outer lip thickened; folds on the columella; aperture generally wide; apex papillary; including *Scaphella, Harpula, Volutilithes, Cymbiola.* Fig. 433, 436.

    5. MELO. Shell comparatively light; spire short, sometimes hidden; apex round, spiral; folds on the columella laminar. Fig. 435.

    6. CYMBA. Upper edge of the aperture separated from the body whorl by a flat disc; apex mammillated, irregular; folds on the columella thick. Fig. 434.

    7. VOLVARIA. Cylindrical; aperture long, narrow; folds on the columella small; spire hidden. Fig. 439.

COLUS. Humphrey. 1797. FUSUS COLUS, Lamarck, and similar species. Pl. xviii. fig. 387.

COMPLANARIA. Swainson, 1840. A subgenus of ALASMODON, (Unio), thus described, "shell winged; the valves connate; the bosses very small and depressed; cardinal teeth two or three; lateral teeth represented by irregular grooves. C. gigas (Unio), Sow. Man. fig. 141. Alasmodon complanatus, (Say) C. Rugosa, Sw."

COMPRESSED. Pressed together, or flattened. The application is the same as in common use. A Patella may be described as a vertically compressed cone. A Ranella, on account of the two rows of varices skirting the whorls, appears, as it were, laterally compressed. A bivalve shell is said to be compressed when it is flat, that is, when only a small cavity is left in the deepest part when the valves are closed. Perhaps the Placuna placenta, fig. 184, is the most remarkable instance of this character.

CONCAMERATIONS. (*Con*, with, *camera*, a chamber.) A series of Chambers joining each other, as in Nautilus, Spirula, &c.

CONCENTRIC. A term applied to the direction taken by the lines of growth in spiral and other shells, (*longitudinal* of some authors.) Every fresh layer of shelly matter forms a new circle round an imaginary line, drawn through the centre of the spiral cone, down from the nucleus. When the edges of the successive layers are marked by any external characters, the shell is said to be concentrically striated, banded, grooved, costated, &c. A fine illustration of the latter character is to be seen in the Scalaria or Wentletrap, fig. 351. Lines, bands, ribs &c. in the opposite direction, (*transverse* of some authors), are "radiating" in bivalves, as the ribs of Cardium, fig. 123, and "spiral" in univalves, that is, following the direction of the whorls, as the bands of colour in

Pyramidella, fig. 342.

CONCHACEA. Bl. The eighth family of the order Lamellibranchiata, Bl. The shells are described as follows: nearly always regular, valves closed all round; apices curved towards the anterior: dorsal hinge complete, with teeth and ligament; the latter external or internal, short and thick; two distinct muscular impressions, united at the lower part by a parallel impression, which is frequently sinuated at the posterior. The genera described in this family are divided into three sections. First, those which are regular, and have distant lateral teeth, Cardium, Donax, Tellina, Lucina, Cyclas, Cyprina, Mactra, and Erycina. Second, those which are regular, and have no distant lateral teeth, Crassatella and Venus. Third, those which are irregular, Venerupis, Coralliophaga, Clotho, Corbula, Sphænia, and Ungulina.

CONCHACEA. Lam. A family of Lamarck's order Conchifera Dimyaria. Regular, unattached in general, closed at the sides. They are always more or less inequilateral. The *Marine* Conchacea are those which inhabit the sea. The fluviatile Conchacea are those which are found in rivers, ponds, &c. Each of these contain various genera, which may be arranged as follows:—

Fluviatile

    1. CYRENELLA. Three cardinal teeth; ligament long; shell thin. Fig. 114.

    2. CYCLAS. Thin, oval; cardinal and lateral teeth; anterior side shortest, including *Pera.*

    3. PISIDIUM. The same, with the posterior side shortest. Fig. 112.

    4. CYRENA. Thick; cardinal and lateral teeth. Fig. 113.

    5. POTAMOPHILIA. Two thick cardinal teeth. Fig. 115.

Marine

    1. CYPRINA. Two cardinal teeth, and one remote lateral tooth. Fig. 116.

    2. VENUS. Three cardinal; no lateral teeth. Fig. 118, 119, 119*a*.

    3. CIRCE. Short lateral tooth, like Cytherea; no sinus in the palleal impression.

    4. CYTHEREA. Several cardinal teeth; one very short lateral tooth. Fig. 117, 117*a*, 117*b*, 117*c*, 117*d*.

    5. MEROE. Short lateral tooth, like Cytherea; wedge-shaped, with a deeply hollowed hinge area.

    6. PULLASTRA. Cardinal teeth notched, shape long, otherwise like Venus. Fig. 120.

    7. ASTARTE. Three cardinal teeth; ligament short. Fig. 110.

CONCHIFERA. Lam. The 11th class of Invertebrata, consisting of all those animals which have bivalve shells. Lamarck divides the class into Dimyaria, which have two adductor muscles; and Mononyaria, which have but one.

CONCHODERMA. Olfers, 1814. A name under which Mr. Darwin, in his recent work on Cirripedes, unites the pedunculated cirripedes commonly known and described in this book as "CINERAS" and "OTION."

CONCHOLEPAS. Lamarck, 1801. (CONCHA, a shell; lepas, a stone or rock.) *Fam.* Pupurifera, Lam. Entomostomata, Bl.—*Descr.* Oval, imbricated, thick; with a very short spire and large oval patelliform aperture, terminating anteriorly in a slight emargination; outer lip crenated, with two produced points or teeth towards the anterior; inner lip smooth, nearly flat, reflected over the last whorl, so as nearly or entirely to cover it; operculum horny. Marine, only one species known, from Peru.—*Obs.* This shell is placed near Patella by Lamarck, on

165. Malleus Vulgaris.
  Himantopoda, chum.

  Fam. Brachopoda

167. Catillus Lamarckii. Inoceramus,
  Sow. (from Blainville.)
168. Crenatula
  mytoloides.   (from
169. Gervillia   Sowerby's
  aviculoides.   Genera.)
170. Pulvinites
  Adansonii.

  Fam. Pectinides

171. Pecten varius. Janera, Schum.
172. —— Plica. Decadopecten,
  Rüppell.
173. Hinnites Pusio. Pecten Pusio,
  Lam.
174. Lima squamosa.
175. Dianchora striata, (from Sow.
  Min. Con:)
176. Plagiostoma spinosum, (from
  Sow. Min. Con.)
177. Spondylus Americanus, Hinge.
  (See Frontispiece.)
178. Plicatula gibbosa. Harpax,
  Parkinson.
179. Pedum Spondyloideum, (from
  Sow. Gen.) Hemipecten, fig.
  580. To be added.

  Fam. Ostracea

180. Ostrea edulis.
181. —— Folium. Dendostrea, Sw.
182. Gryphæa incurva.

account of its large open aperture; but having a horny operculum, and resembling Purpurea in other respects. Concholepas Peruviana. Pl. xix. fig. 418.

CONCHOTRYA. Gray. (*Concha*, a shell; Τρυο, (*tryo*) to bore.) *Order*, Pedunculated Cirripedes, Lam.—*Descr*. Five pieces, two pairs ventral, one single; shaped like Pentelasmis. Found in holes.

CONCHYLIOMORPHITE. A term used by De Blainville to designate the cast or model of a fossil shell, formed by a siliceous substance which has entered or surrounded it when in a liquid state, and subsequently become hardened into flint. The shell has afterwards decomposed or fallen off by accident, leaving its external or internal characters to be conjectured from the monumental impressions that remain.

CONE. A common name for shells of the genus Conus.

CONE. This mathematical term is used by conchologists in its utmost latitude of signification to express a body, which in its formation, commences in a small point, called the apex, and increases in width towards the base. It is applied to all shells, whether the increase in width be gradual or sudden; or whether in its growth it takes a straight, oblique, curved, or spirally-twisted course. In this sense, a bivalve would be described as a pair of rapidly enlarging, oblique cones, and the aperture of every spiral shell would be its base. But this phraseology being in disuse, it is only mentioned here that it may be understood when occasionally met with.

CONELLA. Swainson. A genus composed of species of the genus Columbella, Lam. which have a conical form, and which, on that account, are considered by Swainson as belonging to his family of Coninæ. Swains. Lardner, Cyclop. Malac. described at p. 312. C. picata, Sw. fig. 17. a. p. 151.

CONFLUENT. A term applied to two parts of a shell when they gradually flow into each other, as, for instance, the inner and outer lips of Univalves when they pass into each other at the anterior extremity, without the intervention of a notch or angle.

CONIA. Leach. *Fam.* Balanidea. *Order*, Sessile Cirripedes, Lam.—*Descr*. Four rather irregular valves, of porous structure, placed side by side, so as to form a circular cone, supported at the base on a shelly plate, and closed at the aperture by an operculum consisting of four valves in pairs. Distinguished from Creusia by its porous structure and by its flat support; that of Creusia being cup-shaped. Conia porosa. Pl. i. fig. 21.

CONICAL. A term applied in the ordinary sense, and not as explained above, under the word CONE.

CONIDEA. Swainson. A genus separated from Columbella, Lam. thus described, "Mitra shaped, fusiform; spire equal to or longer than the aperture; the whorls tumid; outer lip slightly gibbous above, contracted below; margin not inflected; striated within; inner lip terminating in an elevated ridge, but with the teeth obsolete. C. semipunctata, (*Columbella*, Lam.) Mart. 44. fig. 465, 466." Africa.

CONILITES. *Fam.* Orthocerata, Lam. & Bl.—*Descr*. "Conical, straight or slightly curved; having a thin external covering, independent of the nut or alveole, which it contains. Alveole transversely chambered, sub separable." (Translated from Lam.)—*Obs*. The difference between Belemnites and Conilites is that the external sheath of the latter is thin, and not filled up with solid matter, from the point of the alveole to the apex, as in the former. De Blainville places in this genus the genera Thalamulus, Achelois and Antimomous, Montf. two of which are figured, Knor. Sup. Fab. iv. fig. 1. 1. 8, 9. Conilites Pyramidatus, Pl. xxii. fig. 470.

CONILITHES. Swainson. A sub-genus of Coronaxis, Sw. (Coni, with coronated whorls) thus described, "Conic; spire considerably elevated;

the aperture linear, C. antediluvianus, Sow. Gen. fig. 1."

CONOHELIX. Swainson, 1843. IMBRICARIA, Schum. 1817. (*Conus and Helix*.) The generic name given to those species of Mitra which are conical in form. C. marmorata, Pl. xx. fig. 432.

CONOPLÆA. Say. *Order*, Sessile Cirripedes, Lam. A genus composed of Balani, attached to the stems of Gorgonia, having their bases elongated. *Ex*. Balanus Galeatus, Pl. i. fig. 27.

CONOPLEURA. Hinds, Voyage of the Sulphur. P. 24, pl. vii. fig. 223. Described as "coniform, or involute, with the spire conically elevated, with a deep posterior sinus, the edge of which is callous; outer lip smooth, columella rather lengthened; aperture linear; scarcely any canal." (Translated.) Remarkable for the series of fossils formed by the successive elevations of the edge of the sinus at the suture. Only one species is known. *Ex*. C. strians, Pl. xxviii. fig. 596.

CONORBIS. Swainson. A genus composed of species of CONUS, such as C. dormitor, (Sowerby, gen. fig. 8) which have elevated spires and the upper part of the outer lip deeply sinuated. Mr. Swainson considers these fossil species as analogous to the Pleurotomæ. Sw. Lard. Cyclop. Malac. p. 312.

CONOVULUS. Lamarck, 1812. MELAMPUS, Montfort, 1810. Conical species of Auricula, which have the outer lip simple. *Ex*. fig. 298, Auricula coniformis.

CONTIGUOUS. A term applied to the whorls of spiral shells when they rest upon, or touch each other. This is the case in a great majority of instances. When, on the contrary, there is a space between the whorls, they are said to be non-contiguous, detached, or free. Examples of non-contiguous whorls are to be seen in Scalaria, fig. 351 (in this case, the distance between the whorls is small), and in Crioceratites, fig. 482. A "*Columella contiguous to the axis*," is when in the centre of the shell and takes the place of the imaginary line which forms its axis.

CONTINUOUS. Carried on without interruption, as the siphon in Spirula, the varices in Ranella, fig. 394, which, occurring in a corresponding part of each whorl, form a continuous ridge.

CONULARIA. Miller. A genus of Orthocerata, described as conical, straight, or nearly so, divided into chambers by imperforate septa; aperture half closed; apex solid, obtuse; external surface finely striated. Resembling Orthoceras, but wanting the siphon. Pl. xxii. fig. 449.

CONUS. Linnæus. (Κωνος, a cone.) *Fam.* Enroulées, Lam. Angyostomata, Bl.—*Descr*. Conical, convolute, with a short spire, consisting of numerous whorls; and narrow lengthened aperture, terminating in a slight emargination at each extremity; outer lip thin; epidermis thin; operculum small, pointed, horny.—*Obs*. This well-known genus of shells is easily distinguished from any other, by its conical form, its smooth columella, its narrow aperture, and thin outer lip. The form of the spire varies from flat and even partially concave, to a regular pyramidal cone; and the upper edges of the whorls are rounded in some species, angulated in others, and in some are waved or coronated. The variety of marking and the numerous delicate tints of these shells have caused them to be highly appreciated by amateur collectors; and many species, as the C. Ammiralis, or admiral; the C. Gloria Maris, or Glory of the Sea; the C. Cedonulli ("I yield to none"), and others, have always produced good prices in the markets. We give figures of the principal forms, as expressed in the genera proposed by De Montfort, of Rhombus, Hermes, Rollus and Cylinder, in figures 459 to 462. Many new species were brought to this country by Mr. Cuming, and are represented in parts 24, 25, 28, 29; 32, 33, 36, 37; 54, 55, 56, 57; 147, 148; 151 to 158 of the Conchological Illustrations, by G. B. Sowerby, jun. See CORONAXIS, Swainson. The cones are mostly tropical, some are found as far north as the Mediterranean, and south as

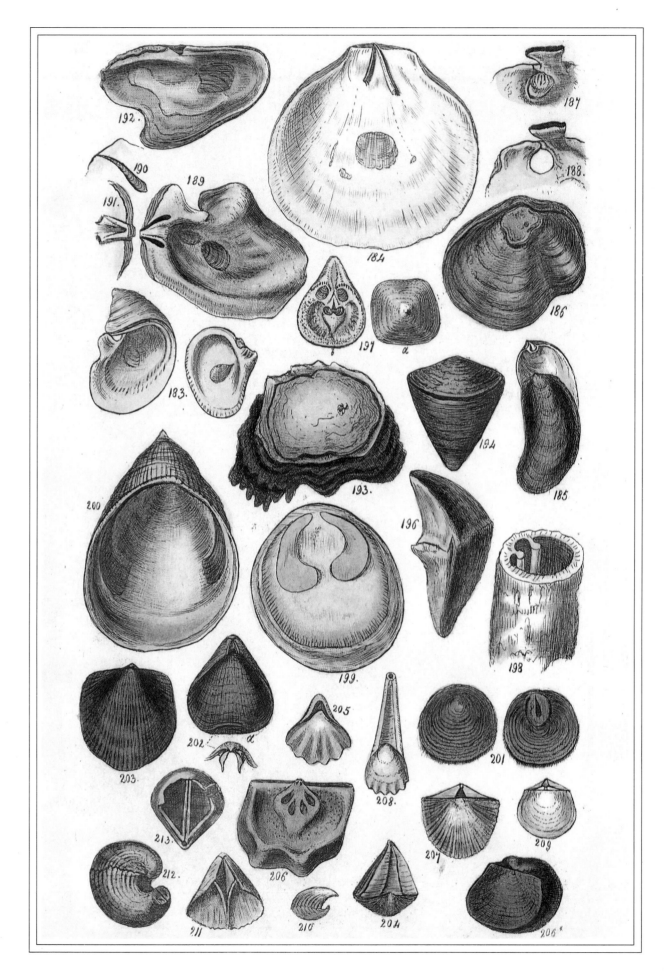

183. Exogyra conica, (from Sow. Min. Con.)
184. Placuna Placenta. *Gen.* Placenta, Schum.
185. Vulsella lingulata.
186. Anomia Ephippium.
187. Hinge of the same, with bony process.
188. Hinge, shewing the fissure.
189. Placunanomia Cumingii.
190. Hinge of the same, shewing the fissure.
191. Hinge of the unattached valve.
192. Mulleria. (from Sow. Gen.)

Fam. Rudistis

193. Sphærulites foliacea. (Radiolites is more conical.)
194. Calceola Sandalina.
196. Birostrites inæquiloba, internal cast of Sphærulites.
197. *a.* Crania personata, dorsal valve; *b.* C. antiquata, interior. (This would be more properly placed in Brachiopoda.)
198. Hippurites Cornucopia, (from Blainville.)
199. Hipponyx Cornucopia, attached valve.
200. Upper valve of the same.
201. Orbicula lævis.
202. Terebratula Psittacea; *a.* anterior margin.
203. Atrypa reticularis. Trigonoteta, König.
204. Cyrtia exporrecta.
205. Delthyris plycotes, (from Dalman.)
206. Leptæna depressa, Dalman. Producta, Sow. (from Sow. Gen.)
206*. Producta antiquata.
207. Orthis basalis, Dalman. Strophomena, Rafinesque.
208. Trigonosemus Lyra, König.
209. Magas pumilus, Sow.
210. Gypidia conchidium, (from Dalman.)
211. Interior of the large valve of the same, (from Dalman.)
212. Pentamerus Aylesfordii, (from Sow. Min. Con.)
213. —— lævis.

the Cape of Good Hope. The most beautiful species are from the East and West Indies. Pl. xxi. fig. 459 to 462.

CONVOLUTÆ. (Enroulées, Lam.) A family of the 2nd section of the order Trachelipoda, Lam. the genera of which may be distinguished as follows:—

1. CYPRÆA. Lips thickened, inflected, with teeth; spire hidden including *Cypræovulum, Luponia, Trivia.* Fig. 444 to 450, and Cyprædia. Pl. xxvi. fig. 564.

2. OVULUM. Lips thickened, inflected, with slight crenulations; spire hidden. Fig. 440 to 443.

3. ERATO. Lips thickened, inflected; spire visible; a groove down the back. Fig. 454.

4. TEREBELLUM. Cylindrical, open at the anterior extremity; columella smooth; suture of the spire canaliculated. Fig. 451, 452.

5. OLIVA. Columella plaited, swelled into a varix at the anterior. Fig. 457, 458.

6. ANCILLARIA. The same, but the suture of the spire covered with enamel. Fig. 455, 456.

7. CONUS. Turbinated, numerous whorls; spire flat or short, conical: columella smooth. Fig. 459 to 462.

CONVOLUTE. (*Con*, together; *volvo*, to revolve.) This term can be strictly applied only to symmetrical shells, signifying that the volutions are parallel to each other in a horizontal direction, as in the Ammonites, &c.; but the term is also commonly used in describing such shells as Conus, in which, the direction of the whorls being scarcely oblique, the last whorl almost entirely covers those which precede it. This is the case with Lamarck's family of Enroulées. Fig. 440 to 462.

CORALLIOPHAGA. Blainville, 1825. CYPRICARDIA Coralliophaga, Lam.—*Descr.* Oval, elongated, finely striated from the apex to the base, cylindrical, equivalve, very inequilateral; umbones slightly raised and quite anterior; hinge nearly the same in both valves; two small cardinal teeth, one of which is bifid, placed before a kind of lammellated tooth, beneath a very slender external ligament; two small, distant, muscular impressions, united by a striated palleal impression, which is strongly striated posteriorly.—*obs.* This shell, which is found in the empty holes of dead Lithodomi, in some instances conforming its shape to its situation, differs from Cypricardia of Lamarck, principally in its cylindrical form. C. Carditoidia, Pl. iv. fig. 92.

CORBICULA. Megerle, 1811. Part of CYRENA, Lam.

CORBIS. Cuvier, 1817. (*A basket.*) *Fam.* Nymphacea, Lam.—*Descr.* Transverse, oval, thick, ventricose, equivalve, sub-equilateral, free, cancellated, with denticulated internal margins; hinge with two cardinal and two lateral teeth in each valve; of the latter, one near and one remote from the umbones; muscular impressions lunulate, two in each valve, united by an entire palleal impression, without a sinus.—*Obs.* This genus, of which only two or three recent species are known, resembles many species of Venus and Cytherea in general form; but differs in having lateral teeth, and in the palleal impressions, which in all the Veneres, &c. is sinuated. From Lucina it may be known, not only by its oval form, but also by the muscular impressions, which, in Lucina, are produced into an elongated point; it will also be distinguished from Tellina, by the want of a posterior fold in the valve, for which that genus is remarkable. C. Fimbriata is an inhabitant of the Indian Ocean. Several fossil species are found in the recent formations, above the chalk, at Grignon and Hautville. Pl. v. fig. 101.

CORBULA. Bruguière, 1792. (*A little basket.*) *Fam.* Corbulacea, Lam. Conchacea, Bl.—*Descr.* Inequivalve, sub-equilateral, transverse, gibbose, not gaping; cardinal tooth in each valve, conical, curved,

prominent, inserting its extremity into a pit in the opposite hinge; cartilage attached to the tooth of the smaller valve, and the pit in the larger; muscular impressions, two in each valve, distant, rather irregular; palleal impression posteriorly angulated. *Obs.* The shells composing this genus were placed in Mya by Linnæus, but differ from the true Myæ in having a sinus in the palleal impression, and a prominent ligamentiferous tooth in each valve, whereas the Myæ have but one. The Corbulæ are marine, some species inhabiting the British coasts. Fossil species occur abundantly in green sand, London clay, crag, and corresponding formations. C. Nucleus, Pl. iv. fig. 89.

CORBULACEA. (Corbulées, Lam.) A family of the order Conchifera Dimyaria, Lam., containing the genera:—

1. CORBULA, with a prominent curved tooth. The Fresh-water species has been separated under the name *Potamomya.* Fig. 89.

2. PANDORA. Thin, pearly, no teeth. Fig. 90.

CORDIFORM. (*Cor*, a heart.) Heart-shaped, a term applied generally to any shell which may be fancied to resemble a heart in shape, as Isocardia, fig. 126, and Cardium Dionæum, fig. 122.

CORETUS. Adamson, 1757. Planorbis.

COREPHIUM. Browne. CHITON echinatus, and similar species with spires on the marginal integument.

CORIACEOUS. (*Corium*, leather.) Of the substance of leather. *Ex.* the integument into which the valves of Chitones are inserted.

CORIOCELLA. Bl. The animal designated by this name is described by De Blainville as being without any traces of shell, either internal or external. This must have arisen from the imperfection of the specimen described, probably deprived by accident of its shell. The testaceous appendage of the Coriocella is now well known to naturalists. It is a milky white, transparent shell, shaped like Sigaretus.

CORNEA, and PISUM, Megerle. CYCLAS, Lam.

CORNEO-CALCAREOUS. A term used to express the mixture of horny and shelly matter which enters into the composition of some shells, Aplysia, for instance. It is also applied to those Opercula, which are horny on one side, and testaceous on the other, as that of Turbo.

CORNEUS. Horny. A species of Patella has had the specific name corneus given to it, because its texture more nearly resembles that of a horn than that of a shell. The epidermis of fresh-water shells is of a similar composition.

CORNUCOPIA. Humph. LEPAS, Linn.

CORONALES. See CORONULAR MULTIVALVES.

CORONATED. (*Corona*, a crown.) Applied to shells when ornamented with a series of points, tubercles, &c. round the upper edges of the volutions. *Ex.* Conus Nocturnus, fig. 459.

CORONAXIS. One of the two genera into which Swainson divides the genus Conus, consisting of those species which have a row of tubercles on the upper edge of the whorls, an arrangement by which he would in many instances, not only separate between two individuals of the same species, but also between two parts of the same shell; for instances occur in which the earlier whorls are coronated, while the body whorl and the penultimate are perfectly plain.

CORONULA. (*Corona*, a crown, dim.) *Order*, Sessile Cirripedes, Lam. *Fam.* Balanidea, Bl.—*Descr.* Six radiated valves, joined side by side in a circle, forming a depressed cone; internal structure of the valves, porous or chambered; thickened at the base; operculum consisting of four valves in pairs; imbedded horizontally in a cartilaginous substance.—*Obs.* The shells composing this genus are found partly imbedded in the skin of whales, and the shells of tortoises, and are therefore destitute of the shelly foundation on which the Balani and other Coronular Multivalves are supported. C. Testudinaria, (CHELO-

214. Spirifer trigonalis.   Trigonotrata, König, (from
215. ——dorsatus.   Sow. Gen.)
216. Thecidium recurvirostrum.
    (Here should come Crania, see
    Rudistes.)
217. Pycnodonta radiata, (from
    Fischer.)
218. Hinge of the same.
219. Lingula Anatina.

Class, MOLLUSCA

Order, PTEROPIDA

220. Atlanta helicialis.
221. Cleodora cuspidata.
222. Creseis spinifera.
223. Cuviera columella.
224. Spiratella limacinea, with
    animal; Limacella, Lam.
    Limacina, Cuvier. (from
    Blainville.)
225. Vaginula Daudinii.
226. Hyalæa tridentata. Archonte,
    Montf. Spiralis, fig. 581.

Order, GASTEROPODA

Fam. Phyllidiana

227. Chiton spinosus.
228. Chitonellus striatus, (from Sow.
    Gen.)
229. Patella oculus; *a.* anterior.
230. Patella pellucida. Helcion,
    Montf. Ansates, Klein.
231. Patelloida Antillarum. Lottia,
    Gray.
231*.Siphonaria Sipho.
    Phakellopleura, fig. 506.
    Amicula, fig. 507.

Fam. Semiphyllidiana

232. Pleurobranchus membranaceus.
233. Umbrella indica. Gastroplax,
    Bl.

Fam. Calyptracea

234. Calyptræa Equestria.
235. ——extinctorium.
236. ——auriculata.
237. ——Pileus. Infundibulum,
    Montf.
238. Side view of the same.
239. Crepidula Porcellana.
240. Capulus ungaricus, two views.
    Pileopsis, Lam.
241. Emarginula fissura.
242. Parmophorus elongatus. Scutus,
    Montf.

NOBIA, Leach), fig. 15. C. Balænarum, (CETOPIRUS, Ranz.) fig. 16. C. Diadema, (DIADEMA, Ranz.) fig. 17. Pl. i. fig. 15, 16, 17.

CORONULAR MULTIVALVES are those which have their parietal valves joined together side by side in a circle, surrounding the body of the animal, so as to form a sort of coronet. This is the characteristic of the Sessile Cirripedes of Lamarck's system, the Balanidea of De Blainville.

CORRODED. (*Corrodo*, eat away, consume.) The umbones, apices, and other thick parts of shells, are frequently worn away or consumed by the action of the element in which they exist. As the thickest parts of some shells are the most subject to this operation; it appears to the author to arise from the outer surface of the shell, being less under the influence of the animal juices than the other parts; and therefore, more exposed to the influence of the surrounding element. This, however, is not the case with respect to the Nayades and other fresh-water shells; with these, corrosion does not take place until after the thick epidermis which covers them, becomes wounded by some means or other, and then the animal thickens its shell within as fast as it is corroded without.

CORTALUS. Montf. (Conch. Syst. 1. 115.) A genus of microscopic Foraminifera, placed by De Blainville in a division of the genus Rotalites.

COSTATED. Ribbed, as Cardium Angulatum, fig. 123.

COSTELLARIA. A sub-genus of the genus Tiara, Sw. (Mitra.) C. rigida. Swainson, Zool. Ill. 1st series, pl. 29.

COWRY. A common name for shells of the genus Cypræa.

CRANIA. Retzius, 1788. (*Cranium*, a skull.) *Fam.* Rudistes, Lam. *Order*, Pallio-branchiata, Bl.—*Descr.* Inequivalve, equilateral, irregular, sub-quadrate; upper valve patelliform, conical, with the umbo near the centre; lower valve attached by its outer surface; muscular impressions, 4 in each valve; two large, posterior, distant; two small, near to each other, central. No hinge teeth; no ligament.—*Obs.* This genus properly belongs to the Brachiopoda, Lam. It differs from Orbicula in the mode of attachment, which in the latter, is by a byssus passing through the lower valve, and not by the valve itself. Hipponyx has only two muscular impressions in each valve. The name of this genus is derived from the inner surface of the attached valve, which presents a remarkable resemblance to the facial portion of a human skull. The appearance is caused by the situation and elevated edges of the muscular impressions. Coasts of Britain and Mediterranean. The monograph in Thesaurus contains four species. Pl. xi. fig. 197.

CRASSATELLA. Lamarck, 1801. (*Crassus*, thick.) *Fam.* Mactracea, Lam. Conchacea, Bl.—*Descr.* Equivalve, inequilateral, close, thick, rounded anteriorly, rostrated posteriorly, with denticulated margins, smooth, or ribbed transversely; hinge with a triangular pit containing the cartilage, two anterior cardinal teeth, and a posterior depression in one valve; one anterior tooth and a slight anterior marginal elevation, and a posterior elevation in the other valve. Muscular impressions distant, strongly marked. Palleal impression not sinuated.—*Obs.* The few recent species known are marine, several being brought from the coasts of New Holland. Fossil species are found in Calcaire-grossier and London clay. The Crassatella are known from the Veneres, &c., by the ligamentary pit in the hinge, and from Lutraria and Mactra by the thickness and closeness of the shell. C. rostrata. Pl. iv. fig. 84.

CRASSINA. Lamarck, 1818. ASTARTE. J. Sowerby, 1816.

CRASSIPEDES. Lam. (*Crassus*, thick; *pes*, foot.) The first section of the order Conchifera Dimyaria, Lam. In this section the foot of the animal is thick, and the shell gapes considerably. It is divided into the families Tubicolæ, Pholadidæ, Solenidæ, and Myaria. Fig. 44 to 76.

CRASSISPIRA. Swainson. A sub-genus of COLUMBELLA, Auct. for which Mr. Swainson quotes "Pleurotoma Bottæ, Auct." Crassispira fasciata, Sw. Lardn. Cyclop. Malac. p. 313.

CRENATED. (*Crena*, a notch.) Applied to small notches, not sufficiently raised or defined, to be compared with teeth. *Ex.* The hinge of Iridina, fig. 150.

CRENATULA. Lamarck, 1819. *Fam.* Malleacea, Lam. Margaritacea, Bl.—*Descr.* Compressed, foliated, irregular, sub-equivalve, inequilateral, oblique; umbones terminal; hinge linear, nearly straight, with a series of excavations, containing the cartilage, while the intervening ridges are covered with the ligament, properly so called. Muscular impression oblong, indistinct.—*Obs.* This genus is known from Perna by the hinge, which in the latter is composed of a series of regular, straight, ligamentary grooves placed across it. In Crenatula also there is no passage for the byssus, as in Perna. C. Mytiloides, pl. x. fig. 168.

CRENELLA. Brown. A genus composed of MODIOLA discors and similar species, having an oblique division between the anterior and posterior portions of the shell, and a crenulated hinge margin.

CRENELLA. ——? See TRIGONOCÆLIUS. Pl. vii. fig. 136.

CRENULATED. Finely crenated or notched.

CREPIDULA. Lamarck, 1801. CRYPTA, Humph. is used in Gray's Synopsis as being the prior name, although it only appeared by name in a catalogue. (*Crepidula*, a little slipper.) *Fam.* Calyptracea, Lam. and Bl.—*Descr.* Oval, irregular, patelliform: apex lateral, incurved, or sub-spiral; external surface convex, smooth, with a flattish septum reaching nearly half across the cavity; epidermis light brown.—*Obs.* The difference between this genus and Calyptræa is that in the latter the septum is more free from the sides of the shell, so that, instead of forming a regular plate, covering half the aperture, it assumes a variety of shapes, and in some is cup-shaped, in others forked, and in some forms a little angular shelf. Indeed, the variations are so numerous that I think it would be better to throw the two genera into one, and then divide them into smaller groups. Some species of Calyptræa are farther removed from each other with respect to the characters of the septum and general form of the shell, than they are from the Crepidulæ. Fig. 239. Mediterranean, North and South America, East and West Indies, New South Wales, &c. Pl. xii. fig. 239.

CREPIDULINA. Bl. CRISTELLARIA, Lam. Microscopic.

CRESEIS. Rang. 1828. *Order*, Pteropoda, Lam.—*Descr.* Thin, fragile, transparent, pyramidal, pointed; with a dorsal ridge produced into a point at the edge of the aperture.—*Obs.* The species found in the Mediterranean is named C. Spinifera, from its resemblance to a thorn. Pl. xii. fig. 222.

CREUSIA. Leach. (*Creux*, se. Fr. a cavity.) *Fam.* Balanidea. Bl. *Order*, Sessile Cirripedes, Lam.—*Descr.* A depressed cone, consisting of four valves, supported upon, and jointed to, a cup-shaped cavity formed in the Madrepores, in which it resides. Aperture quadrilateral, closed by an operculum of four valves.—*Obs.* This genus is distinguished from Pyrgoma, which is supported on the edge of a similar cup-shaped cavity, by the paries being composed of four valves, whereas in Pyrgoma, it consists of a single piece. East Indies. C. Gregaria. Pl. i. fig. 28.

CRICOSTOMATA, Bl. The second family of Asiphonibranchiata, Bl. It is thus described: "shell equally (with the animal) variable in general form, but of which the aperture, always nearly round, is completely closed by the shelly or horny operculum; whorls few, and apex sublateral." This family agrees in some measure with the family Turbinacea of Lamarck, and with the genus Turbo in the system of Linnæus. It contains the genera Pleurotomaria, Delphinula, Turritella,

Proto, Scalaria, Vermetus, Siliquaria, Magilus, Valvata, Cyclostoma, and Paludina.

CRIOCERATITES. A genus composed of species of Ammonites, with disconnected whorls. C. Duvallii. Pl. xxiii. fig. 482.

CRIOPUS. Poli. CRANIA, Auct.

CRISTACEA. Lam. The third family of Polythalamous Cephalopoda, Lam. This family is described as including shells of the following characters: "Multilocular, flattened, nearly reniform; the chambers gradually increasing in length, as they approach the outer arched margin, and appearing to revolve round an eccentric, more or less marginal axis. The Cristacea contain the genera Renulina, Cristellaria, and Orbiculina."

CRISTACEA. Bl. The third family of Polythalamia, Bl. containing the genera Crepidulina, (Cristellaria, Lam.) Oreas and Linthuris.

CRISTARIA. Schum, 1817. DIPSAS Plicatus, Leach. ANODON tuberculatus, Fer.

CRISTELLARIA. Lam. CREPIDULINA, Bl. *Fam.* Cristacea, Lam. and Bl.—*Descr.* Semidiscoidal, chambered; whorls contiguous, enlarging progressively; spire eccentric, sublateral; septa imperforate. Microscopic.

CRUCIBULUM. Schum. 1817. The "cup and saucer" division of Calyptræ.

CRYPTA. Humph. See CREPIDULA, Lam.

CRYPTELLA. Webb, 1833. (Κρυπτω, to conceal.) TESTACELLUS Ambiguus of Ferrusac. Published in Sowerby's Genera of Shells as PARMACELLA calyculata.—*Descr.* A small patelliform shell, with a very short papillary spire; and the aperture irregularly expanded. Canary Islands. Pl. xiii. fig. 256.

CRYPTOCHITON. Gray, 1847. Chiton Amiculatus. The valves of which are entirely covered.

CRYPTOCONCHUS. Bl. A genus composed of species of Chiton, the valves of which are covered by the integument, as Chiton porosus of Burrows. Ch. amiculatus of Pallas.

CRYPTOCONCTUS. Bl. Chiton porosus, the valves of which are covered, with the exception of a narrow dorsal ridge.

CRYPTODIBRANCHIATA. Bl. The first order of the class Cephalophora, Bl. containing families of molluscous animals destitute of shells.

CRYPTODON. Turton, 1822. A genus of Lucinæform shells, differing from that genus in the character of the hinge and palleal impressions, and having a fold at the posterior side of the shell. Partially described by J. Sowerby, under the name Axinus, and named Thyatira, besides several other names by Leach. C. Sinuosum. Pl. xxvii. fig. 575.

CRYPTOTHALMUS. Ehrenherg. A sub-genus of Bullidæ, the shells of which are thus described in Adams's Monograph, No. 11 Sowerby's Thesaurus: "Shell fragile, horny, scarcely involute, destitute of columella and spire; aperture wide."

CRYPTOSTOMA. Bl. 1825. Differs from SIGARETUS, Lam. principally in the soft parts of the animal. De Blainville remarks that he is acquainted with only two species (from the Indies), which he can with decision refer to the genus, but he thinks that many of the Lamarckian Sigareti may very properly be found to belong to it, as soon as the soft parts shall be known. The species which he figures is Cryptostoma Leachii. (Manuel de Malacologie, pl. xlii. fig. 3.)

CTENOCONCHA. Gray. Described as having many characters common with the Solens, the teeth like Nucula, but the cartilage entirely external. SOLENELLA, Sow.?

CUCULLÆA. Lamarck, 1801. (*Cucullus*, a hood.) *Fam.* Arcacea, Lam.—*Descr.* Sub-quadrate, nearly equivalve, sub-equilateral, deep; hinge rectilinear, with a series of angular teeth, small near the umbones; larger and more oblique towards the extremities; umbones separated by a flat external area, on which the ligament is spread. Anterior muscular impression produced into a sharp-edged plate or ledge, projecting from the side of the shell. Posterior muscular impression flat and indistinct.—*Obs.* This genus very much resembles Arca in general form, but differs in the oblique, lengthened character of the remote teeth, and in the singularly prominent edge of the muscular impression. China. C. Auriculifera. Pl. vii. fig. 133.

CUCUMIS. Klein. MARGINELLA, Auct.

CULTELLUS. Schum. 1817. *Ex.* L. Solenoides. Pl. iii. fig. 78.

CUMA. Humph. Part of FUSUS and FASCIOLARIA, Lam.

CUMINGIA. Sowerby, 1833. *Fam.* Mactracea, Lam.—*Descr.* Equivalve, inequilateral, transverse, rounded anteriorly, subrostrated posteriorly. Hinge with a central spoon-shaped cavity in each valve, containing the cartilage; a very small anterior cardinal tooth in each valve; two lateral teeth in one valve, none in the other: muscular impressions two in each valve, distant; palleal impression with a very large posterior sinus.—*Obs.* The species known at present are found in sand, in the fissures of rocks in Tropical climates. They resemble Erycina in general form and character, but differ in having the internal cartilage placed in a prominent spoon-shaped process, while that of Erycina is contained in a hollow which sinks under the umbones. This genus should be placed near Amphidesma. Cumingia mutica. Pl. iv. fig. 87.

CUNEIFORM. (*Cuneus*, a wedge.) Wedge-shaped, as Donax, fig. 108.

CUNEUS. Megerle, 1811. MEROE, Schumacher, 1817. Pl. vi. fig. 117. *a.*

CURVED. Arched or bent. *Ex.* Dentalium, fig. 2.

CUVIERIA. Rang. 1827. (Baron Cuvier.) *Class*, Pteropoda, Lam.—*Descr.* Thin, transparent, glassy, cylindrical, rounded and inflated at the closed extremity, compressed towards the opening, so as to render it oval. This genus differs from Vaginula in being rounded, instead of pointed, at the lower extremity. Mediterranean. C. Columella. Pl. xii. fig. 223.

CYCLAS. Brug. *Fam.* Conques Fluviatiles, Lam. Conchacea, Bl.—*Descr.* Orbicular, thin, subovate, ventricose, sub-equilateral, equivalve; cardinal teeth minute, one more or less complicated in the left valve, two divering in the right; lateral teeth elongated, compressed, laminar, acute doubled in the left valve; ligament external; epidermis thin, horny.—*Obs.* The Cyclades are viviparous, and abound in ditches, ponds, slow streams, &c. in Europe and North America. The genus Pisidium has been separated on account of a difference in the animal, and may be known from Cyclas by being less equilateral, and the anterior side being the longest. C. Rivicola. Pl. v. fig. 3.

CYCLOBRANCHIATA. Bl. The third order of the second section of Paracephalophora Monoica, Bl. containing no genera of Testaceous Mollusca.

CYCLOCANTHA. Swainson, 1840. A genus of "Trochidæ," consisting of Turbo stellaris and T. Calcar, and corresponding with the genus Calcar, Montf.

CYCLONASSA. Swainson. A genus of "Nassinæ," Sw. consisting of Nassa Neritoidea, and corresponding with the genus Cyclops, Montf.

CYCLOPHORUS. Montf. 1810. A generic name proposed for those species of Cyclostoma, Auct. which have an umbilicus. C. Involvulus would be the type of this genus. Pl. xiv. fig. 304.

CYCLOPS. Montf. Nassa Neritoidea, Auct. Pl. xix. fig. 424.

CYCLOSTOMUS. Montf. 1810. (κυκλος, *cyclos*, round; στομα, *stoma*, mouth.) *Fam*. Colimacea, Lam. Cricostomata, Bl. A genus of land shells varying in shape from that of Pupa to that of a flat orb; the aperture is generally circular and the peritreme uninterrupted, thickened, and sometimes reflected, the operculum is shelly and spiral. Two other genera of land shells are provided with opercula, and consequently might be confounded with this genus. In Helicina, the operculum is concentric and the peritreme is not continuous; while in the small genus hitherto almost unknown of Pupina, the peritreme is not continuous, and there is a glassy enamel over the whole of the external surface. The Monograph in Sowerby's Thesaurus contains 175 species. The generic names Cyclostoma, Licina, Cyclophorus, Cyclotus, Myxostoma, Pterocyclos, Farcinea, Myodoctoma, and Pomatias, represent the principal forms. Pl. xiv. fig. 303, 304. Pl. xxv. fig. 529.

CYCLOTUS. Guild. A sub-genus of Cyclostoma, consisting of those species which are discoidal, as C. Planorbulum. Thesaurus Conchylium. Pl. xxv. fig. 83 to 86; and the species in our plate xxv. fig. 531.

CYLICHNA. Loven. Cylindrella, Swainson. Volvaria. Brown. A sub-genus of Bullidæ, consisting of animals with shells, thus described in Adams's Monograph, No. 11, Sowerby's Thesaurus: "Cylindrical; sphire none; apex umbilicated; columella callous, with a single plait."

CYLINDER. Montf. 1810. Conus textile, Auct. (fig. 461) and other species having a cylindrical form.

CYLINDRA. Schumacher, 1817. Voluta crenulata, Lamarck, and other species like Conohelix, but cancellated.

CYLINDRELLA. Sw. Cylichna.

CYLINDRICAL. (Κυλινδρος, a cylinder.) This like other mathematical terms is used with great latitude by Conchologists, and applied to any shell the sides of which are nearly parallel, with the extremities either rounded, flat, or conical. *Ex*. Oliva, fig. 457.

CYLLENE. Gray, 1839. *Fam*. Purpurifera, Lam.—*Descr*. Oval, thick, with a short acute spire; an oval aperture terminating anteriorly in a slight emargination, posteriorly in a short canal; a fold at the lower end of the body whorl; outer lip thick, striated within; angle of the whorls tuberculated.—*Obs*. This genus of small marine shells resembles Voluta in general character, but differs in having a smooth columella without folds. Recent, Pacific Ocean; Fossil, London clay. Pl. xix. fig. 425.

CYMBA. Broderip. (*Cymba*, a boat or skiff.) *Fam*. Columellaria, Lam.—*Descr*. Smooth, ventricose, with a very short, mammillated, rude spire; and a very large, wide aperture, terminated anteriorly in a deep emargination; posteriorly in a flat ledge, which separates the outer lip from the body whorl; columella with three or four oblique, laminar, projecting folds, terminating in a point; outer lip thin, with its edge sharp; epidermis smooth, brown, covered partly or entirely by the glassy enamel, which, commencing with the outer lip, spreads over the body of the shell.—*Obs*. These very elegant shells, found in Africa, are distinguished from the true Volutes by the shapeless, mammillated apex of the short spire, by the large size of the aperture, and by the horizontal ledge which separates the outer lip from the body whorl. The genus Melo, also separated by Mr. Broderip from the Volutes, agrees with Cymba in some respects, but differs in the regularity of the spire. Pl. xx. fig. 434, C. Porcina. Nine species are enumerated in the Monograph by the Author, pt. 8. Thes. Conchyliorum.

CYMBIOLA. Swainson, 1840. The generic name for a group of Volutes, described as "armed with spinous tubercules, sometimes smooth, but never ribbed; spiral whorls gradually diminishing in size, but not

distorted; apex thick and obtuse; pillar with four plaits." Mr Swainson remarks that this genus is chiefly distinguished by the obtuse, but not irregular spire. The typical species are stated to be V. Rutila and V. Vespertilio, fig. 433. Tropical.

CYMBIUM. Adanson, Melo, Broderip.

CYMBULIA. Peron and Leseur, 1810. (Dim. from *Cymba*.) *Fam*. Pteropoda, Lam. An extremely light, cartilaginous covering of a molluscous animal, so named from its similarity in shape to a boat. We mention it here on account of its similarity to the shelly or glassy covering of other Pteropods, to which, although membranaceous, it is evidently analogous. The Cymbuliæ are found in the Mediterranean.

CYNODONTA. Schum. 1817. Scolymus, part. Swainson. Represented by our figure 382.

CYPRÆA. Linnæus. *Fam*. Enroulées, Lam. Angyostomata, Bl.—*Descr*. Oval or oblong, ventricose, convolute, covered by an enamel, generally smooth and shining. Spire short, nearly hid. Aperture long, narrow, terminating in a short canal at both extremities. Outer lip dentated, thickened, inflected. Inner lip dentated, thickened, reflected over part of the body whorl.—*Obs*. These shells are so distinguished by the two rows of teeth arranged on each side of the aperture; the thickened front formed by the inner and outer lips; and the enamel deposited over the back of the shell from the mantle of the animal which envelopes it, that there is no danger of confounding them with any other genus, except in a young state. Before they have arrived at the full growth, the front is not thickened, and the outer lip is thin, not inflected, nor are the teeth formed. In this state the shell resembles, in some degree, an Oliva. Some species are striated, ribbed or tuberculated, but the generality are smooth. Most species belong to tropical climates, only one to Great Britain. The C. Moneta is current as money in some parts of Africa, and many species are worn as ornaments by the South Sea Islanders. The colouring in most species is exceedingly rich, and arranged in every variety of spots, patches, rings, lines, bands and clouds. The species most esteemed by collectors are C. Mappa, C. Testudinaria, C. Pustulata, C. Aurora, C. Princeps, of which only two specimens are known, C. Leucodon, &c. See also Cypræovulum, Trivea and Luponia. The fossil species are principally from the Calc-grossier, the London Clay, Crag, &c. The latest revision of this genus has been effected by Mr. G. B. Sowerby, sen., who has published a complete catalogue in the author's Conchological Illustrations. This catalogue enumerates 130 species, the whole of which are figured in parts 1 to 8, 101 to 131 of the above mentioned work. Pl. xxi. fig. 445 to 450.

CYPRÆCASSIS. Stutch. (Cypræa and Cassis.)—*Descr*. Shell, when young, striated, reticulated, or tuberculated; outer lip simple: when mature, outer lip involute and toothed; columellar lip also toothed; aperture straight, anteriorly terminated by a recurved canal, posteriorly by a shallow channel. Animal with the mantle bilobed; operculum none.—*Obs*. The reasons given for separating this genus from Cassis, are, 1st, That the shells of the latter have an operculum, while those of the proposed genus have none. 2nd, That the Cypræcassides do not form a complete, thickened lip, before the full period of their growth, like the Cassides. 3rd, That the Cypræcassides have no epidermis. The species mentioned as probably belonging to Cypræcassins are C. rufa, the type; C. coarctata, and C. Testiculus, Auct. The establishment of this genus has been opposed on the ground that indications of epidermis are discoverable in some specimens of C. rufa; that some specimens of the same species and Testiculus have been examined, and found to have formed slightly thickened and dentulated outer lips at very early periods of growth, while many of the other Cassides are destitute of varices, and

that an operculum of C. coarctata was brought to this country by Mr. Cuming. It is probable, however, that an increased knowledge of facts might go far to establish the separation. C. Testiculus, Pl. xix. fig. 412.

CYPRÆADIA. Swainson, 1840. A genus of the family "Cypræidæ," Sw. thus described:—"Cypræform; the base contracted; the body whorl not flattened beneath; shell cancellated; aperture of equal breadth throughout; a few thickened, short teeth on the pillar; lip at the base, which is not internally concave. C. cancellata, Sw. Fossil only, differing from Trivea in its contracted base, in the inequality of its aperture, and the equal convexity of the inner lip within." (Sw. Lardn. Cyclop. Malac. p. 325.) Cyprædia, Pl. xxvi. fig. 564.

CYPRÆLA. Swainson. Calpurnus, Montf. Ovulum verrucosum, fig. 441.

CYPRÆOVULUA. Gray. 1832. A genus of Cypræidæ thus described, "shell like a cowry, but front end of columella covered with regular cross-ribs, like the rest of the base, internally produced into an acute toothed ridge. Shell pear-shaped, cross-ridged." C. capense. South Africa. Pl. xxi. fig. 444.

CYPRICARDIA. Lam. Fam. Cardiacea, Lam.—Descr. Equivalve, inequilateral, subquadrate, transversely elongated, with the anterior side very short; hinge with three cardinal teeth and one remote lateral tooth in each valve; ligament external.—Obs. This genus is distinguished from Cardita by the three cardinal teeth. The mollusca of this genus are marine. Pacific Ocean. C. angulata, Pl. vi. fig. 125.

CYPRINA. Lamarck, 1818. Fam. "Conques Marines," or Marine Conchacea.—Descr. Equivalve, inequilateral, sub-orbicular; umbones curved obliquely; hinge with three diverging cardinal and one remote lateral teeth in each valve; ligament external; muscular impressions two in each valve; palleal impression having a slight posterior sinus; epidermis thick, rough brown.—Obs. The Cyprinæ belong to the Northern Hemisphere. The recent species are not numerous. Fossil species are found in the tertiary deposits. Cyprina may be known from Venus by the remote lateral tooth and the thick epidermis. C. vulgaris, Pl. v. fig 116.

CYRENA. Lamarck, 1818. Fam. Fluviatile Conchaceæ, Lam. Conchacea, Bl.—Descr. Suborbicular, equivalve, inequilateral, ventricose, corroded at the umbones, thick, covered with a thick epidermis; hinge with three cardinal and two remote lateral teeth in each valve. Muscular impressions two in each valve; palleal impression not sinuated.—Obs. This genus is distinguished from Venus, Cytherea and Cyprina, by having two remote lateral teeth; and from Cyclas by the thickness of the shell. This genus is mostly fluviatile; the recent species are tropical, and the fossil are found in the newest formations. C. fuscata. Pl. v. fig. 113.

CYRENELLA. Desh. See CYRENOIDA.

CYRENOIDA. Joannis, 1835. CYRENELLA, Desh. Fam. Conques Fluviatiles, Lam.—Descr. Equivalve, subequilateral, ventricose, thin, covered with a reddish brown epidermis, coroded at the umbones, with a slight posterior fold. Hinge thin, with three diverging cardinal teeth in each valve, and a very slight posterior fold in the right valve. Ligament not very tumid.—Obs. This fresh-water shell differs from Cyclas and Cyrena in the lateral teeth, and from the later in the thinness of the shell. Pl. v. fig. 114.

CYRTIA. Dalman. (Κυρτος, curtos, gibbose.) Fam. Brachiopoda, Lam.—Descr. "Hinge rectilinear; with the back elevated into a semicone or half-pyramid, the cardinal side perpendicularly plane."—Obs. This genus of fossil Brachiopoda forms part of the genus Spirifer, Sow. C. exporrecta, (Anomites exporrecta, Nonnull.) Pl. xi. fig. 204.

CYTHARA. Schum. 1817. Cancellaria Cytharella. LAMARCK.

CYTHEREA. Lam. Fam. "Conques Marines," Lam.—Descr. Equivalve, inæquilateral, oval, lenticular, or sub-trigonal; hinge with two or more short, diverging cardinal teeth, and one anterior approximate lateral tooth in each valve.—Obs. The Cythereæ are distinguished from the Veneres by the lateral tooth. The Monograph of this genus, in No. 12. Thesaurus Conchyliorum contains, apart from Meroe, Artemis and Circe, 115 species. See MERETRIX. C. MERETRIX. Pl. vi. fig. 117, and 117, a. b. c. d.

CYRTULUS. Hinds. 1844. A genus founded on a turbinella-like shell, thus described, (translation) "fusiform; the two last whorls turbinated, the spire suddenly rising; aperture linear, ending in a short effuse canal; columella much arched, callous above; outer lip acute; umbilicus small; epidermis smooth." C. scrotinus. Pl. xxviii. fig. 594.

DACTYLINA. Gray. Syn. B. Mus. Pholas Dactylus, and other species, with several accessory valves. Pl. ii. fig. 55.

DACTYLUS. Schum. 1837. Species of ACTÆON or TORNATELLA, which have a duplicate fold at the lower part of the columella. T. solidula.

DACTYLUS. Humph. MARGINELLA, Auct.

DAPHNELLA. Hinds. Voyage of the Sulphur, p. 25. Pl. vii. fig. 19, 20, 21. "Among the smaller Pleurotomaceæ are a few shells of a thin fragile structure, elongated in form, the outer lip acute and separated from the last whorl so as to leave a sinus, aperture of a lengthened oval, scarcely any canal, and with the surface usually transversely striated. These form a very distinct group, and may be separated with advantage under a proper head; the best known of these is probably Lymnæformis Kiener." Ex. D. Marmorata, our Pl. xxviii. fig. 593.

DARACIA. Gray. A subgenus of Pyrgoma, including a species which is remarkable for the irregularity of its form. It grows upon a species of Monticularia, and the margin takes the shape of the lobes by which it is surrounded. The aperture is large, and completely closed by the operculum. Daracia (Pyrgoma) Monticulariæ. Pl. xxiv. fig. 489, 490.

DATE. A common name given to shells of the genus Pholas, on account of their cylindrical form and consequent resemblance to the fruit. For the same reason the name Pholas Dactylus has been given by Naturalists to the species which we represent, fig. 66.

DEAD SHELL. A term used among collectors to signify that the shell has been exposed on the sea-shore after the animal has ceased to live. A shell in this condition is worn down by attrition, and loses its beauty and brilliancy of colouring by being subject to the action of salt water. A dead shell may be known by a certain hoary whiteness spread over its surface.

DECACERA. Bl. The second family of the order Cryptodibranchita, Bl. containing the genera Calmar and Sepia, which have no shells.

DECADOPECTEN. Rüppell. PECTEN Plica, Linn. Having a plicated hing. Pl. x. fig. 172.

DECOLLATED. (Decollari, to be beheaded.) The apex or nucleus of some shells being composed of a more fragile substance than the rest, has a tendency to fall off. The reason of this probably is that the animal withdrawing from that part, leaves it unprotected. When the part falls off, the hole is stopped up by a septum filling the cavity of the volution, so as to exclude the air: the shell is then said to be decollated. Ex. Bulinus decollatus, fig. 289.

DECUSSATED. Intersected by striæ crossing each other. Ex. Rissoa, fig. 346.

DELPHINULA. Montf. (Delphinus, a dolphin.) Fam. Scalariens, Lam. Cricostomata, Bl.—Descr. Orbicular, depressed, thick, rugose; whorls few, angulated, branched at the angles; aperture pearly, rounded or

sub-quadrate; peritreme continuous, thickened; operculum horny, composed of numerous whorls.—*Obs.* Several fossil species are found in the tertiary deposits. D. laciniata. Pl. xvi. fig. 352. Recent species belong to tropical climates.

DELTHYRIS. Dalman. *Fam.* Brachioponda, Lam.—*Descr.* Hinge more or less rounded, with distant umbones; both valves convex; with the umbo of the largest rostrated and deltoid, with a hollow. This genus forms part of the genus Spirifer, Sow. D. Plycotes, Dalman. Pl. xi. f. 205.

DELTOID. (Δ, *delta.*) Triangular.

DENDOSTREA. Swainson, (1840). (Δευδρον, *dendron*, tree; οστρεον, *ostreon*, oyster.) Ostrea *Crista-galli*, and other species which are attached to stems of sea-weed and corallines, by means of arms thrown out from the innter surface of the lower valve. Ostrea Folium. Pl. x. f. 181.

DENTALIUM. Linnæus (*Dens*, a tooth.) *Fam.* Maldania, Lam. *Order*, Cirrobranchiata, Bl.—*Descr.* Tubular, arched, increasing in size towards the anterior extremity, open at both ends; small aperture sometimes having a lateral fissure; large aperture round; external surface ribbed, striated or smooth.—*Obs.* The well known shells composing this genus are shaped very much like an elephant's tusk, and are not liable to be confounded with any other genus. The fossil species are sometimes termed Dentalithes, from *dens*, a tooth, and *lithos*, a stone. The Dentalia, being true molluscs, are not rightly placed among the Annelides. D. octogonum. Found on sandy shores in most climates. Pl. i. f. 2.

DENTATED. Having teeth or raised points.

DENTICULATED. (Denticulatus, Lat.) Having little teeth or raised points.

DEPRESSED. Flattened, pressed down, as the spires of some shells.

DEXTRAL Spiral Shells. Place the point of a spiral shell towards the eye, with its mouth downwards; if, as in most instances, the aperture be on the right side of the axis, it is a *dextral* shell, if otherwise, it is *sinistral* or *reversed*. Balea (fig. 296), and Clausilia (fig. 295), are examples of reversed shells.

DEXTRAL Valve. Take a bivalve shell closed, place it before the eye, with the umbones uppermost, and the posterior side, which may be known by the ligament towards the observer, whose right side will then correspond with the right valve of the shell.

DIADEMA. Ranz. Coronula Diadema, Auct. Pl. i. fig. 17.

DIADORA. Grey. Cemoria, Leach.

DIANCHORA. Sowerby. *Fam.* Pectinides, Lam. *Order*, Palliobranchiata, Bl.—*Descr.* Inequivalve, attached, oblique, subtriangular; attached valve, having an opening in the place of the umbo; the other valve auriculated, with an obtuse umbo; hinge without teeth.—*Obs.* The green sand fossils contained in this differ from Plagiostoma in being attached. D. striata. Pl. x. f. 175.

DIAPHANOUS. (Δια, *dia*, through; φαινω, *phaino*, to shine.) Transparent.

DIAPHRAGM. (διαφραγμα, a partition.) This term is applied to the septa, by which the chambers of multilocular and other shells are divied from each other.

DICERAS. Lamarck. (Δυς, *dis*, double; Κερας, *ceras*, horn.) *Fam.* Chamacea, Bl. and Lam.—*Descr.* Inequilateral, inequivalve, attached by the point of the umbo of the larger valve; umbones prominent, spirally twisted and grooved; hinge with one large thick tooth in the larger valve; muscular impressions, two in each valve.—*Obs.* The prominent spiral umbones, which gives to this genus its name, with the circumstance of its being attached by the point of one of them, is

sufficient to distinguish it from any other. Although it appears to approach Isocardia in some characters, in others it will be found still more nearly to resemble Chama. In fact, from being attached and irregular, the shells composing this genus have been regarded as Chamæ with produced umbones. The singular fossil shells composing this genus, are found in granular limestone, near Geneva in Normandy. D. perversum. Pl. ix. fig. 154.

DICHÆLASPIS. Darwin. Cirrip, p. 115. Octolasmis, Gray. Heptalasmis, Leach. A genus of pedunculated cirripides, the shell of which is thus described: "Valves 5, generally appearing like 7, from each section being divided into two distinct segments, united at the rostral angle; carina generally extending up between the terga, terminating downwards in an imbedded disc, or fork, or cup." Ex. D. Warwickii (imperfect figure.) Pl. 2. f. 41.

DIDONTA. Schum. Saxicava. Auct.

DIFFUSE. (*Diffundo*, to spread out, to dilate.) A term applied to the aperture of a univalve shell, when it is spread out or widened into a flat surface, or digitations. *Alated* is another term used to express the same character. Thus the shells belonging to the family of Alatæ, in the system of Lamarck, are *diffuse* in the outer lip. Fig. 402 to 406.

DIGITATED. (*Digitus*, finger.) Branched out in long points, as Ricinula, fig. 413.

DILATED. Expanded, spread. This term has the same application as diffuse and alated, explained above. The outer lip of Rostellaria Columbaria, fig. 403 (Hippochrenes, Montf.), will serve as an example.

DIMORPHINA. D'Orb. A genus of microscopic Foraminifera.

DIMYARIA. (Δις, *dis*, double; μυον, *myon*, muscle.) The first order of Conchifera, Lam, including those molluscs which have two adductor muscles, and consequently two muscular impressions in each valve. The Conchifera Dimyaria are divided into Crassipedes, Tenuipedes, Lamellipedes, and Ambiguæ, fig. 44 to 155.

DIODONTA. Deshayes. A genus formed for the reception of Tellina fragilis. Hanley, in Sowerby's Thesaurus Conchyliorum. P. 319, pl. lvi. fig. 14, and similar species.

DIOICA. Bl. The first division of the class Paracephalophora, Bl. It is divided into the orders Siphonobranchiata and Asiphonibranchiata, Bl.

DIONE. A generic term used to distinguish the group of Cytheræa represented by C. Dione. See Monograph of Cytheræa, No. 12, pl. cxxxii. fig. 98. Sowerby's Thesaurus Conchyliorum.

DIPLODON. Spix. Hyria Syrmatophora, Lam. fig. 144, and Unio multistriatus, Lea, are doubtfully quoted by Lea as belonging to this apparently ill-defined genus of Nayades.

DIPLODONTA. Brown. Resembles Lucina, but without the ligneate elongation of the muscular impression. D. rotundata. Forbes and Hanley, British Mollusca. Our figure, pl. xxvii. fig. 576.

DIPSAS. Leach, 1817. A genus or sub-genus of Nayades, the distinctive character of which is "having a linear tooth under the dorsal edge." D. plicatus, pl. viii. fig. 142.

DISCINA. Lam. Orbicula, Auct.

DISCODOMA. Sw. A sub-genus of Lucerninæ, Sw. (Helix), thus described, "teeth none; aperture angulated; the inner lip nearly obsolete; the outer only slightly thickened; margin carinated."

DISCOIDAL. (*Discus*, a circular plane.) A spiral shell is said to be discoidal, when the whorls are so horizontally convolute as to form a flattened spire. *Ex.* Planorbis, fig. 311. Orbulites Discus, fig. 479.

DISCOLITES. Montf. A genus of microscopic Foraminifera.

DISCONTINUOUS. Interrupted. *Ex.* The siphon of Nautilus is discontinuous, i.e. its termination in one chamber does not reach to its

349. Cirrus nodosus, Sow.
350. Euomphalus pentangulus, (from
    Sow. Min. Con.)
351. Scalaria Pallassii. Aciona,
    Leach.
352. Delphinula laciniata.
    Chemnitzia, 585. ⎫ To be
    Alvania, 586. ⎬ added to
    Odostomia, 587. ⎭ this family.

Fam. Turbinacea

353. Solarium perspectivum.
354. ——Bifrons. Bifrontia and
    Omalaxis, Desh.
355. Orbis Rotella, (from Lea.)
356. Another view of the same.
357. Rotella vestiaria, Pitonellus,
    Montf.
358. Trochus stellaris, Lam. Calcar,
    Montf. Turbo, Sow.
359. ——maculatus. Tectus, Montf.
360. ——agglutinans. Phorus.
361. ——Pharaonis. Clauculus,
    Montf.
362. Margarita tæniata.
363. Littorina vulgaris.
363*.Assiminea Grayana.
364. Lacuna pallidula.
365. Planaxis sulcata.
366. Monodonta labeo; Odontis,
    Sow.
367. Phasianella variegata.
368. Turbo setosus. Marmarostoma,
    Sw.
369. Tuba striata, (from Lea.)
370. Turritella imbricata.
371. Monotygma, Gray.
    Chrysostoma, fig.
        542.
    Elenchus, fig. 543. ⎫
    Adeorbis, fig. 588. ⎪ To be
    Teinostoma, fig.   ⎬ added
        589.   ⎪ to this
    Camitia, fig. 589. ⎪ family.
    Mesalia, fig. 591. ⎪
    Eglesia, fig. 592. ⎭

Fam. Canalifera

372. Cerithium Aluco, front.
374. Nerinea Goodhallii, (from Geol.
    Trans.)
375. Triphora plicata, (from
    Deshayes.)
376. End view of the same.
379. Pleurotoma Babylonia; *a, a,*
    extremities of the anix.
381. ——strombiformis, Clavatula,
    Lam.

commencement in the next. The varices of Triton, occurring in different parts of the whorls, do not form the continuous ridges which characterize the generality of the Ranellæ.

DISCORBITES. Lam. A genus of microscopic Foraminifera.

DISTANT. The teeth on the hinge of a bivalve shell are said to be distant when they are said to be remote from the umbones.

DIVARICATED. Diverging, meeting in a point, as the teeth on the hinge of Placuna, fig. 184.

DOLABELLA. Lamarck (Dim. from *Dolabra*, a hatchet.) *Fam.* Aplysiacea, Lam. and Bl.—*Descr.* Hatchet-shaped, arched, covered with a horny epidermis; posteriorly attenuated, thickened, sub-spiral, anteriorly plane, broad, thin; posterior margin reflected.—*Obs.* The two or three species of Dolabella known are inhabitants of the Indian Ocean. They were placed by Linnæus in his very convenient genus Bulla, under the name of B. dubia. Pl. xiii. fig. 255, Dolabella Rumphii.

DOLIUM. Brown, (1756.) (*a tun.*) *Fam.* Purpurifera, Lam. Entomostomata, Bl.—*Descr.* Thin, ventricose, oval, or globular, with a short spire; large aperture terminating in a reflected canal, and spirally ribbed or grooved external surface; outer lip crenated; inner lip reflected over part of the body whorl, which terminates in a tumid varix; epidermis light, horny. Mediterranean and East Indian.—*Obs.* This genus is distinguished from Cassis by the outer lip, which is not reflected. The species which are not so round as the others, as D. Perdix, Auct. have been separated under the name Perdix, as if generically distinct. Mr. Reeve's Monograph contains fourteen species. Dolium Maculatum. Pl. xix. fig. 420.

DONAX. Linnæus. *Fam.* Nymphacea, Lam. Conchacea, Bl.—*Descr.* Equivalve, inequilateral, trigonal, with the anterior side short, straight, plane; the posterior side elongated, drawn to a narrow, rounded termination; hinge with two cardinal teeth in one valve, one in the other, and one or two, more or less remote lateral teeth; ligament external; muscular impressions two in each valve; palleal impression sinuated posteriorly.—*Obs.* The Capsæ have not the crenated margins, the short anterior side, and the distinct lateral teeth, which characterise the Donaces. Some species of Erycina resemble Donax in general form, but are at once distinguished by the ligamentary pit in the hinge. The Donaces inhabit sandy shores in all climates. D. cuneatus. Pl. v. fig. 108.

DORSAL. A dorsal shell is one placed upon the back of the animal. The dorsal margin of a bivalve shell is that on which the hinge is placed; the opposite margins are termed ventral. The dorsal surface of a spinal univalve is that which is seen when the aperture is turned from the observer. The dorsal valve is the uppermost in Brachiopodous bivalves. The dorsal part of a symmetrical convolute univalve, such as the Nautilus and Ammonite is that part of the whorls which is at the greatest distance from the spire, that is, the outer part of the whorls. Thus the situation of the siphon is said to be dorsal when it pierces the septum near the outer edge of the whorls. The dorsal part of symmetrical conical univalves, such as Patella, is the upper part, on which the apex is placed.

DORSALLIA. Lam. (*Dorsum*, the back.) The first family of the order Annelides Sedentaria, Lam. containing the genera Arenicola, not a shell, and Siliquaria, fig. 1, which is now considered as a true mollusc, and placed next to Vermetus.

DOSINA. Schum. VENUS Verrucosa, Casina, and similar species. Fig. 119, *a*.

DREISSINA. 1835. MYTILUS Polymorphus. Auct. fig. 159. This genus differs from Mytilus principally in the characters of the animal. The shell is characterized by a small septiform plate under the hinge within.

Fluviatile, Europe and Africa. Pl. ix. fig. 159.

EBURNA. This name belongs to the species "glabrata," described in this book as an Ancillaria. "Latrunculus" is given by Gray for the present genus. Ancillaria glabrata, fig. 455. (*Eburneus*), ivory. *Fam.* Purpurifera, Lam. Entomostomata, Bl.—*Descr.* Oval, thick, smooth, turrited, umbilicated; spire angulated, acute, nearly as long as the aperture; aperture oval, terminating anteriorly in a canal, posteriorly in a groove; outer lip slightly thickened with an anterior notch, which terminates in a spiral fold surrounding the body whorl; umbilicus generally covered by the thickened columellar lip.—*Obs.* (A. glabrata, fig. 455.) The Eburnæ resemble in some respects the genus Buccinum, but a glance at the figure will enable the reader to distinguish a true Eburna from all other shells. Fig. 426 is Eburna Zeylanica. A catalogue of 9 species is given in part 20 of the Conchological Illustrations published by the Author, accompanied by figures of several species.

ECHIDNIS. Montf. Described as a straight, chambered, annulated, fossil shell, computed from the extremely gradual increase in diameter of the fragments to be at least sixteen feet long. Found in marble from the Pyrenees.

ECHINELLA. Swainson. A sub-genus of Monodonta. Sw. Malac. page 352.

EFFUSE. (*effundo*, to pour out.) The aperture of an univalve shell is said to be effuse when there is a notch in the margin which would suffer a liquid to escape, and thus prevent it being filled to the brim.

EGEON. Montf. A genus of microscopic Foraminifera.

EGERIA. Lea. (Contrib. to Geol. p. 49, pl. 1.) A genus of fossil bivalves, described as very variable in form, with or without lateral teeth, sometimes a crenated margin, &c. The only certain characters appear to be that they have two diverging cardinal teeth in each valve, one of which is bifid; and an external ligament. Lea states that the Egeriæ should be placed between the Sanguinolariæ and the Psammobiæ, which two latter genera have been united by Sowerby. E. Triangulata, from the tertiary formation of Alabama. Pl. v. fig. 103.

EGLESIA. Gray. Reeve's Monograph (2 species.) Conch. Iconica. "Shell elongated, turrited; whorls numerous; sutures depressed; columella flatly thickened; squarely angled at the base; aperture small, rounded; margins almost joined, not reflected." Distinguished from Turritella by the angular depression of the upper part of the whorls, and by the consequent straightness of the outer lip.—*Obs.* There are certain species of so-called Scalariæ; such as Sc. Australis, Sc. Diadema, Sc. Crenata, &c. of Sowerby's Thesaurus, which perhaps might be added to this genus with propriety. See our Pl. xxviii. fig. 592.

ELENCHUS. Humph. A genus composed of TROCHUS Iris, Auct. and other similarly formed species. It is the same as CANTHARIDUS of Montfort. Pl. xxv. fig. 543.

ELEPHANT'S TUSK. The common name given by dealers to shells of the genus Dentalium. *Ex.* D. octogonum, fig. 2.

ELEVATED. A term which is applied by some conchological writers to the spire of an univalve shell when it consists of numerous whorls drawn out into a telescopic form. Other authors use the term *elongated*, or the more simple one '*long*,' to express the degree of elevation.

ELLIPSOLITHES. Montf. (Ελλειψις, *ellipsis*, oval; λιθος, *lithos*, stone.) A genus composed of Ammonites, which instead of being regularly orbicular, take an elliptical or oval form. This character appears to be accidental, as some individuals of the same species, both of Nautilus and Ammonites, are round, while others are compressed into an oval form.

ELLIPSOSTOMATA. Bl. (Ελλειψις, *ellipsis*, oval; στωμα *mouth*.) The third family of the class Asiphonibranchiata, Bl. The shells of this family are described as of various forms, generally smooth; the aperture longitudinally or transversely oval, completely closed by a horny or shelly operculum. This family contains the genera Rissoa, Phasianella, Ampullaria, Helicina, and Pleuroceras.

ELLIPTICAL. (Ελλειψις, *ellipsis*.) Oval. Applied to any shell or part of a shell, having that form.

ELMINEUS. Leach. *Order*, Sessile Cirripedes, Lam.—*Descr*. Four unequal valves, arranged circularly side by side, forming a quadrate cone; aperture large, sub-quadrate, irregular; operculum composed of four valves, in pairs.—*Obs*. This genus differs from Conia in the structure of the shell, the latter being porous. Elmineus Leachii. Pl. i. fig. 22.

ELPHIDIUM. Montf. (Conch. Syst. t. 1. p. 15.) A genus of microscopic Foraminifera.

EMARGINATED. (*e*, out; *margo*, border.) Notched or hollowed out. Applied to the edges or margins of shells, when instead of being level they are hollowed out, as the outer lip of Oliva, fig. 457, at the base, and the ventral margins of some bivalves.

EMARGINULA. Lamarck, 1801. (*e*, out; *margo*, border.) *Fam*. Calyptracea, Lam. Branchifera, Bl.—*Descr*. Patelliform, oblong or oval; anterior margin notched or emarginated; apex posteriorly inclined; muscular impressions wide.—*Obs*. Emarginula elongata, of some Authors, Parmophorus of De Blainville is commonly called the Duck's bill limpet, from its shape. The Emarginulæ may be known from Patellæ and other neighbouring genera, by the notch or slit in the anterior edge. In the genus Rimula, Defr. fig. 243, this slit is near the apex, and does not reach the margin. Recent species occur in all climates, but are not numerous. Fossil species are still more rare, occurring in the Calcairegrossièr, Crag and Oolite. E. fissurata, Pl. xiii. fig. 241.

ENDOSIPHONITES. A genus composed of Ammonites, having the siphon close to the body whorl. Pl. xxii. fig. 476.

ENDOTOMA. Rafinesque. A genus of microscopic Foraminifera.

ENOPLOCHITON. Gray. Chiton niger, &c.

ENROULEES. Lam. See Convolutæ.

ENSATELLA. Swainson, 1840. Ensis, Schum. 1817.

ENSIS. Schum. 1817. Solen ensis. Auct. and similar species, fig. 60.

ENTALIS. Defr. Dentalium duplicatum, Bl. Pharetrium, König. This genus is described as a small tube, within a larger one, the smaller extremity of the inner tube projecting beyond that of the outer one. Deshayes, who describes this genus, expresses a conviction that the soft parts of the animal must be entirely different from those of the animal of Dentalium. The genus Pharetrium, as described by König in his "Icones Fossilium Sectiles," is evidently identical with Entalis. It is placed by him in the family of Pteropoda, but being a fossil shell, there is some difficulty in finding its place in the system. See plates, fig. 3.

ENTELLITES. Fischer. A genus composed of species of Terebratula, Spirifer, and Productus, Auct. having the hinge large and the umbones short. Orthis? Dalman.

ENTIRE. (Integra.) Not interrupted, not emarginated. The peritrême of a univalve shell is said to be entire when not interrupted by canals or by the body whorl. *Ex*. Cyclostoma, fig. 304. The palleal impression is entire, when continued without interruption, or without a sinus.

ENTOMOSTOMATA. Bl. The second family of the order Siphonibranchiata, Bl. The shells of this family are described as differing but little from those contained in the family of Siphonostomata of the same author, both with regard to the soft parts, and their testaceous covering. This family partly answers to the Purpuriferæ in the system of

Lamarck, and contains the genera Subula, Cerithium, Melanopsis, Planaxis, Terebra, Eburna, Buccinum, Harpa, Dolium, Cassidaria, Cassis, Ricinula, Cancellaria, Purpura, Concholepas.

EOLIDES. Montf. A genus of microscopic Foraminifera.

EPIDERMIS. (Επι, *epi*, over or upon; δερμα, *derma*, skin.) The fibrous, horny, external coating of shells, called by the French, "*Drap marin*," or marine cloth. Lamarck objects to the name Epidermis, because he does not consider the substance as answering to the cuticle or scarf skin of the human body, but more analogous to the nails and hair. Gray calls it the Periostracum, from the membranous skin covering the bones of quadrupeds.

EPIPHRAGM. The membranaceous or calcareous substance by which some species of molluscs close the aperture of the shell, when they retire within it to hibernate. When the animal wishes to come forth from his hiding-place, again to breathe the air, the edges of the Epiphragm are detached by a chemical process, so that it drops off. The name *Hibernaculum* has also been given to this covering. It must not be confounded with the operculum, which is a permanent portion of the shell, and is used as a door, fitted to the foot of the animal and moved at will to pen or close the aperture of the shell, whereas the Epiphragm is produced for the occasion from a mucous secretion of the animal and dissolved at the edges when no longer, wanted, when it drops off.

EPISTYLA. Swainson, 1840. A subgenus of the genus Helix. E. conical. Sw. Helix Epistylium, fig. 281.

EPONIDES. Montf. A genus of microscopic Foraminifera.

EQUILATERAL. (*Æquus*, equal; *latus*, side.) Equal-sided. A term applied to bivalve shells, when a line drawn down perpendicularly from the apex would divide the shell into two equal parts. *Ex*. Pectunculus pilosus, fig. 134.

EQUIVALVE. (*Æquus*, equal, *valva*, a valve.) A term applied to a bivalve shell when the valves are equal to each other in dimensions.

ERATO. Risso, 1826. *Fam*. Convolute, Lam.—*Descr*. Ovate, more or less angulated, smooth or granulated, with a dorsal scar, spire short, aperture large, angulated, emarginated; columella slightly crenated; outer lip reflected, denticulated on the inner edge. Suture of the whorls covered with enamel.—*Obs*. This genus of shells resembles Marginella in form, but has no folds on the columella. Having a scar or groove down the back it may be considered intermediate between Marginella and Cypræa. In the Author's Conchological Illustrations, seven species are enumerated and figured. E. Maugeriæ. Pl. xxi. fig. 454.

ERUCA. Sw. A subgenus of Clausilia. Sw. Malac. p. 334.

ERVILIA. Turton, 1822. A genus described as "oval, equivalve, equilateral, closed. Hinge with a single erect tooth closing between two small diverging ones in the opposite valve: lateral teeth none. Ligament internal. E. nitens. Turt. Mya. nitens, Auct." Pl. xxiv. fig. 497.

ERYCINA. Lam. *Fam*. Mactracea, Lam. Conchacea, Bl.—*Descr*. Ovate or triangular, transverse, equivalve, inequilateral, smooth; hinge with a ligamentary pit, two diverging cardinal and two lateral teeth in each valve; muscular impressions two in each valve; palleal impressions sinuated. East and West Indies and Mediterranean.—*Obs*. This genus is distinguished from *Mactra* and *Lutraria* by the cardinal teeth being placed one on each side of the ligamentiferous pit; whereas in the last named genera they are both placed on the anterior side. E. Plebeja. Pl. iv. fig. 86.

ESCUTCHEON. The impression on the posterior dorsal margin of some bivalve shells. That on the anterior margin is named the lunule. The escutcheon is pointed out by the letter *e* in some of the figures of Cythereæ. Fig. 117, *a. b. c.*

ETHERIA. Lam. 1808. *Fam*. Chamacea, Lam. and Bl.—*Descr*. Irregu-

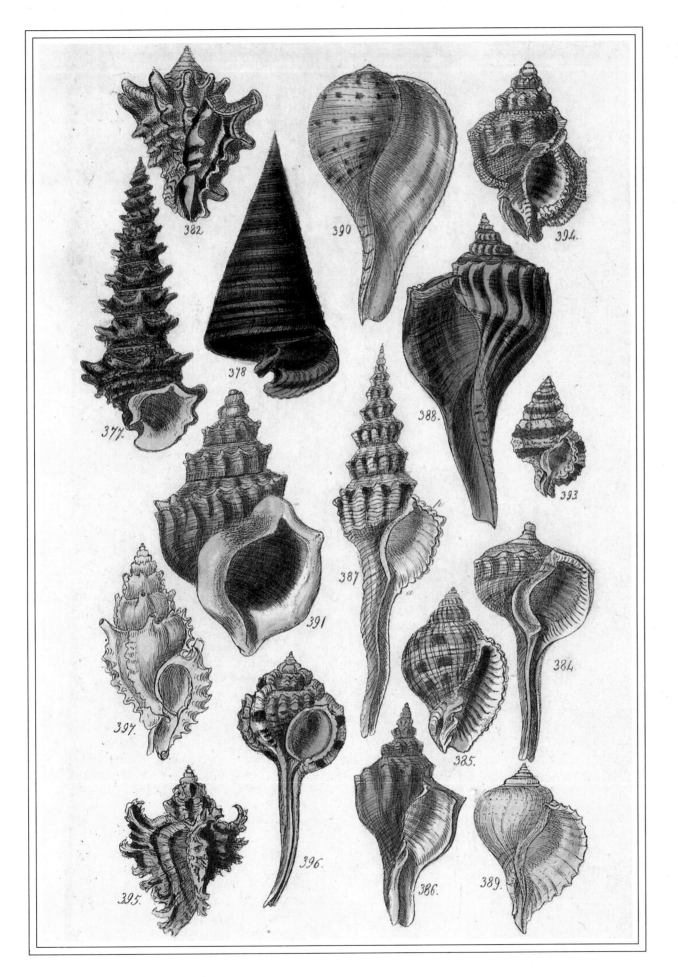

377. Potamis muricata. Pyrazus,
    Montf. Tympanostomata,
    Schum.
378. Cerithium Telescopium. *Gen*.
    Telescopium.
382. Turbinella corniger. Scolymus,
    Swainson.
384. Spirillus. *Gen*. Pyrella, Sw.
    Turbinella spirillus, Auct.
385. Cancellaria reticulata.
386. Fasciolaria Trapezium.
387. Fusus Colus; *a*, anterior of the
    aperture; *p*. posterior.
388. Pyrula perversa. Fulgur,
    Montf.
389. ——papyracea. Rapanus,
    Schum. bulbus, Humph.
    Rapella, Sw.
390. ——Ficus. Ficula, Sw.
391. Struthiolaria straminea.
393. Ranella ranina. Apollon, Montf.
394. ——neglecta. Bufo, Montf.
395. Murex inflatus. Chicoreus,
    Montf.
396. ——haustellum. Brontes,
    Montf.
397. Typhis tubifer, (from
    Deshayes.)

lar, inequivalve, inequilateral, foliaceous, pearly within, covered by an olive green epidermis without; hinge callous, undulated, destitute of teeth; ligament partly external, partly internal, passing through the hinge on a somewhat raised, callous area in the lower valve. Muscular impressions elongated, two in each valve, united by a slender palleal impression. Rivers of Africa.—*Obs.* The irregular, unequal air-bubbles of the inner surface, whence this genus derives it name, are very brilliant in some species, and atone, in some measure, for the rugged ugliness of the exterior. In its irregular form, foliated structure, and toothless hinge, it resembles OSTREA, from which it differs in having two muscular impressions. E. semilunata. Pl. ix. fig. 155.

EULIMA. Risso, 1826. *Fam.* Scalareins, Lam.—*Descr.* Elongated, smooth, pyramidal; spire long, composed of numerous whorls; apex acute, slightly tortuous; aperture oval, rounded anteriorly, acute at the posterior union with the body whorl; outer lip slightly thickened; columella smooth. Fig. 347, E. labiosa, fig. 348, E. splendidula. A complete illustrated Monograph of this genus of pretty shining little shells, consisting of 15 known species, is given in parts 52 and 53 of the Conchological Illustrations by the author. Pl. xv. fig. 347, 348.

EUOMPHALUS. J. Sowerby. *Fam.* Scalariens, Lam.—*Descr.* Orbicular, planorbular spire, with three or four volutions, imbricated above; smooth below; aperture of a round polygonal form; umbilicus large, penetrating to the apex of the shell.—*Obs.* This genus of fossils very nearly resembles Delphinula. The main difference appears to be that the whorls do not increase so rapidly in size in the former as in the latter. Fossil, in the Carboniferous Limestone. Pl. xvi. fig. 350.

EUTROPIA. Humphrey. Gray's Synopsis, Phasianella, Lamarck.

EXOGYRA. Say. A genus of fossil bivalves described as resembling Chama in shape and Ostræa in structure, having but one muscular impression in each valve. Pl. xi. fig. 183.

EXSERTED. Standing out, protruding.

EXTERNAL. An external shell is one which contains the animal and is not covered by the mantle.

FARCIMEN. Troschel, 1847. Pupæform species of CYCLOSTOMA. *Ex.* C. tortum. Thesaurus Conchyliorum, Pl. xxviii. fig. 181, 182: and our figure. Pl. xxv. fig. 529.

FASCIATED. (*fascia*, a band.) Banded or striped. *Ex.* Carocolla marginata, fig. 277.

FASCICULATED. (From fasciculum.) A little bunch of hairs or bristles against each end of each valve, characterizes some species of the genus Chiton, which are termed fasciculated species.

FASCIOLARIA. Lamarck, 1801. *Fam.* Canalifera, Lam. Siphonostomata, Bl.—*Descr.* Elongated, fusiform, ventricose; spire conical, consisting of a few rounded or angulated whorls; aperture wide, terminating in a long straight open canal: columella lip with several oblique folds, the lower of which is larger than the rest; operculum horny, pyriform.—*Obs.* This genus is known from Fusus by the folds on the columella; from Turbinella, by their obliquity and the last being larger than the rest. Mr. Reeve's Monograph contains 16 species. East and West Indies and Australia. F. trapezium. Pl. xvii. fig. 386.

FASTIGIELLA. Reeve. Zool. Proc. 1851. A genus composed of the single species figured, whose characters (as to the shell) place it half way between Turritella and Cerithium. *Ex.* F. carinata, Reeve. Pl. xxviii. fig. 598.

FAUNUS. Montf. Part of MELANOPSIS, Auct.

FERRUGINEOUS. Of an iron rust colour.

FERUSSINA. Grateloup. STROPHOSTOMA, Deshayes. The latter being the Latin name must be dropped. *Ex.* Pl. xxv. fig. 534–5–6.

FIBROUS. A shell is said to be of a fibrous structure when a fracture would present a series of perpendicular fibres, as Pinna.

FICULA. Swainson, 1840. A generic group of shells, consisting of those species of PYRULA. Auct, which have the true pear-shaped character. P. Ficus. Pl. xvii. fig. 300.

FIMBRIA. Megerle. CORBIS, Cuvier.

FIMBRIATED. Fringed; as Murex fimbriatus, a delicate white species, with broad fringed varices.

FISSURE. (*Fissura*, a slit.) A slit or cut, a narrow perforation, as in Emarginula and Fissurella.

FISSURELLA. Lamarck, 1801. (*Fissura*, a fissure.) *Fam.* Calyptracea, Lam. Branchifera, Bl.—*Descr.* Patelliform, oval or oblong, radiated; apex anterior, perforated.—*Obs.* The Fissurellæ are known from Patellæ by the performation in the apex. Fig. 245. The catalogue published by the author in the Conchological Illustrations, enumerates 68 species. Pl. xiii. fig. 245.

FISTULANA. Lam. (*Fistula*, a pipe.) *Fam.* Tubicolæ, Lam. Adesmacca, Bl.—*Descr.* A transversely elongated, equivalve, in equilateral bivalve, enclosed by a septum within the widest, closed extremity of a straight calcareous tube. Fistulana is known from Gastrochæna by the straightness of the tubes, and the oblong state of the valves. Fistulana Clava. Pl. ii. fig. 53, 54.

FLEXUOUS. Having windings or bendings. *Ex.* The Tellinæ are known by the twist or flexuosity in the posterior ventral margin of the shell.

FLORILLUS. Montf. A genus of microscopic Foraminifera.

FLUVIATILE. (Fluviatilis.) Belonging to a river or running stream. *Ex.* Limnæa fluviatilis.

FLUVIATILE CONCHACEA. See CONCHACEA.

FOEGIA. Gray, 1840. ASPERGILLUM. Novæ Zelandiæ.

FOLIATED, or FOLIACEOUS. (From *folium*, a leaf.) When the edges of the successive layers of which a shell is composed are not compacted but placed apart from each other, projecting like tiles, the shell is said to be of a foliated structure. The common Oyster, fig. 180, presents a familiar example.

FORAMINIFERA. D'Orb. (*Foramen*, a hole or pit) An order established for minute many chambered internal shells, which have no open chamber beyond the last partition. Lamarck, D'Orbigny, and other writers have placed them among the Cephalopoda in their systems, but Du Jardin, on comparing the fossils with some recent species of the same class, arrived at the conclusion, now generally adopted, that they constitute a distinct class, much lower in degree of organization than even the Radiata. Not recognizing these microscopic bodies as shells, properly so called, but considering them sufficiently numerous and interesting to form a distinct branch of study, I do not think it desirable to describe the genera, or to present any arrangment of them in this work.

FORNICATED. Arched or vaulted, as the exfoliations on the costæ of Tridacna Elongata, fig. 157.

FORSAR. Gray, 1840. Is it not a Trichotropis?

FOSSIL SHELL. A shell is considered to be in a fossil state when, the soft parts having ceased to exist, it is deprived of all its animal juices, has lost all, or nearly all its natural colour, and its thus changed in its chemical composition, when little or nothing is left but a mere bone, which is embedded in a sedimentary deposit. In this state it is fragile, prehensible to the tongue, and either destitute of colour or tinged with the diluted mineral matters which prevade the stratum in which it lies. In some cases, the mineral composition of the shell is so completely changed as no longer to present its proper structure, consisting of

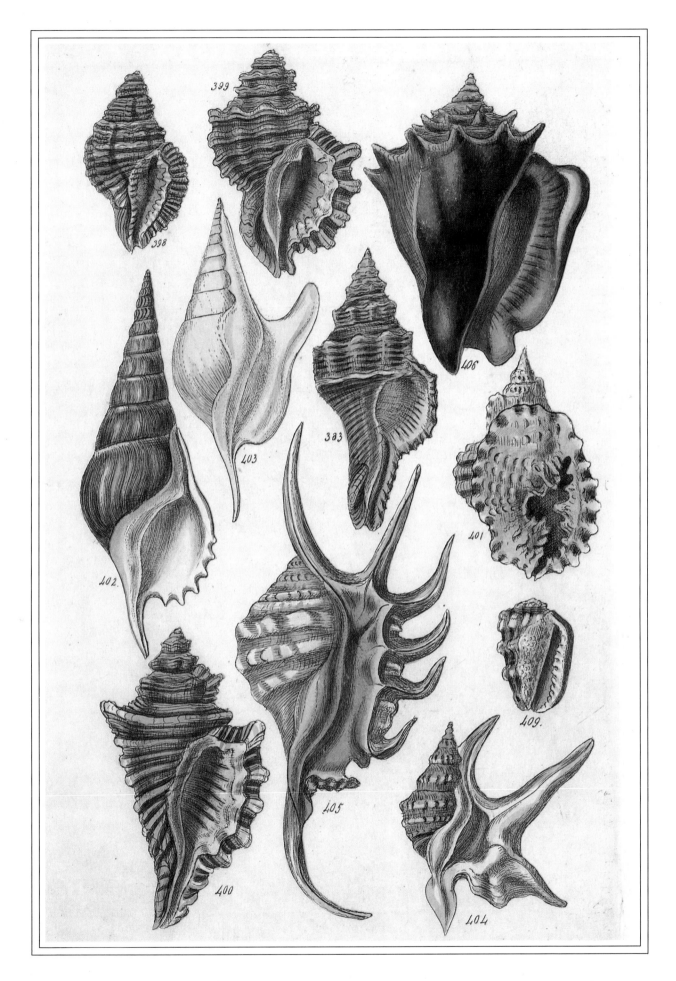

383. ——polygona. Polygonum,
   Schum.
398. Triton pilearis.
399. ——cutaceus. Aquillus, Montf.
400. ——Lotorium. Lotorium,
   Montf.
401. ——anus. Persona, Montf.

Fam. Alatæ

402. Rostellaria curvirostrum.
403. ——columbaria.
   Hippochrenes, Montf. (from
   Sow. Gen.)
404. ——Pes-pelicani. Aporrhais,
   Petiver.
405. Pteroceras aurantiacum.
406. Strombus pugilis.
   Clavalithus, fig.
      548.
   Leiostoma, fig. 549.
   Pyrella, fig. 550.
   Tomella, fig. 551.
   Myristica, fig. 552.
   Vitulina, fig. 553.
   Cyrtulus, fig. 594.
   Trophon, fig. 595.
   Conopleura, fig.
      596.
   Mangelia, fig. 597.
   Frastigiella, fig.
      598.
   Hindsia, fig. 599.

   To be
   added
   to this
   family.

Fam. Purpurifera

409. Oniscia Oniscus. Cassidaria.

successive oblique layers of shelly matter; but is altered into a fibrous structure, composed of rhomboidal particles. An example of this will be found in the Belemnites, which if broken, shew the perpendicular fibres. In other cases, the matter which has entered and filled up the cavities of the shell has become silicified, or changed into flint, and the shell itself has been decomposed and fallen off, so as to leave nothing but an external or internal cast of its form, in flint. This is called a Conchyliomorphite by continental writers. Some of the most important of Geological data are obtained by a minute comparison of fossil shells, found in various beds, with recent ones presenting the nearest resemblance to them. Some species of fossil shells are considered as identical with recent species. And many Geologists seek to fix the chronology of the different strata by the number of species which they inclose bearing a resemblance to the recent species. Indeed, all who would study Geology with success, will find it indispensably necessary to obtain a thorough knowledge of Conchology.

FRAGELLA. Swainson, (1840.) CLANCULUS, Montf. 1810. A sub-genus of Monodonta, consisting of M. Pharaonis (fig. 361), and similar species.

FRAGILE. (*Fragilis.*) Tender, easily broken.

FREE SHELL. One that is not attached.

FREE VALVE. In attached bivalve shells, one only is fixed; the other is then *free*, as far as to the action of opening and shutting.

FRESH-WATER SHELLS, (sometimes described as aquatic) are those which inhabit rivers, running pools and ditches, in which case they are *fluviatile*; or wells and ponds of standing water, &c. Fresh-water shells are either thin and horny in their texture, as the Limneana of Lamarck; or are covered with a compact, smooth, horny epidermis. They are generally simple in form, subject to corrosion where the epidermis is wounded or broken, and are circumscribed with regard to the classes and genera to which they belong. The family of Nayades includes nearly all the fresh-water bivalves; and the Melaniana and Limneana are the principal among univalves.

FRONDICULARIA. Defr. A genus of microscopic Foraminifera.

FRONT. The surface of a shell on which the aperture appears.

FULCRUM. That part of a shell on which any other part rests or turns. The term is applied more particularly to the tumid part in the hinge or bivalve shells on which the ligament is fixed.

FULGUR. Montf. 1810. PYRULA perversa, Auct. and such other species as have an angulated spire. Fig. 388.

FUSIFORM. (*Fusus*, a spindle.) Shaped like a spindle, swelling in the centre and tapering at the extremities. *Ex.* Fusus, fig. 387.

FUSUS. Lamarck, (1801.) (A spindle.) *Fam.* Canalifera, Lam. Siphonostomata, Bl.—*Descr.* Fusiform, turrited, with many rounded whorls; aperture generally oval, terminating in a long straight canal; operculum horny, pyriform.—*Obs.* The Fusi are subject to considerable variations in form. The recent species are numerous and do not appear to be confined to any climate. The fossil species are also numerous, chiefly abounding in the tertiary formations. Mr. Reeve's Monograph contains 79 species. The recent species are mostly tropical. Pl. xvii. fig. 387, F. Colus. Priority has been claimed for the generic name "Colus," used by Humphrey in 1797, but without any description.

GADILA. Synopsis of Brit. Mus. Dentalium Gadus. Martyn.

GALATHÆA. Brug. 1798, POTAMOPHILA, Sow. MEGADESMA. Bowd.

GALEA. Klein. PURPURA, Auct.

GALEOLARIA. Lam. (From Galea, a helmet or crest.) A genus composed of species of SERPULA, Auct. Distinguished as being fixed by the side of the shell, and having the anterior extremity erect, the aperture terminating in a tongue-shaped projection.—*Obs.* This genus is said by Lamarck to resemble Vermilia in other respects, but to differ in having the anterior part raised. Africa and Australia. G. decumbens. Pl. i. fig. 6.

GALEOMMA. Turton, 1835. *Fam.* PHOLADARIA, Lam.—*Descr.* Thin, oval, equivalve, equilateral, with the ventral margin gaping; hinge with one cardinal tooth in each vale; muscular impressions two, approximate; palleal impression interrupted, not sinuated; ligament small, partly internal, partly external, fixed on a prominent fulcrum.—*Obs.* The wide hiatus in the ventral margins of this equilateral shell prevents the possibility of confounding it with any other. Four or five recent species are known, one of which is found on the coast of Sicily, and also in the British Channel. *Fam.* "Kelliadæ." G. Turtoni. Pl. ii. fig. 28, 29.

GALERICULUS. (*Galericulum*, a little cap or bonnet.) VELUTINA, Auct. fig. 337.

GALERUS. Humph. Species of CALYPTRÆA, Lam. With an obliquely spiral septum. *Ex.* C. Chinensis.

GAPING. (*Hians.*) Bivalve shells are said to gape when the margins do not meet all round. *Ex.* Gastrochæna, fig. 52.

GASTEROPODA. Lam. (Γαστηρ, *gaster*, belly; πους, ποδος, *pus, podos*, a foot.) The second order of the class Mollusca, Lam. containing those molluscous animals whose organs of locomotion are ventral. Most of the shells belonging to this order are patelliform, placed upon the back of the animals, which rest or crawl upon the belly. This order is divided into Pneumonobranchiata, that is, those which breathe air, or land molluscs; and Hydrobranchiata, or those which breathe water, marine or fresh-water molluscs. Fig. 227 to 263.

GASTEROPTERA. Meckel. A genus of Bullidæ without any shell.

GASTRANEA. Schum.? CORBULA, Act.

GASTRIDEA.? Pseudoliva Swainson, 1840. Eburna plumbea. Sowerby. Pl. xxvi. fig. 547.

GASTROCHÆNA. Spengler, 1780. (Γαστηρ, *gaster*, belly; χαινω, *chaino*, gape.) *Fam.* Pholadaria, Lam. Pyloridea, Bl.—*Descr.* Equivalve, regular, inequilateral, with a wide, oblique, ventral hiatus, inclosed in a curved pyriform tube. Differing from Galeomma in being a free, oblique shell; from Fistulana, in the oval shape of the valves, and the curve of the tube; from Aspergillum and Clavagella, in both valves being free.—*Obs.* The Gastrochænæ are found in the hollows of massive shells or other marine substances. G. Modiolina. Pl. ii. fig. 62.

GASTROPLAX. Blainville. UMBRELLA, Lam. De Blainville described this genus from a specimen in which the shell had been, probably by accident, placed upon the under part of the animal, and not discovering his error until afterwards, gave it the above name.

GENA. Gray. Part of Stomatella, Lamarck.

GEOMITRA. Swainson. A sub-genus of Geotrochus, Sw. founded on a trochiform species of Helix, with coronated nodules on the whorls. Helix bicarinata, Sow. Zool. Journ. 1, pl. iii. fig. 7. Sw. page 166 and 332.

GEOPHONUS. Montf. Conch. Syst. t. 1, p. 19. A genus of microscopic Foraminifera.

GEOTROCHUS. Swainson, (1824.) HELIX pileus, Auct. (fig. 278), and other trochiform species. Divided into the sub-genera Pithohelix, Geotrochus, Hemitrochus, Gonidomus, and Geomitra. Sw. p. 165 and 166, described at page 331. Pl. xiii. fig. 278.

GEOVULA. Swainson. A sub-genus of Melampus (Auricula), consisting of oval species, resembling Auricula Midæ, fig. 297.

GERVILLIA. Defr. *Fam.* Margaritacea, Bl. Malleacea, Lam.—*Descr.*

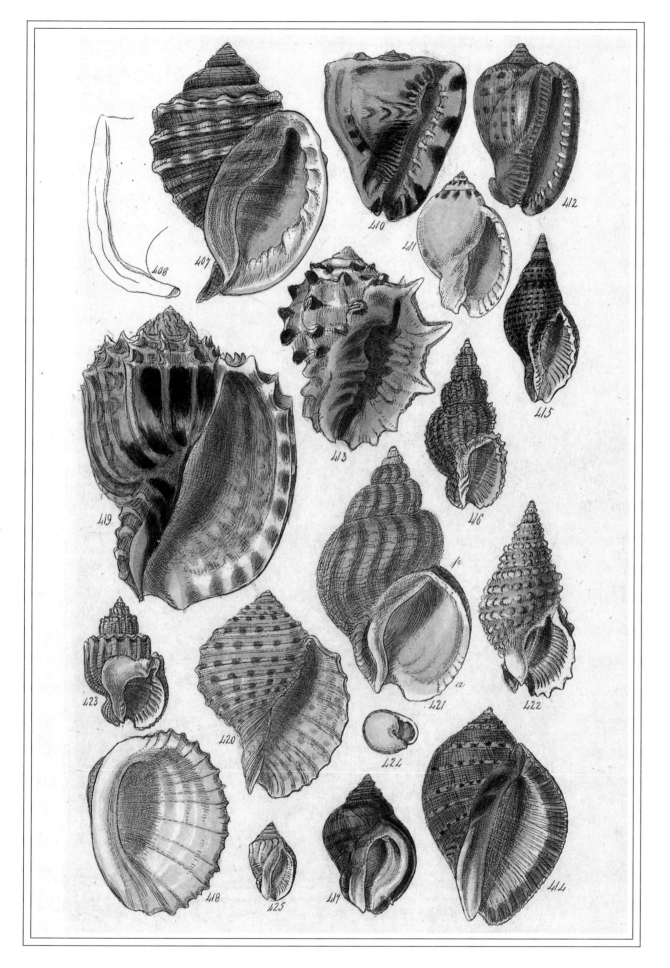

407. Cassidaria echinophora. Morio,
     Montf.
408. Side view of the outer lip, to
     shew the canal.
410. Cassis tuberosa, reduced.
411. ——erinaceus. Cassidea, Sw.
412. ——testiculus. Cypræcassis,
     Stutchbury.
413. Ricinula horrida. Sistrum,
     Montf.
414. Purpura persica.
415. Tritonidea (*Pollia*, Gray.)
     articularis.
416. Phos senticosa.
417. Monoceros crassilabrum.
418. Concholepas Peruviana.
419. Harpa ventricosa.
420. Dolium maculatum.
421. Buccinum undatum; *a*, anterior
     of the aperture; *p*. posterior.
422. ——papillosum. Alectrion,
     Montf.
423. Nassa arcularia.
424. ——neritoidea. Cyclops,
     Montf.
425. Cyllene, Gray.

Equivalve, oblong, oblique; hinge long, straight, having small, irregular, transverse ligamentary pits.—*Obs*. This genus of fossil shells, found at various geological periods, from the Lias to the Baculite limestone in Normandy, is now extinct. In general form it resembles Avicula, but in the hinge it approaches Perna. G. Avicularis. Pl. x. fig. 169.

GIBERULA. Sw. A genus separated from MARGINELLA, Auct. and thus described, "sub-oval; spire slightly prominent; top of the outer lip dilated and gibbous; base of the inner lip with plaits; inner lip broad, spreading, G. Zonata. Enc. Méth. 374, f.6."

GIBBOSE or GIBBOUS. (*Gibbosus*.) Bunched out, embossed, having a lump or swelling of any kind. *Ex*. Bulinus Lyonetianus, (fig. 284) named Gibbus by De Montfort. Ovulum gibbosum.

GIBBUS. Montfort, (1810.) BULINUS *Lyonetianus*, Lam. PUPA, Bl. Pl. xiv. fig. 284.

GLABELLA. Swainson, 1840. MARGINELLA Glabella (fig. 437), Goodallii, Auct. and similar species.

GLANDINA. Schum. 1817. POLYPHEMUS, Montf.

GLANDIOLUS. Montf. A genus of microscopic Foraminifera.

GLAUCONOME. Gray, 1829. *Fam*. Solenacea, Lam.—*Descr*. Oblong or oval, transverse, slightly ventricose, equivalve, inequilateral; margins close, rounded anteriorly, somewhat acuminated posteriorly; hinge teeth, three in each valve, of which the central in one, and the posterior in the other, are bifid; muscular impressions anterior, elongated, marginal; posterior sub-quadrate; palleal impression, having a long sinus; ligament oblong, external; epidermis thin, horny, green, folded over the margins.—*Obs*. C. Chinensis was the first species described, since which eight more have been added, in a monograph by Reeve, several of which were brought by Mr. Cuming from the Philippine Islands. Pl. iii. fig. 64.

GLOBIGENERA. D'Orb. A genus of microscopic Foraminifera.

GLOBOSE. (*Globosus*.) Rounded like a globe or ball, as the species of Helix, represented in fig. 268.

GLOBULARIA. Swainson, 1840. A sub-genus of Natica, consisting of globose species. (Sw. p. 345.) *Ex*. N. Lineata, fig. 328.

GLOBULUS. Sow. Min. Con. Part of AMPULLARIA, Auct.

GLOSSUS. Poli, 1795. ISOCARDIA Moltkiana, and similar species. Pl. vi. fig. 126.

GLYCIMERIS. Lamarck, 1799. *Fam*. Solenacea, Lam. Pyloridea, Bl.—*Descr*. Equivalve, transverse, oblong, thick, compressed, gaping at both extremities; hinge callous, without teeth; ligament large, external, prominent; epidermis thick, black, horny, folded over the margins; muscular impressions two, distant, running into the irregular palleal impression which unites them.—*Obs*. But few species of this singular genus are known; Lamarck describes two species from the Northern Seas. Blainville is of opinion that they belong to the family of the Nayades. G. Siliqua. Pl. 3. fig. 67.

GNATHODON. Gray, 1837. (Γναθος, *gnathos*, jaw-bone; οδος, οδοντος, *odontos*, tooth.) *Fam*. Mactracea, Lam.—*Descr*. Ovate, posteriorly angulated, equivalve, thick, ventricose, inequilateral, covered with a greenish brown epidermis; umbo distant, prominent; hinge having in one valve a sharp, angular, notched, cardinal tooth, and two lateral teeth, the posterior of which is elongated, and the anterior angulated, tortuous, shaped like a jaw-bone; in the other valve, two cardinal and two lateral teeth, the anterior of which is wedge-shaped; ligament internal, cuneiform, placed in a deep cardinal pit proceeding from the umbones; muscular impressions two; palleal impression having a slight sinus.—*Obs*. Only one species is known, G. cuneatus, fig. 83, from New Orleans. It is known from all other shells by the character of the hinge. Pl. iv. fig. 83.

GONIATITES. De Haan. A genus composed of species of Ammonites, Auct. in which the last whorl covers the spire and the sinuations of the septa are angulated. Pl. xxiii. fig. 480. G. striatus.

GONIDOMUS. Swainson. A sub-genus of Geotrochus, Sw. PUPA pagodus, Auct. Sw. p. 332. Pl. xxv. fig. 519.

GONIOSTOMA. Swainson, 1840. A sub-genus of Bulimus, thus described, "spire elongated, of few whorls; aperture contracted at each end; lips margined; the pillar curving inwards; the base slightly notched. G. erubescens, *Sw*. Zool. Journ. i. pl. 5, f. 2." Sw. p. 335.

GONIOSTOMATÆ. Bl. A family belonging to the order Asiphonibranchiata, Bl. containing the genera Solarium and Trochus.

GONOSPIRA. Swainson, 1840. A sub-genus of Pupa, thus described, "spire perfectly cylindrical, of equal thickness, the tip obtuse, with the whorls large; aperture oval; lips thickened; pillar with or without a plait. G. polanga, *Desh*. Lesson, Voy. pl. 8, f. 8." Sw. p. 333.

GRANULATED. (*Granum*, a grain.) Covered with minute grains, rough. The granulated lip of Oniscia, (fig. 409) will serve as an example.

GRATELOUPIA. Desmoulins, 1828. *Fam*. Nymphacea, Lam.—*Descr*. Equivalve, inequilateral, sub-cuneiform, rounded anteriorly, sub-rostrated posteriorly; hinge with three cardinal teeth, a series of five or six irregular, small diverging teeth behind the umbones, and one lateral anterior tooth in each valve; ligament external; muscular impressions two; palleal impression sinuated posteriorly.—*Obs*. This genus (Donax irregularis, Bast.) is only known in a fossil state. Pl. v. fig. 102. G. Moulinsii.

GRYPHÆA. Lamarck, 1801. (From Gryps, a griffin.) *Fam*. Ostracea, Lam.—*Descr*. Inequivalve, free; lower valve large, concave; with the umbo prominent, incurved: upper valve small, flat, opercular; hinge toothless, with a curved, depressed area; one muscular impression.—*Obs*. These shells, which approach the Oysters, are of a more regular form, and are remarkable for the curved, produced beak of the lower valve. They are only known in a fossil state, belonging to the more ancient strata. Fig. 182, G. incurva. The recent species mentioned by Lamarck is not a true Gryphæa. Pl. x. fig. 182.

GYMNOLEPAS. A generic name used by De Blainville to include OTION and CINERAS, Leach. See CONCHODERMA.

GYMNOSOMATA. Bl. The second family of the order Aporobranchiata, in the system of De Blainville. The animals belonging to this family are destitute of shells.

GYPIDEA. Dalman. A genus of Brachiopoda, thus described, "Larger valve with the umbo rostrated, remote from the hinge; with the canal large, deltoid; bilocular within." PENTAMERUS, Sow. G. Conchidium, copied from Dalman. Pl. xi. figs. 210, 211.

GYROGONA. Lam. A genus of microscopic Foraminifera.

GYROIDINA. D'Orb. A genus or microscopic Foraminifera.

HALIA. Risso. PRIAMUS, Beck. Fig. 545.

HALIOTIDÆ. Sw. A sub-genus of Calyptræa. CALYPTRÆA dilatata. Sowerby's Genera of Shells, fig. 9.

HALIOTIS. Linnæus. (αλς, *als*, sea; ους, ωτος, *otos*, ear.) *Fam*. Macrostomata, Lam. Otides, Bl.—*Descr*. Auriform, broad, depressed, pearly within, rough, costated, tuberculated without; spire short, flat, consisting of one or two whorls; aperture wide; ovate; columella laminar, flat, oblique; a spiral series of perforations running along the dorsal margin.—*Obs*. The splendid shells belonging to this genus are remarkable for the pearly iridescence of the inner surface, and the row of holes following the course of the spire. The soft parts are eaten in Guernsey and Jersey, and reckoned delicious. They belong to temperate and tropical climates. Fig. 338, H. rubra. 339, Padollus, Montf. Mr. Reeve's monograph contains 73 species.

HALIOTOID. (*Haliotis*, and ειδος, *eidos*, form.) Ear-shaped.

HAMIFORM. (*Hamus*, a hook.) Curved at the extremity.

HAMINEA. Leach. A genus of Bulridæ, the shells of which are thus described by Adams in his Monograph, No. 11, Sowerby's Thesaurus, "shell convolute, horny, thin, transversed, grooved, destitute of columella or spire."

HAMITES. Parkinson. (*Hamus*, a hook.) *Fam.* Ammonacea, Lam.—*Descr.* Elongated, cylindrical, chambered, recurved at the smaller extremity, annulated; septa lobed and sinuated.—*Obs.* This remarkable fossil from the Baculite limestone in Normandy, differs from Baculites in being curved at one extremity, a circumstance from which its name is derived. Some small species are found in chalk-marl, Folkestone. H. cylindricus. Pl. xxiii. fig. 484.*

HARPA. Humphry, 1797. (*Harpa*, a harp.) *Fam.* Purpurifera, Lam. Entomostomata, Bl.—*Descr.* Oval, ventricose, longitudinally and regularly costated; spire short, with rounded, dome-like whorls; aperture wide, emarginated; outer lip thickened, reflected, composing the last costa or rib; inner rib polished, spread over part of the body whorl, terminating in a point.—*Obs.* This beautiful genus of shells is so clearly defined by the regular, longitudinal ribs that adorn the external surface, suggesting the idea of a stringed instrument, that there is no danger of confounding it with any other. H. multicostata; (Buccinum costatum, Linn.) and H. ventricosa, are among the most elegant of the testaceous productions of the sea both in form and colouring; the former is rare. The recent species are not numerous, they inhabit the Indian Ocean. A fossil species occurs at Grignon, near Paris. Mr. Reeve's Monograph contains 9 species. *Ex.* H. ventricosa. Pl. xix. fig. 419.

HARPAX. Parkinson. Part of PLICAULA, Auct.

HARPULA. Swainson, 1840. A group of shells separated from VOLUTA, Auct. thus described, "shell generally tuberculated or longitudinally ribbed; apex of the spire papillary, smooth, and in general distorted; pillar with numerous distinct plaits; the upper, small and slender, the lower, thickest and shortest."—*Type*, H. Vexillum. (Voluta, Auct.) Thesaurus Conchyliorum. Pl. l. fig. 54, 55; Pl. xxvi. fig. 557.

HAUSTATOR. Montf. A genus proposed to include those species of TURRITELLA, Auct. which have angulated whorls.

HAUSTELLARIA. Swainson, 1840. BRONTES. Montf. 1810. A sub-genus of Murex, consisting of species with long canal and no spines. Murex haustellum, fig. 396.

HAUSTRUM. Humph. PURPURA, Lamarck.

HELCION. Montfort, 1810. A genus composed of species of Patella, which have the apex distinctly and prominently bent forwards. *Ex.* P. pellucida. Pl. xii. fig. 230.

HELENIS. Montf. A genus of microscopic Foraminifera.

HELICELLA. Fer. One of the sub-genera into which De Ferussac has divided the genus Helix, consisting of depressed species with large umbilicus, such as Helix Algira, (Gonites Montf.) fig. 279.

HELICIFORM. Shaped like shells of the genus Helix.

HELICIGONA. One of De Ferussac's sub-genera of the genus HELIX, consisting of angulated species, such as Carocolla Lamarckii, fig. 277.

HELICINA. Lamarck, 1801. ROTELLA, Lamarck, 1822.

HELICINA. Lamarck, 1822. OLYGIRA, Sacy. *Fam.* Colimacea, Lam. Ellipsostomata, Bl.—*Descr.* Globose, compressed, or angulated, generally light and thin; aperture trigonal or semi-lunar; outer lip thickened and generally more or less reflected; inner lip spread over the body whorl, frequently callous near the columella, which is short, and terminates in a notch, angle, or slight callosity.—*Obs.* This genus of land shells, distinguished from the genus Helix, by having an operculum and a thickened columellar lip, differs also from Cyclostoma in having the apterture semicircular or angular, the peritrême discontinuous and the operculum concentric. These shells are generally small in size, and simple in form. Lamarck describes only three or four species. Mr. Gray described some others in the Zoological Journal. 73 species are given in the Monograph, No. 1, Sowerby's Thesaurus. "Oligyra" of Say is given to this genus in Gray's Synopsis, because Lamarck applied "Helicina" first to Rotella. Helicina Major and similar species having a notch in the peritrême, have been separated under the name Alcadia (our figs. 306, 307.) H. Aureola, Thesaurus Conchyliorum, Pl. i. fig. 43, 4, 5, having a peculiar contraction near the outer lip, is named genus "LUCIDELLA," and the sharp-keeled, Carocolla-formed species (our figs. 532, 533), has been named genus "TROCHATELLA." The passage by intermediate species is, however, so gradual, that these generic distinctions can hardly be maintained.

HELICITES. Bl. Part of the genus NUMMULITES, Lam. ROTALITES and EGEON, Montf.

HELICOGENA. Fer. A sub-genus of Helix, consisting of species, which, like the common garden snail, fig. 268, are globose and simple in form.

HELIOCOLIMAX. Fer. VITRINA, Drap. H. Pellucida, Pl. xiii. fig. 263.

HELICOPHANTA. Fer. A sub-genus of Helix, consisting of ear-shaped species with large open apertures.

HELICOSTYLA. Fer. A sub-genus of Helix, consisting of species with numerous whorls, as H. Epistylium, Pl. xiv. fig. 281.

HELISOMA. Sw. A sub-genus of Planorbis. Sw. p. 337.

HELIX. Linnæus. *Fam.* Colimacea, Lam.—*Descr.* Orbicular, light, generally globular; spire short, last whorl ventricose, aperture oblique, peritreme reflected, interrupted by the most prominent part of the body whorl; columella confluent with the outer lip, and contiguous to the axis of the shell. No operculum; a thin epidermis.—*Obs.* The land shells composing this genus are found in all parts of the world; the common snail, H. Aspersa, is well known as a destructive animal in our gardens. The genera Helix, Achatina, Bulinus, Clausilia, Anostoma, &c., have been united under one generic name by De Ferussac, and again divided under the following sub-generic names, each of which we shall illustrate by a figure. GENUS HELIX: *Sub-genus 1, Helicophanta,* consisting of species with large apertures, like Vitrina; Helix brevipes. *S. gen. 2, Cochlohydra,* Succinea Amphibia, Drap. *S. gen. 3, Helicogena,* consisting of the common species with the last whorl large; Helix Hæmastoma, H. Contusa, (Streptaxis, Gray,) H. Aspersa. *S. gen. 4, Helicodonta,* consisting of species with teeth or folds on the columella; Polydonta, Montf. Anostoma, Helix Nux-denticulata. *S. gen. 5, Helicigona,* Carocolla, Geotrochus. *S. gen. 6, Helicella,* consisting of depressed species with a large umbilicus; H. Citrina (Nanina, Gray.) *S. gen. 7, Helicostyla,* consisting of species with a simple aperture, like the Helicogenæ, but with the whorls increasing very gradually; H. epistylium. *S. gen. 8, Cochlostyla,* Bulinus. *S. gen. 9, Cochlitoma,* Achatina. *S. gen. 10, Cochlicopa,* Polyphemus Glans. *S. gen. 11, Cochlicella,* Bulinus decollatus. *S. gen. 12, Cochlogena,* Azeca tridens. *S. gen. 13, Cochlodonta,* Pupa Uva. *S. gen. 14, Cochlodina,* Clausilia macascarensis, Balea fragilis. The last three sub-genera are included in the genus Odostomia of Fleming. We give an example of each of these sub-divisions, for the sake of presenting the reader with the principal variations to which the genus is subject. The established genera will be characterized in their places. Pl. xiii. fig. 254 to 281.

HELIXARION. Ferussac, 1819. VITRINA, Drap. Differing from Helicolimax in the structure of the animal. Pl. xiii. fig. 262.

HEMICARDIUM. Swainson, 1840. (ημισυς, *hemisus*, half, Καρδια, *cardia*, heart.) CARDIUM Hemicardium, and several similar species. Pl. vi. fig. 123***.

HEMICYCLA. Sw. A sub-genus of Helix.

HEMICYCLONOSTA—see CARDILIA.

HEMICYCLOSTOMATA. Bl. The fourth family of Asiphonibranchiata, Bl. described as "more or less globular, thick, flattened on the under side; spire very short; aperture large, semilunar, entire; its outer edge hollowed; its inner or columellar edge straight, sharp and septiform." This family answers to the genus *Nerita* of Linnæus, and to the family Neritacea of Lamarck. It contains the genera Natica, Nerita, Neritina, and Navicella.

HEMIMACTRA. Swainson, 1840. A sub-genus of Mactra, thus described: "General form of *Mactra*, but the cardinal teeth entirely wanting; cartilage internal, central, in a large triangular cavity; lateral teeth ½, distinct, lateral, striated: connected to the *Glycimeri*. H. gigantea, *Lam*. v. 472. No. 1. grandis, *Sw*. Sp. Nov." Sw. p. 369.

HEMIMITRA. Sw. A sub-genus of Paludomus, Sw. (Melanianæ.)

HEMIODON. Sw. A sub-genus of Anodon, described as having "Tubercles or undulations on the hinge margin. H. undulatus, purpurascens and areolata."

HEMIPECTEN. Adams and Reeve. Mollusca of the Samarang. A genus belonging to the family of Pectinidæ, thus described, "attached, inæquivalve, irregular, hyaline, upper valve simple anteriorly, very slightly auriculated posteriorly; lower valve simple anteriorly, conspicuously auriculated posteriorly, deeply sinuated and denticulated beneath the auricle; hinge edentulate, ligament slightly marginal with a small cartilage in a central cavity. Hemipecten Forbesianis, *Reeve*. Conch. Icon." Our Plate xxvii. fig. 580.

HEMISINUS. Sw. A sub-genus of Melania, thus described: "General shape of *Melania*; but the base of the aperture is contracted and emarginate; outer lip crenated. H. lineolata, Griff. Cuv. xii. pl. 13. fig. 4."

HEMITOMA. Sw. A sub-genus of Emarginula, thus described: "Patelliform; the fissure not cut through the shell, but merely forming an internal groove. H. tricostata, *Sw*. Sow. Gen. fig. 6."

HEMITROCHUS. Sw. A sub-genus of Geotrochus, Sw. H. hæmastroma. Sw. p. 331.

HEPTALASMIS. Leach. ('Επτα, *hepta*, seven; ελασμα, *elasma*, plate.) A small shell resembling Pentelasmis, from which it differs in the number of valves, being composed of seven valves according to Leach, and of eight according to Gray, who counts the dorsal valve, which is jointed, as *two*, and names his genus Octolasmis, the appearance of seven valves being caused by the scuta being entirely or partially divided into two segments. M. Darwin has decided not to retain either of the names, implying the apparent number of valves but to name the genus. DICHELASPIS. *Ex*. D. Warwickii. Pl. ii. fig. 41.

HERCOLES. Montf. A microscopic shell, appearing from De Montfort's figure to resemble TROCHUS *Imperialis* in shape.

HERION. Montf. LENTICULINA, Bl. Microscopic.

HERMAPHRODITA. Bl. The third sub-class of Paracephalophora, Bl. divided into, Sect. 1, *symmetrical*, containing the orders Cirrobranchiata and Cervicobranchiata; Sect. 2, *non-symmetrical*, order, Scutibranchiata.

HERMES. Montfort, 1810. A genus composed of CONUS *Nussatella*, Auct. and other elongated, cylindrical, striated species. Pl. xxi. fig. 460.

HETEROBRANCHIATA. Bl. The fourth order of the class Acephalophora, Bl. containing no testaceous mollusca.

HETEROPODA. Lam. The fifth order of the class Mollusca, Lam. This order contains but one genus of shells, viz. Carinaria, fig. 488.

HETEROSTEGINA. D'Orb. A genus of microscopic Foraminifera.

HIATELLA. Daudin. Fam. Lithophagidæ, Lam. A genus composed of species of Saxicava, Auct. which have sharp, angulated, posterior ridges, a circumstance which occurs to many species in a young state, which afterwards become rouonded off. Hiatella biaperta. Pl. iv. fig. 95.

HIATULA. Sw. A genus proposed to include those species of Oliva, Auct. which have widened apertures. *Ex*. O. Subulata. Pl. xxi. fig. 458.

HIBOLITHES. Montf. A genus composed of species of Belemnites, Auct. which are swelled towards the apex, and contracted near the centre. B. Hastatus, Auct. Pl. xxii. fig. 468.

HIMANTOPODA. Schum. MALLEUS, Auct.

HINDSIA. A. Adams, Zool. Prac. 1851. A genus composed of Triton Acuminata, (Reeve's Monograph) and similar species, of which there are about a dozen, agreeing with each other remarkably well in characters, which separate them from other groups. They have no distinct varices, properly so called, such as distinguish the true Tritons, excepting a large one immediately behind the aperture, which is rather small, with the lips produced and detached. The general form over the back, but long and slightly recurved. *Ex*. T. acuminatum. Pl. xxviii. fig. 599.

HINGE. The edge of the bivalve shells near the umbones, including the teeth and ligament.

HINNITES. Defrance, 1831. A generic name proposed for PECTEN PUSIO, Auct. remarkable for the irregularity of the outer surface, which would almost lead to the belief of its being an attached shell. The monograph of this genus in the Author's Thesaurus Conchyliorum contains three species. Pl. xx. fig. 173, H. Pusio.

HIPPAGUS. Lea. (*Horse boat*.) A minute fossil shell, resembling Isocardia in form, but destitute of hinge teeth. H. Isocardioides. Pl. vi. fig.f 128.

HIPPOCHRENES. Montfort, 1810. Species of ROSTELLARIA, Auct. with the outer lip spread. R. Columbaria. Pl. xviii. fig. 403.

HIPPONYX. Defrance, 1819. ('Ιππος, *hippos*, horse; ονυξ, *onyx*, nail or hoof.) *Fam*. Rudistes, Lam.—*Descr*. Inequivalve, sub-equilateral, rather irregular, destitute of ligament and hinge teeth; lower valve attached, flat, sub-orbicular, with a muscular impression, composed of two lunulate portions, meeting at one extremity, and presenting the form of a horse-shoe; upper valve conical; with the apex inclined backwards, and the muscular impression marginal.—*Obs*. The earlier naturalists having only met with the upper valve of these shells, placed them among the patelliform univalves; to some of which, particularly Pileopsis, they bear a very strong resemblance. The species of Hipponyx are numerous, and till lately only known in a fossil state. The recent species belong to tropical climates: the fossil species are found in the tertiary beds. The monograph in the Thesaurus Conchyliorum contains five species. H. cornocopia. Pl. xi. figs. 199, 200.

HIPPOPODIUM. Conybeare. J. Sowerby, 1819. *Fam*. Cardiacea, Lam.—*Descr*. Equivalve, obliquely transverse, heavy, deep, inequilateral, umbones incurved; ventral margin sinuated, so as to give a bilobed appearance to the shell; hinge incrassated, with one rugged oblique tooth.—*Obs*. These fossils are found in the upper beds of Lias. H. Ponderosum. Pl. vii. fig. 129.

HIPPOPUS. Lam. ('Ιππος, *hippos*; πους, *pous*, foot.) *Fam*. Tridacnacea, Lam.—*Descr*. Equivalve, inequilateral, regular, subquadrate;

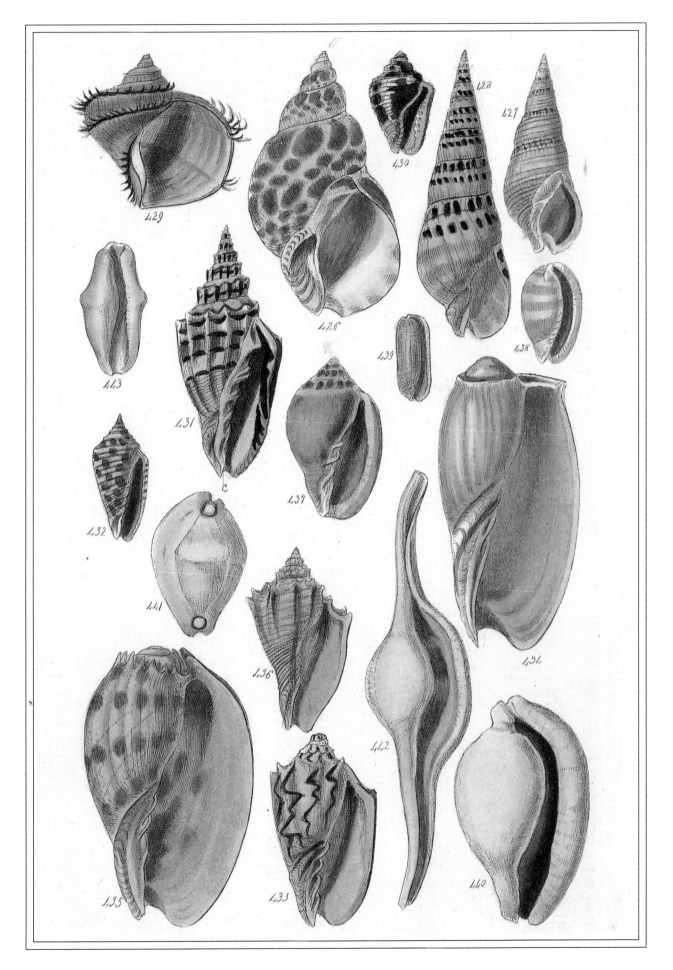

426. Eburna Zeylanica.
427. Bullia vittata.
428. Terebra maculata. Subula, Bl.
429. Trichotropis bicarinata.
Polytropa, fig. 546.
Vexilla, fig. 544. } To be
Gastridium, fig. } added
545. } to this
Daphnella, fig. 593. } family.

Fam. Columellata

430. Columbella mercatoria.
431. Mitra plicaria; *c.* termination of the columella.
432. Conohelix marmorata.
433. Voluta Vespertilio. Cymbiola, Sw.
434. Cymba porcina.
435. Melo Æthiopicus.
436. Volutilithes spinosus.
437. Marginella Glabella. Glabella, Sw. Cucumis, Klein.
438. ——persicula. Volutella, Sw. Persicula, Schum.
439. Volvaria concinna.
Harpula, fig. 557.
Mitreola, fig. 558. } To be
Mitrella, fig. 559. } added
Nitidella, fig. 560. } to this
Pachybathron, fig. } family.
600. }

Fam. Convolutæ

440. Ovulum Ovum.
441. ——verrucosum. Culpurnus, Montf.
442. ——Volva. Radius, Montf.
443. ——gibbosum. Ultimus, Montf.

lunule closed, flat, with crenulated edges; ventral margin deeply undulated; external surface fluted, with radiating ribs, which are transversely fringed with rows of tubular spines; hinge margin thick, with two long, compressed posterior lateral teeth in one valve, three in the other; ligament marginal, external.—*Obs*. The shell thus described is rightly separated from Tridacna, on account of the anterior dorsal margins being closed; whereas in Tridacna there is a wide hiatus. Only one species of this genus is known, which receives its name from its resemblance in form to a horse's foot, when held with the flat anterior dorsal margin downwards. Few shells are found to concentrate so many beauties as the Hippopus Maculatus, commonly called the Bear's-paw-clam; the delicate whiteness of the interior, the undulating edge, the radiated fluted columns, adorned at intervals by crisped fringes, and the richness of the variegated colouring, are such as to secure the admiration of the most superficial observer. From the Indian Archipelago. H. Maculatus. Pl. ix. fig. 156.

HIPPURITES. Montf. *Fam*. Orthocerata, Lam. Rudistes, Bl.—*Descr*. Tubular, rude, irregular, attached; lower valve cylindrical, more or less lengthened, apparently divided into sections by septa (considered by some authors as merely projecting layers of growth) having one or two lateral tubes within; upper valve round, flat, fixed on the aperture of the tubular valve like an operculum.—*Obs*. This genus is known only in a fossil state, and but very imperfectly. Lamarck places it among his chambered Cephalopoda, &c. De Blainville, considering it a true Bivalve, enumerates it among his Rudistes. Cretaceous group. H. Cornucopia. Pl. xi. fig. 198.

HYALÆA. Lamarck, 1799. (*Hyalus*, glass.) *Fam*. Pteropoda, Lam. Thecosomata, Bl.—*Descr*. Globose, glassy, transparent, with a triangular opening at the upper part where the dorsal portion advances beyond the ventral; ventral portion vaulted; dorsal more flat; lower extremity tridentate.—*Obs*. The singular structures composing this genus were formerly taken for bivalves, and named Anomia Tricuspidata, &c. They are now known to belong to the class of molluscous animals, called Pteropoda, from the wing-shaped organs of locomotion. A species of Hyalæa occurs in Sicily in a fossil state. Recent species are found in the Mediterranean, Atlantic, and Indian Oceans. H. Tridentata. Pl. xii. fig. 226.

HYALINA. Schumacher, 1827. Marginella pallida, Thesaurus Conchyliorum, Pl. viii. Marginella, Pl. lxiv. fig. 108.

HYALINA. Studer. VITRINA, Drap.

HYALINE. (*Hyalus*, glass.) Glassy, thin, transparent.—*Ex*. Carinaria Mediterranea, fig. 488.

HYDATINA. Schumacher. A sub-genus of Bullidæ, the shells of which are thin and inflated, and have flat, visible spires. B. venillum is an example of four species described in M. Adams' Monograph, Part 11, Sowerby's Thesaurus.

HYDROBRANCHIATA. Bl. The first section of the order Gasteropoda, Lam. containing Molluscs which breathe water only; divided into the families Tritoniana, Phyllidiana, Semiphyllidiana, Calyptracea, Bullæana, and Aplysiana.

HYGROMANES. Fer. A sub-division of Helix, containing H. limbata, Auct. &c. Gray's Turton, p. 143.

HYPOTHYRIS. Phillips, King, 1846. A genus represented by Terebatula psittacea. Pl. xi. fig. 202.

HYRIA. Lamarck, 1819. A genus composed of species of Nayades, distinguished by their alated dorsal margins, and lamellated lateral teeth. South America. HYRIA corrugata, fig. 143, Hyria Syrmatophora. Pl. viii. fig. 144.

HYRIDELDA. Swainson, 1840. A genus of "Hyrianæ," Sw. described as differing from HYRIA, Auct. in having a cardinal as well as a lateral tooth in each valve. Sw. p. 380.

HISTRIX. Humphrey, 1797. RICINULA, Auct.

IBDRUS. Montf. CAROCOLLA, Lam.

IBLA. Leach, 1825. *Fam*. Pedunculated Cirripedes, Lam.—*Descr*. Four valves, posterior pair elongated, anterior pair short, triangular; pedicle cylindrical, contracted at the base, hairy.—*Obs*. I. Cuveriana, is brought from Kangaroo Island. Pl. ii. fig. 40.

ICTHYOSARCOLITES. Desmarest. *Fam*. Ammonacea, Lam.—*Descr*. Chambered, slightly arcuate, laterally compressed; septa simple, leaving triangular articulations imbricated like the thick muscles of a fish.

ILOTES. Montf. ORBICULINA, Bl. A genus of microscopic Foraminifera.

IMBRICARIA. Schumacher, 1817. CONOHELIX, Sw. 1833. See MITRA.

IMBRICATED. (*Imbrex*, a tile.) A shell is said to be imbricated when the superficial laminæ are arranged over each other in the manner of tiles.

IMPERATOR. Montfort, 1810. A genus composed of species of the genus TROCHUS, Auct. with whorls angulated and stellated, having an umbilicus. *Ex*. T. Imperialis.

IMPRESSION. See MUSCULAR IMPRESSION.

INCRASSATED. (*Crassus*, thick.) Thickened, as the hinge of Glycimeris, fig. 67.

INCURVED. Turned inwards or bent forwards. Applied to symmetrical shells, when the point of the apex turns towards the anterior extremity, as in Patella. The apex of a shell is said to be curved when it is bent inwards, but not sufficiently so to be described as spiral. *Ex*. Ammonocesas, Lam. fig. 477.

INDENTED. (*In*, in; *dens*, a tooth.) Exactly the reverse of DENTATED; meaning a series of small cavities, such as might be produced by the entrance of teeth. The cast of a dentated surface would be indented.

INEQUILATERAL. (*Æquus*, equal; *latus*, a side.) A term applied to a bivalve shell when its extent on one side of the umbones is greater than that on the other. When the sides are nearly equal, the term *subequilateral* is used.

INEQUIVALVE. (*in*; *æquus*, equal; *valva*, valve.) The two principal valves differing from each other in diameter or convexity.

INFERIOR VALVE is that which is attached to sub-marine bodies. Only applied to attached bivalves.

INFEROBRANCHIATA. Bl. The fourth family of the second section of Paracephalophora Monoica, Bl. containing no testaceous mollusca.

INFLATED. Swelled, as Bulla, fig. 250, 252. This term can only be applied to rotund shells of a light, thin texture.. In other cases we should use the word VENTRICOSE.

INFLECTED. Turned inwards. This term is applied to the outer lip of a spiral shell when it turns towards the body whorl. This is the case in Cypræa, fig. 446. See REFLECTED.

INFUNDIBULUM. Montfort, 1810. (*A funnel*.) A genus formed of those species of CALYPTRÆA, Lam. which, having a spiral septum, so nearly resemble Trochus that some authors have placed them in that genus. One species named Patella Trochiformis. Recent from South America, fossil from the tertiary beds. Calyptræa (Infundibulum) Pileus. Pl. xii. fig. 237, 238.

INNER LIP. That edge of the aperture of a univalve shell which is near to the imaginary axis, as distinguished from the outer lip, or that which is on the opposite side.

INOCERAMUS. Sow. *Fam*. Malleacea, Lam. Margaritacea, Bl.—*Descr*. Thick, inequivalve, sub-equilateral, triangular, deep, with the umbones incurved; hinge formed of a series of transverse grooves.—

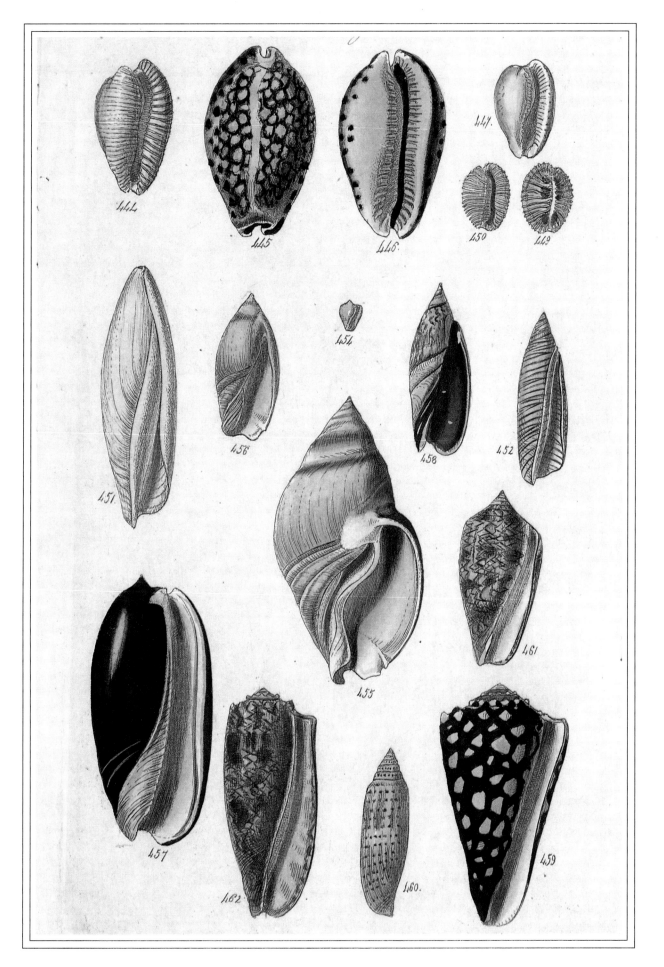

444. Cypræovulum capense.
445. Cypræa arabica, back.
446. The same, front.
447. Cypræa Algoensis. Luponia,
    Gray, front.
449. ——Pediculus. Trivia, Gray,
    Back.
450. The same, front.
451. Terebellum convolutum.
    Seraphs, Montf.
452. ——subulatum, front.
454. Erato Mangeriæ.
455. Ancillaria glabrata. Anolax,
    Brongn.
456. ——cinnamonea.
457. Oliva Maura.
458. ——subulata. Hiatula, Sw.
459. Conus nocturnus. Rhombus,
    Montf.
460. ——Nussatella. Hermes,
    Montf.
461. ——Textile. Cylinder, Montf.
462. ——geographus. Rollus,
    Montf.
    Lamprodoma,
      fig. 561.   } To be added
    Cyprædia,   } to this family.
      fig. 564.

Obs. The larger valves of these fossil shells resemble the larger valve of Gryphæa; but the hinge is quite distinct. The species described in Mineral Conchology are found in the blue marl, at Folkestone, and in the chalk. I. Lamarckii, (Catillus, Brong.) Pl. x. fig. 167.

INTERNAL CAST. The mould of a fossil shell, composed of matter which entered the shell in a soft state, and has subsequently hardened, when, the shell dropping off, the hardened substance which filled it is left to represent its internal form.

INTERNAL LIGAMENT. A term used by some conchological writers signifying that the ligament of a bivalve shell is placed within the closed part of the hinge, so as not to be seen when the valves are shut. But the substance, formerly called the internal ligament, is now distinguished from the true ligament both in structure and use; and is now more properly called the cartilage, so that when the ligament is said to be internal, it must be understood that the internal cartilage is unaccompanied by any ligament properly so called, and when a shell is described as having two ligaments, as in the case of Amphidesma, it means that the two substances are so far removed from each other in the hinge that they are no longer confounded together.

INTERNAL SHELL is one which is enclosed in the soft parts of the animal, as a bone is enclosed in the flesh of a human body. The Limax, or common garden slug, which as a testaceous shield beneath its mantle, is an instance of this.

IO. Lea, 1842. A genus composed of several species of fresh-water shells which are considered as differing from Melaniæ in having the anterior termination of the aperture produced into a point in some degree resembling the caudal canals of shells belonging to the family of Canalifera, which are marine. Io fusiformis and spinosus are described and figured in Lea's work.

IPHIGENIA. Schum. 1817. Capsa, Lamarck.

IPHIGENIA. Gray, 1821. A sub-genus of Clausilia, C. biplicata, &c. Auct. Gray's Turton, p. 214.

IRIDEA. Sw. A genus of "Hyrianæ," Sw. thus described:– "Oblong ovate; bosses small, depressed, sulcated; inner cardinal tooth placed between the outer. I. granosa, *Lam.* En. Méth. 248. fig. 9."

IRIDINA. Lamarck, 1818. A genus belonging to the Nayades, and resembling the Anodontæ, Auct. but its peculiar characteristic is that the hinge lamina is tuberculated or crenulated in its whole length. Sowerby unites all the genera of the family into the genus Unio. I. Elongata. Pl. viii. fig. 150.

IRREGULAR SHELLS, are those which, being attached to, or imbedded in other marine bodies, have no constant form, but are modified in shape according to the substances to which they are fixed, as the Chamacea, fig. 153 to 155.

IRUS. Oken. Comprehending Pandora, Petricola, Saxicava, &c.

ISCHNOCHITON. Gray. Chiton vestitus, and similar species.

ISOCARDIA. Lamarck, 1801. (Ισος, *isos*, similar; Καρδια, *cardia*, heart.) *Fam.* Cardiacea, Lam. Chamacea, Bl.—*Descr.* Cordiform, regular, equivalve, ventricose, with distant, diverging, involute, free umbones; hinge with two compressed cardinal teeth in each valve, and one distant compressed lateral tooth; ligament external, bifid, diverging in the direction of the umbones.—*Obs.* The shells composing this genus are remarkable for the beautiful curvature of the diverging umbones. European and Chinese Seas, I. Moltkiana. Pl. vi. fig. 126.

JANIRA. Schum. 1817. A genus composed of species of Pecten, Auct. having oblique plicæ or calli on each side of the ligamentary pit. *Ex.* P. plica, fig. 172. Decadopecten, Rüppell.

JANTHINA. Bolton, 1798. (*Janthum*, a violet.) *Fam.* Neritacea, Lam. Oxystomata, Bl.—*Descr.* Sub-globose, thin, fragile; spire short, con-

sisting of few whorls; aperture angulated, at the anterior junction of the inner and outer lips; columella tortuous, contiguous to the axis; outer lip thin, sinuated in the centre.—*Obs.* The shells composing this genus are celebrated for their beautiful purple colour. The animal possesses a small vesicular process, which keeps it floating on the surface of the water; it exudes a purple secretion when irritated. It is occasionally floated on to the shores of most temperate and tropical countries. J. Fragilis. Pl. xv. fig. 333.

JATARONUS. Adanson. Chama, Auct.

JEFFREYSIA. Alder. A genus of small shells separated from Rissoa on the ground of a peculiarity in the operculum. *Ex.* J. Diaphana, Forbes and Hanley. British Mollusca, No. 30. Pl. cli. fig. 76.

JESITES. Montf. A minute fossil resembling Galeolaria.

JODAMIA. Defr. A genus resembling Birostrites, except that in Jodamia one valve overwraps the other, while in Birostrites the circumference of the valves is equal.

JOUANNITIA. Desmoulins. Pholas semicandata.

KATHARINA. Gray. Chiton lumiatus, &c. The external part of the shell is small.

KEEL. A flattened ridge, resembling the keel of a ship. As that on the back of Carinaria vitrea, fig. 488, and those on the whorls of some spiral shells. A shell characterized by a keel or keels is said to be carinated.

KELLIADÆ. A family of small bivalve shells divided into the following genera, viz.—

 Montacuta, Turton. M. bidentata? Pl. xxvii. fig. 570.
 Turtonia, Hanley. T. minuta. Pl. xxvii. fig. 567.
 Kellia, Montagu. K. orbicularis. Pl. xxvii. fig. 569.
 Poronia, Recluz. P. rubra. Pl. xxvii. fig. 568.
 Lepton, Turton. L. squamosum. Pl. iii. fig. 62.
 Galeomma, Turton. G. Turtoni. Pl. ii. fig. 58, 59.

With the exception of the two latter, the distinctions of the above genera depend so much on anatomical grounds that our readers must be content for the present with a characteristic figure of each.

 Pythina, Hinds, may be added to this family. Pl. xxvii. fig. 571.

KELLIA. Turton. See Kelliadæ, K. orbicularis. Pl. xxvii. fig. 569.

LABIS. Oken. Monodonta, Lam.

LABIUM, or inner lip,—is used to express that side of the aperture which is nearest to the axis and generally contiguous to the body whorl. The lower part of this, when sufficiently distinct from that part which overwraps the body whorl, is called the Columella.

LABRUM, or outer lip,—is the edge of the aperture at the greatest distance from the axis.

LACINEA. Humph. Chama, Lam.

LACUNA. Turton, 1828. *Fam.* Turbinacea, Lam.—*Descr.* Globose, thin, covered with a smooth epidermis; spire short, consisting of few rapidly increasing whorls; aperture semilunar, rounded at the extremities; columella oblique, reflected over part of the umbilicus; umbilicus forming a lengthened area behind the columella. Northern shores. L. Pallidula. Pl. xvi. fig. 364.

LAGENULA. Montf. A genus of microscopic Foraminifera.

LAMELLARIA. Montagu. Sigaretus. Auct. (The thin, hyaline species.)

LAMELLATED. (*Lamella*, a thin plate.) When the layers of which a shell is composed, instead of being compacted into a solid mass, are separated, overlaying each other in the manner of tiles, with the edges prominent, the structure is said to be lamellated or foliaceous.

LAMELLIBRANCHIATA. Bl. The third order of the class Acephalophora, Bl. consisting of bivalve shells, divided into the families

Ostracea, Subostracea, Margaritacea, Mytilacea, Polydontes, Sybmytilacea, Chamacea, Conchacea, Pylorides, Adesmacea.

LAMELLIPEDES. Lam. (*Lamella*, a thin plate, *pes*, a foot.) The third section of the order Conchifera Dimyaria, containing bivalves, with the foot of the animal broad and thin; divided into the families Conchacea, Cardiacea, Arcacea, Trigonacea, Nayades. Fig. 111 to 152.

LAMPAS. Montf. LENTICULINA, Bl. A genus of microscopic Foraminifera.

LAMPRODOMA. Swainson. A genus of "Olivinæ," Sw. thus described:– "Mitriform; spire produced, conic; resembling MITRELLA in shape, but the suture is channelled; the aperture effuse at the base, contracted above; lower half of the pillar with 6 to 7 plaits. Volutella, Zool. Ill. ii. series, pl. 40. f. 1. (*fig.* 86.)" Sw. p. 321. Pl. xxvi. fig. 561.

LAMPROSCAPHA. Sw. A sub-genus of "Anodontinæ," Sw. thus described:– "Shell not winged, elongated, pod-shaped; teeth none; bosses near the anterior extremity. Tropical America only? L.? elongata. *Sw.* Zool. Ill. i. 176. ensiforme, *Spix*. Braz. Test. siliquosa. Braz. Test. pygmæa. Ib." Sw. p. 381.

LANCEOLATE. Lengthened like a lance.

LANISTES. Montfort, 1810. Reversed species of AMPULLARIA. Pl. xv. fig. 319.

LAPLYSIA. See APLYSIA.

LAPLYSIACEA. Lam. (properly Aplysiacea.) A family belonging to the first section of the order Gasteropoda, Lam. containing the genera Aplysia and Dolabella. Fig. 254, 255.

LARVA. Humph. Part of FISSURELLA, Lam.

LATERAL. (*Latus*, a side.) The lateral teeth are those which, taking their rise near the umbones, proceed to some distance towards the sides of the shell; as distinguished from the cardinal teeth, which receive their full development close to the umbones. Lateral muscular impressions are those which are placed at a distance from each other, on the opposite sides of the shell.

LATIAXIS. Sw. A genus of "Eburninæ," Sw. corresponding with the genus Trichotropis. Sow. (Sw. Malac. p. 306.)

LATRUNCULUS. Gray. The name "Eburna" being used for Ancillaria Glabrata, this is required for the genus described in this book as "Eburna."

LATIRUS. Montfort, 1810. A genus composed of a species of FUSUS, Auct. which have an umbilicus and are turriculated. L. polygonus.

LAURIA. Gray, 1840. A sub-genus of PUPA, containing P. umbilicata, & c. (Gray's Turton, p. 193.)

LEDA. Schum. 1817. Those species of Nucula, Lamarck, which have a rostrated form. Leda caudata. Pl. xxvii. fig. 578.

LEGUMINARIA. Schum. 1817. SILIQUA, Megerle, 1811. A genus composed of species of SOLEN, Auct. which have an internal longitudinal bar or rib. Fig. 61. S. Radiatus, Lam.

LEILA. Gray, 1840. Described as having the hinge smooth like Iridina, but having a "sharp siphonal inflection." (Syn. B. M. p. 142.) Anodon esula.

LEIODOMUS. Sw. A genus of "Buccininæ," Sw. consisting of Terebra vittata and other similar species. This genus corresponds with Bullia, Gray.

LEIOSTOMA. Swainson. A genus of "Fusinæ," Sw. thus described, "Equally fusiform," (with Fusus) "but ventricose in the middle; shell entirely smooth, almost polished; inner lip thickened, and vitreous; base of the pillar very straight. Fossil only. (*fig.* 75.) L. bulbiformis. En. Méth. 428. f. 1." Pl. xxvi. fig. 549.

LEMBULUS. Leach. A genus composed of oval species of NUCULA,

resembling N. margaritacea, fig. 137.

LENDIX. Humph. PUPA, Lam.

LENGTH. See MEASUREMENT.

LENTICULAR. (*Lens*.) Of a circular, convex form, as Pectunculus, fig. 134.

LENTICULINA. Lam. A genus of microscopic Foraminifera.—*Descr.* Lenticular, sub-discoidal, compressed, convolute, symmetrical; aperture notched; chambers few in number; visible on the exterior, radiating from the centre of the disk.

LEPADICEA. Bl. The first family of the class Nemantopoda, Bl. This family consists of the same animals which constitute the Pedunculated Cirripedes of Lamarck, and part of the genus Lepas in the system of Linnæus. It contains the genera Gymnolepas, Pentalepas, Polylepas and Litholepas.

LEPAS. (Δεπας, *lepas*, a rock.) The Linnæan name Lepas contains all the Cirripedes or Multivalves, the different kinds of which are not distinguished in the accounts given by early writers of the habits of the animals. (Fig. 14 to 43.) It was formerly applied to the Limpets or Patella. In fact, the ancient definition was "Concha petræ adhærens," and would apply to any shells attached to rocks. Mr. Darwin, however, in his work on the Lepadæ, has very properly restricted the term "Lepas" to the genus described in this work as Pentelasmis. Pl. ii. fig. 34.

LEPTÆNA. Dalman. A genus belonging to the Brachiopoda; and thus described:– "Hinge compressed, rectilinear, frequently exceeding the width of the shell." It forms part of the genus Producta, Sow. Fig. 206, L. depressa.

LEPTOCHITON. Gray. Chiton Cinereus, Chiton Cajetanus, and similar species.

LEPTOCONCHUS. Rüppell. (Λεπτος, *leptus*, thin; Κογχος, *conchos*, shell.) This shell resembles a young MAGILUS in general appearance, although the animal is said to differ. In the young Magilus also, the inner lip is reflected over the body whorl, which is not the case in Leptoconchus. Red Sea. Pl. i. fig. 11.

LEPTOCONUS. Swainson. A sub-genus of Conus, consisting of Conus grandis, amadis, duplicatus, Australis, &c. Sw. p. 312.

LEPTOLIMNEA. Swainson. A sub-genus of Limnea, described as being nearly cylindrical. Limnea elongata, Sow. Gen. fig. 6.

LEPTON. Turton, 1822. SOLEN Squamosus, Montague, and other species described as "flat, nearly orbicular, equivalve, inequilateral, a little open at the sides. Hinge of one valve with a single tooth, and a transverse linear lateral one on each side; of the other valve, with a cavity in the middle and transverse deeply cloven lateral tooth on each side, the segments of which divaricate from the beak." See KELLADIÆ, L. squamosum. Pl. iii. fig. 62.

LEPTOSPIRA. Swainson. A sub-genus of Bulinus, thus described: "Spire excessively long, sub-cylindrical; body whorl largest; outer lip thickened; aperture oval; no teeth, striata, *Sw.* Chem. 153. f. 1226. signata *Sw.*" Sw. p. 335.

LEUCOSTOMA. Swainson. A genus of "Achatina," Sw. described as resembling Achatinella, but having a "thick pad," at the top of the "upper lip," and another over the base. L. variegata, Sw. Lardn. Cyclop. Malac. fig. 24. 172.

LEVENIA. Gray, 1847. Cassis Coarctatum, &c.

LICINA. Browne, 1756. CISTULA. Humphreys, 1797. CYCLOSTOMA fimbriata, and Thesaurus Conchyliorum. Pl. xxviii. fig. 145, 146, and similar species having a broad fringed margin.

LICIUM. Humph. OVULA, Lam. (Ovulum.)

LIGAMENT. (From *Ligo*, to bind.) The true ligament is always external, and serves the purpose of binding the two valves of a shell together externally by the posterior dorsal margins. There is another substance, called by Gray the *Cartilage*, which is elastic and of a condensed fibrous structure, placed within the ligament, either close to it, or at a more interior part of the shell; it is sometimes contained in a pit, formed for its reception, in the centre of the hinge. The substance, being elastic, keeps the valves open, unless drawn together by the counteracting force of the adductor muscles. When conchologists speak of a shell as having the ligament external, the real meaning is that these two substances are so close together as in appearance to constitute one body placed outside the shell so as to be seen when the valves are closed. When two ligaments are spoken of, as in Amphidesma, the meaning is that the cartilage occupies a separate place on the hinge.

LIGAMENTIFEROUS. (*Ligamentum*, a ligament, *fero*, to bear.) Having or containing the ligament, as the cardinal pit in Mya, fig. 71.

LIGULA. Leach. A genus containing the more rounded and less gaping species of Lutraria, Auct. Fig. 77, Lutraria Papyracea.

LIGULATE. (*Ligula*, a slip, a shoe-latchet.) Thin, slender, like a slip, or neck of any thing, as the anterior muscular impression of Lucina, fig. 104.

LIGUMIA. Swainson. A sub-genus of Unio, thus described:– "Very long and pod-shaped; bosses depressed; cardinal teeth moderate. S. recta, Lam. vi. l. p. 74." Sw. p. 378.

LIGUUS. Montf. 1810. A genus containing species of Achatina, Auct. which have rounded apertures and lengthened spires, differing from his Polyphemi, which have lengthened apertures. A. virginea, Auct. fig. 286, is the type of this genus.

LIMA. Brug. 1797. (Lima, a file.) *Fam.* Pectinides, Lam. Subostracea, Bl.—*Descr.* Equivalve, inequilateral, compressed, oblique, auriculated, oval, radiately ribbed or striated, imbricated, covered with a light brown epidermis; hinge with a triangular disc between the umbones, divided in the centre by a triangular ligamentary pit without teeth; muscular impression one, sub-lateral, sub-orbicular.—*Obs.* The shells thus described are marine, two or three species being found on our coasts, and fossil species occuring in Lias, inferior Oolite, Calcaire-grossiér, &c. They differ from Pecten in having a wide hiatus for the passage of a byssus, by which they are occasionally attached, and also in the triangular disc, which separates the umbones. The animal makes use of the valves of his shell for swimming, working them like fins or paddles, and by this means proceeding at a rapid rate through the waters. The Monograph of this genus in the Author's Thesaurus Conchyliorum contains 13 species. Plates 21, 22. L. Squamosa, Pl. x. fig. 174.

LIMACINA. Cuv. (*Limax*, a snail.) Fam. Pteropoda, Lam.—*Descr.* Papyraceous, fragile, planorbicular, sub-carinated, obliquely convolute; spiral side rather prominent, the other side umbilicated; aperture large, entire, not modified, peristome sharp.—*Obs.* This is Spiratella, Bl. The shell figures as Limacina in Sowerby's Genera, under "pteropoda," is an *Atlanta*. Our representation of Spiratella Limacinea, fig. 224 is copied from Blainville.

LIMACINEA. Lam. A family of the order Gasteropoda, Lam. including the following genera:–

    1. Cryptella. Spire mammillated; a septum. Fig. 256.
    2. Parmacella. Flat, haliotoid, spiral. Fig. 257, 258.
    3. Testacellus. Sub-spiral. Fig. 261.
    4. Limax. Incomplete. Fig. 259.
    5. Plectrophorus. Conical. Fig. 260.
    6. Vitrina. Heliciform, hyaline. Fig. 262, 263.

LIMACINEA. Bl. The third family of the order Pulmobranchiata, Bl.

Described as containing shells very variable in form, most frequently inclining to globular or oval; the apex always obtuse; aperture variable, but never emarginated. All the Limacinea are phytophagous and terrestrial. This family answers to the genus Helix of Linnæus and to the Colimacea of Lamarck, leaving out the Auriculacea. It contains the genera Succinea, Bulinus, Achatina, Clausilia, Pupa, Partula, Helix, Vitrina, Testacella, Limacella, Limax.

LIMAX. Linnæus. Limacinea, Lam. and Bl.—*Descr.* Internal irregular, sub-quadrate, scutiform, crystalline; apex rounded, indistinct; epidermis, light brown, thin, extending beyond the margin.—*Obs.* The shell is placed under the scutellum of the common garden slug. L. Antiquorum. Pl. xiii. fig. 259.

LIMNACEA. Bl. The first family of the order Pulmobranchiata, Bl. The shells of this family are described as thin, with the outer lip always sharp. It contains the genera Limnea, Physa, Planorbis.

LIMNEANA. Lam. A family of the order Trachelipoda, Lam. containing the following genera:–

    1. Limnæa. Spire produced; including *Physa*. Fig. 308 to 310.
    2. Planorbis. Spire orbicular; including *Planaria*. Fig. 311, 312.

LIMNEA. Lamarck, 1801. (Λιμνας, *limnas*, lacustrine.) Fam. Limnacea, Lam. and Bl.—*Descr.* Oblong, light, thin; spire variable in length, acute; last whorl large, aperture large, longitudinal, entire; inner lip spread over a portion of the last whorl; columella forming an oblique fold; outer lip rounded at each extremity, thin.—*Obs.* These light horn-coloured shells are common in standing pools, ponds and ditches, in various parts of Europe. They resemble the Amber shell (Succinea) in shape, but the animal of the latter is amphibious, and the shell of a bright amber colour. L. Stagnalis, fig. 308. L. auricularia, fig. 309. (Radix, Montf.) The reversed species have been separated under the name Physa, fig. 310. Other generic names have been given to other species. Pl. xiv.

LINES OF GROWTH. The concentric striæ or lines formed by the edges of the successive layers of shelly matter deposited by the animal by which it increases the shell. The outer edge of the aperture is always the last line of growth.

LINGUIFORM. (*Lingua*, tongue; *forma*, form.) Tongue-shaped.

LINGULA. Lam. 1801. (Dim. from *lingua*, tongue.) *Fam.* Brachiopoda, Lam. Palliobranchiata, Bl.—*Descr.* Equivalve, oblong, depressed, thin, equilateral, gaping and pointed at the umbones, gaping and truncate or trilobate at the opposite extremities, attached by a fleshy pedicule fixed to the umbones.—*Obs.* This is the only bivalve shell which is pedunculated, in which respect it constitutes a singular anomaly. The ancient writers, seeing the valves separate, placed it in their systems under the name Patella Unguis. There are several recent species found in the Moluccas, and some fossils in sandy indurated marl, and in alluvium of Suffolk. L. Anatina, fig. 219, is so named from its resemblance to a duck's bill. Mr. Sowerby's Monograph of this genus in the Author's Thesaurus Conchyliorum contains 7 species. Plate 67. See our Plate xii. fig. 219.

LINGULINA. D'Orb. A genus of microscopic Foraminifera.

LINTERIA. Adams. Sowerby's Thesaurus, Pl. 11. 1850. A sub-genus of Bullidæ, the shells of which are thus described: "oval, depressed; aperture with a slight canal above; inner lip with a cup-shaped appendage, spiral within."

LINTIIURIS. Montf. Conch. Syst. 2. 154. A genus of microscopic Foraminifera.

LIP. See Labium and Labrum.

LIPPISTES. Montf. A genus of microscopic Foraminifera.

LITHODOMUS. Cuv. (Λιθος, *lithos*, stone; Δωμα, *doma* house.)

Fam. Mytilacea, Lam.—*Descr*. Transverse, elongated, cylindrical, equivalve, with the extremities rounded, and the posterior extremity rostrated; umbones not prominent, terminal; hinge straight, destitute of teeth; ligament linear, most conspicuous within; muscular impressions two.—*Obs*. The shells composing this genus differ from Modiola, not only in the cylindrical form, but also in the circumstance from which the generic name is derived, *i.e.* of their living in stones. Thus, while the form and structure of the shell bring it near the Mytili or Muscle shells, the habits of the animal cause it to approach the Lithophagi, or rock-eating molluscs of Lamarck. L. Dactylus is the Mytilus Lithophagus of ancient authors. Pl. ix. fig. 161.

LITHOLEPAS. Bl. (ΛιΘος, *lithos*, stone; λεπας, *lepas*, rock.) De Blainville, Lithotrya, Sowerby.

LITHOPHAGIDÆ. Lam. (ΛιΘος, *lithos*, stone; Φαγω, *phaga*, eat or gnaw.) A family of the Conchifera Dimyaria, Lam. consisting of terebrating bivalves, gaping anteriorly, having no accessary valves; and containing the genera Saxicava, Petricola, Venerupis, to which are added other genera enumerated in explanation of figures 91 to 97. Notwithstanding the numerous genera which have been created, I think that the most convenient arrangement will be to reduce them to two, thus–

1. Petricola, with distinct cardinal teeth, including Clotho, Venerirupis and Coralliophaga. Fig. 91, 92, 97.
2. Sacicava, without teeth, including Biapholius, Hiatella, Sphænia, Byssomya, and Thracia. Fig. 93 to 96.

LITHOPHAGUS. Megerle, 1811. Lithodomus. Cuvier, 1817.

LITHOTRYA. G.B. Sowerby. (ΛιΘος, *lithos*, stone; τρυω, *truo*, to bore through.) *Fam*. Pedunculated Cirripedes, Lam.—*Descr*. Eight unequal valves, forming a laterally compressed cone, the lower central valves being very minute; pedicle fleshy, scaly at the upper extremity; fixed at the base in a patelliform shelly support.—*Obs*. This genus derives its name from the power possessed by the animal of making dwelling holes in stones or pieces of rock. The remarkable shelly cup at the base of the pedicle is regarded as analogous to the shelly base of the Balanus, so that this genus seems to form an intermediate link between the Sessile and Pedunculated Cirripedes of Lamarck. West India Islands. L. dorsalis, Pl. ii. fig. 39.

LITIOPA. Rang. 1829. *Fam*. Turbinacea, Lam.—*Descr*. "Shell not very thick, horny, with a slight epidermis, rather transparent, conical with whorls somewhat rounded; the last being larger than all the rest together; with the apex pointed, longitudinally grooved; aperture oval, larger anteriorly than posteriorly, with the lips disunited, the right lip simple, separated from the left by a rather indistinct notch, or a slight sinus in the contour. The left slightly reflected backwards, so as to form a kind of salient margin with the anterior extremity of the columella, which is united, rounded, arcuated and slightly truncated at the anterior."—*Obs*. The Molluscous animals, whose shells are thus described, are found in the Mediterranean, and are remarkable for the power of suspending themselves from the sea-weed on which they live, by a thread resembling a spider's web. The general appearance of the shell presents a medium between Phasianella and Littorina, but it is apparently destitute of an operculum.

LITTORINA. Ferussac. (*Littus*, the sea-shore.) *Fam*. Turbinacea, Lam.—*Descr*. Turbinated, thick; spire acuminated, consisting of a few whorls, about one-third of the axis in length; aperture entire, large, rounded anteriorly; outer lip thickened within, acute; columella rather flattened; operculum horny, spiral with rapidly increasing volutions.—*Obs*. The shells composing this genus are known from Turbo and

Phasianella by the horny operculum; and from Trochus, which has also a horny operculum, by the small number of the whorls. The Littorinæ, among which may be enumerated the common Periwinkle, are, as the name implies, found on sea shores, feeding upon sea-weed, in all parts of the world. L. Vulgaris. Pl. xvi. fig. 363.

LITUACEA. Bl. The second family of Polythalamacea. Bl. The shells are described as chambered, symmetrical, convolute in part of their extent, but constantly straight towards the termination. The genus Spirula, which is admitted into this family, does not properly belong to it, any more than to the Lituolæ of Lamarck, in which it is also placed. It does not agree with the descriptions of either. This family partly corresponds with the "Lituolées," Lam. and contains the genera Lituola, Ichthyo, sarcolites, Spirula, Hamites and Ammonoceras.

LITUACEA. Lam. A family of the order Polythalamous Cephalopoda, Lam. containing the genus Spirula, fig. 471.

LITUITUS. Montf. Spirolina, Lam. Microscopic.

LITUOLA. Lam. A genus of microscopic Foraminifera.

LITUOLÆ. Lam. The third family of Polythalamous Cephalopoda, Lam. the shells of which are described as partially spiral, the last whorl continuing in a straight line. The transverse septa which divide the chambers, are in general pierced by a siphon which breaks itself off before it reaches the succeeding septum. This family contains the genera of microscopic Foraminifera Lituola and Spirolina. The genus Spirula, also placed in this family, does not by any means agree with Lamarck's definitions, "the last whorl continuing in a straight line."

LITUUS. Hump. Cyclostoma? Lam.

LIVID. (From *lividus*.) Of a pale, dull, blue colour. The adjective is sometimes used as a specific name. *Ex*. Conus *lividus*, Sanguinolaria *livida*.

LOBARIA. Schum. Sanguinolaria rosea, Lam. (fig. 98) and other similar species.

LOBATE or LOBED. Divided into two parts.

LOBATULA. Fleming. A genus composed of two very minute species of chambered shells. Serpula lobata and S. concamerata, Mont. Test. Brit. 515.

LOMASTOMA. Rafinesque. An imperfectly defined genus, probably belonging to the Limnacea.

LONGITUDINAL. Lengthwise. Longitudinal striæ, ribs, &c. are those which radiate from the apex and follow the spiral direction of the whorls, in spiral shells; and from the umbo to the ventral margin in bivalves. The term "decourantes" is employed by French conchologists. The bands in Achatina, fig. 286, are longitudinal or spiral.

LOPHUERUS. Poli. Chiton squamosus, and similar species. The marginal insegment in regular scales.

LORICULA pulchella. G.B. Sowerby, Jun. Ann. Nat. Hist. Vol. XII. 1843, p. 260. Darwin, Fossil lepadæ, p. 84. A very beautifully formed Cirripede, found in the lower chalk, near Rochester, Kent. The specimen is in Mr Wetherell's collection.

LORIPES. Poli. A genus composed of a species of Lucina. Auct. in which the cartilage is wholly internal. *Ex*. Lucina divaricata.

LOTORIUM. Montf. 1810. A genus composed of species of Triton, Auct. in which the aperture is effuse. T. Lotorium, Pl. xviii. fig. 400.

LOTTIA. Gray, 1833. Patelloida, Quoy and Gaimard.

LUCERNA. Humph. A generic name applied to some species of Helix included in De Ferussac's sub-genus Helicogena.

LUCERNELLA. Sw. A genus of "Lucerninæ," Sw. thus described: "Teeth on both sides of the aperture; surface regularly and distinctly striated. Circumference convex."

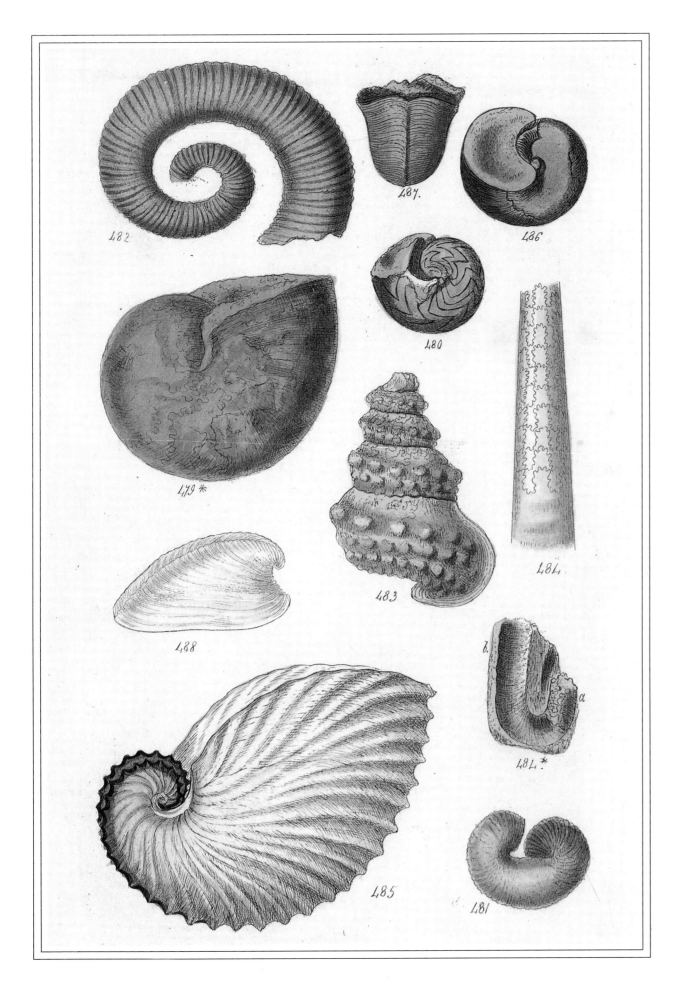

479*.——discus. Aganides, Montf.
480. Goniatites striatus.
481. Scaphites æqualis.
482. Crioceratites Duvallii.
483. Turrilites tuberculatus.
484. Baculites Faujasii. Portion near
    the centre.
484*.Hamites cylindricus; *a*, internal
    cast of part of the shell; *b*,
    hollow external cast of the
    remainder.

   Second Division. Monothalamous
          Cephalopoda

485. Argonauta Argo.
486. Bellerophon tenuifasciata, (from
    Sow. Gen.)
487. The same, shewing the dorsal
    keel.

     Order. HETEROPODA

488. Carinaria Mediterranea

LUCIDELLA. Swainson, 1840. HELICINA or OLIGYRA, species contracted near the outer lip. H. aureola. Thesaurus Conchyliorum, Pl. i. fig. 43, 4, 5.

LUCIDULA. Sw. A sub-genus of "Lucerna," Humph. thus described: "Aperture transverse, both lips much thickened and united; the outer with marginal obsolete teeth at the base; umbilicus closed. Barbadensis, *Lam.* No. 49. p. 78. Fêr. Moll. pl. 47, 2, 3, 4."

LUCINA. Brug. 1792. *Fam.* Nymphacea, Lam. Conchacea, Bl. *Descr.* Equivalve, inequilateral, orbicular, lenticular, radiately striated; hinge with, generally, two minute cardinal teeth, which are sometimes nearly obsolete, and two lateral teeth, on each side of the umbo in one valve, one in the other; ligament external, partly hidden by the margins of the valves when closed. Muscular impressions two in each valve, the anterior one produced into an elongated, ligulate band, the posterior short and semi-rotund; impression of the mantle not sinuated.—*Obs.* The shells of this genus resemble Amphidesma in general form, but are distinguished by the external ligament, the elongated muscular impression, and the want of a sinus in the palleal impression. East and West Indies, and European shores. L. Tigerina. Pl. v. fig. 104.

LUCINOPSIS. Forbes and Hanley. Nov. 1848. VENUS undata pennant. Differing slightly from Artemis in the hinge and palleal sinus. See Sowerby's Thesaurus, Pl. 13.

LUNULATE. (*Luna*, the moon, dim.) Moon-shaped, having the form of a crescent. Applied most frequently to muscular impressions. The word semilunar is sometimes used, perhaps with greater accuracy, to express the same shape.

LUNULE. An impression on the anterior dorsal margin of some bivalve shells. The similar impression on the posterior dorsal margin is called the *escutcheon.*

LUPONIA. Gray, 1832. A genus composed of species of CYPRÆA, Auct. which are described as having the anterior of the columellar lip crossed by several irregular ridges, without any distinct marginal ones, internally narrow, flat; the shell pear-shaped, smooth, or cross-ribbed. *Ex.* C. Algoensis, Luponia Algoensis, Gray, Pl. xxii. fig. 447.

LUTRARIA. Lamarck. 1799. (*Lutum?* mud.) *Fam.* Mactracea, Lam.— *Descr.* Thin, equivalve, inequilateral, transverse, oblong or ovate, gaping at both extremities; hinge with one double and sometimes one single cardinal tooth in each valve, and a triangular, oblique pit with a prominent margin, containing the ligament; muscular impressions distant; palleal impression having a large sinus.—*Obs.* This genus differs from Mactra in the entire absence or indistinctness of lateral teeth. Fig. 77, L. Papyracea. (Ligula, Leach.) Fig. 78. L. Solenoides. Sandy and muddy shores. Pl. iii. fig. 77, 78.

LUTRICOLA. Blainville, 1825. LUTRARIA. Lam. 1799. Fig. 77, 78.

LYCOPHRIS. Montf. A microscopic fossil described as resembling NUMMULITES, but having a granulated surface.

LYMNADEA. Sw. A sub-genus of "Mysca," Turton, in the family of Nayades, Lam. thus described: "Posterior hinge margin elevated and winged; the valves connate; the surface smooth. L. alata *Sw. Ex.* Conch. (fig. 48.) fragilis. *Sw.* Zool. Ill. compressa, *Lea.* Am. Tr. iii. pl. 12. f. 22." Sw. p. 379.

LYMNEA. See LIMNEA.

LYMNEUS. Lam. See LIMNEANA.

LYONSIA. Turt. Inequivalve, species of ANATINA, Auct. which have no spoon-shaped cavity in the hinge, but an accessary piece. L. striata, Pl. xxiv. fig. 491, 492.

LYRIA. Swainson. Voluta Nucleus, Thesaurus Conchyliorum, Pl. v. fig. 108.

LYRODON. Goldf. TRIGONIA?

MACLURITES. Lesœur. Journ. des Scienc. Nat. Philad. t. 1. p. 312. pl. 13. fig. 2, 3.

MACOMA. Leach. VENUS tenuis, Bl. and similar species, described as "Clothed with an epidermis; striated, compressed, oval; the summits not very prominent; two bifid teeth upon the right valve and a single undivided one upon the left."

MACRODITUS. Montf. LENTICULINA, Bl. A genus of microscopic Foraminifera.

MACROSPIRA. Guild. 1840. SUBULINA, Beck, 1837. A genus composed of HELIX Octona, Auct. *Ex.* Subulina octona, Pl. xxv. fig. 514.

MACROSTOMATA. Lam. (Μακρος, *macros*, long; στομα, *stoma*, mouth.) A family belonging to the first section of the order Trachelipoda, the shells belonging to which are described as haliotoid or ear-shaped, with a very large aperture, destitute of an operculum. This family contains the following genera, which may be thus distinguished.

   1. VELUTINA. Globose, with velvety epidermis. Fig. 337.

   2. STOMATIA. Ear-shaped; pearly within; including STOMATELLA. Fig. 335, 336.

   3. SIGARETUS. The same, not pearly; including *Cryptostoma*, Fig. 334.

   4. CORIOCELLA. The same, thin, transparent.

   5. HALIOTIS. The same, not thin, nor transparent; with holes; including *Padollus.* Fig. 338, 339.

   6. SCISSURELLA. Heliciform, with a slit near the aperture. Fig. 340.

   7. PLEUROTOMARIA. Trochiform, with a slit at the edge of the aperture. Fig. 341.

MACTRA. Linn. (*Mactra*, a kneading trough.) *Fam.* Mactracea, Lam. Conchacea, Bl.—*Descr.* Usually thin, equivalve, sub-equilateral, subtrigonal, slightly gaping at the extremities; hinge with one cardinal tooth, divided into two parts, diverging from the umbo, with sometimes a very small laminar tooth close to its side; a deep triangular pit near the centre, containing the cartilage; one long, lateral tooth on each side of the umbo in one valve, received between two in the other; muscular impressions two, lateral; palleal impression with a small sinus.—*Obs.* This genus contains many species of beautiful shells found in various parts of the world, some of which are common in Britain. Fossil species are not numerous, they occur in the tertiary strata. The principal forms are represented by M. Splengleri, fig. 81. (SCHIZODESMA) M. gragilis, fig. 80, (SPISULA) M. bicolor, fig. 82, (MULINEA) and M. Stultorum, fig. 79. Pl. iv. fig. 79 to 82.

MACTRACEA. Lam. A family of the order Conchifera Dimyaria, Lam. Sect. Tenuipes. The cartilage placed in a trigonal pit with a small external ligament. The genera may be thus distinguished.

   1. LUTRARIA. No lateral teeth, shell gaping. The short species constitute the genus *Ligula.* Fig. 77, 78.

   2. MACTRA. Lateral teeth, shell closed. This genus has been divided into mactra, Mulinia, Schizodesma and Spisula, by Mr. Gray. Fig. 79 to 82.

   3. GNATHODON. Teeth serrated, thick, one angular. Fig. 83.

   4. CRASSATELLA. Shell thick, lateral teeth. Fig. 84.

   5. AMPHIDESMA. A distinct external ligament, internal ligament oblique. Fig. 85.

   6. ERYCINA. A short tooth on each side of the cartilaginous pit in each valve. Including Mesodesma. Fig. 86.

   7. UNGULINA. Ligament flat, divided. Fig. 88.

MACULATED. (From *Macula*, a spot.) Spotted or patched. This term is applied by conchological writers, to those shells which are coloured in spots or small patches. In the same sense it is also used as a specific

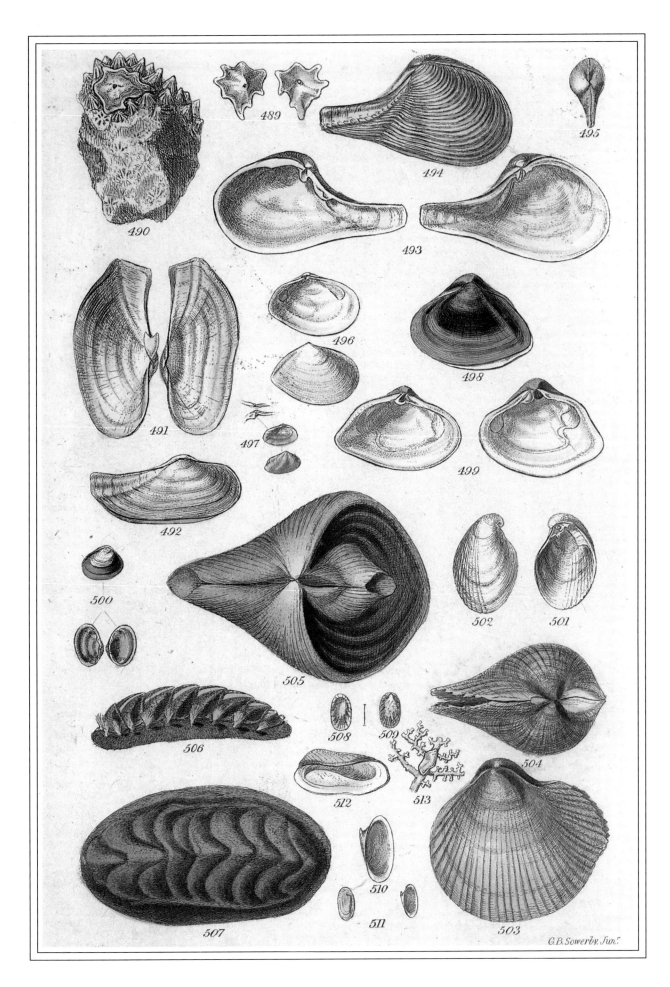

489. Pyrgoma monticularia. *Subgenus*, Daracia, Gray, back and front.
490. The same, in situ.
491. Lyonsia Norvegica. Anatina, Nonnul. Inside view of both valves.
492. Outside, with the valves closed.
493. Næara longirostrum, Anatina longirostris, Lam. Inside of both valves.
494. Outside, with both valves closed.
495. A smaller species of Næara, shewing the inequality of the valves.
496. Amphidesma tennis. Abra. Leach.
497. Ervillia nitens.
498. Potamomya, of some authors. A fresh-water shell, resembling Corbula. Outside, valves closed.
499. Inside of both valves.
500. Cyclas amnica. Pera, Leach.
501. Cardilia semisulcata. Isocardia semisulcata. Lam. Internal view.
502. External view of the same valve.
503. Cardium apertum. Papyridea, Sw.
504. The same, shewing the umbones.
505. Pleurorynchus, fossil, (from Mineral Conchology.)
506. Chiton fascicularis. Phakellopleura, Guild.
507. —— amiculatus. Amicula Gray.
508. Scutella, Brod. Internal view.
509. External view of the same.
510. Ancylus, a reversed species, illustrating the genus Velletia, Gray, enlarged view.
511. The same, natural size.
512. Pedicularia. Enlarged figure, (copied from Swainson.)
513. The same, natural size, growing on coral.

name. As for instance, Cytherea maculata, fig. 167, c. and Hippopus maculatus, fig. 156.

MAGAS. Sow. (Μαγας, *magas*, a board, a deck.) *Fam.* Brachiopoda, Lam.—*Descr.* Equilateral, inequivalve; one valve convex, with a triangular area, divided by an angular sinus in the centre; the other valve flat, with a straight hinge line and two small projections; a partial longitudinal septum, with appendages attached to the hinge within. Differing from Terebratula in having a triangular disc, and not a circular perforation. Magas pumilus. Fossil in chalk. Pl. xi. fig. 209.

MAGILUS. Montf. *Fam.* Cricostomata, Bl. Serpulacea, Lam.—*Descr.* Thick, tubular, irregular, contorted; rounded above, keeled beneath, free; apical extremity convolute, heliciform, ovate or sub-globose; aperture elliptical.—*Obs.* This shell when in a young state presents the characteristics of a regularly formed spiral univalve, living in holes in madrepores. As the madrepore increases in bulk, the animal gives an eccentric course to the shell, in order to have its aperture even with the surface, and leaving the nucleus or young shell behind, fills it up with calcareous matter to reside in the open extremity of the tube. Red Sea and Mauritius. Campulotus is the original name for this genus. Pl. i. fig. 9, 10.

MALACOTA. Schum. OTION. Leach. CONCHODERMA.

MALACOZOA. Bl. (Μαλακος, *malacos*, soft; εν, *in*, τεμνω, *temno*, cut; Ζωον, *zoon*, animal.) Or articulated mollusca. The sub-type in De Blainville's system, comprehending those with multivalve shells.

MALDANIA. Lam. The second family of the order Annelides Sedentaria. The only genus of shells described in this family is Dentalium, fig. 2, to which may be added Pharetrium, König, fig. 3. It is doubtful however whether the latter do not belong to an unknown genus of Pteropodous Mollusca.

MALEA. Valenciennes. A genus composed of DOLIUM latilabrum, Kiener, and other similar species. D. ringens, &c.

MALENTOZOA. Bl. (Μαλακος, *malacos*, soft; εν, *in*, τεμνω, *temno*, cut; Ζωον, *zoon*, animal.) Or articulated mollusca. The sub-type in De Blainville's system, comprehending those with multivalve shells.

MALLEACEA. Lam. A family belonging to the order of Conchifera Monomyaria. Containing the following genera of irregular pearly bivalves.

1. AVICULA. Hinge linear, simple, including *Meleagrina*. Fig. 163, 164.
2. PERNA. Hinge with linear grooves, including *Pulvinites*. Fig. 166, 170.
3. GERVILLIA. Shaped like Modiola, with irregular grooves. Fig. 162.
4. CRENATULA. Hinge with a series of pits. Fig. 168.
5. CATILLUS. Like Perna, but more regular and convex. Fig. 167.
6. MALLEUS. A triangular disc on the hinge, and two auricles. Fig. 165.

MALLEUS. Auct. (*Malleus*, a hammer.) *Fam.* Malleacea, Lam. Margaritacea, Bl.—*Descr.* Equivalve, inequilateral, foliaceous, trilobate, undulated, irregular, attached by a byssus passing through a sinus in one valve; hinge rectilinear, lengthened by two auricles; with a small disc under the umbones, containing the ligament, and a groove containing the cartilage; muscular impressions one in each valve, large, uniform, and one or two others extremely minute.—*Obs.* Malleus Vulgaris, the type of this genus, is a most singular shell, commonly called the "Hammer Oyster," from the peculiarity of its shape. It belongs to the Linnean genus Ostrea, from which it differs in being attached by a byssus. M. Vulgaris, Pl. x. fig. 165.

MAMILLARIA. Sw. A sub-genus of NATICA, corresponding with Polinices of Montfort, having the spire small and the umbilicus filled. *Ex.* Natica Mamilla, Auct. fig. 327.

MAMMILLA. Schum. 1817. Natica melanostoma.

MAMMILLATED. (*Mammula*, a little teat.) A term applied to the apex of a shell when it is rounded like a teat. *Ex.* Voluta Vespertilio, fig. 433.

MANGELIA. Leach. A genus consisting of small shells which approach the clavate form of the Pleurotomæ. They are angularly fusiform, ribbed, and turrited; the aperture is long and narrow, the outer lip thickened, turned inwards and denticulated, with an angle and slight sinuosity above; the inner lip is more or less granulated or denticulated. *Ex.* M. Citharella, Leach. This was the first species known, and it was placed by Lamarck among the Cancellariæ, to which it has little affinity. M. Reeve's Monograph contains about 70 species, the great majority of which were brought new from the Philippines by Mr. Cuming. Mangelia Coronata, Hinds. Pl. xxviii. fig. 597.

MARGARITA. Leach. (*Margarita*, a pearl.) A genus of small shells resembling the genus Trochus, from which it differs in having an operculum consisting of few whorls. M. tæniata, fig. 362. Mr. G. B. Sowerby, sen. has enumerated 15 species in a list accompanying the figures published by the author of this manual in Nos. 132 to 134 of his Conchological Illustrations.

MARGARITACEA. Bl. The third family of Lamellibranchiata, Bl. The shells belonging to it are described as irregular, inequivalve, inequilateral, black or horny without, pearly within; hinge auriculated, scarcely developed, and without teeth. The ligament is variable and there is a large sub-central muscular impression. This family contains the genera Vulsella, Malleus, Pinna, Crenatula, Inoceramus, Catillus, Pulvinites, Gervillia and Avicula.

MARGARITACEOUS. (*Margarita*, a pearl.) Pearly.

MARGARITANA. Schum. 1817. ALASMODONTA. Say, 1840. A sub-genus of Uniones, composed of species having "one cardinal tooth," and no lateral teeth. *Ex.* M. Complananta, fig. 141.

MARGARITIFEROUS. (*Margarita*, pearl; *fero*, to bear.) Pearl-bearing. Applied to shells which form pearls; as Meleagrina Margaritifera, or Pearl-bearing Oyster.

MARGINAL. Near the margin or edge.

MARGINATED. (*Margo*, edge.) Having an edge or border thicker than the rest of the shell, from which circumstance the little genus Marginella derives its name.

MARGINELLA. Lamarck, 1801. PORCELLANA. Adanson, 1757. (A little rim or border.) *Fam.* Columellaria, Lam. Angyostomata, Bl.—*Descr.* Ovate, smooth, shining, with a short, sometimes hidden spire; aperture narrow, emarginated; columella with several oblique folds; outer lip neatly reflected.—*Obs.* This genus of pretty little shells differs from Voluta, in the reflection of the outer lip. The animal covers the greater part of the shell with the mantle, and by continually depositing vitreous matter gives it a bright polish, which, together with the delicately neat arrangement of colours in most species, renders them exceedingly beautiful. The Marginellæ are marine and tropical. A few fossil species are found in the Calc-grossier. Fig. 437. M. Glabella, genus GLABELLA, Sw. Sowerby's Monograph in Thesaurus Conchyliorum enumerates 108 species. It will be seen that priority may be claimed for the name "Porcellana" for this genus. Pl. xx. fig. 437.

MARGINULINA. D'Orb. A genus of microscopic Foraminifera.

MARINE CONCHACEA. See CONCHACEA.

MARINE TESTACEA. Those shell-fish which inhabit seas, lakes, &c.

of salt water, in distinction from the *Aquatic* Testacea, or those which are found in rivers, ponds or stagnant pools of fresh water: and also from the *Land* Testacea, which live on land and breathe air. The great proportion of shells belong to the former class, those of the latter two classes being limited in their nubmer, and in the genera to which they belong.

MARINULA. King. A genus of small shells resembling Auricula and Pedipes, described as "Ovate, sub-solid, with aperture ovate entire; columella bidentate, uniplicated towards the base, with large sub-remote teeth; the largest uppermost; no operculum."

MARISA. Gray, 1824. CERATODES, Guilding. AMPULLARIA Cornu-arietis, Lamarck. See our fig. 323.

MARMAROSTOMA. Sw. A genus of "Trochidæ," Sw. thus described: "Umbilicus deep; spire of few whorls, much depressed, and obtuse; inner lip obsolete; base even more produced than in *Senectus*, but never distinctly channeled. M. versicolor. Mont. 176. f. 1740, 1741', undulata. Chem. 169. f. 1640, 1641." Sw. p. 348. The operculum is thick, rounded, and with a canal near the outer edge.

MARPESSA. Gray. A sub-genus of Clausilia, C. bidens, &c. Auct. Gray's Turton, p. 212.

MARTESIA. Leach. A genus composed of those species of PHOLAS, Auct. which are described as short, cuneiform, nearly closed at both extremities, having several accessary pieces on the middle of the back, and two marginal, lower down. The Monograph of the genus PHOLAS, in Sowerby's Thesaurus Conchyliorum, No. 10. Ph. striata, sp. 29, fig. 40 to 44, and other similar species.

MEASUREMENT. The most usual method of stating the measurements of various kinds of shells is as follows: *symmetrical convolute univalves*, the length is from anterior to posterior; the depth from ventral to dorsal; the breadth, from side to side of the aperture, as marked on the diagram, page 18. Of *symmetrical conical univalves*, length, from front to back; breadth from side to side; depth from apex to base. Of *spiral univalves*, length, from apex to anterior of the columella or axis of the shell; breadth, across from the outer lip to the opposite side. Of *non-symmetrical bivalves*, the length is from the anterior to the posterior margin; breadth, from the greatest convexity of one valve to the corresponding part of the other; depth, from the ventral to the dorsal margin. See Introduction.

MEGADESMA. Bowd. (Μεγας, *megas*, great; δεσμα, *desma*, ligament.) POTAMOPHILA, Sow. GALATHÆA, Lam.

MEGADOMUS. Sw. A sub-genus of Unio, thus described: "Only one lateral tooth in each valve; cardinal teeth two; posterior hinge margin winged. M. gigas, *Sw.*." Sw. p. 378.

MEGALODON. Sow. (Μεγας, *megas*, great; οδος, *odos*, tooth.) *Fam.* Cardiacea, Lam.—*Descr.* Equivalve, longitudinal, acuminated at the umbones, thick; hinge forming an incrassated septum across the cavity of the shell, with a large bifid tooth in the right valve, and one irregular and one pointed in the left; ligament long, external.—*Obs.* The general form, the thickened hinge reaching across the cavity of the valve and the terminal umbones serve to distinguish this genus from Cardita, to which, however, it is nearly allied. M. cucullatus, Pl. vii. fig. 127.

MEGALOMASTOMA. Guild. A sub-genus of Cyclostoma, thus described: "Cylindrical, resembling *Pupa*, but has a horny operculum; spire not thickened; teeth or fold on the pillar none, flavula *Sw.* En. Méth. 461. f. 6. brunnea *Guild.* (*fig. 97. g. h.* 1.) Sw. p. 336." Mr. Gray applies the name to those species which have "a groove or ridge in front of the mouth near the pillar." *Ex.* Cyclostoma Flavulum, Sowerby's Thesaurus Conchyliorum, Pl. xxiv. fig. 66, 67; and our fig. (same species?) Pl. xxv. fig. 529.

MEGARIMA. Rafinesque. A genus proposed to include species of TEREBRATULA, Auct. which are smooth and nearly equivalve. T. lævis, T. crassa, T. truncula.

MEGASPIRA. Lea. (Μεγας, *megas*, great, and spire.) M. Ruschenbergiana, (fig. 294) is a pupiform land shell, remarkable for the length of its spire, which consists of no less than twenty-five close set, narrow, gradually increasing whorls. The outer lip is simple, slightly thickened; the inner lip has a tooth on the body-whorl, and two folds on the columella. Only one species of this singular shell is known. Pl. xiv. fig. 294.

MEGATHYRUS. D'Orbigny. A genus of Brachiopoda represented by M. cistellula. Forbes and Hanley, British Mollusca, and Teretrabula decollata, Sowerby's Thesaurus Conchyliorum. Pl. lxxi. fig. 68 to 70.

MEGATREMA. Leach. M. S.? A genus composed of those species of PYROGOMA, Auct. which have a large aperture. Pl. i. fig. 33.

MELACANTHA. Sw. A sub-genus of Melania. Sw. p. 341.

MELAFUSUS. Sw. A sub-genus of Melanopsis. Sw. p. 341.

MELAMPUS. Montf. CONOVULUM, Lam. A genus composed of species of AURICULA, Auct. of a conical form. A. conoidalis, fig. 298.

MELANIA. Auct. (Μελας, *melas*, black.) *Fam.* Melaniens, Lam. Ellipsostomata, Bl.—*Descr.* Turrited; spire generally elongated, acute; aperture entire, oval or oblong, pointed at the posterior extremity, rounded anteriorly, with a kind of indistinct canal or sinuosity; epidermis thick, generally black.—*Obs.* In common with other fresh-water shells, the Melaniæ are frequently found with corroded apices. This genus is known from Melanopsis by the absence of the notch at the anterior part of the aperture. The Melaniæ occur in rivers of warm climates. The fossil species are frequent in upper marine formations. Pl. xiv. fig. 313.

MELANIANA. Lam. (Melaniens.) A family belonging to the first section of the order Trachelipoda. The genera contained in it may be distinguished as follows.

    1. MELANOPSIS. Aperture notched; columellar lip thickened above; including *Pirena*. Fig. 315, 316.

    2. MELANIA. Aperture not notched; columellar lip not thickened; including *Auculosa, Pasithœa, Io.* Fig. 313, 314, 317.

MELANITHES. Sw. A sub-genus of Melanopsis. Sw. p. 341.

MELANOIDES. Olivier. MELANOPSIS. Fer.

MELANOPSIS. Fer. *Fam.* Melaniana, Lam. Entomostomata, Bl.—*Descr.* Oval or oblong, fusiform; spire acute, sometimes elongated; aperture oblong or oval, pyriform, with a distinct notch at the anterior extremity; columella tortuous, callous, thickened at the extremity near the spire; epidermis thick, horny, generally black. Subtropical.—*Obs.* This description includes the two first species of the genus Pirena, Lam. The Melanopsides are known from the Melaniæ by the notch in the aperture. M. costata. Pl. xiv. fig. 315.

MELAS. Montf. MELANIA, Auct.

MELATOMA. Sw. A sub-genus of Melanopsis. Sw. p. 341.

MELEAGRINA. Lam. MARGARITA. A genus composed of the Pearl Oyster and similar species, separated from Avicula on account of the roundness of their general form, but re-united by Sowerby. For generic characters, see Avicula. M. margaritifera. Pl. ix. fig. 164.

MELEAGRIS. Montf. TURBO Pica, Auct. and similar species, having the aperture oblique, the columella gliding imperceptibly into the outer lip, and having an umbilicus.

MELINA. Schum. BERNA, Auct.

MELO. Brod. (*Melo*, a melon.) *Fam.* Columellaria, Lam.—*Descr.* Light, ventricose, oval, with a light greenish brown epidermis, spire short, papillary, regular, sometimes hidden by the last whorl; aperture

514. Achatina? octona. Macrospira, Guild.
515. Stenopus cruentatus, Guild. Under side.
516. ——lividus.
517. Helix, the aperture covered by the epiphragm.
518. Pupa secale, Drap. Abida, Leach.
519. ——pagoda. Gonidomus, Sw.
520. Truncatella, enlarged figure.
521. The same, natural size.
522. Auricula caprella. *Gen.* Caprella, Nonnul. Front view.
523. The same, dorsal view.
524. Pupina vitrea.
526. ——antiquata.
527. ——Namezii.
528. ——lubrica. Callia? Gray.
529. Cyclostoma, flavulum. Megalomastoma, Guild.
530. ——Planorbulum. Cyclotus, Guild.
531. ——a smaller species, with the complicated notch at the posterior part of the aperture. Pterocyclos, Benson.
532. Helicina acutissima, nobis. View of the under side. Trochatella, Sw.
533. The same in profile.
534. ⎫
535. ⎬ Strophostoma, Desh. Three views.
536. ⎭
537. Paludina impura. Bithinia, Gray?
538. Ampullaria avellana. *Amphibola Schum.*
539. A species of Ampullaria, having a thickened ledge on which the shelly operculum rests. Pachystoma, Guild. changed to Pachylabra, Sw.
540. Ringicula, Desh. A fossil species, front view.
541. Back view of the same.
542. Turbo nicobaricus. Chrysostoma, Sw.
543. Trochus Iris. Elenchus, Humph.
544. Purpura vexilla. *Gen.* Vexilla, Sw.
545. Halia. Achatina priamus, Auct.

large, nearly as long as the whole shell, emarginate anteriorly; outer lip thin; columella slightly curved, with four or five laminar, oblique, prominent plaits.—*Obs.* The genus Melo has been separated from *Voluta* principally on account of the largeness of the aperture, the lightness of the shell and the thinness of the outer lip. Melo differs from Cymba in the regularity of the spiral apex, and in the greater rotundity of the shell. The Melons are beautifully coloured large shells, found in the seas of the old world. The Melo Indicus has a certain resemblance to a Melon. Ten species are enumerated in the Monograph, Pt. viii. Thesaurus Conchyliorum, by the author. M. Æthiopicus. Pl. xx. Fig. 435.

MELONIA or MELONITES. A genus of microscopic Foraminifera.

MERCENARIA. Schum. Venus Mercenaria, Auct. The Money shell which passes current for cash, under the name "Wampum," among the North American Indians.

MERETRIX. Lam. 1801. Original name for Cytherea, Lam. 1818. In the British Museum Synopsis it is proposed to confine this genus to the species resembling Cyth.'meretrix, &c. After, however, removing Meroe, Circe, and Arthemis, from Lamarck's Cytheræa, it appears difficult to make any further divisions. In preparing the Monograph for No. 12 of the Thesaurus Conchyliorum, the author found the succession of forms so gradual, that it was impossible to make a rest at any given point. Pl. vi. fig. 117, *a. b. c. d.* d.

MEROE. Schum. Cuneus, Mergerle, (prior.) Cytherea Meroe, sulcata, scripta, hians, Auct. and similar species. The Monograph, Thesaurus Conchyliorum, No. 12, contains seven species. Pl. vi. fig. 117, *a.*

MESALIA. Gray. Reeve Conch. Icon. "Shell acuminately turrited, rounded at the base, columella flatly twisted, receding; margin of the aperture below the columella sinuated and reflected;" distinguished from Turritella by the character of the columella, which is receding and flattened. Reeve's Monograph contains three species. *Ex.* M. brevialis. Pl. xxviii. fig. 591.

MESODESMA. Desh. Erycina, Lam. according to G. B. Sowerby.

MESOMPHYX. Rafinesque. A genus proposed to be separated from Helix, Auct.

MICROTOMA. Sw. A genus of "Purpurinæ," Sw. thus described, "Pillar very broad and curving inwards; aperture effuse; the notch at the base small and nearly obsolete; spire very short, patula. Mart. 69. f. 758, 759. Persica. En. Méth. 397. f. 1. unicolor. *Sw.* Chem. f. 1449. Sw. p. 301." Purpura Persica. Fig. 414.

MILIOLA. Lam. A genus of microscopic Foraminifera.

MISILUS. Montf. A genus of microscopic Foraminifera.

MITRA. Lam. (*Mitre.*) *Fam.* Columellaria, Lam. Angyostomata; Bl.—*Descr.* Oblong, thick, covered with a light brown epidermis; spire long, turrited, acute; aperture emarginated anteriorly; outer lip thickened; columella with several oblique, thick plaits.—*Obs.* The pretty shells composing this genus differ from Marginella, not only in general form, but in the outer lip not being reflected. Some species of Voluta, of a more elongated shape than the rest, present a near approach to the most ventricose of the Mitræ. The apex of Mitra, however, is always acute, while that of Voluta is generally papillary. The aperture of the former is narrow and the inner lip thickened, the contrary being the case with the latter. The shells of this genus are varied in colouring, which is generally rich; and also in form, some being angulated, some plicated, some coronated and others smooth. The species are mostly tropical; very few occur so far north as the Mediterranean. Fossil species are numerous in the Eocene beds. Fig. 431. M. Plicaria. Fig.

432. Conohelix marmorata, Sw. Pl. xx.—The Mitræ are thus divided in Gray's British Museum arrangement: *Mitra*, typified by the common M. episcopalis; *Zierliana*, Gray, certain short, thick-lipped strombiform species, M. Ziervoglii; *Turris*, Montf. of which our figure is an example; *Cylindra*, like Conohelix, but cancellated, M. Dactylus; and Conohelix (our fig. 432), to which is given the prior name, Imbricaria, Schum.

MAITRELLA. Sw. A genus consisting of Mitra Fissurella, casta, Olivæformis, and similar species, described as "Rather small; olive-shaped; unequally fusiform; always smooth and polished, and sometimes covered with an epidermis; base obtuse and effuse; spire nearly or quite equal to the aperture; plaits of the pillar few, oblique, and extending beyond the aperture, which is smooth internally." Sw. p. 321. M. Fissurata, E.M. 371. f. 1. Olivarii, f. 2. Dactylus, 372. f. 5. *Ex.* Mitra bicolor. Pl. xxvi. fig. 559.

MITREOLA. Sw. A genus of "Mitranæ," Sw. thus described: "Small; unequally fusiform; the base obtuse; inner lip, typically thickened, inflected, and either toothed or tuberculated; plaits on the pillar distinct, the inferior largest; tip of the spire sometimes papillary; aperture without either striæ or groove." Sw. p. 320, M. Monodonta, M. Trebellum. Zool. Illustr. II. 128. f. 1. f. 2. dPl. xxvi. fig. 558.

MODIOLA. Lam. (*Modiola*, a little measure.) *Fam.* Mytilacea, Lam.—*Descr.* Equivalve oblique, cuneiform, inequilateral, thin, with the anterior side short and narrow, slightly gaping to admit the passage of a byssus, and the posterior side elongated, broad, sub-quadrate; hinge thin, toothless, rectilinear, with a long, partly external ligament; muscular impressions two in each valve; palleal impression irregular, not sinuated.—*Obs.* This genus differs from Mytilus, to which the common muscle belongs, in the anterior margin being rounded out beyond the umbo, which in Mytilus is terminal. The Lithodomi may be known from this genus by their cylindrical form. M. Tulipa. Pl. ix. fig. 160.

MODULUS. Gray, 1840. Species of Monodonta. Lamarck, typified by Trochus modulus.

MOLLUSCA. (From *Mollis*, soft.) The twelfth class of invertebrated animals with univalve shells or none; divided into the following orders: Pteropoda, Gasteropoda, Trachelipoda, Cephalopoda, Heteropoda, fig. 220 to 488. The term mollusca is also used in a general sense to include the classes Conchifera and Molusca of Lamarck, corresponding with the type Malacozoa of De Blainville.

MONEY COWRY. Cypræa Moneta, which passes current in some parts of Africa and the East Indies.

MONILEA. Sw. A sub-genus of Monodonta. Sw. p. 352.

MONOCEROS. Lamarck. Acanthiza, Fischer. (Μονος, *monos*, single; Κερας, *ceras*, horn.) *Fam.* Purpurifera, Lam.—*Descr.* Ovate, thick, covered with a brown epidermis; spire short, consisting of few whorls; aperture emarginated anteriorly; columella rather flat; outer lip thick, with a prominent tooth near the extremity.—*Obs.* This genus resembles Purpura, in every respect, except in having the tooth from which the name is derived. A catalogue of 16 species by Mr. Sowerby, sen. is published with figures of 14, in parts 48 to 67 of the Conchological Illustrations by the author. The species belong to the South American coasts of the Pacific Ocean. Priority is claimed for the name Acanthiza (Fischer, 1807) for this genus. Pl. xix. fig. 417.

MONOCONDYLÆA. D'Orb. A sub-genus of Uniones, described as equivalve, inequilateral, sub-rotund or angulated; hinge consisting of a large, obtuse, round cardinal tooth in each valve, with no lateral teeth. Monocondylæ (Unio) Paraguayana. Pl. viii. fig. 149.

MONODONTA. Lam. ODONTIS, Sow. A genus separated from Trochus, Auct. on account of the tooth or notch with which the columella abruptly terminates. M. labeo. Pl. xvi. fig. 366.

MONOICA. Bl. The second sub-class of the class Paracephalophora, Bl. divided into the orders Pulmobranchiata, Chismobranchiata, Monopleurobranchiata, in the first section; and Aporobranchiata, Polybranchiata, Cyclobranchiata, Inferobranchiata, and Nucleobranchiata, in the second.

MONOMYARIA. Lam. (Μονος, monos, single; μυον, myon, muscle.) The second order of Conchifera, consisting of those bivalve shells which have but one principal muscular impression in each valve. The Monomyaria are thus divided: First section, containing the families Tridacnacea, Mytilacea, Malleacea; second section, containing the families Pectinides, Ostracea; third section, containing the families Rudistes, Brachiopoda.

MONOPLEUROBRANCHIATA. Bl. The second order of the first section of Paracephalophora Monoica, Bl. The animals are described as having the lungs branched, situated at the right side of the body and covered more or less completely by the operculiform mantle, in which there is sometimes enveloped either a flat or a more or less involute shell, with a large entire aperture. They have either rudimentary or auricular tentacula, or none. This order, which includes mollusca with haliotoid or patelliform shells, is divided into the following families: Fam. 1. Subaplysiacea; 2. Aplysiacea; 3. Patelloidea; 4. Acera.

MONOPTYGMA. Lea. A genus of small shells resembling Tornatella, but having a strong, oblique fold in the centre of the columellar lip. M. elegans. Pl. xv. fig. 344.

MONOTHALAMIA. (Μονος, monos, single; Θαλαμος, thalamos, chamber.) The second division of Cephalopoda, Lam. containing only one genus, namely Argonauta.

MONOTHYRA. A term used by Aristotle to designate spiral univalves.

MONOTIGMA. Gray. A genus founded on the species represented. It is a turrited shell, but we are unacquainted with the characters of the genus. Pl. xvi. fig. 371.

MONTACUTA. Turton, 1822. (See KELLIADÆ.) M. bidentata. Pl. xxvii. fig. 570.

MOPALIA. Gray. CHITON, Hindsii, &c.

MORIO. Montf. 1810. CASSIDARIA, Lamarck, 1812. (The former should be used.) C. Echinophora, fig. 407.

MOTHER OF PEARL. This beautiful substance, which is so much resorted to for ornamental purposes, constitutes the thickened coating of the internal surface of the shell named by scientific collectors, Meleagrina Margaritifera, commonly called the Pearl Oyster, a young specimen of which is figured (164) in our plates. The reason why this substance is called mother-of-pearl is that the true pearls are produced from its surface. They arise principally from accident or disease, and are sometimes artificially produced by pricking the outside of the shell while the animal is living. The animal is allowed to live until it has formed a pearl over the wounded part.

MOULINSIA. Grateloup. PUPINA, Vignard. A genus of small land shells with enamelled surface and spiral operculum. See PUPINA.

MOURETIA. Gray. "Gadin," Adanson. A genus of patelliform shells, described as differing from SIPHONARIA (the original Mouretia of Adanson) in the situation of the siphon, which in Mouretia is close to the place where the muscular impression is interrupted to leave a space for the head; while in Siphonaria it is nearly half way between the anterior and posterior ends of the shell.

MOUTH. The aperture or opening of univalve shells.

MULINIA. Gray. A genus composed of species of MACTRA, Auct.

described as having the ligament (properly so called) internal, and lateral teeth simple. M. bicolor; Mactra, Auct. Pl. iv. fig. 82.

MULLERIA. Fer. Fam. Ostracea. Lam.—Descr. Irregular, subquadrate, inequivalve, inequilateral, foliaceous, attached, pearly within, green, horny without; hinge irregular, with a partly external ligament, passing to the interior, through a sort of sinus.—Obs. This remarkable shell resembles Etheria in general form and appearance, but is distinguished by having only one muscular impression. It is so rare that, although not very beautiful, a specimen has been known to produce £20. at a sale. Pl. xi, fig. 192.

MULTILOCULAR. Many chambered.

MULTISPIRAL. (Multus, many; spira, spire.) A term applied to a shell when the spire consists of numerous whorls; or to an operculum of numerous volutions.

MULTIVALVE. (Multus, many; valva, valve.) Consisting of numerous valves. There are three kinds of multivalve shells: 1st. Those in which the valves are arranged in pairs, and produce a flattened figure, as Pedunculated Cirripedes, fig. 34 to 43; 2nd. Those in which they are arranged circularly, as Sessile Cirripedes, the valves of which are of two kinds; the opercular, consisting of several valves, which close the aperture, and the parietal, consisting of those which surround the body of the animal in a circular form, fig. 14 to 33. 3rd. Those in which they are arranged in a straight line, as Chiton, fig. 227.

MUREX. Linn. (A sharp rock.) Fam. Canalifera, Lam. siphonostoma, Bl.—Descr. Turrited, ventricose, thick, with three or more longitudinal, continuous, branched, spinose or fringed varices; spire prominent, acute; aperture oval, terminating in a posterior, partly closed canal, outer lip varicose, inner lip smooth, laminar; operculum horny, concentric, pointed.—Obs. This genus contains some of the most exquisitely beautiful shells in existence, the richness of their colouring, the ramifications of their varices, would render most species the finest possible subject for the exercise of the painter's art in still life. The most remarkable are the Rosebud Murex, with its pink-tipt fringes, the Venus Comb, with its long rows of parallel spines; the Ducal Murex, the Royal Murex, and many others, which follow each other in a tortuous direction on the spire. The Ranellæ have only two rows of varices, and have a posterior as well as an anterior canal. The genus Typhis consists of several small species resembling Murex in every respect, excepting that of having a tubular opening on the upper part of the whorl between each varix. See TYPHIS. The most beautiful Murices are brought from tropical climates. Pl. xvii. fig. 395, 396. The genus Trophon, consisting of Murex Magellanicus, &c. may very well be separated from the other types. M. Reeve's Monograph of Murex, including the latter, contains nearly 200 species.

MURICANTHUS. Sw. A sub-genus of Murex, thus described: "Varices numerous, foliated; spire short; margin of the outer lip with a prominent tooth near the base; Radix. Sw. Zool. Ill. 2nd series, pl. 113, Melanomathus. En. Méth. 418. f. 2." Sw. p. 296. The latter of the two species quoted, however, does not agree with the description, having no prominent tooth on the margin of the outer lip.

MURICATED. (Muricatus.) Having sharp points or prickles.

MURICIDEA. Sw. A genus of "Muricinæ," Sw. thus described: "Spire more produced, as long or longer than the body whorl; varices numerous; no internal channel at the top of the aperture." Sw. p. 297, and consisting of the following incongruous species, "Lamellosa. Chem. f. 1823, 4. Magellanica. En. M. 419. f. 4. Peruviana. Ib. f. 5. senticosa, Ib. f. 3. scaber. En. Méth. 419. f. 6. hexagona. Ib. 418. f. 3. erinacea. Mart. f. 1026." Sw. p. 297.

MUSCULAR IMPRESSIONS are the marks or areas formed on the

interior surface of shells by the muscular fibres which attach the animals to them. Lamarck has divided the Conchifera into two kinds: 1st. Monomyaria, those which have but one adductor muscle, and consequently have but one impression in each valve, as the Common Oyster, fig. 180; wnd. The Dimyaria, those which have two, and consequently have two impressions in each valve. There are other smaller impressions in some shells besides the principal. The palleal impression is a mark or scar passing near the margin of the shell. See Introduction.

MYA. Auct. *Fam.* Myaria, Lam. Pyloridea, Bl.—*Descr.* Transverse, oval, thick, gaping at both extremities, rounded anteriorly, acuminated posteriorly; hinge with one large dilate, compressed tooth in one valve, and a suture in the other, containing the cartilage; muscular impressions two, distant, large, irregular; palleal impression with a large sinus.—*Obs.* Mya may be known by the large, prominent, broad tooth in one valve. In Anatina there is one in each valve, and, in Lyonsia, accessory pieces. Lutraria has cardinal teeth and a ligamentary pit. Few species of Mya are known. They belong to the Northern Hemisphere. M. truncata. Pl. iii. fig. 71.

MYCETOPODA or MYCETOPUS. D'Orb. *Fam.* Nayades, Lam. *Descr.* Shell elongated, soleniform, inequivalve, inequilateral, gaping anteriorly; muscular impressions very complex.—*Obs.* These shells are said to terebrate like Pholas. M. solenoides. Pl. viii. fig. 151.

MYARIA. Lam. A family belonging to Lamarck's order Conchifera Dimyaria. Containing the following genera:

1. ANATINA. Ligament in a spoon-shaped prominence on the hinge of each valve, shell thin. Fig. 69.
2. MYA. Spoon-shaped prominence in one valve; shell thick. Fig. 71.
3. ANATINELLA. A spoon-shaped process in both valves. Fig. 70.
4. LYONSIA. An internal bony appendage on the hinge. Fig. 491, 492.
5. MYOCHAMA. Flat valve attached, a bony appendage on the hinge. Fig. 73.
6. CLEIDOTHÆRUS. Deep valve attached, a bony appendage. Fig. 75, 76.
7. CUMINGIA. Ligamentary pit in both valves, spoon-shaped. Fig. 87.

MYOCHAMA. Stutch. (*Mya* and *Chama.*) *Fam.* Myaria, Lam.—*Descr.* Inequivalve, irregular, attached, subequilateral; attached valve flat, with two marginal, diverging teeth, and one end of a little testaceous appendage fixed between them by a horny cartilage; free valve convex, with umbo incurved and two very minute, diverging teeth, between which the other end of the testaceous appendage is placed; external surface of both valves conforming to the grooves or undulations of the shell to which the specimen is attached; muscular impressions two in each valve; palleal impressions with a short sinus.—*Obs.* This new genus, of which only one species is known, the M. anomoides from New South Wales, differs from Anomia and Anatina in being attached by the surface of one of the valves, from which circumstance the word Chama is added to its name; the little testaceous appendage bringing it near the Myariæ. M. anomoides. Pl. iii. fig. 73, 74.

MYOCONCHA. Sow. (*Mya* and *Concha.*) *Fam.* Cardiacea, Lam. *Descr.* Oval, equivalve, oblique; umbones terminal; ventral margin rounded; hinge with an external ligament, and one oblique, elongated tooth in the left valve; impression of the mantle not sinuated.—*Obs.* The fossil genus has the general form of Mytilus or Modiola, but the hinge of the Conchæ generally.

MYODORA. Gray. Reeve, Conch. Icon. Bivalve, for the most part triangular, inæquivalve; left valve concave, right valve flat; anterior side rounded; posterior side flexuous, truncated; hinge, with linear projections on each side of a triangular ligamentary pit, and a bony appendage. *Ex.* Myodora striata, Pl. xxvii. fig. 574.

MYOPARA. Lea. (*Myoparo*, a piratical oar-galley.) *Fam.* Arcacea, Lam. A genus founded on a minute fossil bivalve shell, somewhat resembling Isocardia in form, but having a series of teeth placed on each side of the umbones. M. costatus, Pl. vii. fig. 135.

MYRISTICA. Sw. A genus of "Pyrulinæ," Sw. thus described: "Subpyriform; spire strong, spiny, or tuberculated, nearly as long as the base; umbilicus either partially or entirely concealed; inner lip vitreous, thin; the outer with an internal and ascending canal; the basal channel wide. Hippocastanea. En. M. 432. f. 4. lineata, Ib. f. 5. melongena. En. Méth. 435. f. 3. nodosa. Chem. 1564. 5." Sw. p. 307. *Ex.* P. Melongena. Pl. xxvi. fig. 552.

MYRTEA. Turt. VENUS spinifera, Auct. LUCINA spinifera Nonnull. The shells of this genus are described as "Oval, triangular, equivalve, nearly equilateral, closed. Hinge of one valve with a single tooth, and lateral one on each side; of the other valve with two teeth, the lateral ones obscure. Ligament external." British Channel and Mediterranean.

MYSCA. Turt. A genus composed of species of UNIO, Auct. which are distinguished by having "strong, transverse, notched, cardinal and long lateral teeth." Unio pictorum.

MYSIA. Leach. A genus composed of TELLINA rotundata, montagu and other similar species.

MYTILACEA. Bl. The fourth family of Lamellibranchiata, Bl. The shells are described as regular, equivalve, frequently with a thick, horny epidermis. A toothless hinge and a linear ligament. This family contains the genera Mytilus and Pinna.

MYTILACEA. Lam. A family belonging to the first section of Conchifera Monomyaria, Lam. described as having the ligament partly interior, occupying the greater part of the hinge line, which is straight. The shell is rarely foliaceous. The Mytilaceæ cannot easily be confounded with the Malleaceæ, because the former are generally regular and the latter are irregular, and have a thick internal coating of pearl, beyond which the external coating extends. The genera may be thus distinguished:

1. MYTILUS. Umbones terminating in a point. Fig. 158.
2. DREISSINA. The same, with a septiform plate. Fig. 159.
3. MODIOLA. Anterior margin rouonded beyond the umbones. Fig. 160.
4. PINNA. Open at the posterior extremity. Fig. 162.
5. LITHODOMUS. Cylindrical, living in holes. Fig. 161.

MYTILUS. Auct. *Fam.* Mytilacea. Lam.—*Descr.* Equivalve, cuneiform, oblique, smooth, with umbones terminal, pointed, and posterior side broad, rounded; hinge linear, with a long, partly internal ligament; muscular impressions two in each valve, that on the posterior side large, irregular; that on the anterior small; palleal impression irregular.—*Obs.* The Linnæan genus Mytilus included the Modiolæ, which differ from the mytili in the rounded anterior side; and the Pinnæ, which are large shells, gaping at the posterior extremity. M. achatinus, Pl. ix. fig. 158.

MYXOSTOMA. Troschel, 1847. Cyclostoma Peteveriana, Thesaurus Conchyliorum, Pl. xxv. fig. 100, 101.

NÆARA. Gray. A genus composed of ANATINA longirostrum, Lam. and other similar species. Pl. xxiv. fig. 493, 494, 495.

NAIA. Sw. A sub-genus of Castalia, Lam. thus described: "Oval cardinal teeth beneath the bosses, and deeply sulcated, C. corrugata. *Lam.* En. Méth. 248. f. 8, picta, *Sw.* En. Méth. 248. f. 6." Sw. p. 379. Pl. viii. fig. 148.

George Sowerby, Sc.

565. Cæcum trachea.
566. Triomphalia globosa.
567. Turtonia minuta.
568. Poronia rubra.
569. Kellia orbicularis.
570. Montacuta
  videntata.
571. Pythina
  Deshayesiana.

See
Kelladiæ

572. Syndosmya alba.
573. Cochlodesma prætenuis.
574. Myodora striata.
575. Cryptodon sinuosum.
576. Diplodonta rotundata.
577. Circe scripta.
578. Leda caudatu.
579. Nucinella miliaris.
580. Hemipecten Forbesianus.
581. Spiralis.
582. Stoastoma pisum.
583. Paludomus neritoides.
584. Vanicoro cidaris.

NANINIA. Gray. A genus composed of the planorbicular species of HELIX, with large umbilici, and outer lip thin, included in the sub-genus Helicella, Fer. *Ex.* H. citrina. Pl. xiv. fig. 280.

NASSA. Lam. A genus of small shells united to Buccinum by some authors, but separated by others on account of the little tooth-like projection terminating the columella. N. arcularia. Pl. xix. fig. 423.

NATICA. Brug. *Fam.* Neritacea, Lam. Hemicyclostomata, Bl.—*Descr.* Globose, thick, generally smooth; spire short, pointed, with few volutions; aperture semilunar, entire; outer lip thin; columellar lip oblique, nearly straight, callous; umbilicus with a spiral callosity, terminating behind the columella, and sometimes filling up the cavity; operculum shelly in some species, horny in others; epidermis thin, light, semitransparent.—*Obs.* The straight, callous, smooth edge of the columella and the callosity serve to distinguish this genus from Nerita, Neritina, Neritopsis and Helix. Pl. xv. fig. 327, 328.

NATICARIA. Sw. A sub-genus of Natica, thus described: "Oval; convex above; umbilicus small, open, placed very near the top of the aperture; inner lip reflected; small. N. melanostoma, Mart. 189. f. 1926, f1927. cancellata, *Sw.* Ib. 189. f. 1939. bifasciata, Griff. Cuv. 1. f. 2." Sw. p. 346.

NATICELLA. Guild. A sub-genus of Natica, thus described: "Operculum horny; shell globose, but generally depressed; umbilicus nearly filled up by a vitreous deposition of the inner lip; spire obtuse. N. aurantia. Mart. 189. f. 1934, 1935." Sw. p. 345.

NAVICELLA. Lamarck, 1822. CATILLUS, Humphrey (named in a catalogue) 1817. CIMBER, Montf. 1810. (*A little ship.*) *Fam.* Neritacea, Lam. Hemicyclostomata, Bl.—*Descr.* Transversely oval, symmetrical, smooth; aperture entire, oval; dorsal surface convex; outer lip thin; inner lip flat, straight edged; spread over the front surface of the body whorl, and sometimes hiding the apex; apex incurved; operculum testaceous, flat, sub-quadrate, with a lateral articulation.—*Obs.* This well known genus, of which there are several species, is named Cimber by Montfort. The shells are brought from India, the Isle of Fance and the Moluccas. Fifteen species are enumerated in a Monograph of the genus by the Author, Thes. Conch. No. 11. Ex. n. Elliptica. See our Pl. xv. fig. 323.

NAUTELLIPSITES. Parkinson. A generic name proposed to include such species of Nautilus as have been compressed, so as to assume an oval instead of round form. The genus Ellipsolites of De Montfort consists of species of Ammonites similarly deformed.

NAUTILACEA. Bl. The fifth family of Polythalamacea, Bl. the shells of which are described as more or less discoidal, compressed, symmetrically convolute; the last whorl much larger than the others; which are entirely hidden beneath it and advancing beyond the last but one, so as constantly to form a large oval aperture, which is always, however, modified by the last whorl. The septa are united in the greater number of instances and pierced by a siphon. This family contains the genera Orbulites, Nautilus, Polystomella and Lenticulina.

NAUTILACEA. Lam. The sixth family of Polythalamous Cephalopoda, Lam. containing the genera Discorbites, Siderolites, Polystomella, Vorticialis, Nummulites, Nautilus. To these may be added Simplegas and Endosiphonites. Fig. 472 to 476.

NAUTILUS. Auct. (*A little boat.*) *Fam.* Nautilacea, Lam. and Bl.—*Descr.* Convolute, discoid, chambered, symmetrical; spire partly or entirely concealed by the last whorl; aperture modified by the last whorl, wide, sinuated on the dorsal margin; interior surface pearly; septa dividing the chambers simple: siphon discontinuous.—*Obs.* The shell named Nautilus by Pliny is the Argonauta of modern authors, a thin shell, not chambered. The Nautili are known from the Ammonites

by the septa being simple, not sinuated as in the latter genus, and in general the volutions of the spire are not visible. Three or four species are known inhabitants of the Pacific Ocean and Australian Ocean. The fossil species are found in the tertiary, and also in the secondary strata, as low down as the Mountain limestone. Five species are described in Pl. ix. of the Author's Thesaurus Conchyliorum. N. pompilius, Frontispiece.

NAYADES. Lam. A family of the order Conchifera Dimyaria, Lam. described as containing fresh-water bivalve shells, with or without teeth on the hinge. They are all pearly within, and have a thick, rather smooth epidermis without. This family contains a great variety of shells, which have been separated into an immense number of genera, but which G. B. Sowerby, sen. gives very good reasons for uniting under one generic name. The most generally received distinctions are as follows:

1. CASTALIA. Two cardinal, one lateral, ribbed teeth. This genus is removed from the family of Trigonacea. Fig. 140.
2. UNIO. Teeth various. Fig. 142, 145, 149, 148, 147, 151, 141.
3. HYRIA. Trigonal, alated. Fig. 143, 150.
4. ANODON. No teeth. Fig. 152.
5. IRIDINA. Hinge crenated. Fig. 150.

NEARA. Gray, 1830. A genus composed of bivalve shells, formerly included in the genus Anatina, having a small spoon-shaped process and posterior lateral tooth in one valve, and an undefined ligamental pit, with no lateral tooth in the other. *Ex.* N. longirostratum, fig. 493, 4; and another species, fig. 495.

NECTOPODA. Bl. The first family Nucleobranchiata, Bl. containing the genera Carinaria and Firola; the latter is not a shell.

NEMATOPODA. Bl. The first class of the sub-type Malentozoa, Bl. containing all the mollusca with multivalve shells, except Chiton, and divided into the families Lapadicea and Balanidea, corresponding with Lamarck's sessile and pedunculated Cirripedes, and with the Linnean genus Lepas.

NEMATURA. Benson. *Fam.* Turbinacea, Lam.—*Descr.* Thin, nearly oval, somewhat compressed from back to front; spire acute, consisting of few rounded whorls; last whorl large, but contracted near the aperture; aperture small, oblique, rounded anteriorly; peritreme continuous, thin; operculum spiral, horny, with few volutions.—*Obs.* The distinguishing character of this genus is the contraciton of the last whorl near the aperture, in which respect it is nearly resembled by the shell called Cyclostoma lucidum. Two recent and one fossil species, all very minute, are described by Sowerby in Loudon's Magazine of Natural History, New Series. Pl. xiv. fig. 305.

NERINEA. Defr. *Fam.* Canalifera, Lam.—*Descr.* Turrited, oblong, sub-canaliculated, consisting of numerous whorls; aperture with a strong fold on the columella, one on the outer lip, and one on the inner lip at the edge of the body whorl.—*Obs.* This genus is only found in a fossil state, and usually in the Oolitic beds; no other shell resembles it; the strong, prominent folds on the three upper angles of the subquadrate aperture presents a singular appearance in a section. One species has been named N. Hieroglyphus. *Ex.* N. Goodhalii. Pl. xvi. fig. 374.

NERITA. Auct. *Fam.* Neritacea, Lam. Hemicyclostomata, Bl.—*Descr.* Smooth or ribbed, semiglobose; spire short, sometimes flat, consisting of few volutions; aperture large, semi-lunar; outer lip thick, entire; inner lip thickened, dentated at the edge, spread over the body whorl, forming a flattened disc; operculum shelly, spiral, with an appendage by which it is locked under the sharp edge of the columella.—*Obs.* These marine shells are known from Neritina by the thickness of the

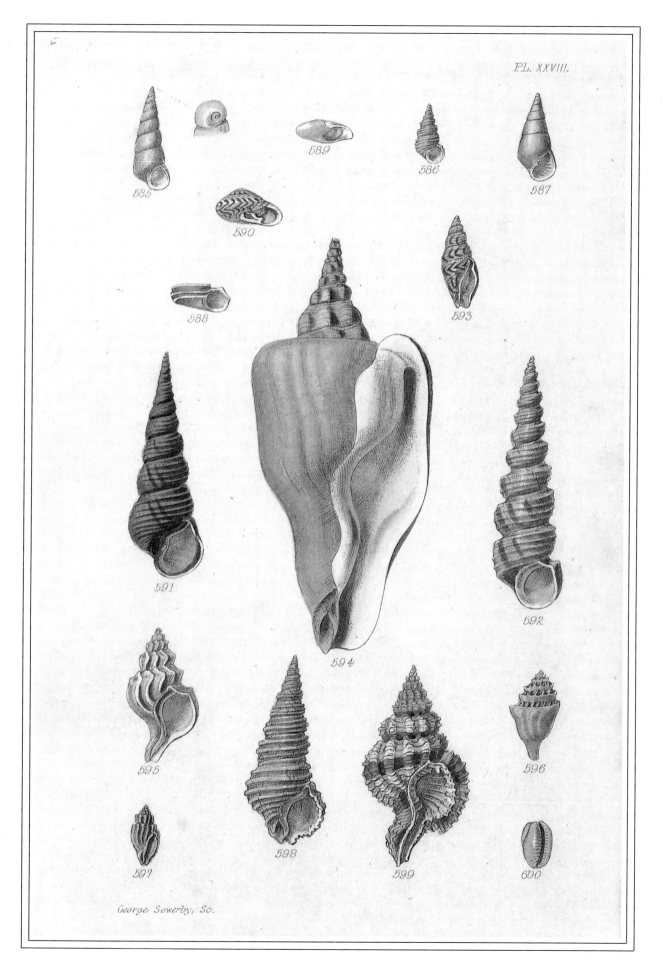

George Sowerby, Sc.

585. Chemnitzia varicula.
586. Alvania ascaris.
587. Odostomia plicata.
588. Adeorbis sub-carinata.
589. Teinostoma politum.
590. Camitia pulcherrima.
591. Mesalia brevialis.
592. Eglesia spirata.
593. Daphnella marmorata.
594. Cyrtulus serotinus.
595. Trophon scalariformis.
596. Conopleura striata.
597. Mangelia coronata.
598. Fastigiella carinata.
599. Hindsia acuminata.
600. Pachybathron marginelloides.

shell and the want of the thick, horny, dark coloured epidermis; from Natica, by the flat area produced by the spreading of the thickened columellar lip. N. Peloronta. Pl. xv. fig. 330.

NERITACEA. Lam. A family of the first order of Trachelipoda. Lam. containing the following genera:

1. NAVICELLA. Apex terminal, not spiral; inner lip septiform. Fig. 323.
2. NERITA. Columellar lip septiform, edge with distinct teeth; shell thick. Fig. 330.
3. NERITINA. Shell thin; columellar lip septiform, edge denticulated; generally a thick, dark coloured epidermis. Fig. 324 to 326.
4. NATICA. Having an umbilicus behind the columellar lip, with a spiral callosity. Fig. 327, 328.
5. NERITOPSIS. Edge of the columellar lip with a deep notch. Fig. 331.
6. PILEOLUS. Patelliform; apex central; columellar lip septiform, leaving the aperture small. Fig. 322.
7. JANTHINA. Columellar lip linear; aperture angulated. Fig. 333.

NERITELLA. Humph. 1797. NERITINA, Lamarck, 1822.

NERITINA. Lamarck, 1822. NERITELLA, Humph. *Fam*. Neritacea, Lam.—*Descr*. Thin, semiglobose, obliquely oval, smooth, flattish in front; spire short, sometimes depressed, consisting of few rapidly increasing whorls; aperture semicircular; outer lip thin, sharp; columellar lip broad, flat, its inner edge straight, denticulated; operculum testaceous, semicircular, sub-spiral, with an articulating process on the inner edge.—*Obs*. This genus of fresh-water shells differs from Nerita in the minuteness of the denticulation of the columellar, as well as in the characters mentioned in our observations upon the latter genus. N. Spinosa, (Clithon, Montf.) fig. 352. N. virginea, fig. 324. N. perversa, Lam. (Velates, Montf.) fig. 326. The Monograph, in Pl. 10 of the Thesaurus Conchyliorum, contains 116 species. Our Plate xv. fig. 324, 325.

NERITOPSIS.Gray. *Fam*. Neritacea, Lam.—*Descr*. Sub-globose, thick, cancellated; spire short, composed of few rapidly increasing whorls; aperture transverse, sub-orbicular; outer lip thickened within; columellar lip thick, rather flat, with a large rounded notch in the centre of its inner edge.—*Obs*. This genus most nearly resembles Nerita, from which it differs in the peculiar notch of the columella. N. granosa. Pl. xv. fig. 331.

NICANIA. Leach. ASTARTE, Sowerby. The same as CRASSINA of Lamarck.

NEVERITA. Risso, 1826. NATICA glaucina, and similar species.

NISSO. Risso, 1826. The perforate species of EULIMA; Genus BONELLIA, Deshayes, 1836.

NITIDELLA. Sw. A genus of "Columbellinæ," Sw. thus described: "Bucciniform, small, ovate, smooth, glassy; aperture effuse; outer lip slightly thickened, faintly inflexed, and generally striated internally; inner lip somewhat flattened above; base of the pillar with one or two slight internal folds, or a single angular projection. Columbella nitida, *Lam*. (fig. 17, *c*. 151.)" Sw. p. 313. Pl. xxvi. fig. 560.

NOBIA. Leach. *Order*, Sessile Cirripedes, Lam. This genus resembles Pyrgoma, Auct. consisting of a conical paries, supported upon a funnel-shaped cavity in the madrepore, but differs in its operculum, which consists of two valves, whereas that of Pyrgoma has four. N. grandis. Pl. i. fig. 29.

NODOSARIA. Lam. and ORTHOCERA have been united by Sowerby under the name of the first. *Fam*. Orthocerata, Lam. and Bl.—*Descr*.

Straight, chambered, elongated; chambers more or less ventricose; septa perforated by a central siphon.—*Obs*. This genus consists only of fossils found in sub-appenine tertiary beds. It is placed by De Blainville in one of his divisions of the genus Orthoceras, which is characterized as "species not striated, and with chambers very much inflated." N. æqualis. Pl. xxii. fig. 465.

NODOSE. Having tubercles or knobs.

NOGROBS. Montf. A fossil appearing from the figure and description to resemble Belemnites.

NONION. Montf. A genus of microscopic Foraminifera.

NONIONINA. D'Orb. A genus of microscopic Foraminifera.

NOTREMA. Rafinesque. A shell described as composed of three integral valves, concerning which De Blainville puts the query, "ne seroit-ce pas plutôt une Balanide mal observée?"

NOVACULINA. Benson. (*Novacula*, a razor.) *Fam*. Solenacaea, Lam.—*Descr*. Equivalve, inequilateral, transversely elongated; external ligament communicating with the interior of the shell by an oblique channel; beaks prominent; hinge line nearly straight, with one narrow curved cardinal tooth in one valve, entering between two similar teeth in the other; siphonal scar long; extremities of the shell gaping; epidermis thin, light brown, folding over the edges and connecting the dorsal margins. *Hab*. Jumna, Gooti, and Ganges. Pl. iii. fig. 63.

NUCINELLA. S. Wood. Biv. Crag. 1850. A genus formed for the reception of a very minute crag fossil belonging to the same family as the Nuculæ and Pectunculi; but differing in the arrangement of the teeth. N. miliaris. Pl. xxvii. fig. 579.

NUCLEOBRANCHIATA. Bl. The fifth order of the second section of Paracephalophora Monoica, Bl. the shells of which are described as symmetrical, more or less curved, or longitudinally rolled up and very thin. This order contains, *Fam*. 1. Nectopoda, containing Carinaria; *Fam*. 2. Pteropoda, containing Atlanta, Spiratella and Argonauta.

NUCLEUS. (*A kernel*.) Anything forming a centre around which matter is gathered. The nucleus of shells is the first formed part; the first deposit of shelly matter to which the successive layers are added; the apex of the spiral cone, of which most shells are composed. (See CONE.) The nucleus is formed within the egg in oviparous, and within the old shell in viviparous mollusca. It is frequently more transparent and light than the remainder of the shell, and sometimes falls off; when this occurs the shell is said to be decollated.

NUCULA. Lamarck, 1801. (*A small nut*.) *Fam*. Arcacea, Bl. and Lam.—*Descr*. Equivalve, inequilateral, transverse, covered with an epidermis; hinge linear, with a series of sharp, angulated teeth, arranged in a line on each side of the umbones, and central ligamentary pit; muscular impressions two, simple; palleal impressions not sinuated.—*Obs*. The row of teeth on each side of the umbones, and the ligamentary pit in the centre of the hinge prevent the pretty little shells of this genus from being confounded with any other. Thirty-four figures are enumerated in the catalogue by Sowerby, sen. which accompanies the Conchological Illustrations of the author. The new species, to the amount of 24, have been figured in parts 14 to 16, of the above mentioned work. Recent Nuculæ are found from the frozen to the torrid zones, and the fossil species occur in nearly all the beds from the Pliocene to the Carboniferous system. Pl. vii. fig. 137.

NUMMULACEA. Bl. The third family of Cellulacea, Bl. described as containing shells or calcareous bodies, which are characterized as discoidal, lenticular; without the slightest traces of whorls to be seen externally. The whorls are numerous, internal, and divided into a great number of cells, which are separated from each other by imperforate septa. This family contains the genera Nummulites, Siderolites, Vorticialis, Helicites, Orbiculina, Placentula.

NUMMULITES. Lam. (*Nummus*, money.) *Fam.* Nautilacea Lam.— *Descr.* Orbicular, convolute, shewing no trace of spire externally; interior divided into cells spirally arranged.—*Obs.* The singular fossils composing this genus receive their name from their external resemblance to a battered coin. N. lenticulina. Pl. xxii. fig. 472, 473.

NUX. Humph. CYCLAS, Lam.

NYMPHACEA. Lam. A family belonging to the order Conchifera Dimyaria, Lam. Ligament external, placed on a prominent fulcrum. This family contains the following genera:

1. SANGUINOLARIA. Rostrated, gaping; two cardinal teeth in each valve, including *Soletellina* and *Lobaria.* Fig. 98, 99.
2. PSAMMOBIA. Quadrate; valves closed, including Psammotæa. Fig. 100.
3. CORBIS. Thick, fimbriated; a cardinal tooth in the centre of a pit. Fig. 101.
4. GRATELOUPIA. A series of small teeth filling a triangular area. Fig. 102.
5. EGERIA. One single and one double cardinal tooth. Fig. 103.
6. LUCINA. Rounded; anterior muscular impression tongue-shaped. Fig. 104.
7. TELLINA. An anterior fold in the ventral margin; lateral teeth. Fig. 105, 106.
8. TELLINIDES. No anterior fold; no lateral teeth. Fig. 107.
9. DONAX. Margin denticulated; shell wedge-shaped. Fig. 108.
10. CAPSA. Margin not denticulated, no lateral teeth. Fig. 109.

OBELISCUS. Humph. PYRAMIDELLA (part.) Lamarck.

OBLIQUE. (*obliquus*, lat.) In a slanting direction. The whorls of spiral univalves generally take an oblique direction in reference to the imaginary axis of the shell. A bivalve is said to be oblique when it slants off from the umbones. An example of this is seen in Avicula, fig. 163.

OBSOLETE. (*obsoletus*, lat.) Worn out, out of use. This term is used to express an indistinctness of character, which sometimes is used to express an indistinctness of character, which sometimes results from the action of sea-water upon unprotected parts of the shell, and sometimes from the deposits of enamel formed in age, and covering the early striæ, ribs, teeth, &c. thereby rendering them less acute.

OBTUSE. (*obtusus*, blunt.) The application of this term is not peculiar to conchology. It is most frequently used to express the character of the spire. *Ex.* The apex of Megaspira, fig. 294.

OCEANUS. Montf. ("Corne d'ammon vivant," Fr.) NAUTILUS umbilicatus, Auct.

OCTHOSIA. Ranz. CLITIA, Leach.

OCTOCERA. Bl. The first family of the order Cryptodibranchiata, Bl. containing the genus Octopus. A species of which being found in the Argonauta, or Paper Sailor, has given rise to the long continued controversy as to whether it is really the constructor of the shell, or whether it is a mere pirate, and having destroyed the true animal of the Argonaut, has possessed itself of the habitation. This question is now set at rest. See ARGONAUTA.

OCTOGONAL. (*octogonum.*) Having eight angles. For an example, see Dentalium, fig. 2.

OCTOMERIS. Sow. (οκτω, *octo*, eight; μερος, *meros*, part.) *Fam.* Balanidea, Bl.—*Order*, Sessile Cirripedes, Lam.—*Descr.* Eight principal valves circularly arranged, forming a compressed cone, attached by a jagged base; aperture enclosed by an operculum, consisting of four valves in pairs.—*Obs.* The only genus of Sessile Cirripedes agreeing

with this in the number of principal valves in Catophragmus, Sow. which is, however, sufficiently distinguished by the several rows of smaller valves by which the principals are surrounded at the base. O. angulosus. Pl. i. fig. 24.

ODONTIS. Sow. MONODONTA, Lam.

ODOSTOMIA. Fleming, 1842. *Descr.* "Shell conical; aperture ovate; peristome incomplete, retrally, and furnished with a tooth on the pillar." A genus originally composed of several small species of land shells. Turbo plicatus, Spiralis, Unidentatus, &c. Mont. Since applied to some minute marine shells, nearly resembling Chemnitzia. *Ex.* O. plicata. Pl. xxviii. fig. 587.

OLIVA. Auct. (*An olive.*) *Fam.* Convoluta, Lam. Angyostomata. Bl.— *Descr.* Oblong, cylindrical, thick, smooth, shining; spire very short, with sutures distinct, aperture elongated, notched at both extremities; outer lip generally thick; columella thick, obliquely striated, terminated by a tumid, oblique, striated varix; a raised band passing round the lower part of the body whorl.—*Obs.* The shells composing this well known genus present a great variety of rich markings and brilliant colours. They are marine and tropical. Fossil species are found sparingly in the London Clay and Calcaire-grossièr. The ancillariæ are distinguished from this genus by the sutures of the whorls being covered by enamel. Mr Reeve's Monograph contains 99 species. The genus is thus divided in the British Museum arrangement, STREPHONA and OLIVELLA, the O. porphyria and the common form; SCAPHULA, the wide-mouthed cymbiform species, O. auricularia; AGARONIA, Gray, the thin subulate species, with the mouth widening at the bottom. Pl. xxi. fig. 457.

OLIVELLA. Sw. A genus of "Olivinæ," Sw. thus described: "Oliviform; spire (typically) rather produced; the tip acute; inner lip not thickened; outer lip straight; base of the pillar curved inwards, and marked by two strong plaits; upper plaits obsolete or wanting; aperture effused at the base only; biplicata, Tank. Cat. 2332. purpurata. Zool. Ill. ii. 58, f. 1. mutabilis. *Say.* eburnea. Zool. Ill. ii. 58, f. 2. conoidalis. *Lam.* No. 57. oryza. *Lam.* No. 62."

OLYGYRA. Say. "Helicina," Lamarck, was first applied by Lamarck to Rotella, and afterwards to the genus of operculated land shells, to which "Olygyra" should perhaps in strictness be now given.

OMALAXIS. Desh. Subsequently BIFRONTIA. Desh. Fig. 354.

ONISCIA. Sow. (G. B.) *Fam.* Purpurifera, Lam. Entomostomata, Bl.—*Descr.* Oblong, sub-ovate, slightly turbinated, cancellated; spire short; aperture elongated; terminating anteriorly in a very short, recurved canal; outer lip thickened, denticulated within; inner lip spread over a portion of the body whorl, granulated.—*Obs.* The granulated inner lip is the principal character by which this genus is distinguished from Cassidaria. In Oniscia the canal is not so produced. Mr. Reeve's Monograph contains 7 species. C. oniscus, Pl. xviii. fig. 409.

ONUSTUS. Humph. A genus proposed by Humphrey and adopted by Swainson who describes it thus: "Shell trochiform, the surface irregular, and often covered with extraneous bodies, cemented and incorporated with the calcareous substance of the shell; the under part of the body whorl flattened or concave, umbilicate. O. Solaris. Mart. 173. f. 1700, 1701. Indicus. Ib. 172. f. 1697, 1698." A thin lamina extending beyond the angle of the body whorl from the outer lip gives a concavity to Phorus Indicus, and is considered by some authors sufficient to distinguish it from the genus Phorus.

ONYTHOCHITON. Gray. Chiton undulatus, and similar species.

OPERCULAR. Of, or belonging to, the operculum. A term applied to the valves which compose the operculum of multivalve shells, as distinguished from the parietal valves, or those which are arranged circularly and form the body of the shell.

OPERCULINA. D'Orb. A genus of microscopic Foraminifera.

OPERCULUM. (*A cover or lid.*) The plate or plates with which many molluscous animals enclose the aperture of their shells, when retired within them. The operculum is sometimes *horny*, as in Trochus; and sometimes *testaceous* or shelly, as in Turbo. It is *spiral* when from a central or sub-central nucleus, the successive layers take a revolving direction, as in Trochus. It is *concentric* or *annular* when the outside edge of each layer entirely surrounds the preceding one. It is *unguiculated*, when the laminæ are placed side by side, as in Purpura. The opercula of multivalve shells are composed of two or four pieces, which are called the opercular valves. The shelly or membranaceous plate with which some of the animals enclose the aperture of their shells, during the wintry part of the year, for the purpose of protecting them while in a torpid state, and which they get rid of by dissolving the edges, when preparing to emerge from their temporary retirement, must not be considered as the operculum, as it does not belong to or form part of either the animal or its shell, but is produced for the occasion by a secretion of the animal, being deposited in a soft state and subsequently hardening. It is called the *epiphragm*, and may easily be distinguished from the true operculum by the texture, and by the circumstance of their being soldered to the edge of the aperture. The operculum, on the contrary, is moveable, and is always composed of a series of successive layers, corresponding with the growth of the shell.

OPIS. Defr. A genus described by De Blainville as consisting of species of Trigonia which have the umbones sub-spiral, with a large, striated tooth on the hinge. Opis cardissoides, Trogonia, Lam. Opis similis, Sow. Min. Con. pl. 232. f. 2.

ORAL. (*Os, oris,* mouth.) Applied to that part of a shell which corresponds with the mouth of the animal, but very seldom used in this sense.

ORBICULA. Lam. (*Orbis,* an orb.) *Fam.* Brachipoda, Lam. Palliobranchiata, Bl.—*Descr.* Inequivalve, irregular, sub-orbicular, compressed, attached by a fibrous substance passing through a fissure near the centre of the lower valve; upper valve patelliform, with the umbo central; muscular impressions four in each valve, semilunar. South America and West Indies.—*Obs.* Discina, Lam. is an Orbicula. Crania is known from this genus by having no fissure in the lower valve, but being attached by its substance. Hipponyx has only two muscular impressions in each valve. Mr. Sowerby's Monograph of this genus in the author's Thesaurus Conchyliorum contains 6 species. O. lævis, Pl. xi. fig. 201.

ORBICULAR. (*Orbiculus,* a little orb.) Of a round or circular form.

ORBICULINA. Lam. A genus of microscopic Foraminifera.

ORBIS. Lea. A minute fossil, described as "orbicular, with flat quadrate whorls and aperture square," in other respects resembling Solarium. O. Rotella, Pl. xvi. fig. 355, 356.

ORBITINA. Risso. A genus said to be established upon the nuclei of two land shells.

ORBULITES. Lam. a genus separated from Ammonites on account of the last volution covering the spire. This is generally considered as characterizing the Nautili, and distinguishing them from the Ammonites; but there are so many gradations that it seems impossible to maintain the distinction in this respect. Fig. 479, O. crassus, fig. 480, O. discus. Pl. xxii.

OREAS. Montf. Part of CRISTELLARIA, Lam. A genus of microscopic Foraminifera.

ORTHIS. Dalman. (ὀρθος, *orthos,* straight.) *Fam.* Brachiopoda, Lam. One of the generic divisions of Brachiopoda by Dalman, thus described: "Hinge rectilinear, with umbones distant; the larger valve with a transverse, basal, smooth area, with a triangular pit." O. basalis, Pl. xi. fig. 207.

ORTHOCERA. Lam. See NODOSARIA.

ORTHOCERATA. Lam. A family of Polythalamous Cephalopoda, Lam. containing the following genera:—

1. CONULARIA. Conical, externally striated; no siphon. Fig. 469.
2. AMPLEXUS. Cylindrical; margins of the septa reflected. Fig. 463.
3. ORTHOCERATITES. Straight, gradually conical; septa simple; siphon central. Fig. 464.
4. NODOSARIA. Divided externally into lobes. Fig. 465.
5. BELEMNITES. Straight, conical; septa simple; siphon lateral; apex solid; internal cast, or nucleus, pyramidal, separable. Fig. 466 to 468.
6. CONILITES. Like Belemnites, but external shell thin at the apex. Fig. 470.

ORTHOCERATA. Bl. The first family of Polythalamacea, Bl. containing the genera Belemnites, Conularia, Conilites, Orthoceras and Baculites. De Blainville remarks that the genera included in this family are all fossils, and known very imperfectly, in consequence of the greater number of the specimens being only casts.

ORTHOCERATITES. Auct. *Fam.* Orthocerata, Lam. and Bl.—*Descr.* Straight, conical, divided into numerous chambers by simple septa perforated by a central siphon. O. annulata, Pl. xxii. fig. 464.

OSTEODESMA. Desh. PERIPLOMA, Schum.

OSTRACEA. (*Ostracées,* Lam.) A family belonging to the second section of the order Conchifera Monomyaria, the shells of which are described as irregular, foliaceous, sometimes papyraceous, with the ligament wholly or partly interior. The principal difference between the Ostracea and the Pectinides consists in the absence of the auricles and the foliated structure of the shells, for, although the Spondylus has ex-foliations or spines upon the external surface, the shell itself is compact and firm. This family contains the genera Gryphæa, Ostrea, Vulsella, Placuna, Anomia, which may be thus distinguished:—

1. PEDUM. Flat, turned up at the sides, an hiatus for the passage of a byssus. A triangular disc on the hinge. Fig. 179.
2. OSTREA. Foliaceous, irregular, hinge on a small triangular disc. Including Dendostrea, Ostræa, Exogyra, Gryphæa. Fig. 180 to 183.
3. PLACUNA. Two diverging ribs near the umbones. Fig. 184.
4. PLACUNANOMIA. The same, but attached by fibres passing through a hole in one valve. Fig. 189 to 191.
5. ANOMIA. No hinge ribs, attached by a bony substance passing through a hole in one valve. Fig. 189 to 191.
6. VULSELLA. Tongue-shaped, a ligamentary pit on the hinge. Fig. 185.
7. MULLERIA. Doubtful. Fig. 192.

OSTRACEA. Bl. The first family of the order Lamellibranchiata, Bl. containing the genera Anomia, Placuna, Harpax, Ostrea (including Dendostrea, Sw.) and Gryphæa.

OSTREA. Auct. (οστρεον, *ostreon,* a bone.) *Fam.* Ostracea Lam. and Bl.—*Descr.* Irregular, inequivalve, generally inequilateral, foliaceous, attached by part of the lower valve; hinge sometimes slightly crenated; destitute of teeth; with a ligament spread upon the lower part of a central, triangular area, which is divided into three parts; upper valve much flatter than the lower; muscular impressions one in each valve,

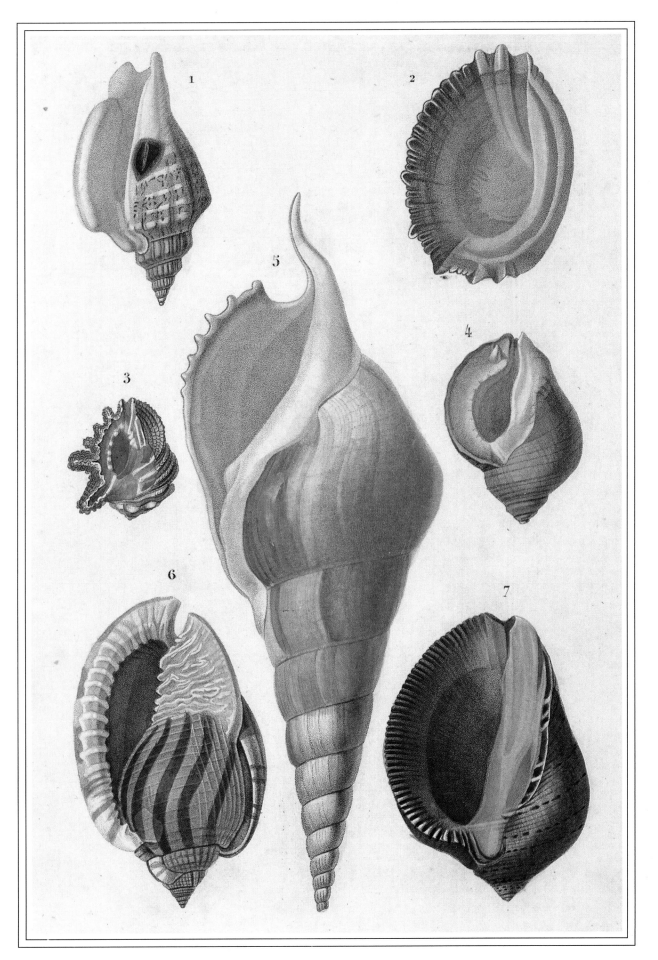

1. *Strombe variable*. (Strombus variabilis, *Swain*.)
2. *Concholépas du Pérou*. (Concholepas Peruvianus, *Lamk*.)
3. *Ricinule digitée*. (Ricinula digitata, *Lamk*.)
4. *Licorne lèvre épaisse*. (Monoceros crassilabrum, *Lamk*.)
5. *Rostellaire bec-arqué*. (Rostellaria curvirostris, *Lamk*.)
6. *Casque xèbre*. (Cassis undata, *Martini*.)
7. *Pourpre persique*. (Purpura persica, *Lamk*.)

large, sub-central, sub-orbicular; with one very minute.—*Obs*. The Linnean genus Ostrea includes the Pectens and many other genera so different from each other, that without any desire to increase the number of genera, it was found necessary by subsequent authors to separate them. The common Oyster is the type of this genus as at present constituted, and is well known to be abundant in various parts of the world. Those which depart farthest from this type are the Gryphæa, Lam. with a prominent, incurved umbo in the lower valve. The Dendostrea, Sw. with margins characterized by strongly angulated folds, throw out arms from the lower valve, by which they are attached to stems of sea-weed, &c. Fig. 180, O. edulis. Fig. 181. O. folium. (Dendostrea, Sw.) Fig. 182, Gryphæa incurva. Fig. 183, Exogyra conica. Pl. x.

OTIDES. Bl. The first order of Scutibranchiata, Bl. containing the genera Haliotis and Ancylus.

OTION. Leach. (ωτιον, a little ear.) Included by Darwin in his work on Cirripedes, with CINERAS, under the name CONCHODERMA defers. *Order*. Pedunculated Cirripedes, Lam.—*Descr*. Body sub-quadrate, supported on a fleshy pedicle with a gaping aperture and two posterior auricular tubes; valves five, separate, two semilunar, placed at the sides of the aperture, two terminal, very small, one dorsal, minute.—*Obs*. Otion differs from Cineras in having two cylindrical posterior tubes, and in the extreme minuteness of three out of five of the valves. Found on spars floating in the sea, &c. (Lepas aurita, Linn.) O. Cuvieri. Pl. ii. fig. 43.

OTIS. Humph. AURICULA, Lam.

OVATE. (*Ovatus*.) Egg-shaped or oval.

OVEOLITHES. Montf. A microscopic shell resembling Bulla.

OVIPAROUS MOLLUSCA. Those which produce their young in eggs. Used in distinction from the VIVIPAROUS MOLLUSCA, whose young are perfectly formed before they leave the body of the parent.

OUTER LIP. See LABRUM.

OVULUM. Brug. (*Ovum*, an egg, dim.) *Fam*. Convoluta, Lam. Angyostomata, Bl.—*Descr*. Ovate or fusiform, smooth, convolute, spire covered; aperture narrow, with a canal at each extremity; outer lip crenulated, inflected; inner lip smooth, callous towards the spiral extremity; dorsal area wide, sometimes indistinctly marked.—*Obs*. The Ovula were placed by Linnæus in his genus Bulla, from which they are very remote. They differ from Cypræa in having the inner lip smooth. We have given representations of their different forms as follows: O. Ovum, fig. 442. O. verrucosum, (Calpurnus Montf.) fig. 441. O. Volva, the weaver's shuttle (Radius, Montf.) fig. 422. O. gibbosum, (Ultimus, Montf.) fig. 443. The Monograph in the Thesaurus Conchyliorum , Pl. 9, enumerates forty-eight species of this beautiful genus of shells. See our plate xx. fig. 441 to 443.

OXYANASPIS. Darwin. Cirripedes. Lepadæ, P. 133. Pl. iii. fig. 1. A genus of Pedunculated Cirripedes, the shells of which are thus described, "Valves 5, approximate; scuta with their umbones in the middle of the occludent margin; carina rectangularly bent, extending up between the terga, with the basal end simply concave."

OXYSTOMATA. Bl. The fifth family of Asiphonbranchiata, Bl. This family appears to have been formed for the express purpose of providing a place in the system for the genus Janthina, which seems to bear so little analogy with other genera of Mollusca, that conchological writers have been puzzled to known where to place it.

PACHYBATHRON. Gaskoin. A genus established for the reception of a singular shell resembling Marginella, but having the columellar lip spread over the body whorl, and the teeth continued across it in folds,

giving the front of the shell the appearance of a Cypræa. I think Marginella Kieneriana, Petit. Sowerby's Thesaurus Conchyliorum, Pl. lxxviii. fig. 198, 199, 200, will be found to approach this shell, and almost lead it into the Marginellæ. *Ex*. P. Marginelloides. *Gaskoin*. West Indies. Pl. xxviii. fig. 600.

PACHYLABRA. Sw. PACHYSTOMA, Guild. A sub-genus of Ampullaria, the outer lip of which is thickened within. *Ex*. Ampullaria globosa.

PACHYMYA. Sow. (παχυς, *pachus*, thick, and *Mya*.) *Fam*. Cardiacea? Lam.—*Descr*. Obliquely elongated, equivalve, thick sub-bilobed, with beaks near the anterior extremity; ligament partly immersed attached to prominent fulcra.—*Obs*. This singular fossil is shaped like Modiola, but the shell being extremely thick, and the ligament attached to a prominent fulcrum, it is difficult to know where to place it. Pachyma Gigas. Pl. vii. fig. 130.

PACHYSTOMA. Guild. (παχυς, *pachus*, thick; στόμα, *stoma*, mouth.) A genus composed of such species of Ampullaria, Auct. as have the edge of the aperture thickened and grooved within so as to form a sort of ledge upon which the operculum rests. Ampullaria globosa and corrugata are examples of this variation. The name Pachylabra is given to such species by Swainson, who objects to the above name on account of its having been previously used to a genus of fishes. Pl. xxv. fig. 539.

PACHYTOMA. Sw. A sub-genus of Helicina, thus described, "Aperture entire; the inner lip very thick; the spiral whorls hardly convex; P. occidentalis. Zool. J. iii. 15. f. 6–10. viridis, Zool. Journ. i. pl. 6. f. 7." Sw. p. 337.

PACLITES. Montf. A genus composed of species of Belemnites, Auct. described towards the extremity, with a pore, at the apex, and a straight lengthened aperture. *Ex*. B. ungulatus, Bl.

PÆCILASMA. Darwin. Cirrip. P. 99, including TRILASMIS, Hinds. A genus of Pedunculated Cirripedes, the shell of which is thus described, "Valves 3, 5, or 7 proximate; carina extending only to the basal points of the terga; with its lower end either truncated or produced into a deeply imbedded disc, scuta nearly oval, with their umbones at the vertical angle."

PADOLLUS. Montf. 1810. A genus composed of species of HALIOTIS, with a strongly marked spiral groove. *Ex*. H. tricostalis, Lam. Pl. xv. fig. 339.

PAGODELLA. Swainson. Should be PAGODUS, Gray. A sub-genus of Trochus, thus described: "Trochiform; generally thin, and always not pearlaceous; aperture and pillar perfectly united and entire; operculum horny. P. major. Mart. 163. f. 1541, 1542. P. tectum. P. persicum. Ib. f. 1543, 1544." Sw. p. 351.

PAGODUS. Gray, 1839. See PAGODELLA.

PALLEAL IMPRESSION. (*Pallium*, a mantle.) The mark or groove formed in a bivalve shell by the muscular attachment of the mantle, which, being always found near the margin of the shell, is sometimes termed the marginal impression. In bivalves with two muscular impressions it passes from one to the other. If in passing, it takes a bend inwards posteriorly, it is said to be sinuated, and that part is called by Mr. Gray, the Siphonal scar.

PALLIOBRANCHIATA. Bl. The first order of the class Acephalophora. Bl. The animals of this order are described as more or less compressed, included between the two valves of a bivalve shell, one inferior, the other superior, joining at the back and opening in front. The Palliobranchiata in the system of De Blainville correspond with the Brachiopoda in the system of Lamarck, and the shells may be known by their being symmetrical. This order contains in the first section of symmetrical bivalves, Lingula, Terebratula, Thecidium, Strophomena, Plagiostoma, Dianchora and Podopsis; in the second section, Orbicula and Crania.

PALMATED. Flattened like a palm, as the fronds or fringes of some Murices.

PALMINA. Gray. Differing from Otion in having but one auricle.

PALUDINA. Lam. *Fam.* Peristomata, Lam. Cricostomata, Bl.—*Descr.* Varying in form from oval to globose, in some instances oblong, covered with a greenish horny epidermis; spire acute, composed of rounded whorls; aperture ovate; peritreme entire, slightly modified by the last whorl; operculum horny, concentric. Europe, North America, East Indies, China, &c.—*Obs.* The construction of the operculum distinguishes this genus of fresh-water shells from Valvata and Cyclostoma. The Paludinæ are viviparous. P. Achatina, Pl. xv. fig. 321.

PALUDOMUS. Swainson. A genus of the family of "Melanianæ," Sw. described as differing from Melania in having the spire shorter than the aperture. Sw. p. 340. Mr. Reeve's Monograph contains 15 species. See our Plate xxviii. fig. 583.

PANDORA. Brug. *Fam.* Corbulacea, Lam. Pyloridea, Bl.—*Descr.* Thin, inequivalve, pearly within, rounded anteriorly, rostrated posteriorly; right valve flat with a cardinal tooth, or short rib, and a slit containing the cartilage with a narrow plate on the dorsal edge turned towards the left valve; left valve concave, with a receptacle for the cardinal tooth of the right valve and the internal cartilage; no external ligament. Europe, America, Ceylon, &c.—*Obs.* This well known genus is in no danger of being confounded with any other shell. P. rostrata, Pl. iv. fig. 90.

PANOPÆA. Menard. *Fam.* Solenacea, Lam. Pyloridea, Bl.—*Descr.* Equivalve, inequilateral, oval, gaping at both extremities; hinge with an acute cardinal tooth in each valve, and a large callosity near the umbones supporting the ligament; muscular impressions two, distant, oval; palleal impression with a large sinus. Britain, North America, Mediterranean, Australia, &c.—*Obs.* This genus resembles Mya in general appearance, but differs in having an external ligament and a sharp tooth, instead of the broad spoon-shaped process in the hinge of the latter genus. P. Australis. Pl. iii. fig. 65, 66.

PAPER SAILOR. A common name given to the Argonauta.

PAPILLARY. (*Papilla*, a teat.) Shaped like a teat. This term is applied by conchologists when the apex of the spire of a univalve shell is rounded like a teat and not spiral up to the extreme point; as the apex of Cymba, fig. 434.

PAPYRACEOUS. (*Papyrus*, a kind of paper made of the flags of the river Nile in Egypt.) Of a thin, light texture, resembling that of paper. An example of this is to be seen in the Argonauta, commonly called the "Paper Sailor," fig. 485, and in the Pholas papyracea, fig. 56.

PAPYRIDEA. Sw. A sub-genus of Cardium, thus described: "Shell heart-shaped, or transversely oval; inequilateral; the anterior side almost always gaping; representing the Pholadæ. P. Soleniforme, Wood, Conch. pl. 56. f. 3.—apertum, Ib. 56. f. 2.—transversum, Sow. Conch. f. 4.—ringens, Wood, pl. 53. f. 1, 2." Pl. xxiv. fig. 503, 504.

PARACEPHALOPHORA. Bl. The second class of the type Malacozoa, Bl. divided into the sub-classes: P. dioica, P. monoica, P. hermaphrodita.

PARIES. (*A wall.*) The principal part of a multivalve shell, forming a circular wall round the body of the animal, and composed of one or more valves which are called the parietal valves.

PARIETAL VALVES. The principal valves of multivalve shells surrounding the body like a wall; as distinguished from the opercular valves, or those which compose the operculum.

PARMACELLA. Cuv. (*A little cell.*) *Fam.* Limacinea, Lam. and Bl.—*Descr.* Haliotoid, internal, thin; spire flat, consisting of one or two rapidly increasing whorls; aperture as large as the whole shell, with the dorsal margins inflected.—*Obs.* This description applies to Parmacella of Cuvier. The shell figured in Sowerby's Genera under that name is Cryptella of Webb. Pl. xiii. fig. 256, 257, 258.

PARMOPHORUS. Bl. A genus composed of Emarginula elongata, Auct. and other species of a similarly elongated form. Australian. p. elongatus. Pl. xii. fig. 242.

PARTULA. Ferussac. *Fam.* Colimacea, Lam. Auriculacea, Fer.—*Descr.* Conical, smooth; spire equal to the aperture in length, consisting of few whorls; aperture auriform; outer lip reflected, broad; inner lip reflected, with a slight prominence on the columella. 25 species are given in Reeves' monograph. P. australis, fig. 302.

PASITHÆA. Lea. A genus formed of some pyramidal shells, described as resembling Melania, but separated from that genus on account of being marine fossils. P. striata, Pl. xiv. fig. 317.

PATELLA. Linnæus. (*A dish* or *platter.*) *Fam.* Phyllidiana, Lam. Retifera, Bl.—*Descr.* Symmetrical, compresso-conical, nearly regular, oblong or oval; apex sub-central, inclining towards the anterior margin; aperture oval, forming the base of the shell; internal surface smooth; with a muscular impression shaped like a horse-shoe, with the ends bending forwards, encircling and dividing the space all round, except where the interruption occurs to receive the head of the animal; external surface ribbed, grooved, striated or banded radiately. Helcion is a name given to P. pellucida, fig. 230. On rocks and sea-weeds in all climates.—*Obs.* Patelloida differs from Patella in the construction of the animal; Siphonaria, in the lateral siphon; and Ancylus, in the oblique twist of the anix, as well as in the nature of the animal. The Patellæ are marine. P. Oculus. Pl. xii. fig. 229, 230.

PATELLIFORM. (*Patella*, a dish; *forma*, shape.) Shaped like a dish, or like shells of the genus Patella.

PATELLOIDA. Quoy and Gaimard. Lottia, Gray.—*Fam.* Phyllidiana, Lam.—*Descr.* Patelliform, rather flat; apex obtuse, leaning towards the posterior margin; muscular impression not symmetrical, but widest on the right side near the head of the animal; central disc of a variable brown colour. On rocks and sea-weeds in all climates.—*Obs.* The shells of this genus so closely resemble patella that it is almost impossible to make the distinction from the shells alone. They are, however, generally flatter, and have the apex placed somewhat nearer the posterior margin. The animals are very distinct. P. Antillarum. Pl. xii. fig. 231.

PATELLOIDEA, Bl. or patelliform shells. The third family of the order Monopleurobranchiata, Bl.; the animals of which are described as depressed, flattened, covered by a wide external shell, which is patelliform and non-symmetrical. This family contains the genera Umbrella and Siphonaria.

PATROCLES. Montf. A genus of microscopic Foraminifera.

PALULARIA. Sw. A sub-genus of "Anodontinæ," Sw. thus described: "Shell nearly equilateral, round or cordate; no teeth, P. ovata, Sw." *Ex. Conch.* pl. 36, rotundatus, Ib. pl. 137.

PAVONIA. D'Orb. A genus of microscopic Foraminifera.

PAXYODON. Schum. Hyria, Lam.

PECTEN. Brug. (*A comb.*) *Fam.* Pectenides, Lam. Subostracea, Bl.—*Descr.* Inequivalve, ribbed longitudinally, nearly equilateral, with a triangular auricle on each side of the umbones; hinge linear, destitute of

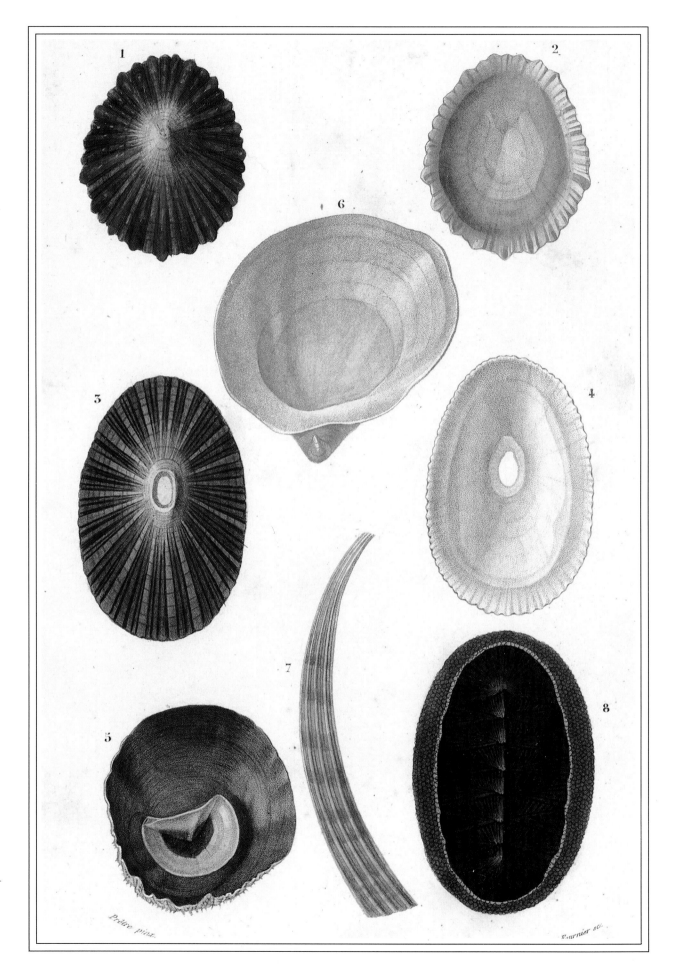

1, 2. *Patelle commune*. (Patella
     vulgata, *Lin*.)

3, 4. *Fissurelle en bateau*. (Fissurella
     nimbosa, *L^k*.)

5. *Calyptrée scabre*. (Calyptraea
     equestria, *L^k*.)

6. *Cabochon bonnet hongrois*. (Pileopsis
     hungarica, *L^k*.)

7. *Dentale éléphantine*. (Dentalium
     elephantinum,)

8. *Oscabrion écailleux*. (Chiton
     squamosus, *Lin*.)

teeth, having a central pit containing the cartilage; muscular impressions one on each valve, large, subcentral.—*Obs.* This genus of beautiful shells, to which the well known Scallop belongs, contains numerous species, some of which are found in the British Seas. The Hinnites Pusio (P. Pusio of some authors) has been separated on account of the irregularity of the external surface of one valve. The Monograph of this genus in Thesaurus Conchyliorum, by the author, contains 101 species. Plates 12 to 20. Fig. 171 to 173. Pl. x.

PECTENIDES. Lam. A family belonging to the second section of the order Conchifera Dimyaria, Lam. including the following genera:

1. PECTEN. Unattached, including *Decatopecten* and *Hinnites.* Fig. 171, 172, 173.
2. LIMA. Unattached, gaping. Fig. 174.
3. PLAGIOSTOMA. Unattached, with an area between the umbones. Fig. 176.
4. DIANCHORA. Attached by the point of the umbo. Fig. 175.
5. SPONDYLUS. Attached, irregular, a triangular area in one valve, divided by a slit. Fig. 177.
6. PLICATULA. Plicated, a very small area in one valve. Fig. 178.

PECTINATED. (*Pecten*, a comb.) Marked in a regular series of ridges.

PECTUNCULUS. (*Pecten*, dim.) *Fam.* Arcacea, Lam. and Bl.—*Descr.* Equivalve, sub-equilateral, orbicular, thick, covered with a velvety epidermis, striated longitudinally; ventral margin denticulated within; hinge semi-circular, with a series of small teeth on each side of the umbones, which are separated by a small triangular disc in each valve bearing the ligament; muscular impressions two in each valve, strongly marked, united by an entire palleal impression.—*Obs.* Linnæan conchologists have mixed this genus with Arca, from which it is, however, totally distinct, not only in the roundness of the general form, but also, and principally, in the curve of the hinge line; in fact the characters of this genus are so strongly marked that there is no danger of confounding it with any other. It does not contain many species; two or three are British. The fossil species occur in London Clay and Calcaire-grossiér. The Monograph by Mr. Reeve contains nineteen species. The generic name, AXINEA of Poli, claims the priority. Pectunculus pilosus. Pl. vii. fig. 134.

PEDICLE or PEDUNCLE (*Pedunculus*, a little foot.) The stem or organ of attachment of the class of shells called in the system of Lamarck "Pedunculated Cirripedes," consisting of a fleshy tendinous tube, by the lower end of which they are attached to sub-marine substances.

PEDICULARIA. Sw. A genus of "Scutibranchia," thus described: "Shell irregular, sub-patelliform; a thick, large, obsolete apex on one of the longest sides, and an internal callous rim within, on one side only; circumference undulated, irregular. P. Sicula, Sw." Sw. p. 357. Sicily. A singular shell probably of the nature of the Cypraedae, which is found attached to corals, conforming its shape to the irregularity of their surface, and fitting closely. *Ex.* Pl. xxiv. Fig. 513.

PEDIPES. Adanson. *Fam.* Auriculacea, Bl. Colimacea, Lam.—*Descr.* Sub-globose, longitudinal, thick, striated; spire equal to the aperture in length; aperture sub-ovate; peritreme sharp, thickened within, modified by the last whorl; columella with three strong plaits on the inner edge; outer lip with one fold.—*Obs.* This genus contains but one or two small recent species, in some respects resembling Auricula, from which it is known by the thickness of its shell, and its globular form. Coast of Africa. Pl. xiv. Fig. 299, P. Adansoni.

PEDUM. Lam. (*A shepherd's crook.*) *Fam.* Pectinides, Lam. Sub-ostracea, Bl.—*Descr.* Irregular, inequivalve, sub-equilateral, attached by a byssus passing through a sinus in the lower valve; hinge toothless, with a triangular area in each valve, separating the umbones; ligament

contained in a groove running across the area; muscular impressions one in each valve, large, sub-orbicular; both valves flat, narrow at the dorsal, broad at the ventral extremities; lower valve with raised edges over-wrapping the upper.—*Obs.* This singular genus, of which only one species is known, differs from all the other Pectinides, not only in shape and structure, but also in the mode of attachment, which is by means of a byssus passing through a sinus in the lower valve; and not, as in Ostræa, by a part of the outer surface. P. Spondyloideum is the only species at present known. Moluccas. Pl. x. fig. 179.

PEDUNCLE. See PEDICLE.

PEDUNCULATED. (*Pedunculus*, a little foot.) Attached to external objects by a hollow fleshy tube, called the Peduncle.

PEDUNCULATED CIRRIPEDES. Lam. An order consisting of molluscs which have multivalve shells, supported on a peduncle. The genera which it contains are thus distinguished:

1. PENTELASMIS. Five valves. Fig. 34.
2. CINERAS. Five very minute valves distant from each other. Fig. 42.
3. OTION. The same, but the animal has two auricles. Fig. 43. The genus Palmina, Gray, has but one.
4. OCTOLASMIS. Shaped like Pentelasmis, abut with 7 or 8 valves. Fig. 41.
5. LITHOTRYA. Five valves, peduncle scaly, with a plate at the base. Fig. 39.
6. SCALPELLUM. Shape square, valves 13, peduncle scaly. Fig. 35.
7. SMILIUM. Same, but the peduncle hairy. Fig. 36.
8. IBLA. Four valves, one pair long, one pair short, peduncle hairy. Fig. 40.
9. BRISMEUS. Even at the base. Fig. 38.
10. POLLICIPES. Principal valves in pairs, with many smaller valves at the base. This genus has been divided into *Pollicepes*, and *Capitellum*, the latter of which is founded upon Pollicepes Mitellus, Auct. Fig. 37 and 37*.

PELAGUS. Montf. A genus composed of species of AMMONITES, which have the spire covered by the last whorl, as in Nautilus, and have an umbilicus. ORBULITES. Bl.

PELLUCID. Transparent.

PELORUS. Montf. POLYSTOMELLA, Bl. A genus of microscopic Foraminifera.

PELORONTA. Oken. NERITA *Peloronta*, Auct. 330.

PENEROPLIS. Montf. A genus of microscopic Foraminifera.

PENICILLUS. Brug. ASPERGILLUM, Auct.

PENTAMERUS. Sow. (Πεντε, *pente*, five; μερος, *mgros*, part.) *Fam.* Brachiopoda, Lam.—*Descr.* Equilateral, inequivalve; one valve divided by a central septum into two parts; the other by two septa, into three parts; umbones incurved, imperforate.—*Obs.* Dalman remarks upon this genus Gypidia, that it is most probably identical with PENTAMERUS, Sow.; but rejects the name for two reasons; 1st. That it has already been applied to a class of insects; 2nd. He disputes the fact of the shell being quinquelocular, *i.e.* not counting the triangular foramen in the hinge of the larger valve as one of the divisions. Pl. xi. Fig. 212, 213.

PENTELASMIS. Leach. See LEPAS. (Πεντε, *pente*, five; 'ελασμα, *elasma*, plate.) *Order.* Pedunculated Cirripedes, Lam.—*Descr.* Compressed, conical, composed of five valves; lower lateral pair sub-trigonal; upper lateral pair elongated, sub-quadrate; dorsal valve accurate, peduncle elongated, smooth. Found on floating wood in the sea.—*Obs.* This genus should have been described under the name

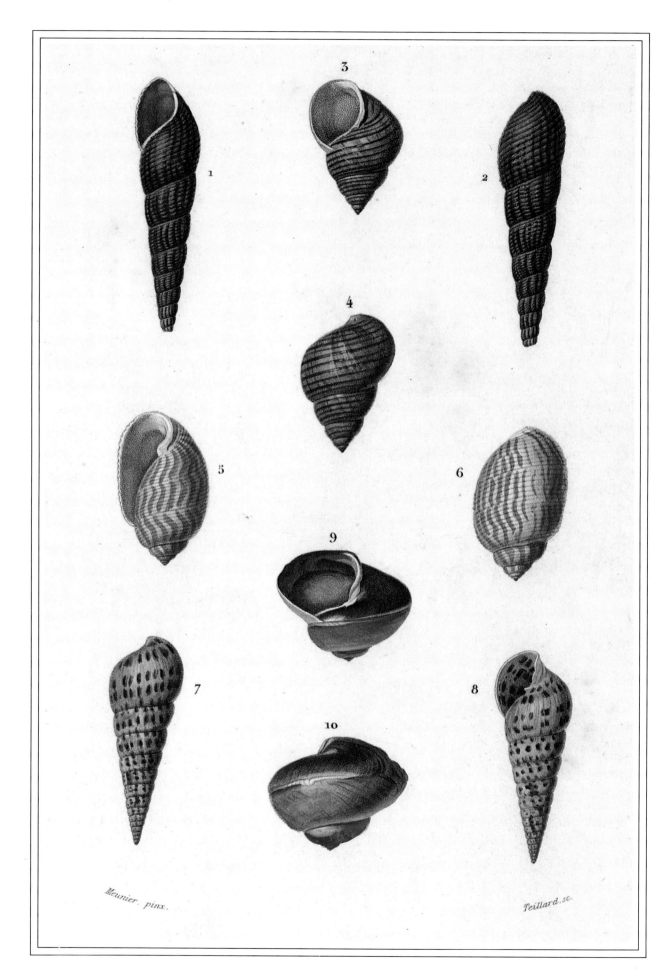

1, 2. *Mélanie tronquée.* (Melania
abra, *Desh.*)

3, 4. *Paludine du Bengale.* (Paludina
Bengalensis, *Lamk.*)

5, 6. *Tornatelle brocard.* (Tornatella
flammea, *Lamk.*)

7, 8. *Pyramidelle tachetée.*
(Pyramidella maculosa,
Lamk.)

9, 10. *Janthine commune.* (Janthina
communis, *Lamk.*)

Meunier. pinx.

Teillard.sc.

LEPAS; it is known from all others of the order by the number of valves. Pentelasmis is the genus Anatifera of Lamarck. Lepas anatifa, Linn. Fossil species of this marine genus are found in the Calcaire-grossièr of Paris, and in other similar beds. P. lævis. Pl. ii. fig. 34.

PENULTIMATE WHORL. The last whorl but one.

PERA. Leach. A genus composed of CYCLAS amnica, and other similar species. pl. xxiv. fig. 500.

PERDIX. Montf. DOLIUM *Perdix*, Auct.

PERFORATED. (*Perforatus*.) Bored through, as the apex of Fissurella, fig. 245, and Dentalium, fig. 2.

PERFORATION. (*Perforo*, to bore or pierce.) A round opening, and having the appearance of being bored, as in Haliotis, fig. 338. Sometimes the term is applied to an umbilicus which penetrates a shell through the axis to the apex, as Eulima splendidula, fig. 348.

PERIBOLUS. Brug. A genus founded upon young specimens of CYP-RÆA, with their outer lips not formed.

PERIOSTRACUM. A name used by Mr. Gray to signify the substance which covers the outer surface of many shells, called the *Epidermis* by most conchological writers. "Drap Marin" is the name given to this substance by French Naturalists.

PERIPLOMA. Schum. *Fam.* Myariæ. A genus thus described: "Shell very thin with the left valve more ventricose than the right; hinge toothless, ligament double, the external portion thin, the internal part thick, placed upon prominent, sometimes spoon-shaped hinge laminæ, and supported by a transverse bone; muscular impressions two, distant, palleal impression sinuated posteriorly." *Genus*, Osteodesma, Deshayes. *Ex.* P. inæquivalvis. Pl. iii. fig. 72.

PERISTOMATA. Lam. A family belonging to the first section of the order Trachelipoda, containing the following genera:–

    1. AMPULLARIA. Globose or discoidal; operculum concentric; in-cluding *Pachystoma, Lanistes, Ceratodes*. Fig. 318 to 320.

    2. PALUDINA. Oval; operculum concentric. Fig. 321.

    3. VALVATA. Globose; operculum spiral. Fig. 322.

PERISTOME. The edge of the aperture, including the inner and outer lips.

PERITREME. A term used to express the whole circumference of the aperture of a spiral shell. In descriptions, it is said to be notched or entire, simple, reflected, round or oval, &c. as the case may be.

PERLAMATER. Schum. (*Mother of Pearl*.) MELEAGRINA Margar-itifera, Lam. The pearl oyster.

PERNA. Auct. ("Pernæ concharum generis," Plin.) *Fam.* Malleacea, Lam.—*Descr.* Sub-equivalve, irregular, compressed, foliaceous; hinge straight, linear, composed of a series of transverse, parallel grooves, containing the cartilage and intermediate spaces bearing the ligament; anterior margin with a sinus for the passage of a byssus; posterior ventral margin oblique, attenuated.—*Obs.* This genus is known from Crenatula by the straightness, number and regularity of the grooves in the hinge and the sinus, for the passage of the byssus. P. Ephippium. Pl. ix. fig. 166. Thesaurus Conchyliorum, Pl. 97, fig. 189 to 191.

PERSICULA. Schum. A genus formed of MARGINELLA *Persicula*, Auct. and other species having the spire concealed. Pl. xx. fig. 438.

PERSONA. Montfort, 1800. (*Mask.* A genus composed of TRITON *Anus*, Auct. and similar species. Pl. xviii. fig. 401.

PETRICOLA. Lam. (*Petrus*, a stone; *cola*, an inhabitant.) *Fam.* Lithophagidæ, Lam.—*Descr.* Equivalve, inequilateral, transversely ovate or oblong, rather irregular, anterior side rounded; posterior side more or less attenuated, slightly gaping; hinge with two cardinal teeth in each valve; muscular impressions two in each valve; palleal impress-ion entire; ligament external.—*Obs.* The Petricolæ are found in holes

made by the animals in rocks, madrepores, & C. They may be known from Saxicava by the regularity of their form and the teeth on the hinge. Pl. iv. fig. 91, 92.

PETRIFIED FINGERS, CANDLES, SPECTRE CANDLES, &c. are vulgar terms by which fossils of the genus Belemnites were formerly known.

PHAKELLOPLEURA. Guild. A genus composed of those species of CHITON, Auct. which have bunches of hairs or hyaline bristles on each side of each valve on the margin. The Chiton fascicularis, found on our own coasts, is a well knwon example. Pl. xxiv. fig. 506.

PHANEROPTHALMUS. *Adams*, Sowerby's Thesaurus, f1850. A sub-genus of Bullidæ, the shells of which are thus described: "con-cealed, oval, entirely open, without more trace of a spire than a curved process at the left border; the right border prolonged into a point slightly turned on itself."

PHARAMUS. Montf. LENTICULINA, Bl. A genus of microscopic Foraminifera.

PHARETRIUM. König. (φαρετρεων, *pharetrion*, a quiver.)—*Descr.* A testaceous body composed of two conical sheaths, one within the other, perforated at the apex, and joined together near the oral margin. In describing this genus, which appears to be the same as ENTALIS of Defrance, Mr. König expresses the supposition that it may probably belong to the class Pteropoda. P. fragile, Pl. i. fig. 3.

PHARUS. Leach. MS. Gray. Syn. Brit. Mus. (undescribed.) CERATI-SOLEN, Forbes. British Mollusca, P. 255.

PHASIANELLA. Lamarck, EUTROPIA. Humphrey, Gray's Synopsis. (*Phasianus*, a pheasant.) *Fam.* Turbinacea, Lam. Ellipsostomata, Bl.—*Descr.* Smooth, oval, variegated; aperture entire, oval; outer-lip thin; inner-lip thin, spread over a portion of the body whorl; columella smooth, rather thickened towards the base; operculum horny, spiral within; testaceous, incrassated without. Britain, Mediterranean, &c.; the fine large species are Australian. Some fossil species are found in the tertiary beds.—*Obs.* The shells composing this genus are richly marked with lines and waves of various and delicate colours, and if the genus be restricted to those species which are smooth, and which have a thick shelly operculum, we may regard it as well defined; but there are some spirally-grooved species of TURBO, Linn. which, from their oval shape, have been considered as belonging to this genus. Such species should not, in our opinion, be retained in this genus; they belong to Littorina. P. variegata, Pl. xvi. fig. 367.

PHILINE. *Ascanias.* A sub-genus of Bullidæ, the shells of which are thus described by Adams in his Monograph in Sowerby's Thesaurus: "shell concealed in the mantle, thin, involute on one side, destitute of distinct spire or columella; aperture large and wide."

PHITIA. Gray. CARYCHIUM, Müller.

PHOLADARIA. Lam. A family of the order Conchifera Dimyaria, Lam. The animals contained in this family live in cavities bored by themselves in rocks, wood, &c. Theya re cylindrical in form. Lamarck here places PHOLAS and GASTROCILÆNA, the last of which belongs more properly to the family of Tubicolaria, where we have enumerated it. Pholas has been divided into *Pholas*, fig. 55, *Martesia*, which has the valves nearly closed; and Pholadidæa, fig. 56, which has the cup-shaped extension. The genus Pholadomya, fig. 67, has been added, although of doubtful character. The genus Galeomma, fig. 58, 59, has also been recently added.

PHOLADIDÆA. Leach. PHOLAS Papyracea, Auct. Remarkable for the cup-shaped process at the posterior extremity. Pl. ii. fig. 56.

PHOLADOMYA. Sow. (*Pholas* and *Mya*.) *Fam.* Pholadaria, Lam.—*Descr.* Thin, rather hyaline, equivalve, inequilateral, ventricose,

1. *Aplysie ponctuée*. (Aplysia punctata, *Cuv*.)

2, 3. *Sigaret déprimé*. (Sigaretus haliotoideus, *Lamk*.)

4, 5. *Natice flammulée*. (Natica canrena, *L*.*k*.)

6, 7, 8. *Bulle banderolle*. (Bulla aplustre, *Lin*.)

9. *Ombrelle de la méditerranée*. (Umbrella mediterranea, *Lamk*.)

posteriorly gaping, elongated, anteriorly short, rounding; ventral margin rather gaping; hinge with an elongated pit, and lateral plate in each valve; ligament external, short, muscular impressions two in each valve, rather indistinct; palleal impression with a large sinus.—*Obs.* The only recent species of this genus is from the island of Tortola. Several fossil occur in rocks of the Oolitic series. P. candida. Pl. ii. fig. 57.

PHOLAS. Auct. (Φωλεω, *pholeo,* to lie hid in a cavity.) *Fam.* Pholadaria, Lam. ADESMACEA, Bl.—*Descr.* Transverse, oblong, equivalve, inequilateral, imbricated, gaping on both sides, the anterior hiatus being generally the largest, although sometimes nearly closed, with the dorsal margin surmounted with one or more laminar accessory valves; hinge callous, reflected, with a long curved tooth protruding from beneath the umbones in each valve.—*Obs.* This genus of marine shells, dwelling in holes formed in rocks, wood, &c. is easily distinguished from any other nearly allied genus by the curved, prominent, rib-like teeth. The monograph of the family in Pt. 10 of Sowerby's Thesaurus Conchylium contains, besides TRIOMPHALIA, 42 species. The principal forms of which are represented by Ph. Costata and Candida, Thes. fig. 21, 22, 23, and 8, 9, with *one* accessory valve. Ph. Dactylus, our fig. 56 (Dactylina) with several accessory valves; Ph. Crispata, Thes. fig. 37. (Zirfœa) with *no* accesssory valve. Ph. tridens, Thes. fig. 60, 61 (Calona) with tube. Ph. papyracea, our fig. 56 (Pholadidæa) with a cup-like termination; and Ph. striata, Thes. f. 40 (Martesia) enclosed by various shields. (P.. ii. fig. 55, 56.)

PHOLEOBIUS. Leach. Part of the genus SAXICAVA, Auct.

PHONEMUS. Montf. A genus of microscopic Foraminifera.

PHORUS. Montf. TROCHUS agglutinanas, &c. Auct. Remarkable for the adhesion of little pebbles, dead shells, &c. to the outer edge of the whorls, which are taken up in the course of the growth of the dead shell. From this circumstance they are called "Collectors, Carriers, &c." Recent species are brought from the East and west Indies; fossil species are fouond in the Tertiary beds. The genus ONUSTUS, *Humphreys,* has for its type, Phorus Indicus, a very thin species, with the margin of the body whorl extending in a broad keel at the angle. Pl. xvi. fig. 360.

PHOS. Montf. *Fam.* Purpurifera? Lam.—*Descr.* Turrited, thick, cancellated, varicose; spire pointed, generally longer than the aperture; aperture rounded or oval; outer lip having internal ridges, with a sinus near the anterior termination; columella with an oblique fold; canal short, forming externally a raised varix.—*Obs.* The raised external surface of the canal, brings this genus near to Buccinum, while, in general appearance, most of the species more resemble Murex. They have, however, no truce varices on the whorls, but merely raised bars. Pl. xvi. fig. 416, P. senticosus.

PHYLLIDIANA. Lam. A family belonging to the first section of the order Gasteropoda, Lam. The genera belonging to this family may be distinguished as follows:

1. CHITON. Composed of eight valves; valves contingent. Fig. 227.
2. CHITONELLUS. The same, with the valves distant. Fig. 228.
3. PATELLA. Conical, symmetrical. Fig. 229, 230.
4. PATELLOIDA. Differing from Patella in the animal. Fig. 231.
5. SIPHONARIA. With a siphonal scar on one side. Fig. 231*.
6. SCUTELLA. Siphonal scar nearer to the side of the head. Fig. 510, 511.

PHYLLONOTUS. Sw. A sub-genus of Murex, thus described: "Canal moderate; varices foliated, laciniated, compressed, or resembling leaves; inflatus. Mart. 102. fig. 980, eurystoma. Zool. Ill. ii. 100. imperialis Ib. pl. 109." Sw. p. 296.

PHYSA. Drap. A genus formed for reserved species of Limnæa, Auct. P. castanea. Pl. xiv. fig. 310.

PHYSETER. Humph. SOLARIUM, Lam.

PILEOLUS. Cookson. (*A little cap.*) *Fam.* Neritacea, Lam.—*Descr.* Patelliform, with the apex sub-central, straight. In the lower disc, or under surface, the centre of which is rather raised or cushion-shaped, is placed the lateral, narrow, semilunar aperture, with the outer lip marginated and the inner lip crenulated.—*Obs.* This interesting genus is known only in a fossil state. Two species are found in the upper layer of Oolite, above the Bradford clay. The spire, although internal, connects this genus in some degree with Neritina. Still there is no danger of confounding them. P. plicatus. Pl. xv. fig. 332.

PILEOPSIS. Lamarck. 1822. CAPULUS, Montf. 1810.

PILIDIUM. Forbes and Hanley. A genus established on anatomical grounds for the reception of a little patelliform shell, the P. fulvum, British Mollusca, p. 441, pl. 62, fig. 6, 7.

PILLAR. The usual English name for the column which forms the axis of spiral shells, around which the whorls revolve. See COLUMELLA.

PINNA. Auct. (*The fin of a fish.*) *Fam.* Mytilacea, Lam.—*Descr.* Equivalve, inequilateral, oblique, wedge-shaped, thin, horny; umbones terminal; hinge rectilinear, without teeth; anterior margin sinuated, to admit the passage of a byssus; posterior margin truncated, gaping; muscular impressions two in each valve; posterior large, sub-central; anterior small, terminal, sometimes double.—*Obs.* The beautiful large shells of which this genus is composed, are possessed of a large, flowing, silky byssus, of which gloves and hose have been manufactured. They have received their name from their resemblance to the pectoral fins of some fishes. some species attain very large dimensions, and measure two feet in length. A fabulous story is told with regard to animals of this genus, namely, that a certain small species of crab is in the habit of taking refuge from its enemies in the shell of the Pinna, into which it is received with great hospitality and kindness by the "*blind slug,*" which inhabits it. In return for which kindness, he occasionally goes abroad to procure food for both. On his return he knocks at the shell, which is opened to receive him, and they share the supplies together in convivial security! Some species are smooth, although the greater number are imbricated or crisped outside. P. saccata. Pl. ix. fig. 162.

PINNATED. (From *Pinna,* a fin.) When a protuberant part of a shell is spread out and flattish, as in Rostellaria columbaria, fig. 403, it is said to be *alated,* or winged, but when the protuberant part is radiated or ribbed, like the fin of a rish, it is *pinnated,* as in Murex pinnatus, and Murex tripterus. (Conch. Illustr.)

PIRENA. Lam. A genus of fresh-water shells, rejected by De Ferussac and other authors, who place Lamarck's two first species with melanopsis, and his two last with Melania. P. terebralis, Pl. xiv. fig. 316.

PISIDIUM. Leach. a genus of river shells separated from Cyclas principally on account of a difference in the animal. The species of Pisidium, however, are less equilateral than the Cyclades, and the posterior or ligamentary side of the latter is the longer, while that of the former is the shorter. Pl. v. fig. 112.

PISIFORM. (*Pisum,* a pea; *forma,* shape.) Shaped like a pea or small globular body.

PISUM. Megerle. (*A pea.*) PISIDIUM, Leach.

PITHOHELIX. Sw. A sub-genus of "Geotrochus," Sw. Sw. p. 332.

PITONELLUS. Montf. ROTELLA, Auct.

PLACENTA. Schum. PLACUNA, Auct.

PLACENTULA. Schum. A genus of microscopic Foraminifera.

PLACUNA. Brug. (πλακους, *placos,* a cake.) *Fam.* Ostracea, Lam. and

Bl.—*Descr*. Compressed, thin, equivalve, nearly equilateral planorbicular, fibrous, foliaceous; hinge flat, with two diverging ribs in one valve, and two corresponding grooves in the other, containing the cartilage; muscular impressions one, large, circular, central, and one or two smaller in each valve.—*Obs*. The two best known species of this well defined genus are the P. placenta, commonly called the Chinese Window Shell, and the P. Sella, called the Saddle Oyster, from the anterior margin being turned up so as to resemble a saddle. The genus may be known from all others by the divering costa on the hinge. Placunanomia is the only genus resembling it in this respect, but this is easily distinguished by a perforation through the shell. These shells are used in China to glaze windows. Pl. xi. 184, P. Placuna.

PLACUNANOMIA. (Sw. *Placuna* and *Anomia*.) *Fam*. Ostracea, Lam. and Bl.—*Descr*. Thin, foliaceous, compressed, sub-equivalve, sub-equilateral, irregular, flat near the umbones, plicated towards the margins, attached by a bony substance passing through a fissure in the lower valve; hinge flat, with two diverging ribs in one valve, corresponding with two diverging grooves, containing the cartilage, in the other; muscular impressions one in each valve, central, sub-orbicular.—*Obs*. The specimens from which Mr. Broderip described this singular genus, were brought by Mr. Cuming from the gulf of Dulce in Costa Rica. Another species is from one of the Philippine Islands. They partake of the characters of several genera, having the hinge like Placuna, and being attached by a process passing through the lower valve, like Anomia. P. Cumingii, Pl. xi. fig. 189, 190, 191.

PLAGIOSTOMA. Sow. Min. Con. (πλαγιος, *plagios*, oblique; στομα, *stoma*, mouth.) *Fam*. Pectenides, Lam. Palliobranciata, Bl.—*Descr*. Sub-equivalve, inequilateral, oblique, auriculated on each side of the umbones, radiately striated; hinge straight in one valve, with a triangular notch in the other.—*Obs*. This genus, one species of which is spinous, and another smooth, is only known in a fossil state. It is found in the Lias and chalk. P. spinosum. Pl. x. fig. 176.

PLAIT or FOLD. A term applied to the prominences on the columellar lip of some univalve shells, particularly in the sub-family of Volutidæ. *Ex*. Voluta, fig. 433; Cymba, 434; and Melo, fig. 435.

PLANARIA. Brown. A minute fossil resembling Planorbis in appearance, but differing in being a marine shell, and having a reflected outer lip. From Lea's Contributions to Geology. P. nitens. Pl. xiv. fig. 312.

PLANAXIS. Lam. (*Plana*, flat; and *axis*.) *Fam*. Turbinacea, Lam. Entomostomata, Bl.—*Descr*. Sub-ovate, pyramidal, solid; spire measuring ½ or ⅓ of the axis, consisting of a few whorls; columella contiguous to the axis, flat, truncated, and separated from the outer lip by a short canal; outer lip thickened and denticulated within; operculum horny, thin, with a terminal nucleus.—*Obs*. This is a genus of small marine shells found in the West Indies, &c. P. sulcata. Pl. xvi. fig. 365.

PLANE. (*Planus*.) Flat, planed, as the columellar lip of Purpura, fig. 414.

PLANORBICULAR. (*Planus*, flat; *orbis*, an orb.) Flat and circular, as Ammonites, fig. 478.

PLANORBIS. Müll. (*Planus*, flat; *orbis*, an orb.) *Fam*. Lymnacea, Lam. and Bl.—*Descr*. Thin, horny, convolute, planorbicular, nearly symmetrical; spire compressed, concave, consisting of numerous gradually increasing whorls, which are visible on both sides; aperture transversely oval, or nearly round; peritreme entire; outer lip thin; inner lip distinct, spread over a part of the body whorl.—*Obs*. This is a genus of shells abounding in all climates in ditches and stagnant pools, not liable to be confounded with any other, excepting the discoidal species of Ampullaria, which may be distinguished by the aperture being broadest in the opposite direction. It is further to be remarked that the discoidal Ampullariæ are dextral shells, and the Planorbes are sinistral or reversed; and although the latter are sometimes so flat and orbicular that it is difficult to know which is the spiral side, it may nevertheless always be ascertained by a careful examination. Fossil species are found in the fresh-water strata of the Isle of Wight, and the neighbourhood of Paris. P. corneus. Pl. xiv. fig. 311.

PLANORBULINA. D'Orb. A genus of microscopic Foraminifera.

PLANULACEA. Bl. The second family of Cellulacea, Bl. The microscopic Foraminifera contained in this family are described as very much depressed, not spiral, chambered, cellular, and having the septa indicated by grooves on the external surface of the shell, which increase in length from the apex to the base: some of the small cellular cavities are to be seen on the margins. This family contains the genera Renulina and Peneroplis.

PLANULARIA. Defr. PENEROPLIS, Montf. A genus of microscopic Foraminifera.

PLANULINA. D'Orb. A genus of microscopic Foraminifera.

PLANULITES. Lam. DISCORBITES of the same author. A genus of microscopic Foraminifera.

PLATIRIS. Lea. (πλατυς, *platus*, wide; ιρις, *iris*.) A genus including several species of Nayades, referred to IRIDINA, Lam. The genus Platiris is divided into two sub-genera. Iridina, species which have crenulated margins; I. Ovata, I. exotica, Spatha, Lea; those with smooth or very slightly crenulated hinges, S. rubeus, S. Solenoides, Mycetopus, D'Orb. Fig. 151.

PLATYLEPAS. (πλατυς, *platus*, wide; λεπας, *lepas*, rock.) *Order*. Sessile Cirripedes, Lam. *Fam*. Balanidea, Bl.—*Descr*. Conical, depressed, consisting of six valves, each divided internally by an angular plate jutting from the centre (like the buttress of a wall); operculum consisting of four valves in pairs.—*Obs*. This genus differs from Balanus, Coronula, &c. in the internal structure of the valves. De Blainville's description of Chthalamus partly agrees with this. Pl. i. fig. 19.

PLAXIPHORA. Gray. Chiton Carmichælis, &c.

PLECTOPHORUS. Fer. (πληκτρον, *plectron*, spur; φορεω, *phoreo*, to carry.) A genus consisting of small testaceous appendages fived on the posterior extremity of a species of slug. P. corninus. P.. xiii. fig. 260.

PLEIODON. Conrad. IRIDINA, Lam. *Fam*. Nayades, Lam.

PLEKOCHEILUS. Guild. AURICULA Caprella, Lam. CARYCHIUM undulatum, Leach. (CAPRELLA, Nonnull.) This proposed genus is described as scarcely umbilical, dextral, oval, spiral; with the spire elevated, obtuse; the two last whorls very large, ventricose; aperture entire, elongated; columella with a single plait; the plait concave, inflected. Fig. 522, 523.

PLEUROBRANCHUS. Cuv. (Πλερα, *pleura*, the side; *Branchiæ*, gills.) *Fam*. Semiphyllidiana, Lam. Subaplysiacea, Bl.—*Descr*. Internal, thin, haliotoid, slightly convex towards the spiral apex; aperture entire.—*Obs*. This is a very light shell, delicately coloured, resembling Aplysia, but differing in the integrity of the margin. P. membranaceus. Pl. xii. fig. 232.

PLEUROCERUS. Rafinesque. A genus very imperfectly described in the "Journal de Physique" as "oval, or pyramidal; aperture oblong; outer lip thin; inner lip truncated at the columella, which is smooth and tortuous, not umbilicated. Operculum horny or membranaceous." De Blainville, in giving this description, remarks that he has neither seen the animal nor the shell of this genus, which he imagines to have been formed from the "Paludine Coupée de M. Say."

PLEURORYNCHUS. Phillips. (Πλευρα, *pleura*, the side; ρυγχος,

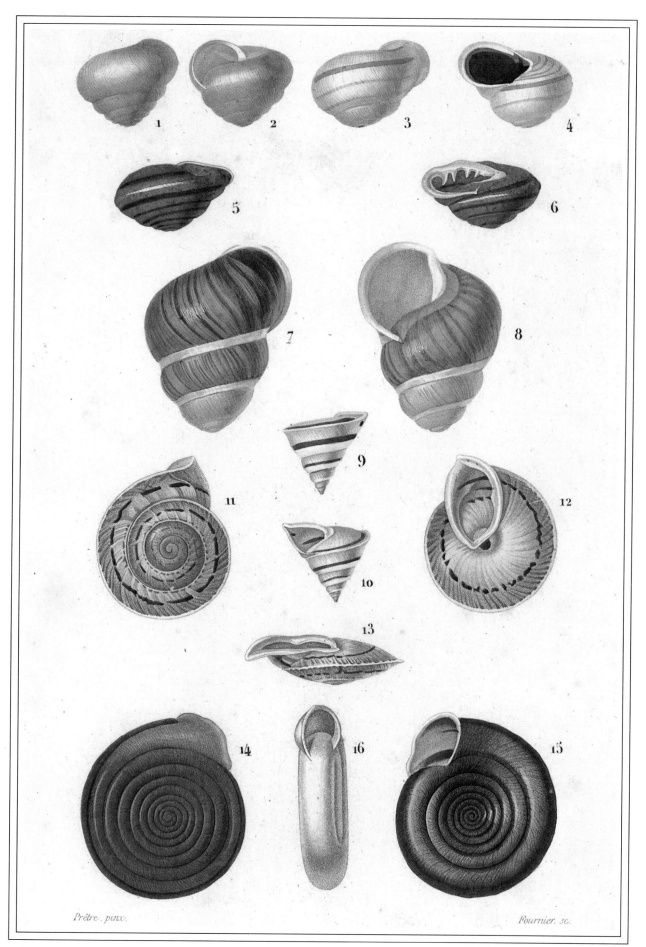

Prêtre. pinx.

Fournier. sc.

1, 2. *Hélice trochiforme*. (Helix epistylium, *Mull.*)
3, 4. *Hélice macrostome*. (Helix vittata, *Mull.*)
5, 6. *Hélice sinuée*. (Helix sinuata, *Mull.*)
7, 8. *Hélice multicolore*. (Helix, polychroa, *Swain.*)
9, 10. *Hélice Pyramidelle*. (Helix pyramidella, *Wagner.*)
11, 12, 13. *Hélice de Lister*. (Helix Listeriana, *Gray.*)
14, 15, 16. *Hélice polygire*. (Helix polygirata, *Born.*)

rynchus, a beak.) A genus founded upon a very singular species of CARDIUM, distinguished by the short anterior side, and the elongation of the hinge line into auricular processes, which are truncated at the extremities. C. Hibernicum from the Black Rock near Dublin, which is vulgarly called "Asses-hoof," and C. elongatum (Sow. Min. Con. vol. 1. 82.), form part of this genus. Pl. xxiv. fig. 505.

PLEUROTOMA. Lam. *Fam*. Canalifera, Lam. Siphonostomata, Bl.— *Descr*. Fusiform, thick, in general ribbed or striated transversely; aperture oval, terminating anteriorly in an elongated canal; outer lip thin, with a fissure near its spiral extremity; columella smooth, nearly straight. Found principally in tropical climates.—*Obs*. This genus, which nearly resembles Fusus in other respects, may be known by the notch in the outer lip. The species differ in the length of the canal. Swainson has designated this genus a family, and divided it into the following genera: Brachytoma, in the description of which he says that the spire and aperture are of equal length, including the species strombiformis: Pleurotoma, in which the channel is so much lengthened, as to be little shorter than the spire: Clavatula, having the long narrow slit of Pleurotoma, in which the channel is so much lengthened, as to be little shorter than the spire: Clavatula, having the long narrow slit of Pleurotoma, but with a very short canal: Clavicantha, having the canal equally short, but the sinus or notch, instead of being linear and long, is short and wide; the surface is rough, and the whorls either coronated with prickles, or with compressed nodules resembling spines: Tomella, which has the spire and canal fusiform, but the spire of very few whorls, and the inner lip considerably thickened within where it joins the outer lip. Fig. 379, 389, P. marmorata; 381, P. Strombiformis, (Clavatula, Sw.) The name "Turris," Humphrey, is prior to the above, and also to the application of "Turris" to the turrited mitres. Mr. Reeve's Monograph of the genus Pleurotoma, contains 369 species, including the Clavatulæ. Pl. xvi.

PLEUROTOMARIA. Defr. *Fam*. Turbinacea, Lam.—*Descr*. Turbinated, spiral; aperture sub-quadrate, with rounded angles; outer lip with a deep slit near its union with the spire.—*Obs*. This genus, which is only known in a fossil state, abounds in inferior Oolite, Oxford clay, and casts are found in a limestone bed in Norway. The Scissurellæ differ in being very minute shells, and are not so trochiform as the species of Pleurotomaria, P. reticulata, Pl. xv. fig. 341.

PLICACEA. Lam. A family of the order Trachelipoda, Lam. containing the following genera:

1. PYRAMIDELLA. Pyramidal, with numerous whorls. Fig. 342.
2. TORNATELLA. Cylindrical, with few whorls. Fig. 343, 344.
3. RINGICULA. Margin reflected. Fig. 540, 541.

PLICADOMUS. Sw. A sub-genus of Pupa, thus described: "spire moderate, regular and thick, but gradually conic; the tip obtuse; aperture perpendicular; inner lip wanting; outer lip semicircular; the margin dilated and reflected. P. sulcata, Chem. 135, f. 1231, 1232." Sw. p. 332.

PLICATED. (*Plicatus*, folded.) Applied to spiral plaits on the columella of some shells. *Ex*. Voluta, fig. 433. Also to the angular bendings in the margins of some bivalve shells. *Ex*. Dendrostæa, fig. 181.

PLICATULA. Lam. (*Plicatus*, folded.) *Fam*. Pectenides, Lam. Subostracea, Bl.—*Descr*. Irregular, sub-equivalve, sub-equilateral, attached by a small part of the surface of one valve, strongly plicated; umbones separated by a small, external ligamentary area; hinge with two cardinal teeth in each valve, two approximate in one valve, received between two distant in the other; cartilage placed between the cardinal teeth; muscular impressions one in each valve.—*Obs*. The cardinal teeth resembling those of Spondylus, distinguish this genus from others

of the Lamarckian family Pectenides. Very few species are yet known, they are brought from the East and West Indies and the Philippine Islands. Fossil species are found in several of the supra-cretaceous beds. Seven species are enumerated in the Monograph by the Author, Part 8, Thesaurus Conchyliorum. *Ex*. Pl. gibbosa, Pl. x. fig. 178.

PNEUMOBRANCHIA. Lam. The second section of the order Gasteropoda, Lam. containing the family Limacinea, fig. 256 to 263.

PODOPSIS. Lam. This genus appears to have been described from specimens of a species of Spondylus, with the triangular disc broken out, so as to present a similarly shaped foramen, which was supposed to afford a passage for a large byssus.

POLINICES. Montfort. 1810. A genus composed of NATICA Mammilla, and other similar species with mammillated spires, and the umbilicus filled with enamel. Pl. xv. fig. 327.

POLLIA. Gray. TRITONIDEA, Sw. The name given by Gray was pre-occupied by a genus of Lepidopterous Insects.

POLLICIPES. Leach. (*Pollex*, a thumb's breadth; *pes*, a foot.) *Order*. Pedunculated Cirripedes, Lam.—*Descr*. Conical, compressed, consisting of numerous valves, mostly in pairs, three or four pairs forming the principal part of the shell, and surrounded at the base by two or three rows of smaller valves, supported on a scaly, short pedicle.—*Obs*. This description will be found to exclude Scalpellum, and Smilium, the valves of which are more equal. The P. Mitellus, Auct. (fig. 37*), has been separated as a genus under the name of Mitellus by some authors, and it is certainly very different from P. polymerus, fig. 37, and P. cornucopia. Pl. ii. fig. 37, 37*.

POLLONTES. Montf. MILIOLA, Bl. A genus of microscopic Foraminifera.

POLYBRANCHIATA. Bl. (Πολυς, *polus*, many; *branchiæ*, gills.) The fifth family of the order Lamellibranchiat6a, Bl. containing the genera Arca, Pectunculus and Nucula, which have a series of small teeth on the hinge.

POLYDONTES. Montf. (Πολυς, *polus*, many; οδος, *odos*, tooth.) A species of Helix, shaped like CAROCOLLA, AND HAVING A NUMBER OF TEETH IN THE APERTURE.

POLYGONAL. MANY-SIDED.

POLYGONUM. SCHUM. (Πολυς, *polus*, many; γωνια, *gonia*, an angle.) A genus composed of species of TURBINELLA, Auct. which have large continuous costæ, so as to present the appearance of many-sided shells. T. polygonus, fig. 383. This generic name may be used to include all those species of Turbinella, Auct. which have very small folds on the columella. Pl. xviii.

POLYGYRA. Say A genus of Heliuciform shells, characterized by the large number of close set whorls, constituting the spire. *Ex*. P. Septemvolvus. Pl. xiii. fig. 275, 276.

POLYLEPAS. Bl. (Πολυς, *polus*, many; λεπας, *lepas*, rock, Linn.) SCALPELLUM, Auct.

POLYMORPHINA. D'Orb. A genus of microscopic Foraminifera.

POLYPHEMUS. Montf. A genus composed of species of ACHATINA, Auct. which have elongated apertures, short spires, and an undulation in the outer lip. P. Glans. Pl. xiv. fig. 288.

POLYPLAXIPHORA. Bl. The second class of the sub-type Malentozoa, Bl. containing the genus Chiton.

POLYSTOMELLA. Lam. A genus of microscopic Foraminifera.

POLYTHALAMACEA. Bl. (Πολυς, *polus*, many; Θαλαμος, *thalamos*, chambers.) The third order of Cephalophora, Bl. the shells of which are described as straight, more or less symmetrically convolute, divided into several chambers. The septa are sometimes, but not always, pierced by one or more siphons. This order is divided into the families,

Orthocerata, Lituacea, Cristacea, Ammonacea, Nautilacea, Turbi-nacea, Turriculacea, all of which contain genera of chambered shells. De Blainville arranges these families according to the degree in which the spires revolve. The first being straight, as the Orthocerata, and the last being so closely coiled up, that the last whorl covers the rest, as in the Nautilacea.

POLYTHALAMIA. Lam. The first division of the order Cephalopoda, Lam. containing the following families of chambered shells, viz. Orthocerata, Lituacea, Cristacea, Sphærulacea, Radiolata, Nautilacea, Ammonacea. Fig. 463 to 484.

POLYTROPA. Sw. A genus of Scolyminæ, Sw. thus described: "Bucci-niform; but the base narrow, and ending in a straight and contracted, but rather short, channel; spire longer, or as long as the aperture; exterior foliated, or tuberculated; inner lip flattened, as in *Purpura*; basal notch small, oblique; no internal channel; crispata. En. Méth. 419, f. 2. Chem. 187, f. 1802. Capilla, Pennant, pl. 72, f. 89, imbricata. Mart. 122. f. 1124. ? rugosa. Chem. f. 1473–4." Sw. p. 305. Pl. xxvi. fig. 546.

POLYXENES. Montf. A genus of microscopic Foraminifera.

POMATIA. Gesner. (Gray, Syn. B. M. p. 133.) A genus of the family of "Cyclostomidæ," described as having "an elongated shell with reflexed lips, and a horny spiral operculum." Also a sub-genus of Snails, containing HELIX pomatia, Auct. (Gray's Turton, p. 135.)

POMATIAS. Hartman, 1821. Species of Cyclostoma, of a turrited tapering form, with reflex lips. Cy. patula, Thesaurus Conchyliorum. Pl. xxviii. fig. 171.

POMUS. Humph. Part of AMPULLARIA, Lamarck.

PORCELLANA. Adanson. MARGINELLA, Auct. Monograph, Thes. Conch. Pl. viii.

PORODRAGUS. Montf. A genus composed of species of Belemnites, placed by De Blainville in the section characterized as swelled near the apex, and straightened towards the base.

PORONIA. Recluz. See KELLIADÆ. P. rubra. Pl. xxvii. fig. 568.

POSIDONIA. Brong. A genus formed on the cast of a bivalve shell, common on schists from Dillemberg.

POSTERIOR. (*After, behind.*) The posterior or hinder part of a bivalve shell, is that in which the siphonal tube of the animal is placed. It is known in the shell, by the direction of the curve in the umbones, which is from the posterior towards the anterior; also by the ligament, which is always placed on the posterior part of the hinge, when it exists only on one side of the umbones; and by the sinus (when there is one) in the palleal impression, which is always near the posterior muscular impression. In some shells, however, it is very difficult for a learner to trace these marks; such bivalves, for instance, as have the ligament spread out on both sides of the umbones; such as are nearly symmetric-al, and have the umbones consequently straight, and a single muscular impression near the centre of the valve. The Brachiopodous bivalves have a different position, with relation to the animal, from the other bivalves, so that the hinge line is the posterior extremity, and the part where the valves open, is the anterior. The posterior extremity of the aperture of a spiral univalve shell, is that nearest to the spire. In patelliform shells the anterior and posterior extremities are disting-uished by the muscular impression, which is annular, enclosing a central disc in the inner surface of the shell, excepting where it is interrupted by the place where the head of the animal lies, which of course is anterior. The posterior is marked *p.* in fig. 119, and 387. See ANTERIOR.

POSTERO-BASAL MARGIN of a bivalve shell is the posterior side of the margin opposite the hinge.

POSTERO-DORSAL MARGIN is the posterior side of the hinge.

POTAMIS or POTAMIDES. Brong. A genus of fresh-water shells resembling Cerithium in the characters of the aperture, but which may be known from that genus by the thick, horny epidermis with which they are coated. (Cerithium, Sow.) We think that these shells should be placed near MELANIA. P. muricata. Pl. xvii. fig. 377.

POTAMOMYA. A genus of shells resembling Corbula, in every respect, except that of being inhabitants of fresh-water. Fig. 498, 499, represents one of these fresh-water Corbulæ. Pl. xxiv.

POTAMOPHILA. Sow. (Ποταμις, *potamis*, river; Φιλιος, *philios*, choice.) "Conques fluviatiles," Lam.—*Descr.* Thick, equivalve, ine-quilateral, trigonal, covered with a greenish brown, smooth, horny epidermis; hinge thickened, broad, with one central, notched cardinal tooth in one valve, and two in the other, with indistinct lateral teeth; ligament large, supported on prominent fulcra; muscular impressions two in each valve, sub-orbicular.—*Obs.* The name given to this shell refers to its place of abode, being found in rivers. It is the Venus sub-viridis of some authors, although being a fresh-water shell, and having an incrassated hinge, and a smooth, thick epidermis, it is most distinct from that genus. It is described by Bowdich under the name Megadesma, on account of its large ligament, and by Lamarck under that of Galathæa, a name previously used by hin for a genus of Crustacea. P. radiata, fig. 115. Megadesma appears to be the prefer-able name, since it has the right of priority over Potamophilia. It is found in Africa. Pl. v. fig. 115.

PRIAMUS. Beck, 1837. Halia, Kisso, 1826. A genus composed of ACHATINA Priamus, Lam. BUCCINUM Stercus-Pulicum, Chemn. Conch. 9. t. 120. f. 1026–7. This shell is ascertained to belong to a marine mollusc, having a horny operculum, and therefore is justly considered to form a distinct genus, allied to the Bucicna and Struthiolariæ. Pl. xxv. fig. 545.

PRISODON. Schum. HYRIA, &c. Auct. Fig. 144.

PRODUCEA. (*Productus*, prominent.) A term applied to the spire of univalve shells, or to any other prominent portion.

PRODUCTA. Sow. (*Productus*, produced.) *Fam.* Brachiopoda, Lam.—*Descr.* Equilateral, inequivalve, thick, striated; one valve generally convex, with the margin reflected; hinge rectilinear, transverse.—*Obs.* The peculiarity of this genus, from which it derives its name, is the manner in which the anterior margins of the valves are drawn out and overwrap each other. The genus is only known in a fossil state. Species occur in Mountain Limestone, and Transition Limestone of older date. P. depressa. Pl. xi. fig. 266*.

PROSERPINA. Gray? Fig. 274, represents a small shell belonging to the Helix tribe, to which it is believed, Mr. Gray has applied the name Proserpina nitida. We do not know how the genus is defined. Pl. xiii. fig. 274.

PROTO. Defr. A fossil shell resembling TURITELLA, but having a spiral band reaching to the centre of each valve. p. terebralis, Bl.

PSAMMOBIA. Lam. *Fam.* Nymphacea, Lam.—*Descr.* Transverse, oblong, slightly gaping at both ends; hinge with two cardinal teeth in one valve, one in the other; ligament supported upon a prominent fulcrum; muscular impressions two in each valve, sub-orbicular, distant; palleal impression with a large sinus; epidermis thin.—*Obs.* The genus thus described includes PSAMMOTÆA of Lamarck, which, according to him, only differs in the number of teeth, and which he says are but "Psammobies dégenerés." The difference appears to be accidental. This genus differs from Tellina in not having a posterior fold in the margin. Pl. iv. fig. 100.

PSAMMACOLA. Bl. (ψαμμος, *psammos*, sand; *cola*, an inhabitant.) A name given by De Blainville to shells of the genus Psammobia, including Psammotæa of Lamarck.

PSAMMOTÆA. See Lam. Psammobia.

PSEUDOLIVA. Sw. A genus of "Eburninæ," Sw. thus described: "Shell thick, oval, oliviform, ventricose: spire very short, acute; base with two parallel grooves, one of which forms a notch at the base of the outer lip; suture slightly channelled; inner upper lip very thick, and turning inwards; aperture with an internal canal. Connects the Turbinellidæ with the Volutidæ. P. plumbea, Chem. 188. f. 1806–1807." Sw. p. 306.

PSILOSTOMATA. Bl. The third family of Aporobranchiata, Bl. containing no genera of shells.

PTEROCEERAS. Auct. (Πτερον, pteron, a wing; κερας, ceras, horn.) Fam. Ailées, Lam.—Descr. Turrited, oval, ventricose, thick, tuberculated,; spire short; aperture oval, terminating in a lengthened canal at both extremities; outer lip thickened, expanded, produced into horn-shaped hollow, thickened spires, with an anterior sinus apart from the canal.—Obs. This genus, containing the shells commmonly called Devil's Claws, Gouty Scorpions, Spiders, &c. is distinguished from Strombus by the digitations of the outer lip. No fossil species are known. Ten recent species are enumerated in Pt. 2. of the Author's Thesaurus Conchyliorum. pl. ii. P. aurantiaca. Pl. xviii. fig. 405.

PTEROCYCLOS. Benson. Syn. B. M. p. 133. A genus formed of species of Cyclostoma, Auct. which have "a groove or hole at the hinder part of the mouth." Ex. Cy. bilabiatum. Thesaurus conchyliorum, Pl. xxv. fig. 82.

PTEROPODA. Lam. (πτερον, pteron, a wing; πους, pous, a foot.) The first order of the class mollusca, Lam. consisting of molluscs whose organs of locomotion consist of a pair of wing-shaped fins. This order contains the genera Hyalæa, Cllio, Cleodora, Spiratella, Cymbulia, and Pneumoderma. To which may be added other genera enumerated in explanation of figures 220 to 226. They may be thus distinguished.

1. Atlanta. Shaped like Nautilus, symmetrical. Fig. 220
2. Spiratella. Spiral, not symmetrical. Fig. 224.
3. Creseis. Straight, thorn-shaped. Fig. 222.
4. Vaginula. Straight, widened in the centre; apex pointed. Fig. 225.
5. Cuvieria. The same; apex blunt. Fig. 223.
6. Cleodora. Aperture with three spines; apex recurved. Fig. 221.
7. Hyalæa. Vaulted, open extremity, three-cornered; apex tridentate. Fig. 226.

PTEROPODA. Bl. The second family of Nucleobranchiata, Bl. the shells of which are described as symmetrical, extremely thin, transparent, longitudinally enrolled, either forwards or backwards. The animals are remarkable for a pair of broad, flat, swimming paddles or membranaceous fins, from which the family derives its name. It contains, in the system of De Blainville, the genera Atlanta, Spiratella, and Argonauta, to which may probably be added Pharetrium, König; Entalis, Defrance.

PULLUSTRA. Sow. Tapes, Megeree. Fam. Conques Marines, Lam.—Descr. Equivalve, ovate or oblong, transverse, inequilateral; hinge with three diverging cardinal teeth in each valve, notched at the terminations; muscular impressions two in each valve; palleal impression having a large sinus; ligament external, partly hidden by the dorsal margin.—Obs. This genus includes the Venerirupes of Lamarck, and several species of his Veneres, they are found in the sand on the shores of temperate and tropical climates. See Monogram in Sowerby's

Thesaurus Conchyliorum, pl. 13, 14; and our figure of P. textile, pl. vi. fig. 120.

PULMONOBRANCHIATA. Bl. The first order of the first section of Paracephalophora monica, containing the families Limnacea, Auriculacea, and Limacinea.

PULVINITES. Defr. (Pulvinus, a cushion.) Fam. Malleacea, Lam.—Descr. Sub-equivalve, inequilateral, compressed, thin, slightly gaping posteriorly; one valve flat, the other rather concave; hinge linear, short, divided into perpendicular grooves; muscular impressions two, one sub-central, the other above it, nearer the hinge.—Obs. This fossil shell is imperfectly known, and it is difficult to give a sufficient reason for separating it from Perna. It comes from the Baculite limestone of Normandy. Pl. x. fig. 170, P. Adansonii.

PUNCTUATED. (Punctatus, spotted or dotted.) For example, see Conus Nussatella. Fig. 460.

PUNCTICULIS. Sw. A sub-genus of "Coronaxis," Sw. (Conus) described in Swainson's Malacology, p. 311.

PUNCTURELLA. Lowe. Cemoria, Leach.

PUPA. Auct. Fam. Colimacea, Lam.; Limacinea, Bl.—Descr. Cylindrical, generally ribbed; spire long, obtuse, composed of numerous slowly increasing whorls; aperture sub-quadrate, rounded anteriorly, entire; outer lip thickened; columella plated.—Obs. This genus is composed of land shells very variable in form, differing from Bulinus in the numerous slowly increasing whorls of the spire, and in the plicæ on the columella, and from Clausilia in the want of a clausium. Britain, Southern Europe, East and West Indies, Mexico, &c. P. Uva. Pl. xiv. fig. 291.

PUPELLA. Sw. A sub-genus of Clausilia. Lard. Cyclop. Malac. p. 334.

PUPILLA. Sw. A sub-genus of Pupa, P. marginata, Auct. (Gray's Turton, p. 196.)

PUPINA. Vignard. Moulinsia, Grateloup. Fam. Colimacea, Lam.—Descr. Pupiform, sub-cylindrical; last whorl less than the preceding; surface brilliantly polished; suture of the spire enamelled; aperture circular; peritreme thickened; a notch at the base of the inner lip; operculum horny, spiral.—Obs. The species upon which this genus was originally founded, and described in the "Annals des Sciences Naturelles," tome 18, p. 439, (December, 1829,) is a small pupiform shell, having nothing to distinguish it but the enamelled suture and the notch in the aperture: characters quite insufficient in themselves for the purpose of generic distinction; at the same time sufficient to lead M. de Ferussac to the suspicion of its having an operculum. The next species, described by Grateloup under the name of Moulinsia Nunezii, (Ann. Soc. Linn. Burd, Nov. 1840), presents more remarkable characters, having the spire turned backwards and the penultimate whorl disproportionately large. Seven additional species have been lately brought to this country from the Philippine Islands by Mr. Cumming. They are described by the author in the Zoological Proceedings for 1841, and an illustrated monograph of the whole genus is published in the Thesaurus Conchyliorum, Part I, by the Author. The genus is divided into the genera "Callia," Gray, "Registoma," Hassell, and "Pupina." It may be observed that in one of the new species, the notch in the peritreme almost disappears, leaving a very slight sinus. Pl. xxv. fig. 524, 526, 527, 528.

PURPURA. Auct. ("The shell-fish from which purple is taken," Plin.) Fam. Purpurifera, lam. Entomostomata, Bl.—Descr. Oval or oblong, thick; spire for the most part short, sometimes rather longer; external surface generally sulcated, granulated, tuberculated or muricated; aperture long, oval, somewhat dilated, emarginated anteriorly; outer lip cren-

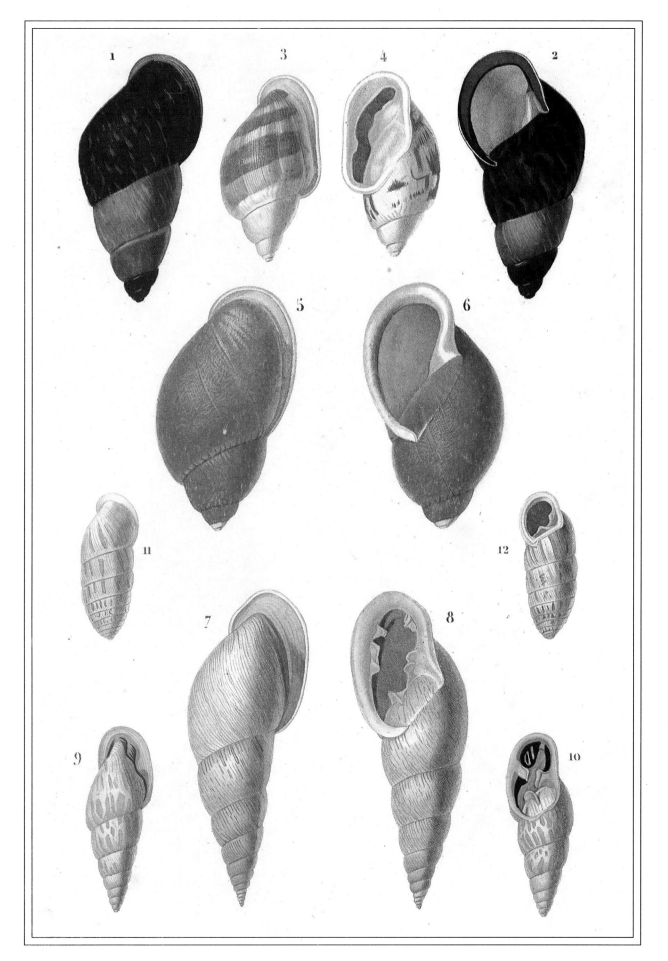

1, 2. *Bulime de Mendor*. (Bulimus
     Mendorensis, *Brod.*)
3, 4. *Bulime buriné*. (Bulimus
     signatus, *Wagn.*)
5, 6. *Bulime pudique*. (Bulimus
     pudicus, *Muller.*)
7, 8. *Bulime pantagruel*. (Bulimus
     pantagruelinus.)
9, 10. *Bulime rongeur*. (Bulimus
     exesus, *Spix.*)
11. 12. *Maillot chrysalide*. (Pupa
     Chrysalis, *Fer.*)

ated, acute; columella flattened; operculum horny, with the nucleus lateral, thin towards the columella.—*Obs.* True purpuræ are to be found in the Lamarckian genera Buccinum, Ricinula, and others. They may be generally distinguished by the flatness of the columellar lip, and by the short canal or emargination, which is not reflected or raised, as in Buccinum. The species are very numerous and very variable in form, inhabiting the seas of temperate and tropical climates. The animals secrete a purple liquor, which has been used advantageously for dyeing; the origin of the famous Tyrian dye. Reeve's Monograph contains about 80 species. *Ex.* P. persicula. Pl. xix. fig. 44.

PURPURIFERA. Lam. (*Purpura*, purple; *fero*, to carry.) A family belonging to the second section of Lamarck's order Trachelipoda, the shells of which are described as having a very short recurved, or ascending canal, or else only a notch between the inner and outer lips. The name Purpurifera has been given to the family, because the animals which it includes and particularly the genus Purpura, contain the colouring matter from which the ancients obtained the well-known splendid purple. This family contains the following genera.

1. CASSIS. Outer lip thick, reflected, denticulated, canal turned suddenly over the back; spire short; including *Cassidea* and *Cypræcassis*. Fig. 410 to 412.

2. CASSIDARIA. Canal turned gently upwards. Fig. 407, 408.

3. ONISCIA. Inner lip granulated; canal short. Fig. 409.

4. BUCCINUM. Outer lip thickened not reflected; canal short; including *Cyllene* and *Phos*. Fig. 416, 421, 422, 425.

5. NASA. The same, with a notch or tooth at the extremity of the columella; including *Cyclops*. Fig. 423, 424.

6. DOLIUM. Swelled, grooved spirally; outer lip not reflected. Fig. 420.

7. PURPURA. Aperture large; columellar lip flat; including Tritonidea. Fig. 414, 415.

8. MONOCEROS. The same, with a tooth on the outer lip. Fig. 417.

9. CONCHOLEPAS. Patelliform; aperture as large as the shell. Fig. 417.

10. RICINULA. Columellar and outer lips granulated, denticulated, outer lip digitated; including *Tribulus*. Fig. 413.

11. TRICHOTROPIS. Hairs on the epidermis, along the keels. Fig. 429.

12. TEREBRA. Elongated, with a spiral groove near the suture of the whorls. Fig. 428.

13. BULLIA. Short; aperture wide; outer lip marginated. Fig. 427.

14. EBURNA. Like Buccinum, but the outer lip not thickened. Fig. 426.

15. HARPA. With varices at regular intervals. Fig. 419.

PUSIA. Sw. A sub-genus of Tiara (Mitra.) (Sw. Malac. p. 320.)

PUSIODON. Sw. A genus of "Lucerninæ," Sw. (Helix) thus described: "Shell flattened, smooth; the body-whorl large, and much dilated at the aperture; spire small, flat, of three or four contracted whorls; aperture very oblique, sinuated, or obsoletely toothed at the base of the outer lip, which is spreading and sub-reflected; inner lip obsolete; umbilicus open. Zonaria Chemn. 132. f. 1188. auriculata, Zool. Ill. I. pl. 6." Sw. Malac. p. 330.

PUSIONELLA. Gray. Fusus Nifal, &c.

PUSIOSTOMA. Sw. A genus of the family "Columbellinæ," Sw. Thus described: "general form of Columbella, but the outer lip is only toothed in the middle, where it is greatly thickened; inner lip convex between the granular teeth; punctata, E. M. 374. f. 4. mendicaria, 375. f. 10. turturina, 314. f. 2. fulgurans. Lam." Sw. malac. p. 313.

PUSTULARIA. Sw. A genus of "Cypræinæ," sw. thus described: "Shell generally marked by elevated pustules; aperture narrow and linear; the extremities more or less produced; the teeth continued beyond, and frequently forming elevated striæ across the lips. P. Cicercula, P. Globulus." Sw. Malac. p. 324.

PYCNODUNTA. Fischer. A genus of brachiopoda. Pl. xii. fig. 117, 118.

PYLORIDEA. Bl. The ninth family of the order Lamellibranchiata, Bl. the shells of which are described as nearly always regular, rarely otherwise, nearly always equivalve, gaping at both extremities; hinge incomplete, the teeth becoming gradually obsolete; two distinct muscular impressions; palleal impression very flexuous posteriorly. This family is divided into: Section 1. Ligament internal; Pandora, Thracia, Anatina, Mya, Lutricola. Section 2. Ligament external; Psammocola, Soletellina, Solen, Sanguinolaria, Solenocurtus, Solinomya, Panopæa, Glycimeris, Saxicava, Byssomya, Rhomboides, Hiatella, Gastrochæna, Clavagella, Aspergillum.

PYRAMIDAL. (*Pyramidalis*.) Resembling a pyramid in form. *Ex.* Cerithium Telescopium, fig. 378.

PYRAMIDELLA. Lam. (*A little pyramid*.) *Fam.* Pliacea, Lam. AURICULACEA, Bl.—*Descr.* Pyramidal, smooth, polished; spire long, pointed, composed of numerous whorls; aperture small, modified by the last whorl, rounded anteriorly; outer lip slightly expanded; columella tortuous, with several folds. This is a genus of small, polished, marine shells. Pyramidella Terebellum. Pl. xv. fig. 342.

PYRAMIS. Schum. 1817. Testus, Montfort, 1810. Trochus Obeliscus. Lamarck.

PYRAZUS. Montf. Part of the genus POTAMIS, Brongniart.

PYRELLA. Sw. A genus consisting of Turbinella Spirilla, Auct. and similar species, having a long channel, a pyriform outline, and one strong plait at the base of the columella, the apex of the spire is enlarged. P. Spirillus, fig. 344. (The proper term would be Spirilla.) Pl. xxxi. fig. 550.

PYRIFORM. (*Pyrum*, a pear; *forma*, shape.) Shaped like a pear, i.e. large and rounding at one end, and gradually tapering at the other. *Ex.* Pyrula, fig. 390.

PYRGO. Defr. A genus of microscopic Foraminifera.

PYRGOMA. Auct. (Πυργος, *pyrgus*, a tower.) *Order* Sessile Cirripedes, Lam.—*Descr.* Composed of a single conical, hollow paries, with a small aperture closed by an operculum of four valves, and supported upon a cup-shaped base.—*Obs.* The genera into which Leach has divided this genus are Pyrgoma, Adna, and Megatrema; his genera Nobia and Savignium differ in having but two valves for the operculum. Pyrgoma differs from Creusia in having the body of the shell, i.e. the parietal cone, simple, not divided into valves. Pl. i. fig. 31. Pl. xxiv. fig. 489, 490.

PYRULA. Lamarck. Family Canalifera, generally turbinate, with few angular whorls; aperture terminating in a canal; columella smooth. The Ficulæ being removed, there remain a considerable number of species under this name, typified by P. Melongena, &c.

PYRUM. Humph. PYRULA, Lam.

PYTHINA. Hinds. Voyage of the Sulphur. P. 70. Pl. xix. fig. 8, 9. A bivalve shell thus described, (translation) "transverse, subæquilateral, æquivalve. One valve with one small central and two lateral teeth; the other valve with two lateral teeth; ligament internal; two rounded muscular impressions; palleal impression rather straight, without a sinus. There is only one species described, the P. Deshayesiana. Pl. xxvii. fig. 571.

QUADRATE. (*Quadratus*.) Square, applied when the outline of shells is formed by nearly straight lines meeting at right angles.

QUINQUELOCULINA. D'Orbigny. A genus of microscopic Foraminifera.

QUOYIA. Desh. MS. Planaxis decollatus Quoy et Gaimard.

RADIATING. (*Radians.*) A term applied to the ribs, striæ, bands of colours, &c. when they meet in a point at the umbones of a bivalve shell, and spread out towards the ventral margin.—*Ex.* The bands of colour in Tellina radiata, fig. 105.

RADICATED. (*Radix*, a root.) Attached, and as it were rooted by means of a fibrous byssus.

RADIOLATA. Lam. A family belonging to the dorer Cephalopoda, Lam. The shells belonging to it are described as discoidal, with the spire central, and the chambers radiating from the centre to the circumference. This family contains the genera Rotalina, Lenticulina, and Placentula.

RADIOLITES. A genus belonging to the family of Rudistes, differing from Sphærulites, in having both the valves more conical.

RADIUS. Montf. A genus composed of Ovulum Volva, Auct. and other similar species, having a long attenuated canal at each extremity. Pl. xx. fig. 442.

RADIX. Montf. A genus composed of species of Limnæa, having a short spire and wide aperture.—*Ex.* L. aperta, fig. 309.

RADSIA. Gray. Chiton Barnesii, and similar species.

RAMIFIED. (*Ramus*, a branch.) Branched out.—*Ex.* The varices of some Murices, &c.

RAMPHIDOMA. Schum. Pollicipes, Leach.

RAMOSE. (*Ramosus*, branched. Spread out into branches.) *Ex.* Murex inflatus, fig. 395.

RANELLA. Auct. (*Rana*, a frog.) *Fam.* Canalifera, Lam. Siphonostomata, Bl.—*Descr.* Oval or oblong, depressed, thick, with two rows of continuous varices, skirting the outline, one on each side; spire rather short, pyramidal, acute, aperture oval, terminating in a canal at each extremity; outer lip thickened within, crenulated, or denticulated, forming an external varix; inner lip spread over a protion of the body whorl.—*Obs.* The shells composing this well-defined genus, are for the most part covered with tuberculations, and granulations, and from the colour and squat shape of some species, have been likened to frogs. The Ranellæ are mostly inhabitants of the East Indian seas. The few fossil species known, occur in the tertiary beds. The two continuous rows of varices skirting the spire, distinguish this genus from Triton, which it nearly approaches, and into which some species run by imperceptible gradations. Mr. Reeve's Monograph contains 50 species. Pl. xvii. fig. 393, 394.

RANGIA. Desmoulins. Gnathodon, Gray.

RAPANUS. Schum? A genus consisting of species of Pyrula, Auct. which are thin, much inflated, with short canals. P. papyracea. Pl. xvii. fig. 389.

RAPELLA. Sw. A genus of "Pyrulinæ," Sw. thus described: "Shell ventricose, generally thin, almost globose; the base suddenly contracted, and forming a short canal, the channel almost obsolete; umbilicus large, partly concealed by the inner lip. R. papyracea. En. Méth. 436, f. 1." Sw. p. 307. Rapanus, Schum. Fig. 389.

RAPHANISTER. Montf. A species of madrepore, described as a shell.

RAPUM. Humph. Turbinella, Lam.

RAZOR SHELL. A common name by which shells of the genus Solen are known in the market.

RECTILINEAR. (*Rectus*, right; *linea*, a line.) In a straight line. *Ex.* The hinge of Byssoarca Noœ, fig. 132.

RECURVED. (*Re*, back; *curvo*, to bend.) Turned backwards; the term,

when applied to symmetrical conical univalves, is used to signify that the apex is turned towards the posterior margin, as in Emarginula, fig. 241.

REFLECTED. (*Reflected*, to fold back.) Turned, or folded backwards. *Ex.* The edge of the outer lip in Bulinus, fig. 282, is *reflected*, while that of Cypræa, fig. 445 to 450, is *inflected*.

REGISTOMA. Hassell, 1824. Pupina vitrœa, Thesaurus Conchyliorum, Pl. iv. fig. 6.

REMOTE. (*Remotus*, distant.) Remote lateral teeth in a bivalve shell, are those that are placed at a distance from the cardinal teeth. *Ex.* The lateral teeth of Aphrodita, (fig. 123) are remote; those of Donax, (fig. 108) are near.

RENIELLA. Sw. A sub-genus of Malleus. Lardn. Cyclop. Malac. p. 886. Gray states it to be only a distorted specimen of Vulsella, Syn. B. M. p. 145.

RENIFORM. (*Ren*, a kidney; *forma*, shape.) Shaped like a kidney. *Ex.* The aperture of Ampullaria, fig. 318.

RENULINA. Lam. A genus of microscopic Foraminifera.

REOPHAX. Montf. A genus of microscopic Orthocerata, Bl.

REPENT. (*Repens*, creeping.) A term applied to those shells, which, being attached by the whole length of their shell, give the idea of creeping or crawling. *Ex.* Vermilia, fig. 7.

RETICULATED. (*Reticulatus.*) Resembling net-work.

RETIFERA. Bl. The first family of the order Cervicobranchiata, Bl. containing the genus Patella.

REVERSED or Sinistral Shells, are those in which the aperture is on the left side of the shell, while it is held with the mouth downwards, and towards the observer. *Ex.* Balea, fig. 296. Attached bivalves are said to be reversed, when the left valve is free, instead of the right; a circumstance which sometimes occurs in Chama and Ostrea.

RHEDA. Humph. Hyalæa, Lam.

RHINOCLAVIS. Sw. A genus of "Cerithinæ," Sw. thus described: "channel curved backwards, in an erect position; inner lip very thick, with a tumid margin; pillar generally with a central plait; operculum ear-shaped; lineatum. En. M. 443, fig. 3, Vertagus. Ib. f. 2, subulatum. Lam. No. 23, fasciatum. Mart. 157, f. 1481. obeliscus, En. Méth. 443, f. 4; faluco, Ib. f. 5, (aberrant), semi-granosum. Ib. 443, f. 1, asperum. Mart. 157, f. 1483.

RHINOCURUS. Montf. A genus of microscopic Foraminifera.

RHINODOMUS. Sw. A genus of "Scolyminæ," Sw. thus described: No internal grove; shell clavate; the spire longer than, or equal with the aperture; the whorls with ridges or longitudinal varices, and rendered hispid by transverse grooves; inner lip wanting; pillar with a terminal fold; aperture striated; outer lip with a basal sinus. R. senticosus, Chem. tab. 193. f. 1864–1866.

RHIZORUS. Montf. A genus described from a microscopic shell, appearing to be a cylindrical Bulla.

RHODOSTOMA. Sw. A sub-genus of "Turbiniæ," Sw. p. 344.

RHOMBOIDAL. (ρομβοειδος, *rhomboeidus.*) Having a rhombic form, i.e. four-sided; two sides meeting at acute, two at obtuse, angles. Conchologists are not very strict in the application of this term, for, indeed, a perfect rhomboidal figure could not be found among shells.

RHOMBOIDES. Bl. A genus described as resembling Byssomya as to the shell, but differing as to the animal. Mytilus rugosus, Gmelin. Hypogæa barbata, Poli.

RHOMBUS. Montf. (ρομβος, *rhombos*, a rhomb.) A genus consisting of species of Conus, having a rhomboidal or quadrilateral form and a coronated spire. *Ex.* Conus nocturnus, fig. 459.

RICINULA. Lamarck, 1812. "Sistrum," Montfort, 1810, has the

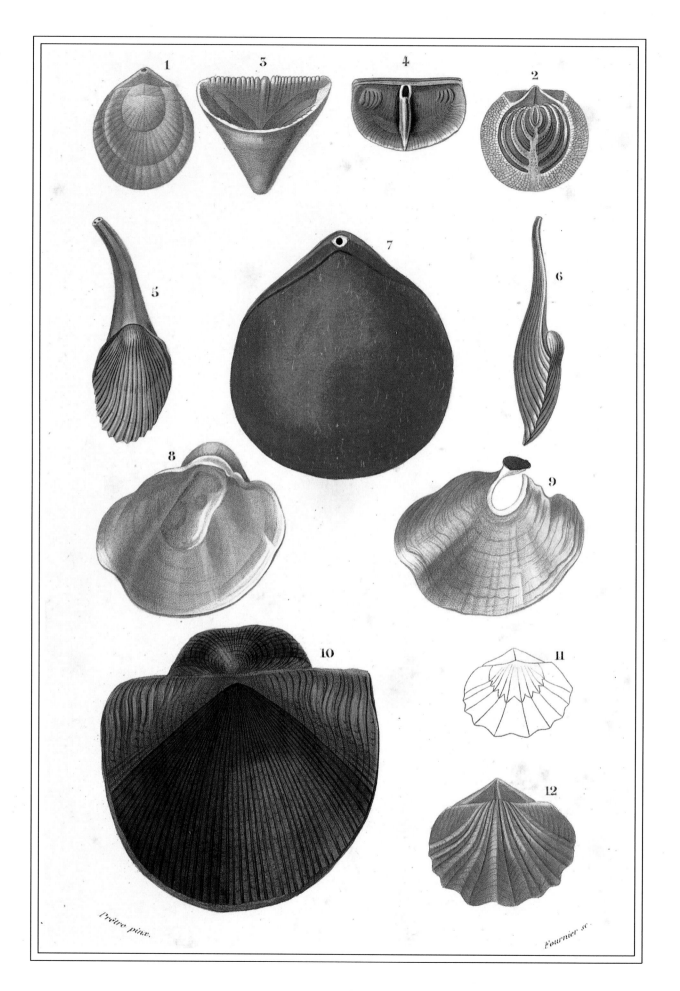

1, 2. *Thécidée rayonnante*. (Thecidea radians, *Def.*)

3, 4. *Calcéole sandaline*. (Calceola sandalina, *Lamk.*)

5, 6. *Térébratule lyre*. (Terebratula lyra, *Lamk.*)

7. *Térébratule lenticulaire*. (Terebratula lenticularis, *Desh.*)

8, 9. *Anomie pélure d'oignon*. (Anomia ephippium, *Lin.*)

10. *Producte treillissé*. (Productus antiquatus, *Sow.*)

11, 12. *Térébratule de Say*. (Terebratula Sayi, *Morton.*)

Prêtre pinx.

Fournier sc.

priority. (Resembling the seed-vessel of the *Ricinus.*) *Fam.* Purpurifera, Lam. Entomostomata, Bl.—*Descr.* Sub-ovate, thick, tuberculated; spire short; aperture narrow, terminating anteriorly in a short canal; outer lip thickened, denticulated within, digitated without; columellar lip spread over a portion of the body whorl, and granulated.—*Obs.* This interesting genus is composed of some neat little shells allied to Purpura, from which they are distinguished by the finger-like branching of the outer lip, and the granulations of the columella. More than 50 species are described in Reeve's Monograph. R. Horrida, Pl. xix. fig. 413.

RIGHT. See DEXTRAL.

RIMULA. Couthoy. CEMORIA, Leach.

RIMULARIA. Defrance. A genus consisting of a minute species of EMARGINULA, Auct. which has a fissure near the margin, but not reaching it. R. Blainvilii, fig. 243.

RIMULINA. D'Orbigny. A genus of microscopic Foraminifera.

RINGICULA. Deshayes. A genus founded on Auricula ringens of Lamarck and several small fossils, resembling in some respects Pedipes of Adanson; they would belong to Tornatella, were it not for the lips being thickened and marginated. Pl. xxv. fig. 540, 541. A. ringens.

RISELLA. Gray, 1840. Small, vertically depressed species of Trochidæ, with flat undersides. Tr. Melanostomus.

RISSOA. Freminville. *Fam.* Ellipsostomata, Bl. Melaniana, Lam.—*Descr.* Oblong, turrited, acuminated; spire long, consisting of numerous whorls; aperture round or oval, pointed posteriorly, dilated anteriorly; outer lip slightly thickened, emarginated, operculum horny.—*Obs.* The Rissoæ are small white, marine shells, considered by some authors as resembling Melaniæ, but placed by Sowerby near the Scalariæ. They are principally from the shores of the Mediterranean, and are also very abundant on the British shores, as well as the East and West Indian. K. reticulata. R. reticulata. Pl. xv. fig. 346.

ROBULUS. Montf. A genus of microscopic Foraminifera.

ROLLUS. Montf. A genus composed of CONUS Geographus, Auct. Pl. xxi. fig. 462, and other species, rather cylindrical in form, and having a coronated spire.

ROSALINA. D'Orb. A genus of microscopic Foraminifera.

ROSTELLARIA. Lamarck, 1801. (From *rostrum*, a beak.) *Fam.* Alatæ, Lam. Siphonostomata, Bl.—*Descr.* Turrited, fusiform, thick, smooth or ribbed; aperture oval, terminating anteriorly in a long canal, posteriorly in a channel running up the spire; outer lip dilated, thickened, sometimes digitated, running up all or part of the spire, with a sinus near the anterior canal; inner lip smooth, spread over part of the body whorl and of the spire. The Red Sea and the Indian Ocean produce the few known species of this genus.—*Obs.* HIPPOCHRENES is the name given by De Montfort, to those fossil species which have the outer lip simple and very much dilated. Four recent species are enumerated in the Thesaurus, Pt. i. by the Author. Ex. R. Curvirostrum. Pl. xviii. fig. 402.

ROSTRATED. (From *rostrum*, a beak.) Having one or more protruding points, as Tellina rostrata.

ROTALIA. Lam. A genus of microscopic Foraminifera. The same as Rotalites of De Montfort.

ROTELLA. Lam. 1822. Previously HELICINA, Lamarck. (*A little wheel.*) *Fam.* Turbinacea, Lam.—*Descr.* Orbicular, generally smooth, shining; spire conical, depressed, short; aperture subtrigonal; outer lip thin, angulated near the centre; inner lip spread over the surface of the whorls, forming a thickened disc. Operculum horny, orbicular, spiral, with numerous whorls.—*Obs.* The pretty little shells thus described are found in seas of tropical climates. They are distinguished from other genera of the family by their lenticular form and the orbicular callosity of the under surface. Fig. 357, R. vestiaria. Pl. xvi.

RUDISTES. Lam. A family of the order Conchifera Monomyaria, Lam. the shells of which are described as irregular, very inequivalve, without distinct umbones; the ligament, hinge and animal entirely unknown. The shells contained in this family may be thus distinguished.

1. CALCEOLA. Large valve conical; attached by a flat space between the umbones, which form the extremities of the shell. Fig. 194.
2. HIPPURITES. Large valve cylindrical, with two internal lobes or varices. Fig. 198.
3. SPHÆRULITES. Large valve attached, including *Radiolites*. Birostrites is proved to be the cast of a Sphærulites. Fig. 193, 196.
4. HIPPONYX. Flat valve attached, upper valve conical. Fig. 199, 200.

RUDISTES. Bl. The second order of the class Acephalophora, Bl. containing the genera Sphærulites, Crania, Hippurites, Radiolites, Birostrites and Calceola.

RUDOLPHUS. Lam. MONOCEROS, Auct.

RUFOUS. Reddish brown.

RUGOSE. Rough, rugged.

RUPELLARIA. Fl. de Belvue. An unfigured shell placed by De Blainville in a division of the genus Venerirupis.

RUPICOLA. Fl. de Belvue. A shell described by De Blainville as an equivalve, terebrating species of ANATINA. A. rupicola, Lam.

SABINEA. A genus of shells resembling small species of LITTORINA, as L. Ulvæ, &c. of our shores.

SADDLE OYSTER. PLACUNA Sella, so called on account of a resemblance in shape to a saddle; the part near the umbones being flat, and the ventral margins being turned up in a sort of fluting or peak.

SAGITTA. (*An arrow.*) An ancient name for Belemnites.

SALIENT. (*Saliens.*) Jutting out, prominent.

SALPACEA. Bl. The second family of the order Heterobranchiata, Bl. containing no genera of shells.

SANDALINA. Schum. CREPIDULINA, Lam. A genus of microscopic Foraminifera.

SANGUINOLARIA. Lamarck, 1801. (*Sanguis*, blood.) *Fam.* Nymphacea, Lam. Pyloridea, Bl.—*Descr.* Equivalve, inequilateral, transverse, sub-ovate, rounded anteriory, sub-rostrate posteriorly, compressed, thin, covered with a shining epidermis, gaping at the sides; hinge with two cardinal teeth in each valve, and an external ligament supported upon a prominent fulcrum; muscular impressions two in each valve, lateral, irregular, palleal impressions with a large sinus.—*Obs.* This description is made to exclude some of Lamarck's species of Sanguinolaria, such as S. occidens, S. rugosa, which are Psammobiæ; and to include others which he has left out. The Sanguinolariæ are sub-rostrated posteriorly, while the Psammobiæ are sub-quadrate, and have a posterior angle. S. rosea. Sandy shores of tropical climates. Pl. iv. fig. 98.

SARACENARIA. Defr. A genus of microscopic Foraminifera.

SAVIGNIUM. Leach. A genus of Sessile Cirripedes, described as composed of four valves soldered together, and a convex bivalve operculum; the ventral and posterior valve on each side being soldered together, in other respects resembling PYRGOMA. Pl. i. fig. 30.

SAXICAVA. Fl. de Belvue. Journ de. Ph. an. 10. (*Saxum*, a stone; *cava*, a hollow.) *Fam.* Lithophagidæ, Lam. Pyloridea, Bl.—*Descr.* Transverse, irregular, generally oblong, inequilateral, sub-equivalve, gaping anteriorly; ligament external; muscular impressions two, lateral; palleal impression interrupted, not sinuated; hinge, when young with sometimes two or three minute, obtuse, generally indistinct, cardinal teeth; which become obsolete when full grown—*Obs*. Several genera have been founded only upon the difference between the young and old shell of the same species of this genus. The Saxicavæ are found in the little hollows of rocks; in cavities on the backs of oysters, of roots of seaweeds, &c. in northern and temperate climates. S. rugosa. Pl. iv. fig. 94.

SCABRICULA. Sw. A sub-genus of Mitræ, consisting of species which have a roughened external surface, &c. Sw. Malac. p. 319.

SCABROUS. Rough.

SCALA. Klein. SCALARIA, Auct.

SCALARIA. Lamarck, 1801. *Fam*. Scalariana, Lam. Cricostomata, Bl.—*Descr*. Turrited, oval or oblong; spire long, composed of rounded, sometimes separate whorls, surrounded by regular concentric ribs; aperture oval, peristome reflected, continuous, entire—*Obs*. The typical species of this genus, commonly called the Wentletrap, (S. pretiosa) is celebrated for the beautiful appearance caused by the numerous ribs encircling the whorls, and formerly produced an immense price in the market. It is brought from China. There are many smaller species, some of which are equally elegant. Fig. 351, S. Pallasii, Kiener. The Monograph in Sowerby's Thesaurus contains 93 species.

SCALARINA. Lam. A family belonging to the first section of the order Trachelipoda, Lam. The shells belonging to it are described as having the inner and outer lips continuous, without a canal, emargination, or other division. In this respect the family is stated to differ from the Turbinacea, and is therefore separated. The genera may be distinguished as follows:-

    1. VERMETUS. Irregularly twisted, like Serpula. Fig. 345.

    2. EULIMA. Pyramidal; apex contorted; including *Bonellia*. Fig. 347, 348.

    3. RISSOA. Pyramidal, straight, consisting of a few whorls. Fig. 346.

    4. SCALARIA. With external varices. Fig. 351.

    5. CIRRUS. Trochiform. Fig. 349.

    6. ENOMPHALUS. Orbicular. Fig. 350.

    7. DELPHINULA. Few whorls, rapidly increasing. Fig. 352.

SCALLOP. The common name for shells of the genus Pecten, the larger species of which were worn by pilgrims to the Holy Land in the time of the Crusades.

SCALPELLUM. Leach. 1817. (A little knife or lancet). *Order*, Pedunculated Cirripedes, Lam. *Descr*. Flat, quadrated, acuminated, composed of thirteen valves, one dorsal, arcuated; one pair apicial, acuminated: one pair ventral; two pair lateral, small, sub-quadrate; pedicle scaly. *Obs*. This genus and *Smilium*, are the only Pedunculated Cirripedes which have thirteen valves; in the latter genus, which we think should at any rate be united to this, the valves are somewhat differently placed, and the pedicle is said to be smooth. Scalpellum vulgare. British. Pl. ii. fig. 35. and S. peronii, Pl. ii. fig. 36.

SCAPHA. Klein. (*A boat*.) NAVICELLA, Auct.

SCAPHA. Voluta vespertilio, &c.

SCAPHANDER. Montf. A sub-genus of Bullidæ represented by BULLA lignaria, Auct. Fig. 251. Several species are described in Adams' Monograph, No. 11. Sowerby's Thesaurus.

SCAPHELLA. Sw. A genus of the family "Volutinæ," Sw. thus described: "Shell smooth, almost polished; outer lip thickened internally; suture enamelled; lower plaits the smallest; apex of the spire various: 1. fusiformis. Sw. Bligh. Cat. 2, undulatus. *Ex*. Conch. pl. 27. 3.

Junonia, Thesaurus Conchyliorum, pl. 49. fig. 44. stromboides. 5. papillosa. Sw. Sow. gen." Sw. Malac. p. 318.

SCAPHITES. (*A boat*.) *Fam*. ammonacea, Lam. and Bl.—*Descr*. convolute, chambered, closely related to the Ammonites, from which it differs in the last whorl being eccentrically straightened, and lengthened, and again incurved towards the extremity. Only known in a fossil state. S æqualis. Pl. xxiii. fig. 481.

SCAPHULA. Sw. A genus of "OLIVINÆ," Sw. thus described: "Spire very short, thick, abtuse, and not defined; aperture very wide, with only two or three oblique plaits at the base. OLIVA patula, *Sow*. Tank. Cat. 2331. (*b*") (Sw. P. 332.) and O. auricularia, Lamarck.

SCARABUS. Montf. (*Scarabæus*, a kind of beetle.) *Fam*. Colimacea, Lam. Auriculacea, Fer.—*Descr*. Oval, somewhat compressed, smooth, with slightly raised varices; spire equal in length to the aperture, pointed, consisting of various whorls; aperture ovate, rounded anteriorly, pointed posteriorly, modified by the last whorl; outer lip sub-reflected, with several prominent folds on the inner edge; inner lip spread over a portion of the body whorls, with several prominent folds.—*Obs*. The shells of this genus are found like the Auriculæ, in marshy places. C. Imbrium is said to have been found on the tops of mountains, by Captain Freycinet. S. imbrium. Pl. xiv. fig. 299.

SCHIZOCHITON. Gray. Ch. incisus, having a notch in the margin.

SCHIZODESMA. Gray. A genus composed of species of MACTRA, Auct. with the ligament placed in an external slit. M. Spengleri. Pl. iv. fig. 81.

SCISSURELLA. D'Orbigny. (*Scissus*, cut.) *Fam*. Turbinacea, Lam.—*Descr*. Sub-globose, umbilicated, with a spiral groove terminating at the margin of the outer lip in a slit; spire short; aperture oval, modified by the last whorl; outer lip sharp, with a deep slit near the spire. Recent on the coast of Britain; fossil in the Calcaire-grossièr.—*Obs*. This genus, consisting of small shells, is known from Pleurotomaria by the shortness of the spire; the latter genus being trochiform. S. elatoir. Pl. xv. fig. 340.

SCOLYMUS. Sw. A genus of the family "Scolyminæ." Sw. (Turbinella) thus described: "Sub-fusiform, armed with foliated spines; spire shorter; pillar with distinct plaits in the middle." The species enumerated are, "cornigerus, pugilaris, Globulus, Rhinoceros, ceramicus, Capitellum, umbilicaris, mitis." Sw. Malac. p. 304.

SCROBICULARIA. Schumacher. A genus belonging to the Tellinidæ, having no lateral teeth, but small cardinal teeth and the internal cartilage placed in an oblique spathular fulcrum in each valve. S. piperita, Forbes and Hanley, Brit. Mollusca, pl. xv. fig. 5.

SCONSIA. Gray, 1847. Cassidaria striata, *Lamarck*, &c.

SCORTIMUS. Montf. A genus of microscopis Foraminifera.

SCROBICULATED. (*Scrobiculus*, a little ditch or furrow.) Having small ditches or furrows marked on the surface.

SCUTELLA. Brod. (*Scutellum*, a little shield.) *Fam*. Phyllidiana, Lam.—*Descr*. Shaped like Ancylus, pearly within; apex posteriorly inclined, central, involute; muscular impressions two, oblong, ovate, lateral; aperture large, ovate.—*Obs*. This genus is intermediate between Ancylus and Patella; while in the aspect of the beak, the observer is reminded of Navicella. BRODERIPIA, Gray, contains part of this genus typified by S. rosea. pl. xxiv. fig. 508, 509. Scutella crenulata.

SCUTIBRANCHIATA. Bl. (*Scutum*, a shield; *branchiæ*, gills.) The third order of Paracepalophora Hermaphrodita, Bl. containing animals with patelliform, but not symmetrical shells, and divided into the families Otidea and Calyptracea.

SCUTUM. Montf (*A shield*) PARMOPHORUS ELONGATUS, Lam.

1, 2. *Galathée à rayons*. (Galathea radiata, *Lamk.*)

3, 4. *Cyrène cordiforme*. (Cyrena cordiformis, *Desh.*)

5, 6. *Astarté d'Islande*. (Astarte Islandica, *Desh.*)

7, 8, 9. *Cyclade des rivières*. (Cyclas rivicola, *Lamk.*)

SECURIFORM. (*Securis*, an axe; *forma*, shape.) Hatchet-shaped. *Ex.* Pedum. fig. 179.

SEDENTARY ANNELIDES. Lam. The third order of the class Annelides, Lam. distinguished from the other two orders by the circumstance of the animal being enveloped by a shelly tube which it never entirely leaves. The order is divided into the families Dorsalia, Maldania, Serpulacea, and Amphitrites. Fig. 1 to 13.

SEA DATE. The common name for PHOLAS Dactylus in the market, given to it on account of its cylindrical shape. Fig. 35.

SEGMENTINA. Fleming, 1824. NAUTILUS Lacustris, Montagu. Test. Brit. Planorbis nitidus, Drap. tab. 2. Fig. 17 to 19.

SEMICORDATE. Half heart-shaped.

SEMIDISCOIDAL. Forming the half of a circular disc.

SEMILUNAR. Half moon-shaped.

SENECTUS. Humph. A genus of "Senectinæ," thus described by Swainson: "Imperforate; the base produced into a broad flat lobe, spire rather elevated and pointed; the whorls convex; aperture perfectly round; not more oblique than *Helix*; inner lip entirely wanting, imperialis. Mart. 180. f. 1790. marmoratus. 1. M. 448. f. 1," Sw. p. 348.

SEMIPHYLLIDIANA. Lam. The second family of the order Gasteropoda, Lam. the genera of which are distinguished as follows:–

   1. UMBRELLA, round, flat; apex central, muscular impression not interrupted. Fig. 332.

   2. PLEUROBRANCHUS, apex lateral, sub-spiral. Fig. 232.

SENOCLITA. Schum. CINERAS, Leach. See CONCHODERMA.

SEPTARIA. Lam. See TEREDO.

SEPTUM. (Lat.) An enclosure, applied to the thin plate of Crepidula, Fig. 239; also to the plates dividing the chambers of multilocular shells.

SERAPHYS. Montf. 1810. TEREBELLUM convolutum, Lam. Fig. 451.

SERPULA. Auct. (*A little serpent.*) *Fam.* Serpulacea, Lam.—*Descr.* Tubular, narrow, pointed at the apex, gradually widening towards the aperture, attached irregularly, sometimes spirally, twisted, imbricated; keeled or plain; aperture generally round, with the edge simple, or angulated by the termination of external ribs or keels.—*Obs.* This description is intended to include the genera Serpula, Spirorbis, Vermilia, Galeolaria, &c. The Serpulæ abound in all seas, on rocky shores, at any time covered by water, attached to any kind of marine substance, whether movable or stationary. The fossil species occur in almost all tertiary strata. Pl. i. fig. 4 to 7.

SERPULACEA. Lam. The fourth family of the order Sedentary Annelides, Lam. containing the following genera of tubular, irregular shells.

   1. SERPULA, attached by a small portion of the shell. Fig. 4.

   2. SPIRORBIS, attached by the whole length, coiled. Fig. 5.

   3. GALEOLARIA, with the open extremity raised, and the aperture tongue-shaped. Fig. 6.

   4. VERMILLA, attached by the whole length, straight or waved. Fig. 5. SPIROGLYPHUS, which hollows a bed in the body to which it is attached. Fig. 8.

      Sowerby* gives satisfactory reasons for reuniting the whole of the preceding under the name SERPULA.

   6. MAGILUS, which burrows in coral; outer lip reflected. Fig. 9 to 10.

   7. LEPTOCONCHUS, outer lip reflected. Fig. 11.

   8. STYLIFER, spiral, thin, globular, living in Starfish. Fig. 12, 13. The three last genera should certainly find some outer place in the system.

SERPULORBIS. Sassi, 1827.

SESSILE CIRRIPEDES. Lam. (*Sessilis*, low, dwarfish.) An order of Cirripedes, consisting of those which are attached by the base of the shells, containing the genera Tubicinella, Balanus, Coronula, Acasta, Pyrgoma, Creusia. To which may be added some other genera enumerated in explanation of figures 14 to 33. The shells of the Sessile Cirripedes consist of two different sets of valves: 1st. The *parietal* valves, or pieces arranged in a circle, side by side, around the body of the animal, (an arrangement designated *coronular* by De Blainville.) 2nd. The *opercular* valves, or pieces placed so as to enclose the aperture. Between those opercular valves the ciliæ protrude which characterize the class. Besides these two sets of valves, there is generally a shelly plate, serving as a sort of foundation to the rest. The Sessile Cirripedes may be thus arranged.

   1. TUBICINELLA. Six parietal valves, tube-shaped, opercular valves perpendicular. Fig. 14.

   2. CORONULA. Six parietal valves, opercular valves horizontal. Fig. 15, 16, 17, 18. These two genera fix themselves in the skin of the Whale. The latter has been divided into the genera Chelonobia, Cetopirus, Diadema, and Chthalamus.

   3. PLATYLEPAS. Valves divided, each having a prominent internal plate. Fig. 19.

   4. CLITIA. Parietal valves four, opercular valves two, valves dove-tailed into each other. Fig. 20.

   5. ELMINEUS. Parietal valves four, opercular valves four. Fig. 22.

   6. CONIA. Parietal valves four, thick and porous at the base. Fig. 21.

   7. OCTOMERIS. Parietal valves eight. Fig. 24.

   8. CATOPHRAGMUS. Parietal valves numerous, irregular. Fig. 23.

   9. BALANUS. Parietal valves six; opercular valves four, placed against each other conically in pairs. This genus has been divided into acasta, Conoplea, Chirona, and Balanus. Fig. 25, 26, 27.

   10. CREUSIA. Parietal valves, four supported on the edge of a funnel-shaped cavity. Fig 28.

   11. PYRGOMA. Paries simple, supported on a cavity. This genus has been divided into the genera Nobia, Savignium, Pyrgoma, Adna, Megatrema, and Daracia. Fig. 29 to 33.

SETIFEROUS. Hairy.

SHANK SHELL. The vulgar name for the shell designated Murex Rapa. It is used in Ceylon for ornamental purposes.

SIDEROLITES. Monft. A genus of microscopic Foraminifera.

SIGARETUS. Lam. *Fam.* Macrostomata, Lam.—*Descr.* Suborbicular, oblique, haliotoid, thick; spire depressed, consisting of two or three rapidly increasing whorls; aperture wide, entire, modified by the last whorl, the width exceeding the length; columella tortuous; inner lip spread thinly over part of the body whorl; epidermis thin.—*Obs.* This genus is distinguished from Natica, by the width of the aperture, and the absence of the umbilical callosity. It may be known from Stomatia, and Stomatella, by the texture, which in Sigaretus, is never pearly as in Stomatia, the former being partly an internal shell. Mostly brought from tropical climates. S. concavus. Pl. xv. fig. 334.

SILIQUA. Megerle. (A husk, or pod.) LEGUMINARIA, Schum. A genus composed of species of SOLEN, Auct. which have an internal rib. Fig. 51, Solen radiatus.

SILIQUARIA. (Lamarck, 1801.) *Fam.* Cricostomata, Bl. Dorsalia,

1. *Ancillaire bordée*. (Ancillaria marginata, *Lamk*.)

2, 3. *Volvaire hyaline*. (Volvaria pallida, *Lamk*.)

4. *Marginelle d'Adanson*. (Marginella Adansoni, *Kiener*.)

5. *Mitre scabriuscule*. (Mitra scabriuscula, *L*.)

6. *Tarière subulée*. (Terebellum subulatum, *Lamk*.)

7, 8. *Ovule intermédiaire*. (Ovula intermedia, *Sow*.)

9. *Olive du Pérou*. (Oliva Peruviana, *Lamk*.)

10. *Porcelaine bouffonne*. (Cyprœa scurra, *Chemn*.)

Lam.—*Descr.* Tubular, regose, spiral near the apex, irregularly twisted near the aperture, with a longitudinal fissure radiating from the apex, and proceeding through all the whorls and sinuosities of the tube.—*Obs.* This genus was included in Serpula by Linnæus, from which, however, it is distinguished by the longitudinal slit. The recent species are found in the sponges with siliceous spiculæ, in the Mediterranean; the fossils in tertiary beds. Pl. i. fig. 1.

SIMPLE. (*Simplex*, lat.) Single, entire, uninterrupted, undivided.

SIMPLEGAS. Mont 1, 83. (*Simplex*, simple; γαστηρ, *gaster*, belly.) A genus described by De Blainville, as being discoidal, and having the spire uncovered like AMMONITES, but having the chambers divided, by simple septa, like Nautilus.—*Obs.* The septa of the shell named Simplegas by De Montfort, are evidently sinuous, according to his figure. S. sulcata, Pl. xxii. fig. 475.

SINISTRAL. (*Sinister*, left.) On the left side. A sinistral shell is a *reversed* one. The sinistral valve of a bivalve shell may be known, by placing the shell, with its ligamentary or posterior part towards the observer; the sides of the shell will then correspond with his right and left side.

SINUOUS. Winding, serpentine. The septa of Ammonites are sinuous. The muscular impression of the mantle, or palleal impression of some bivalve shells, is sinuated near the posterior muscular impression.

SINUS. (*Sinus*, a winding, or bay.) A winding or tortuous excavation. The sinus in the outer lip of Strombus, fig. 406; and that in the muscular impression of Venus, will be indicated by the letter *s*.

SIPHON. (Σιφον, siphon.) A pipe, or tube. A shelly tube passing through the septa of chambered shells. It is said to be *dorsal, central,* or *ventral*, according to its situation near the outer, or inner parts of the whorl. See Introduction.

SIPHONAL SCAR. The name applied by Mr. Gray to the opening or winding sinus in the palleal impression of a bivalve shell, in the place where the siphonal tube of the animal passes.

SIPHONARIA. Sow. (Σιφον, siphon.) *Fam.* Phyllidiana. Lam. Patelloidea, Bl.—*Descr.* Patelliform, depressed, inclining to oval, ribbed; apex nearly central, obliquely inclining towards the posterior margin; muscular impression partly encircling the central disc, but interrupted in front, where the head of the animal reposes, and at the side by a siphon, or canal passing from the apex to the margin.—*Obs.* This siphon, which is in some species very distinct, serves to distinguish this genus from Patella. S. Sipho. Pl. xii. fig. 231*.

SIPHONOBRANCHIATA. Bl. (*Siphon*, and *Branchiæ*, gills.) The first order of Paracephalophora Dioica, Bl. divided into the families Siphonostomata, Entomostomata, and Angiostomata.

SIPHONOSTOMA. Guild. A sub-genus of Pupa, consisting of several elongated species, which have the aperture detached from the whorls; such as P. costata, and fasciata.

SIPHONOSTOMATA. Bl. (Σιφον, siphon; στομα, *stoma*, mouth.) The first family of Siphonobranchiata, Bl., the shells of which are extremely variable in form, but always have a canal or notch at the anterior extremity of the aperture. This family partly answers to the Canalifera of Lamarck and the genus Murex in the system of Linnæus. It contains the genera Pleurotoma, Rostellaria, Fusus, Pyrula, Fasciolaria, Turbinella, Columbella, Triton, Murex, Ranella, and Struthiolaria.

SIPHUNCLE. (Siphunculus.) A small siphon.

SISTRUM. Montf. (1810,) claimed a prior name for RICINULA, Lamarck. Fig. 413.

SKENEA. *Flem.* Typified by S. planorbis. A marine shell of depressed form. Pl. 74, fig. 25.

SMILIUM. Leach. *Fam.* Pedunculated Cirripedes.—*Descr.* Thirteen pieces, ten of which are in pairs, lateral, subtriangular; one posterior dorsal, linear; all smooth; peduncle hairy.—*Obs.* This genus is now included in Scalpellum. Pl. ii. fig. 36, S. Peronii.

SNAIL. The common garden Snail, so destructive to our vegetables, belongs to the genus Helix. The water snail, found in ponds, is Planorbis.

SOL. Humph. A genus consisting of several species of the genus Trochus, and corresponding with the sub-genus Tubicanthus, Sw. Malac. Fig. 349.

SOLARIUM. Lamarck. ARCHITECTOMA, Bolter. (*A terrace or gallery.*) *Fam.* Turbinacea. Lam. Goniostomata, Bl.—*Descr.* Discoidal beneath, conical above, with a wide umbilicus, the spiral margin of which is angulated and crenulated; aperture trapezoidal; peritreme thin, sharp; columella straight; operculum horny, subspiral.—*Obs.* The Solarium Perspectivum, is commonly called the Staircase Trochus, from the angulated edges of the whorls being seen through the umbilicus, which reaches to the apex, and presents the appearance of a winding gallery. The species are not numerous, they belong to tropical climates. A few fossil species occur in the tertiary formations. S. Perspectivum. Pl. xvi. fig. 353.

SOLDIANA. D'Orb. A genus of microscopic Foraminifera.

SOLEN. Auct. (*A kind of shell-fish*, Plin.) *Fam.* Solenacea, Lam. Pyloridea, Bl.—*Desc.* Bivalve, transversely elongated, sub-cylindrical, equivalve, very inequilateral, gaping at both extremities, umbones terminal, close to the anterior extremity; hinge linear, with several small cardinal teeth, and a long external ligament; muscular impressions distant, anterior, tongue-shaped, placed behind the cardinal teeth, posterior irregular, sub-ovate; palleal impression long, bilobed posteriorly.—*Obs.* The above description of the genus Solen, is framed so as to admit only those species which are commonly called Razor Shells, with the umbones terminal, and the anterior muscular impression behind them. They are found buried deep in the sand, in a perpendicular position, their situation being pointed out by a dimple, on the surface. They are abundant in temperate climates. Some of the Lamarckian Solenes will be found in the genus Solenocurtus, Bl. Pl. ii. fig. 60, 61.

SOLENACEA. Lam. A family of the order Conchifera, Dimyaria, Lam. The shells belonging to it are described as transversely elongated, destitute of accessary pieces, gaping only at the lateral extremities; ligament external.—The genera may be thus distinguished.

1. SOLEN. Razor shells, truncated at the extremities. Fig. 60.
2. PANOPÆA. Broad, with prominent tooth. Fig. 65, 66.
3. SOLENOCURTUS. Rounded at the extremities, with internal bar. Fig. 61.
4. SOLENIMYA. No teeth, epidermis over-reaching the shell. Fig. 68.
5. GLYCIMERIS. Thick, fulcrum of the ligament prominent. Fig. 67.
6. LEPTON. Flat, scale-shaped. Fig. 62.
7. NOVACULINA. Umbones nearly central; covered by a thin epidermis. Fig. 63.
8. Glauconome. Oval, margins close. Fig. 64.

SOLENELLA. Sowerby, 1832. (*Solen.*) *Fam.* Arcacea, Lam.—*Descr.* Oval, equivalve, subequilateral, compressed, covered with a thin, shining, olive-green epidermis; hinge with three or four anterior, and numerous sharp posterior lateral teeth, arranged in a straight line; muscular impressions two, lateral; palleal impression with a large sinus; ligament external, prominent, elongated.—*Obs.* This genus partakes of

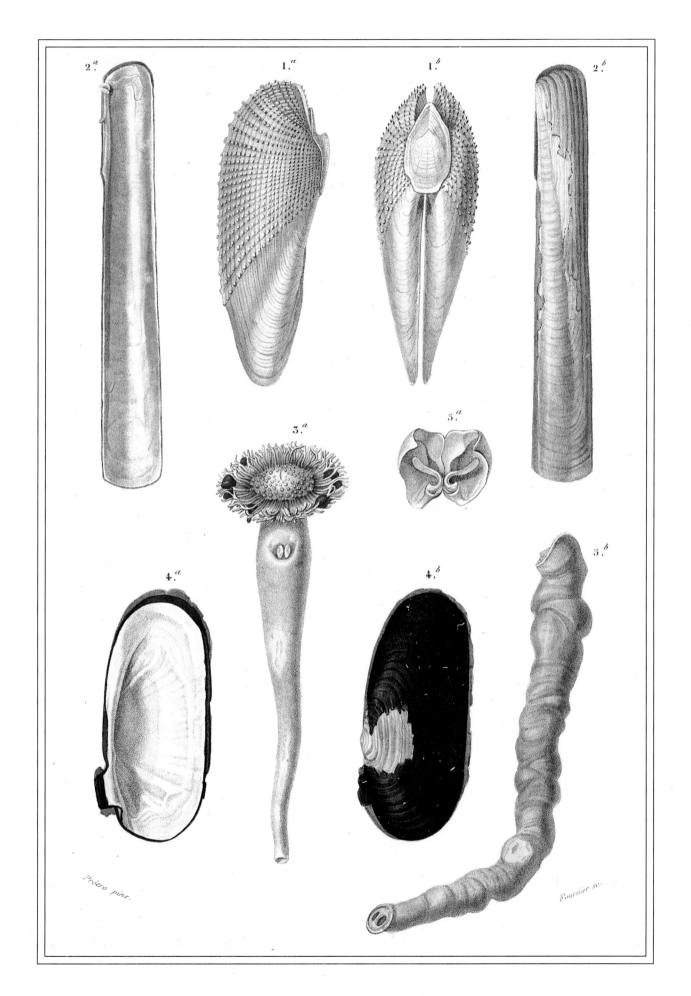

1.*a et* 1.*b Pholade dactyle*. (Pholas
      dactylus, *Lin.*)
2.*a et* 2.*b Solen silique*. (Solen siliqua,
      Lin.)
3. *Arrosoir de Java*. (Aspergillum
      Javanum, *Lamk.*)
4.*a et* 4.*b Glycimère silique*.
      (Glycimeris siliqua, *Lamk.*)
5.*a et* 5.*b Taret commun*. (Teredo
      navalis, *Lin.*)

the characters of the genus Nucula, and of the family Solenacea. A few specimens of the only species known (S. Norrisii) were dredged by Mr. Cuming at Valparaiso. Pl. vii. fig. 138.

SOLENIMYA. Lam. (Solen and Mya.) *Fam.* Mactracea, Lau. Pyloridea, Bl.—*Descr.* Equivalve, inequilateral, transversely oblong, rounded at the extremities with the umbones near the posterior side, covered with a shining brown epidermis extending beyond the edges of the shell; hing without teeth; ligament partly internal, placed in the margin of an oblique, flattish, posterior rib; muscular impressions two, distant, lateral. From the Mediterranean, Australian, and Atlantic Oceans.—*Obs.* Solenimya differs from Solenocurtus and the true Solens in having the posterior side of the shell the shortest; in the internal ligament; and in being destitute of teeth. It resembles Glycimeris, but is not thickened. Solenimya radiata. Pl. iii. fig. 68.

SOLENOCURTUS. Bl. (*Solen* and *curtus*, short.) *Fam.* Pyloridea, Bl. Solenacea, Lam. *Descr.* Oval, elongated, equivalve, sub-equilateral, with the edges nearly straight and parallel, and the extremities rather truncated; umbones not very prominent, sub-central; hinge with or without two or three rudimentary cardinal teeth; ligament prominent, placed upon thick callosities; muscular impressions two, distant, rounded; palleal impression straight, with a deep sinus. East Indies. *Obs.* Distinguished from the true Solenes by the central position of the umbones, and an internal bar reaching partly across the shell. S. radiatus. Pl. iii. fig. 61.

SOLETELLINA. Bl. Sanguinolaria radiata. S. Diphos, f. 99.

SORMETUS Adanson, (1757.) A very questionable genus of Bullidæ, founded on Adanson's doubtful figure of a lengthened, slug-like animal, with a small, square, flat, unspiral shell. S. livida of Sowerby, and similar species, are placed together in this genus. Pl. iv. fig. 99.

SPATHA. Lea. A sub-genus of Iridinæ, consisting of I. rubens, and I. nilotica, which have not distinctly crenulated margins. Spatha solenoides, of Lea, is the genus Mycetopus D'Orbigny. Fig. 151.

SPHÆNIA. Turt. A genus consisting of a small species resembling Saxicava, in general appearance, but having a spoon-shaped process on the hinge of one valve. S. Binghamii. Pl. iv. fig. 96.

SPHÆROIDINA. D'Orb. A genus of microscopic Foraminifera.

SPHÆRULACEA. Bl. The first family of Cellulacea, consisting of the following genera of microscopic Foraminifera: Miliola, Melonia, Saracenaria, Textularia.

SPHÆRULACEA. Lam. The fourth family of Cephalopoda, Lam. described as multliocular, globular, sphærical, or oval, with the whorls enveloping each other; some of them have a particular internal cavity, and are composed of a series of elongated, straight and contiguous chambers which altogether form a covering for the internal cavity. This family contains the genera Miliola, Gyrogona, and Melonia.

SPHÆRULITES. Lam. (*Sphæra*, a sphere.) *Fam.* Rudistes, Lam. and Bl.—*Descr.* Orbicular, inequivalve, irregularly foliated outside; lower valve cup-shaped, depressed; upper valve nearly flat, like an operculum.—*Obs.* These fossils are not regarded as shells by all conchologists. S. folaicea, Pl. xi, fig. 193.

SPHINCTERULUS. Montf. Lenticulina. Bl. A genus of microscopic Foraminifera.

SPINES. (*Spina*, a thorn.) Thin, pointed spikes.

SPINOSE. (Spinosus.) Having spines or elevated points, as Neritina spinosa. Fig. 325.

SPIRAL. (*Spira*, a spire.) Revolving outwards from a central apex or nucleus, like the spring of a watch. A shell or an operculum, may be spiral, without being produced into a pyramid. Bands of colour, striæ,

grooves, &c. commencing from the nucleus and following the volutions of the shell, are described by the above word.

SPIRALIS. Eydoux and Souleyet. A genus of Pteropoda, distinguished by the obliquely spiral form of the shells. Pl. xxviii. fig. 581.

SPIRAMILLA. Bl. A genus of Serpulacea, differing from other Serpulæ principally in the characters of the animal.

SPIRATELLA. Bl. Limacinea, Lam. Pl. xiii. fig. 244.

SPIRE. (*Spira*.) The cone or pyramid produced in a non-symmetrical univalve by its oblique revolution downwards from the apex or nucleus. The spire, in descriptions, includes all the volutions above the aperture. See Introduction.

SPIRIFER. Sow. (*Spira*, a spire; *fero*, to bear.) *Order*, Brachiopoda, Lam.—*Descr.* Transverse, equilateral; hinge linear, straight, widely extended on both sides of the umbones, which are separated by a flat area in the upper and larger valve; this area is divided in the centre by a triangular pit for the passage of the byssus; interior with two spirally convolute appendages.—*Obs.* This genus, which is only known in a fossil state, is distinguished from Terebratula externally, by the flat area in one valve, internally, by the singular spiral process from which the above name is derived. Most of the species belong to the mountain or carboniferous limestone. Pl. xii. fig. 214, 215.

SPIROGLYPHUS. Daudin, 1800. A genus consisting of a Serpula *Auct.* which makes a groove for itself in the surface of shells. Serpula spirorbis, var. Dillwyn. Pl. i. fig. 8.

SPIROLINA. Lam. A genus of microscopic Foraminifera.

SPIROLOCULINA. D'Orb. A genus of microscopic Foraminifera.

SPIRORBIS. Lam. A genus composed of a species of Serpula, Auct. which are coiled round in a spiral disc like a snake at rest. S. nautiloides is the common little white shell, found upon the shell of lobsters. Pl. i. fig. 5.

SPIRULA. (*Spira*, a winding compass.) *Fam.* Lituolata, Lam. Lituacea, Bl.—*Descr.* Convolute, smooth, symmetrical, discoid, with parallel unconnected whorls, divided into numerous chambers by transverse septa; siphon continuous.—*Obs.* This pretty little shell is partly internal, only a part of it being visible when on the animal. Pl. xxii. fig. 471.

SPISULA. Gray. a genus composed of Mactra fragilis, and other similar species, which have the ligament sub-external, marginal, not separate from the cartilage; with the posterior lateral teeth double in one valve, and single in the other. M. fragilis is the species figured for Spisula in Mr. Gray's paper on the Mactradæ, in the second series of London's Magazine of Natural History. We have since learned, however, that it was figured there by mistake, not having been intended for a Spisula, but belonging more properly to the genus Mactra, as defined by Mr. Gray, whose description of Spisula, is as follows:— "Shell ovate, trigonal, sub-angular at each end. Hinge and lateral teeth as in Mactra, but hinge of left tooth small. Siphonal inflexion ovate.' The principal difference between Spisula and Mactra is, that the ligament is not separated from the cartilage in the former. M. fragilis, Pl. iv. fig. 80.

SPONDYLUS. Auct. (*A shell-fish*, Ancients.) *Fam.* Pectenides, Lam. Sub-ostracea, Bl.—*Descr.* Inequivalve, sub-equilateral, irregularly foliaceous and spinose, auriculated, denticulated at the margins, attached by the lower and deeper valve; hinge rectilinear, with two prominent teeth in each valve, locking into corresponding cavities in the opposite valve; umbones separated by a broad, elongated, triangular disc in the lower valve; ligament contained in a groove, dividing the triangular area in the centre; muscular impressions one in each valve,

1.*a* et 1.*b* Gnathodon cuneiforme.
(Gnathodon cuneatum, *Gray.*)

2.*a* et 2.*b* Crassatelle rostrée.
(Crassatella rostrata, *L^k.*)

3.*a* et 3.*b* Mye tronquée. (Mya
truncata, *Lin.*)

4.*a* et 4.*b* Mactre mouchetée. (Mactra
maculosa, *Lamk.*)

5.*a* et 5.*b* Anatine tronquée. (Anatina
truncata, *Lamk.*)

5.*c* Charnière de l'Anatine montrant le
ligament et son osselet.

sub-central, sub-orbicula. The Mediterranean, East and West Indies, and China, produce Spondyli most abundantly.—*Obs*. This genus is remarkable for the richness and beauty of the spines and foliations, which adorn the external surface of most of the species, the splendid colours by which many of them are varied, and the natural groupings formed by their attachment to each other. Forty species are enumerated in the Thesaurus Conchylium, Pl. 8 by the Author, Pl. 83 to 89; our Pl. x. fig. 177, and frontispiece.

SPORULUS. Montf. A genus of microscopic foraminifera.

SQUAMOSE. (*Squama*, a scale.) Scaly, covered with scales, as the pedicule of Pollicipes Mitellus, fig. 37*.

STENOPUS. Guild. (Στενς, narrow) πούς, foot.) A genus nearly "allied to the Linnæn Helices, from all of which it differs in the curious contraction of the pedal disc, and the caudal tentaculum furnished with a gland beneath." The shell is described as heliciform, umbilicated, transparent, with the aperture transverse. The two species described are Stenopus cruentatus and lividus; they are both from the Caribbæan Islands, Guild. Zool. Journ. xii. p. 528, tab. 15, f. 1 to 5. St. cruentata, f. 515, 516. Including Nanina, Gray, Helia, Citrina, f. 280.

STOASTOMA. C. B. Adams. A genus of minute operculated land shells, of a globose form, and semicircular aperture, with a nucleus or concentric operculum. The outer lip is not reflected, and it is produced beyond the columella, from which it is separated by a little groove. In the absence of more accurate knowledge of the animal, I should hesitate to regard this as more than an interesting group of Helicinæ, not more distinct from other groups of the same genus thus they are from each other. Mr. Cuming's collection contains 12 species. En. S. pisum (Jamaica.) Pl. xxviii. fig. 582.

STOMATELLA. See STOMAX.

STOMAX. Montf. 1810. Stomatia, Lamarck, 18701. *Fam*. Mocrostomata, Lam.—*Descr*. Sub-orbicular, oblong, auriform, variegated without, irridescent within; spire depressed; aperture entire, very wide, oblique; peritreme uninterrupted.—*Obs*. This genus is known from Haliotis by being destitute of the series of holes; is distinguished from Sigaretus by the substance of the shell, the latter being internal, and never pearly. Our description includes STOMATELLA, Lam. The Stomatiæ are marine, and belong to the East Indies and New Holland. S. Phymotis. Pl. xv. fig. 335.

STREPHONA. Brown. 1756. Olivia, Lamarck.

STORILLUS. Montf. 1, 131. A genus of microscopic Foraminifera, included in the genus rotallites in M. De. Blainville's system.

STRAPAROLLUS. Montf. A genus containing some species of HELIX. Auct. Generic characters not defined.

STREPTAXIS. Gray. *Fam*. Colimacea, La,.—*Descr*. Ovate, or oblong; when young, sub-hemispherical, deeply umbilicated, with rapidly enlarging whorls. At length the penultimate whorl is bent towards the right and dorsal side of the axis, and the umbilicus becomes depressed, and often nearly closed. The mouth is lunulate, the edge slightly thickened and reflected, and often with a single tooth on the outer side of the inner lip.—*Obs*. This genus of land shells is separated from Helix on account of the eccentricity of the penultimate whorl. S. contusa. Pl. xiii. fig. 269, 270.

STRIATED. (*Stria*, a groove.) Marked with fine grooves or lines.

STRIGOCEPHALUS. Defr. PENTAMERUS, Sow.? GYPIDIA. Dalman.

STROMBUS. Auct. *Fam*. Alatæ, Lam. Angiostomata, Bl.—*Descr*. Oblong, turrited, rather ventricose, solid; aperture generally lengthened, terminating posteriorly in a short canal, and anteriorly in an emargination or truncated canal; outer lip, when young, thin; when full grown, thickened and expanded, lobed at the spiral extremity, sinuated anteriorly, near the caudal canal. *Obs*. This well known genus includes some species of immense size, commonly called conch shells. Most of the recent species are brought from the Indian Ocean. Very few fossil species are known. The young shells have very much the appearance of cones, the outer lips being thin. There are also several species which do not, even when full grown, thicken their outer lips very considerably. The genus Strombus is distinguished from Rostellaria, by the notch in the outer lip, which in the latter genus is close to the canal. Fifty-seven species are enumerated in the Thesaurus Conchyliorum. S. pugilis, Pl. xviii. fig. 406.

STROPHOMENA. Rafinesque. ORTHIS, Dalman.

STROPHOSTOMA. Deshayes, 1827. A fossil shell, of the family of Colimacea, Lam. in some degree resembling Anostoma, having the aperture turned upwards the spire, it is, however, umbilicated, and it is said to have an operculum, resembling that of Cyclostoma. It is the Ferussina of Grateloup, 1826, one year earlier, and therefore the right name. Pl. xxv. fig. 534, 5, 6.

STRUTHIOLARIA. Auct. (*Struthio*, an Ostrich.) *Fam*. Canalifera, Lam.—Descr. Oblong, turrited, thick; spire turrited, composed of several angulated whorls; aperture oval, sub-quadrate, oblique; outer lip thickened, reflected, advancing in the centre, receding towards the extremities; inner lip thickened expanded over the columella and part of the body whorl.—*Obs*. This singular genus, consisting of three of four recent species, is named "Pied D'Autruche" by the French, on account of some resemblance in the outer lip to the foot of the Ostrich. From New Zealand. Fig. 391, S. straminea. Four species are described in the author's monograph, Thesaurus Conchyliorum, Pl. 1. *Ex*. Pl. xvii. fig. 391.

STYLIFER. Brod. (*Stylus*, a style; *fero*, to bear.)—*Descr*. Thin, pellucid, turbinated; apex a little out of the perpendicular, aperture wide anteriorly, gradually narrowing towards the spiral extremity, where it terminates acutely.—*Obs*. This is a genus of small, transparent shells, found burrowing in the rays of Starfish. There are but two or three species at present known, one of which is elongated like Terebra, the other nearly globular. S. astericola. West Indies, Gallapagos, and Britain. Pl. i. fig. 12, 13.

STYLINA. Flem. STYLIFER, Brod.

SUB. (*under*.) Used as a prefix and signifying nearly. Thus a bivalve-shell, the valves of which are nearly alike, would be described as *sub*-equivalve.

SUB-APLYSIACEA. Bl. The first family of the order Monopleurobranchiata, Bl. containing several genera of Mollusca without shells, and the genus Pleurobranchus.

SUB-BIVALVES. A term of distinction applied by De Blainville, to those spiral univalves which have an operculum; these, as they consitute two distinct pieces, he considers as forming a medium between univalves and bivalves.

SUB-MYTILACEA. Bl. The sixth family of the order Lamellibranchiata, Bl. the shells belonging to which are described as free, rather pearly, regular, equivalve; hinge dorsal, laminated; ligament external; two muscular impressions; palleal impression not sinuated. This family, with the exception of the last genus, agrees with the family Nayades of Lamarck, and contains the genera Anodon, Unio, and Cardita.

SUB-OSTRACEA. Bl. The second family of Lamellibranchiata, Bl. the shells of which are described as of a compact texture, sub-symmetrical; with the hinge rather complex; one single, sub-central, muscular impression, without any traces of palleal impression. This family

1, 2. *Lime écailleuse*. (Lima
    squamosa, *Lamk.*)
3, 4. *Spondyle safrané*. (Spondylus
    crocastus, *Desh.*)
5. *Huître feuille*. (Ostrea folium,
    Lamk.)
6, 7. *Pecten tigré*. (Pecten tigris,
    Lamk.)

corresponds with the Pectenides of Lamarck, and part of the genus Ostrea in the system of Linnæus. It contains the genera Spondylus, Plicatula, Himnites, Pecten, Pedum, Lima.

SUB-SPIRAL. Not sufficiently spiral to form a complete volution.

SUBULA. Bl (*An awl.*) A generic name under which M. De Blainville includes TEREBRA maculata, Auct. f. 428, together with nearly all the species of Terebra, enumerated by Lamarck and other authors; only leaving in the latter genus those species, which being more bulbous, or ventricose, nearly resemble Buccinum in general form. These last mentioned species, such as Terebras buccinoidea, have been formed into a new genus by Mr. Gray, under the name Bullia. If both these genera were adopted, the genus Terebra would be extinct. Pl. xx. fig. 428.

SUBULATE. (*Subula*, an awl.) A term applied to shells which are long and pointed as in Terebra. Fig. 427, 428.

SUBULINA. Beck, 1837. A genus founded on the high-spired Helix octona, fig. 514. Macrospira, Guilding, 1840.

SUCCINEA. Drap. (*Succinum*, amber.) *Fam.* Colimacea, Lam. Limacinea, Bl. *Sub-genus*, Cochlohydra, Fer.—*Descr.* Ovate, rather elongated; aperture large, entire, longitudinal; spire short; outer lip thin, continuous with the thin, sharp-edged columella; inner lip spread over a part of the body-whorl.—*Obs.* The shells belonging to this genus of partly amphibious mollusca, are distinguished from Linnæa by not having a fold on the columella. The S. amphibia is of a bright amber colour. Pl. xiii. fig. 265, 266.

SULCATED. (SULCATUS, lat.) Having grooves or furrows.

SULCI. Grooves or furrows.

SUTURE. (*Sutura*, lat.) A seam, stitch, joining together. Applied particularly to the line which marks the joining of the whorls of the spire. The suture is distinguished as *simple*, as in most cases; or *double*, when accompanied by a parallel groove close to it; *marginated*, when produced into a ledge by the matter which fills up and covers it; *obsolete*, when it is filled up so as not to be visible, as in the case of Ancillaria.

SYCOTYPUS. Brown, 1756. A generic name applied to Pyrula ficus, &c.

SYLVICOLA. Humph. CYCLOSTOMA, Lam.

SYMMETRICAL. (συν, *syn*, similar; μετον, *metron*, proportion.) Both sides alike. Although the term is used thus as one of distinction, it is to be observed that no shells are strictly and perfectly symmetrical; even in the Nautilus, the apex verges in a slight degree towards one side of the shell. Two kinds of univalve are symmetrical, or nearly so; 1st. Those which are symmetrically convolute, as the Nautilacea and the Ammonacea, which are spiral; 2nd. Those which are not spiral, but simply conical, as the patelliform shells. Bivalves belonging to the Brachiopoda are also symmetrical. *Ex.* Patella, fig. 229. Ammonites, fig. 478.

SYMPHYNOTA. Lea. A genus of Nayades, in which Mr. Lea proposed to include species of the genus UNIO, the valves of which are connate, or united at the dorsal margin. We believe that this distinction, as a genus, has been abandoned by its author. The fact is, that all the Uniones are Symphynotæ when in a young state. In Unio Alatus, (fig. 147) and Dipsas plicatus, (fig. 142) it will be observed that the valves have not separated at the dorsal edge, but are broken lower down. Pl. vii. fig. 142, 147.

SYNDOSMYA. Recluz. A Tellinæform genus of shells, having a cartilaginiferous pit in each valve, and distinct lateral teeth. *Ex.* S. alba. Pl. xxvii. fig. 572.

TALONA. Gray, 1840. Pholas tridens. See monograph of the genus Pholas in Sowerby's Thesaurus Conchyliorum, Pl. 10. sp. 39, fig. 60, 61.

TAPADA. (Gray Turton. p. 127) A division of the genus HELIX, containing HELIX aperta, Auct. or the Tapada snail.

TAPES. Schum. PULLASTRA. Sow. T. litteratus. See monograph, Thesaurus Conchyliorum, Pl. 13, 14; and our figure, Pl. vi. fig. 120.

TECTURA. "Tecture," Aud. and Edw. Ann. Sci. Nat. 1830. LOTTIA, Gray.

TECTUS. Montf. A genus composed of species of the genus Trochus, having elevated, conical spires, and columella notched or truncated by a spiral fold. Trochus maculatus, presents an example. Pl. xvi. fig. 359.

TEINOSTOMA. H. and A. Adams. A genus formed of two interesting shells collected in W. Colombia, by Mr. Cuming. They are formed like the Rotellæ, and the Nassa neritoidea, but have the aperture quite simple and smooth, with the outer lip produced into a peak. *Ex.* T. politum. Pl. xxviii. fig. 589.

TELEBOIS. Montf. a genus of microscopic Foraminifera.

TELESCOPIUM. Chemn. CERITHIUM Telescopium, Auct. fig. 378.

TELLINA. Linn. *Fam.* Nymphacea, Lam. Conchacea, Bl.—*Descr.* Sub-equivalve, inequilateral, compressed, rounded anteriorly, slightly beaked or angulated posteriorly, the posterior ventral margin having a flexuosity; hinge with two cardinal and generally two lateral teeth in each valve; muscular impressions, two in each valve, remote; palleal impression with a large sinus.—*Obs.* The fold or bending in the posterior margin distinguishes this genus from others which it nearly resembles. It is composed of some bivalves of great beauty and variety, which are dound in nearly all climates. Fig. 105, t. radiata, 106, T. lingua-felis. Mr. Hanley's monograph of this genus in Sowerby's Thesaurus Conchyliorum, contains 207 species, very variable in form. Pl. v. fig. 105, 106.

TELLINIDES. Lam. *Fam.* Nymphacea, Lam.—*Descr.* Subn-equivalve, inequilateral, transverse, compressed, rounded anteriorly, slightly beaked or angulated posteriorly; hinge with two cardinal teeth in each valve, and one lateral tooth in one valve, very near the cardinal teeth. Muscular impressions two, distant, palleal impression with a large sinus. *Obs.* This genus is distinguished from Tellina in having but one lateral tooth near the cardinal teeth. T. rosea, Pl. v. fig. 107.

TENUIPEDES. (*Tenuis*, slender; *pedes*, feet.) The second section of the order Conchifera Dimyaria, divided into the families Mactracea, Corbulacea, Lithophagidæ, Nymphacea.

TERACLITA. Schum. CONIA, Acut.

TEREBELLUM. Browne, 1756. Turritella, Lamarck.

TEREBELLUM. Lamarck, 1801. (*Terebra*, an augur?) *Fam.* Convolutæ, Lam. Angyostomata, Bl.—*Descr.* Smooth, slender, oblong, sub-cylindrical; spire obtuse, short, sometimes hidden; (Seraphs, Montf.) aperture long, narrow posteriorly, wider anteriorly; outer lip slightly thickened, truncated, unconnected at the base with the columella; inner lip thin, smooth, nearly straight, spread over a portion of the body-whorl, continued in a ridge above the sutures of the spire.—*Obs.* Montfort has separated the fossil species with hidden spires, under the name Seraphs. (T. convolutum, Lam.) Only one recent species is known. Of this there are several varieties, one spotted, one marked in sub-spiral lines, another in patches. It is brought from the East Indies. T. convolutum; T. subulatum. Pl. xxi. fig. 451, 452.

TEREBRA. (*An augur, a piercer.*) *Fam.* Purpurifera, Lam. Entomostomata, Bl.—*Descr.* Subulate, elongated, pointed, turrited; spire long, consisting of numerous whorls; aperture small, terminating in a short, reflected canal; outer lip thin; columella tortuous; operculum horny. The recent species are mostly tropical.—*Obs.* Nearly all the species enumerated by Lamarck and other authors are included by De Blainville in his genus Subula; those few species which that conchologist left in the present genus, being shorter and more ventricose than the others, approximate in shape to some of the Buccina, and are distinguished by Mr. Gray under the generic name Bullia. It seems strange, that De Blainville, being convinced of the necessity of separating the two groups, and consequently applying a new generic term to one of them, should have given that term to the larger number and the more typical species of the Lamarckian genus. Fig. 427, Bullia vittata. (Terebra.) Fig. 428, Terebra maculata. (Subula.) The Monograph of this genus in the author's Thesaurus, Pl. v. contains 109 species. Plates 41 to 45. Our Plate xx. gig. 427, 428.

TEREBRALLA. Sw. A genus of "Cerithinæ," Sw. thus described: "Outer lip much dilated, generally uniting at its base to the inner lip; leaving a round perforation at the base of the pillar; channel truncate; operculum round: Palustre. Mart. f. 1472." Sw. p. 315.

TEREBRATING SHELLS. (*Terebro*, to pierce.) Shells which reside in holes pierced in rocks, wood, &c. by means of some corrosive secretion of the animal. *Ex*. Pholas, Teredo, &c.

TEREBRATULA. Brug. (*Terenratis*, bored.) *Fam*. Brachiopoda, Lam.—*Order*. Palliobranchiata, Bl.—*Descr*. Inequivalve, equilateral, oval or sub-trigonal, ventricose, or compressed, attached by a tendon passing through an opening in the dorsal, or upper and larger valve, the umbo of which advances beyond that of the other valve; hinge destitute of a ligament, with two teeth in the dorsal valve, locked into corresponding cavities in the ventral, or lower valve, and with two curious processes originating at the umbo of the lower valve, presenting, in some species, the appearance of fine winding tape, advancing towards the front of the valve, and again receding to the centre, where the ends unite; muscular impressions two, placed near the centre of each valve.—*Obs*. The Terebratulæ are included in the genus Anomia in the system of Linnæus. The recent species are not very numerous – they are found in all climates. The fossil species are more numerous than the recent ones, occurring in the secondary and tertiary formations. Mr. Sowerby, sen's Monograph in the 7th part of the author's Thesaurus Conchyliorum, contains 40 recent species. Plates 68 to 72. P. Psittacea, Pl, xi. fig. 202.

TEREDINA. (From Teredo. *Fam*. Tubicolæ, Lam. Adesmacea, Bl.— *Descr*. Valves equal, inequilateral, with prominent umbones, as it were soldered to the outside of the rounded end of a shelly tube, of which they form a part; aperture of the tube partly divided; a flat accessary valve placed on the unbomes.—*Obs*. This genus, which is only known in a fossil state, is distinguished from Teredo, by the valves being fixed on the tube, and the tube being closed at one extremity. T. personata, Pl. ii. fig. 46, 47.

TEREDO. Auct. (*A piercer*.) *Fam*. Tubicolæ, Lam. Adesmacea, Bl.— *Descr*. Valves equal, inequilateral; presenting when closed, an orbicular figure, with a large angular opening in front, and a rounded opening at the back; placed at the anterior extremity of an irregular, flexuous, elongated tube, open at both ends; the anterior termination divided in a double aperture opened and closed at the will of the animal by two operrcula. *Obs*. This genus of Molluscous animals, is remarkable for boring holes in wood, which are filled by their elongated tubes, and give it a honey-comb appearance. fig. 48. T. Navalis. Fig. 49, a piece of bored wood. Pl. ii.

TERMINAL. When the umbones of a bivalve shell are placed at or near the extremity, as in Mytilus, fig. 158, Pinna, fig. 162, they are said to be *terminal*. The same term is also applied to the nucleus of an operculum, when it forms an extreme point, or is close to one of the edges.

TESSELATED. (Wrought in chequer-work.) A term applied to the colouring of shells, when arranged in regular defined patches like a tesselated pavement.

TESTACELLA. Lamarck, 1801. (*Testa*, a shell.) *Fam*. Limacinea, Lam. and Bl.—*Descr*. Haliotoid, compressed; aperture wide, oblique; columella flat, oblique, spire short, flat, consisting of less than two whorls.—*Obs*. This shell which is extremely small compared with the animal, is placed upon its back, near the posterior extremity. The animal is found in some of our gardens, and very much resembles the common garden slug. t. Haliotoidea. Pl. xiii. fig. 261.

TESTACEOUS. (*Testa*, a shell). Shelly. Testaceous Mollusca, are soft animals having shells. A testaceous operculum is one composed of shelly matter.

TETRACERA. Bl. The first family of the order Polybranchiata, Bl. containing no genera of testaceous mollusca.

TEXTILLA. Sw. A sub-genus of Conus, consisting of Conus ballatus, &c. Sw. Malac. p. 312.

TEXTULARIA. Defr. A genus of microscopic Foraminifera.

THALAMUS. Montf. A genus described as resembling Conilites, but curved and granulated.

THALLEPUS. Sw. A genus of "Aplysianiæ," Sw. thus described: "Body more slender and fusiform;" (than Aplysia,) "the lobes of the mantle short, and incapable of being used for swimming; tentacula two, large, ear-shaped; eyes not visible. T. ornatus, *Sw*. Sp. Now." Sw. p. 349.

THALLICERA. Sw. A generic name under which Swainson distinguishes AMPULLARIA Avellana, Auct. Pl. xxv. fig. 338.

THECIDIUM. *Fam*. Brachiopoda. Lam. *Order*, Palliobranchiata. Bl.— *Descr*. Lower valve concave, sub-trigonal, with the umbo produced into a triangular, slightly incurved beak, and with two short, pointed processes advancing from beneath the umbones; upper valve flat, rounded square, with a short, blunt appendage, formed to fit between the tooth-like process of the other valve; its inner surface ornamented with symmetrically curved ridges. Thecidium Mediterranean, Sowerby's Thesaurus Conchyliorum, Pl. 73. fig. 30, 31, 32. Our Plate vii. fig. 216.

THECOSOMATA. Bl. The family of the order Aporobranchiata, Bl. containing the genera Hyalæa, Cleodora, Cymbulia, Pyrgo.

THELICONUS. Sw. A sub-genus of Conus. Lardn. Cyclop. Malac. p. 312.

THELIDOMUS. Sw. A generic name under which Swainson has described a division of the genus Helix, and which he has also used to designate a genus in the family of "Rotellinæ," founded upon an aggregate of loose particles collected and agglutinated in a spiral form by the larva of an insect. Sw. Malac. p. 330 and 353.

THEMEON. Montf. A genus of microscopic foraminifera.

THEODOXUS. Montf. a division of the genus Nerita. fig. 324, N. virginea.

THETIS. Sow. (*A sea nymph*.) A genus of fossil shells, described as resembling Mactra, but not having the internal ligament, and having several small, acuminated, cardinal teeth, but no lateral teeth. It resembles Tellina in some degree, but has not the posterior fold.

THIARA. Megerle. Part of the genus MELANIA, Lamarck.

THIARELLA. Sw. A sub-genus of Mitra, Lardn. Cyclop. Malac. p. 319.

THRACIA. Leach. *Fam*. Lithophagidæ, Lam. Pyloridea, Bl. A genus described as intermediate between Anatina, and Mya, and in some degree resembling Corbula. T. corbuloides, Pl. iv. fig. 93.

THUNDER-STONES. One of the vulgar appellations which have been applied to shells of the genus Belemnites.

THYATIRA. Leach. A genus composed of AMPHIDESMA *flexuosa*.

Cryptodon. Turton. (First with characters.)

TIARA. Sw. A genus of "Mitranæ," Sw. thus described: "Aperture narrow, linear, or of equal breadth throughout; outer lip and base of the body-whorl contracted, the former generally striated; an internal canal at the upper part of the aperture; shell (typically) turrited, and equally fusiform; representing the *Muricidæ* and Cymbiola." Sw. Malac. p. 319. The principal difference between Tiara and Mitra appears to be that in the latter, the aperture is more linear and contracted in the centre. Mitra Episcopalis is an example.

TINOPORUS. Montf. A genus of microscopic Foraminifera.

TIRANITES. Montf. A division of the genus Baculites.

TOMELLA. Sw. A genus of "Pleurotominæ," Sw. thus described: "Fusiform, smooth; the spire of very few whorls, and not longer than the channel; inner lip with a thick callosity at the top; the slit short and side; lineata, En. Méth. 440, f. 2, clavicularis, IB. f. 4. filosa. En. Méth. 440, f. 6. lineolata. Ib. f. 11." Sw. p. 314. Pl. xxvi. fig. 551.

TOMOGERUS. Montf. 1810. ANASTOMA, Fischer. Described under the later name, ANASTOMA, see fig. 271.

TONICIA. Gray, Syn. B. M. p. 126. A genus composed of those species of Chiton which have the margin smooth. Ch. elegans, &c.

TORNATELLA. Lamarck. ACTEON, Montf. *Fam.* Plicacea, Lam.—*Descr.* Oval, spirally grooved; spire short, rather obtuse, consisting of few whorls; aperture long, narrow, rounded anteriorly; outer lip simple; inner lip thin, slightly spread, columella spiral, incrassated, confluent with the outer lip. The recent species are few. Several fossil species occur in London Clay, Inferior Oolite and Calcaire-grossièr. Monoptygma, Lea, resembles this genus, but has a fold in the inner lip. T. solidula, Pl. xv. fig. 343.

TORNATINA. Adams, 1850. A subgenus of Bullidæ, thus described: "Shell cylindrical or fusiform, spire conspicuous, apex papillated, suture chanelled, columella callous, with a single plate." Sixteen species are described in Mr. Adams' Monograph, Pt. x. Sowerby's Thesaurus.

TORTUOUS. (*Tortuosus*) Twisted. This adjective is sometimes applied as a specific name; as Area tortuosa.

TRACHELIPODA. Lam. (τραχηλος, *trachelos*, a neck; ποδα, *poda*, foot.) The third order of the class Mollusca, in the system, of Lamarck. The trachelipoduos mollusca are described as having the posterior part of the body spirally twisted and separated from the foot; always enveloped in a shell. The foot is free, flat, attached to the case of the neck. Shell spiral, and enclosing the animal when at rest. This order contains the families, Colimacea, Lymnacea, Melaniana, Peristomiana, Neritacea, Janthinea, macrostomata, Scalariana, Plicacea, Canalifera, Alata, Purpurifera, Columellaria, Convolutæ. The genera belonging to these families, are represented in the plates, fig. 264 to 462.

TRANSVERSE. (Crosswise.) A shell is said to be transverse, when its width is greater than its length, that is, when it is longer from one side to the other than from the umbones to the ventral margins. The term is applied by some authors to express the direction of the lines of growth in bivalve shells, and the spiral lines in spiral shells. See CONCENTRIC.

TRAPEZIUM. Meg. CYPRICARDIA, Lam.

TRAPEZIFORM, or

TRAPEZOID. (τοαπεζωον, *trapezion*, trapezium: ειδος, *eidosform*.) Having four unequal and unparallel sides. *Ex.* Cucullæa, fig. 133.

TRIBULUS. Klein. RICINULA, Lam.

TRICHOTROPIS. Brod. and Sow. (Τοιχος, *trichos*, hair; τοοπις, *tropis*, keel.) *Fam.* Purpurifera, Lam.—*Descr.* Turbinated, keeled, thin, umbilicated; aperture longer than the spire; entire; columella obliquely truncated; outer lip thin, sharp; epidermis horny, produced into long hairs at the angels of the shell; operculum horny, with the

nucleus lateral.—*Obs.* Although the shells of this genus have something of the shape of Turbo, they are distinguished from that genus at once by the thinness of the shell. They are also known from Buccinium, by the absence of a canal. Only two or three species are known, which belong to the Northern and Arctic Oceans. T. bicarinata. Pl. xx. fig. 429.

TRIDACNA. Auct. *Fam.* Tridacnacea, Lam. Chamacea, Bl.—*Descr.* Equivalve, regular, inequilateral, radiately ribbed, adorned on the ribs with vaulted foliations, waved at the margins, with a large anterior hiatus close to the umbones, for the passage of a large byssus, by which the animal fixes itself to marine substances; hinge with a partly external ligament; two laminar teeth in one valve, one in the other.—*Obs.* The beautiful shells composing this genus are of a delicate white colour, tinged with buff. One species, the T. gigas, attains a remarkable size, measuring from two to three feet across, and weighing five hundred pounds. Tridacna is distinguished from Hippopus by the large opening in the hinge. t. elongata. Pl. ix. fig. 157.

TRIDACNACEA. Lam. A family belonging to the first section of the order Conchifera Dimyaria, Lam. described as regular, equivalve, solid, and which are remarkable for the deeply sinuated or undulated ventral margin. This family contains the genera:

    1. HIPPOPUS. Valves closed at or near the hinge. Fig. 156.
    2. TRIDACNA. An hiatus near the hinge. Fig. 157.

TRIDENTATE. (*Tridentatus.*) Having three teeth, or salient points. *Ex.* Hyalæa tridentata. Fig. 226.

TRIGONA. Schum.? Triangular species of CYTHEREA, such as C. lævigata, Triplas corbicula, ventricosa, bicolor, &c. The author found, however, in preparing the monograph of Cytheræa, No. 12, Thesaurus Conchyliorum, that the triangular pass by so many gradations into the rounded or oval forms, that it was impossible to find a resting place. Pl. vi. fig. 117*b*.

TRIGONOCÆLIUS. D'Nyst, 1835. A genus of bivalve shells, resembling Pectunculus, but distinguished by a triangular pit in the area of the hinge. *Ex.* T. aurita. Pl. vii. fig. 136.

TRIGONACEA. Lan. a family belonging to the order Conchifera Dimyaria, containing the genera Trigonia and Castalia, the latter of which ought to be removed to the Nayades. Fig. 139, 140.

TRIGONAL. Triangular, having three sides.

TRIGONELLA. Humph. MACTRA, Auct.

TRIGONIA. Brug. (τοιγωνον, *trigonon*, triangular.) *Fam.* Trigonata, Lam. Camacea, Bl.—*Descr.* Equivalve, inequilateral, transverse, sub-trigonal, costated and granulated without, pearly and irridescent within, denticulated on the inner margin, rounded anteriorly truncated posteriorly; hinge with four oblong, compressed, diverging teeth in one valve, receiving between their grooved sides, two similar teeth in the other; ligament external, thick; muscular impressions two in each valve.—*Obs* Only one recent species of this marine genus is known, the T. pectinata, which comes from New Holland; and was formerly so rare, that a much worn odd valve has been sold for a considerable sum. It is of a brilliant pearly texture within, tinged with purple or golden brown. Fossil species occur in Lias, upper and lower Oolite, and Green-sand. t. Pectinata. Pl. vii. fig. 139.

TRIGONOSEMUS. König. A genus composed of species of TEREBRATULA, Auct. which have one valve produced into a beak, perforated, or as it were truncated at the apex, differing from Terebratula lyra, Lam. T. lyra. Pl. xi. fig. 208.

TRIGONOSTOMA. A sub-genus of Helix, with a trigonal aperture. Gray's Turton, p. 139.

TRIGONOTRETA. König. A genus composed of species of Terebratula, Auct. which have the hinge of the larger valve produced into a triangular disc, divided by a triangular foramen in the centre. Spirifer, Sowerby, belongs to this genus. Fig. 214, 215.

TRILASMIS. Hind, Voy. Sulphur, p. 71, Pl. xxi. fig. 5. A small pedunculated Cirripeda, described as having two principal valves and a carina. From the characters of the animal and shell, however, Mr. Darwin has felt obliged to add several species to this group, and those species having the terga developed, and the scuture divided, could not properly be called trilasmis. In Mr. Darwin's work they are described under the name Pæcilasma.

TRILOBATE. (Τοεις, three; λοβος, division, lobe.) Divided into three lobes or principal parts. Ex. Malleus, Fig. 165.

TRILOCULINA. D'Orbigny. A genus of microscopic Foraminifera.

TRIPARTITE. (Tripartitus) composed of or divided into three separate parts.

TRIOMPHALIA. Sowerby, jun. (Τοια, three; ὀμφάλιον, umboes.) Pro. Zool. Soc. and Thesaurus Conchyliorum, p. 500. No. 10. A remarkable form of bivalve shell, differing from the Pholades in several particulars–1st. It has no curved processes in the hinge; 2nd The right valve is produced at the hinder end into a gongue or lappel; 3rd The left valve extends its ventral covering, so as completely to overlap the other anteriorly, Pl. xxvii. fig. 566.

TRIPHORIS. Deshayes. A genus composed of small reversed species of CERITHIUM, Auct. which have the anterior canal closed at the anterior of the aperture, but opened at the extremity, and a small tubular opening on the upper part of the whorls, making three openings on the body whorl. This genus stands in the same relation to Cerithium as the Typhis to Murex. Pl. xvi. fig. 375, 376.

TRIPLEX. Humph. MUREX, Linn.

TRIPLODON. Spix. HYRIA, Auct.

TRIPTERA. Quoy et Gaimard, CUVIERA, Fer. Described in the Voyage de la coquille, and represented as a molluscous animal destitute of a shell.

TRIQUETRA. Bl. Triangular species of VENUS Auct.

TRISIS. Oken. ARCA tortuosa, Auct.

TRISTOMA. Described as TRIPHORA.

TRITON. Montfort, 1810. Fam. Siphonostomata, Bl. Canalifera, Lam.—Descr. Oblong or oval, thick, ribbed or tuberculated, with discontinuous varices placed at irregular distances; spire prominent, mammillated; aperture round or oval, terminating anteriorly in a generally long, slightly raised canal; columellar lip granulated or denticulated; outer lip thickened, reflected, generally denticulated within; epidermis rough; operculum horny.—Obs. However nearly allied the Tritons may apper to the Murices and Ranellæ there are still to be traced in the shells of each of those genera, several constant and well marked distinctions, by which they may be at once recognized. In the Ranellæ, the varices run in two rows along the spire; in the Murices, they form three or more rows; but in the Tritons, they do not follow each other, i.e. they do not occur in the same part of each volution. The large species of Triton are sometimes used as trumpets. The Tritons are brought from the Mediterranean, Ceylon, the East and West Indies, and South Seas. Reeves' Monograph contains 102 species. Fig. 398 to 401.

TRITONIDEA. Sw. A genus of "Buccininæ," Sw. thus described: "Shell bucciniform, but the basal half is narrowed, and the middle more or less ventricose; spire and aperture equal. Pillar at the base with two or three obtuse and very transverse plaits, not well defined; outer lip internally crenated and with a superior siphon; inner lip wanting, or rudimentary." This genus is the same as the one first distinguished by Mr. Gray under the name of Polia. The latter name, as stated by Mr.

Swainson, cannot stand, having been previously occupied for a genus of Lepidopterous Insects. Tritonidea articularis. (Pollia, Gray.) Pl. xix. fig. 415.

TRIVIA. Gray. A genus composed of those small species of CYOPRÆA, Auct. which are characterized by small ridges on the dorsal surface and have the anterior of the columella internally concave and ribbed. C. Pediculus. Auct. Pl. xxi. fig. 449, 450.

TROCHATELLA. Sw. A sub-genus of Helicinæ, consisting of those species which are acute and trochiform. Pl. xxv. fig. 532, 533.

TROCHIA. Sw. A genus of the family Buccininæ, thus described: "shape intermediate between Purpurea and Buccinum; whorls separated by a deep groove; inner lip when young, depressed, when adult, thickened, convex and striated; basal canal very small. T. sulcatus. E. M. 422. f. 4." Sw. Malac. p. 300.

TROCHISCUS. Sowerby. Tr. Norrissii.

TROCHITA. Schumacher. TROCHATELLA, Lesson. INFUNDIBULUM, Montf. The spiral species of Calypræa.

TROCHIDON. Sw. A sub-genus of "Trochinæ," Sw. Lardn. Cyclop. Malac. p. 351.

TROCHILÆA. Sw.? PILEOLUS, Auct.

TROCHURUS. Humph. MONODONTA. Lam.

TROCHUS. Linn. (A top.) Fam. Turbinacea, Lam. Goniostomata, Bl.—Descr. Turbinated, thick, striated, tunerculated or smooth; spire elevated, conical, consisting of numerous whorls; under surface discoid; aperture more or less depressed in an oblique direction, generally angular; columella arcuated, more or less prominent at its union with the outer lip, contiguous to the axis of the shel; operculum horny, orbicular, with numerous whorls.—Obs. Lamarck distinguished this genus from Turbo by the general form, which is more conical, and the aperture, which is angulated, while that of Turbo is rounded. Monodonta or Odontis is only separated on account of the notch at the termination of the columella. But these characters glide so imperceptibly from one genus to the other, that there is no line of demarcation to be found but in the operculum. Accordingly, Sowerby (in Gen. of Sh. 37.) has stated his reasons for considering as Trochi, all the species which have horny opercula; and as Turbines, all those which have testaceous opercula. The Trochi are found in all climates. Pl. xvi. fig. 358 to 360.

TROPÆUM. Sow. CRIOCERATITES.

TROPHON. Montfort, 1801. MUREX Magellanicus, Auct. Fusus Antiquus, and several other species which belong more properly to Fusus than to Murex. T. scalariformis, Wood. Pl. xxviii. fig. 595.

TRUMPET SHELL. A large species of Triton (variegatus), used by the natives of South Sea Islands as a trumpet, to call warriors and herds of cattle together. It answers the purpose tolerably well, producing a very sonorous blast.

TRUNCATED. (truncus, cut short.) Terminating abruptly, as it were cut short. Ex. solenensis, fig. 60.

TRUNCATULANA. D'Orb. A genus of microscopic Foraminifera.

TRUNCATELLA. Risso, 1813. A genus composed of several species of land shells which have been confounded by some authors with Cyclostoma. The genus is thus described: "Shell turriculated, cylindrical, decollated or truncated at the apex, no epidermis; aperture oval, short, with lips continuous, simple." Ex. Truncatella truncatulina, Lowe, Zool. Journ. t, 5. p. 80. Our Plate xxv. fig. 520, 521. It is found on the shores of Britain, the Mediterranean, and West Indies.

TUBA. Lea. A genus of small fossil shells, described as resembling Turbo, but with the aperture more like that of Melania. Lea. Contrib. Geol. Pl. xvi. fig. 369.

TUBERCLE. (*tuberculus*). A small swelling excrescence, or knob.

TUBERCULATED. Having a number of small lumps or pimples, as Turrilites, fig. 483.

TUBICINELLS. Lam. (*Tubicen*, a trumpeter.) *Order*, Sessile Cirripedes, Lam.—*Descr.* A cylindrical tube, composed of six elongated valves jointed together side by side, striated, longitudinally, surrounded by concentric rings; aperture circular, enclosed by an operculum of four valves, placed perpendicularly in an epiphragm.—*Obs.* The Tubicinellæ are found with nearly the whole shell buried in the thick skin of the whale. T. Balænarum. Pl. i. fig. 14.

TUBICOLARIA. Lam (*Tuba*, a tube; *cola*; an inhabitant.) A family of the order Conchifera Dimyaria, Lam. consisting of bivalves soldered as it were within, or connected with, a testaceous tube. The genera contained in this family may be thus distinguished.

1. ASPERGILLUM. Valves fixed, tube perforated and fringed. Fig. 44.
2. TEREDINA. Valves fixed, prominent, tube closed at one end. Fossil. Fig. 46, 47.
3. CLAVAGELLA. One valve fixed, the other free. Fig. 45.
4. TEREDO. Both valves free, tube open at both ends. Fig. 48, 49.
5. FISTULANA. Valves free, tube closed at one end, straight, long. Fig. 53, 54.
6. GASTROCHÆNA. Valves free, tube closed at one end, short, bulbous. Fig. 52.

TUBIVALVES. Bl. Shells composed of two valves connected in a tube, corresponding with the family Tubicolæ of Lamarck.

TULIPARIA. Sw. A sub-genus of "Coronaxis," Sw. Lardn. Cyclop. Malac. p. 311.

TURBINACEA. Bl. The sixth family of Polythalamacea, Bl. containing the genera Cibicides and rosallites, microscopic foraminifera.

TURBINACEA. Lam. A family of the first section of the order Trachelipoda, Lam. containing the following genera.

1. SOLARIUM. With umbilicus reaching to the apex; including *Bifrontia* and *Orbis*. Fig. 353 to 356.
2. ROTELLA. A callosity on the under side. Fig. 357.
3. PHASIANELLA. Oval; operculum shelly. Fig. 367.
4. PLANAXIS, Columellar lip flat; aperture notched. Fig. 365.
5. TURBO. Top-shaped; mouth generally round; operculum shelly. Fig. 368.
6. TROCHUS. Top-shaped; mouth generally angulated; operculum horny, consisting of many whorls; including *Elenchas*. Fig. 358, 359, 361.
7. MARGARITA. Operculum horny, consisting of few whorls; pearly. Fig. 362.
8. LITTORINA. Similar, not pearly; including *Assiminea*. Fig. 363, 363*.
9. PHORUS. Attaching dead shells, stones, &c. Fig. 360.
10. MONODONTA or ODONTIS. A notch and prominent point at the lower part of the aperture. Fig. 366.
11. LACUNA. With an umbilicus. Fig. 364.
12. TURRITELLA. Elongated, screw-shaped. Fig. 369 to 371.

TURBINATED. (*Turbo*, a top.) Top-shaped, the term is applied generally to those shells which are large at one extremity, and narrow to a point at the other. *Ex.* Trochus, fig. 358; Turbinellus, fig. 382.

TURBINELLUS. Lamarck. CYNODONTA. Schum.? SCOLYMUS, Swainson. (*A little top.*) *Fam.* Canalifera, Lam. Siphonostomata, Bl.—*Descr.* turbinated, thick, wide near the apex, generally tuberculated; spire short, depressed, mammillated; aperture rather narrow, terminating anteriorly in an open canal; outer lip thickened within; columella

having from three to five prominent, compressed, transverse folds. The species of this genus are mostly tropical.—*Obs.* The Turbinelli are a well marked genus of marine shells, the species of which are numerous. No fossil species are known. The genus Cancellaris makes the nearest approach to Turbinellus in some characters, but may be distinguished by the roundness of its form, the raised lines inside the outer lip, and the obliquity of the folds on the columellar. Pl. xvii. fig. 382 to 384. Seventy-two species are enumerated in Reeve's Monograph.

TURBO. Auct. (*A top.*) *Fam.* Cricostomata, Bl. Turbinacea, Lam.—*Descr.* Turbinated, solid, ventricose, generally rounded, sub-effuse anteriorly, entire; operculum shelly, solid, incrassated on the outer side, horny and sub-spiral on the inner side. The Turbines are mostly tropical.—*Obs.* The only certain means of distinguishing this extensive genus of marine shells from Trochus, is the operculum, which in the later genus is horny, spiral, and composed of a great number of whorls. The Trochi, however, are in general more conical, and flatter at the under side of whorls, and this constitutes Lamarck's distinction between the genera. Reeve's Monograph contains about thirty species. T. setosus. Pl. xvi. fig. 368.

TURGID. (*Turgidus.*) Puffed up, swollen, inflated. This term is applied synonymously with Ventricose.

TURRICULA. Humph. MELANIA, Auct.

TURRICULACEA. Bl. The seventh family of the Order Polythalamacea, Bl. containing the genus Turrilites, fig. 483.

TURRILITES. Lam. (*Turris*, a tower; λιθος, a stone.) *Fam.* Turriculacea, Lam. Ammonacea, Bl.—*Descr.* Chambered, turrited, spiral; septa sinuous and lobate, perforated by a siphon; aperture rounded, with the outer lip expanded. This genus, which is distinguished from the other Ammonacea by having the spire produced, *i.e.* not being convolute, consists of several species, occurring only in chalk-marl. Pl. xxiii. fig. 483.

TURRIS. Montf. 1810. A genus composed of those species of MITRA, Auct. which have the whorls angulated, with the aperture lengthened and undulated.

TURRITED. The spire of a univalve shell is said to be *turrited* when the whorls of which it is composed are regulated so as to have the appearance of little turrets rising above each other, as in Mitra, fig. 431. Vulpccula, Gray.

TURRITELLA. Lam. TEREBELLUM, Browne. (*A little tower.*) *Fam.* Turbinacea, Lam. Cricostomata, Bl.—*Descr.* Turrited, elongated, generally grooved spirally; spire pointed, consisting of numerous whorls; aperture rounded or angulated; inner and outer lips thin, confluent anteriorly; operculum horny.—*Obs.* The shells composing this well-defined genus, are commonly called screws, a name to which the spiral grooves of most of the species seems to entitle them. Mr. Reeve's Monograph contains sixty-five species. T. imbricata. Pl. xvi. fig. 370.

TURTONIA. Hanley. See "Kelliadæ," T. minuta, Pl. xxvii. fig. 567.

TYMPANOSTOMA. Schum. (*Timbrel mouth.*) POTAMIS, Brongn. Potamus muricata, fig. 377.

TYPHIS. Montf. A genus composed of MUREX tubifer, Auct. and other similar species, which have the canal closed and a perforated tube between each varix on the angulated part of the whorls. Besides the fossil species originally described, there are now five species known, which are figured in part 200, of the Conchological Illustrations by the Author. Typhis tubifer, Pl. xvii. fig. 397. Pl. xxvi. fig. 554, 555, 556.

ULTIMUS. Montf. (*The last.*) A genus composed of OVULUM gibbosum, Auct. and other species in which the canals are not distinctly defined, nor elongated. This fanciful name is given to the genus on account of its being described in the last page of the book. Pl. xx. fig. 443.

UMBILICATED. (*Umbilicatus.*) having an umbilicus, as Nautilus umbilicatus.

UMBILICUS. (*A navel.*) The hollow formed in spiral shells when the inner side of the volutions do not join each other, so that the axis is hollow. The umbilicus is marked with the letter *u* in Helix aglira, fig. 279. The term is also used to express any small, neat, rounded hollow.

UMBO. (*The boss of a buckler or shield.*) The point of a bivalve shell above the hinge, constituting the apex or nucleus of each valve, from which the longitudinal rays diverge, and the lines of growth, commencing at the minutest circle, descend in gradually enlarging concentric layers to the outer margin. The umbones will be marked with the letter *u*, in Cytherea, fig. 117.

UMBRELLA or UMBELLA. (*A little shade.*) *Fam.* Semi-phyllidiana, Lam. Patelloidea, Bl.—*Descr.* Patelliform, sub-orbicular, compressed, rather irregular; apex slightly raised, placed near the centre; margin acute; internal surface with a central, callous, coloured disc, surrounded by a continuous, irregular muscular impression.—*Obs.* This genus is known from Patella, by its continuous muscular impression. It is commonly called the Chinese Umbrella shell. There are but two species at present known; the U. Mediterranea, and the U. Indica. Pl. xii: fig. 233.

UNDATED. (*Unda*, a wave.) Waved.

UNDULATED. (*Undulatus.*) Minutely waved.

UNGUICULATED. (*Unguis*, a nail or hoof.) An unguiculated operculum is one in which the layers are disposed laterally, and the nucleus constitutes part of the outer edge.

UNGULINA. Daud. (*Ungula*, a nail or claw.) *Fam.* Mactracea, Lam. Conchacea, Bl.—*Descr.* Equivalve, sub-orbicular, sub-equilateral, with margins entire, simple, closed all round; hinge with one short, sub-divided cardinal tooth in each valve, and a very minute additional tooth in one valve, an oblong ligamentary pit divided into two portions, one of which receives the cartilage, the external ligament is immediately below the umbones; muscular impressions, two in each valve, oblong; impression of the mantle entire. Coast of Africa. U. transversa, Pl. iv. fig. 88.

UNI-AURICULATED. Having one AURICLE. See AURICULATED.

UNICORNUS. Montf. MONOCEROS, Auct.

UNIO. (*A pearl.*) *Fam.* Nayades, Lam. Submytilacea, Bl.—*Descr.* Inequilateral, equivalve, regular, free, pearly within, covered by a mooth epidermis without; umbones prominent, generally corroded; muscular impressions two in each valve, lateral, distant; the anterior composed of several small divisions; hinge varying in age, species, and individuals.—*Obs.* The above description is framed so as to include all the genera of the Lamarckian Nayades, together with Castalia, which are placed in the family Trigonacea, they are all fresh-water shells, commonly called fresh-water muscles. The distinctions of the various genera into which they have been divided, will be found in their respective places, and under the name of Nayades. They are all represented in figures 140 to 152. Of these fig. 145 to 148, are more generally considered as forming the genus Unio. Pl. viii.

UNIVALVE. (*Unus*, one; *valva*, valve.) A shell consisting of a single piece, as distinguished from Bivalves and Multivalves, which are composed of two or more principal pieces. Spiral shells having an operculum, are called sub-bivalves by some authors.

UPPER-VALVE. The free valve in attached bivalves.

UTRICULUS. Brown. A sub-genus of Bullidæ, the shells of which are thus described by Mr. A. Adams, in his Monograph of Bullidæ in Sowerby's Thesaurus—"Shell small, oblong-ovate; outer lips nearly the whole length of the last whorl, and entire; spire very short, volutions prominent."

UVIGERNA. D'Orb. A genus of microscopic Foraminifera.

VAGINA. Megerle. SOLEN *vagina*, Auct.

VAGINULA. (*A little sheath, the husk of corn.*) *Class*, Pteropoda, Lam.—*Descr.* Pyramidal, slightly inflated in the centre, thin, fragile; aperture oblong, with the edges turned slightly outwards.—*Obs.* The little shells of this genus, which are only known in a fossil state, differ from Cuvieria in being pointed at the extremity. Found in the tertiary beds of Bordeaux. V. Daudinii, Pl. xii. fig. 225.

VAGINULINA. D'Orb. A genus of microscopic Foraminifera.

VALVATA. Muller, 1774. *Fam.* Peristomata, Lam. Cricostomata, Bl.—*Descr.* Thin, turbinated; spire short, composed of from three to six rounded whorls; aperture circular; peritreme acute, entire; operculum horny, spiral.—*Obs.* This genus of small shells resembles Cyclostoma, from which the recent species may be known by the horny texture of the external surface, being fresh-water shells. Europe and North America. The fossils of course belong to the fresh-water formations. V. piscinalis, fig. 322.

VALVES. (*Valva*, a door, a folding piece.) The two pieces composing a bivalve shell, which close upon each other, turning upon a hinge consisting of a ligament, cartilage, and teeth. See BIVALVE, MULTIVALVE, and UNIVALVE.

VALVULINA. D'Orb. A genus of microscopic Foraminifera.

VANICORO. Quay and Gaimard. A genus of beautiful shells, something like Sigaretus in form, admitted by Mr. Sowerby in the genus Neritopsis, but differing from that genus in the form of the columella. The type is Nerita cancellata, Chemnitz. Mr. Cuming's collection contains twenty-four species, all of which are cancelled. The operculum is thin, horny, and semicircular, only half enclosing the animal. Ex. V. cidaris. Pl. xxvii. fig. 584.

VARIX. (*A swelling vein.*) A varix is formed on the outer surface of a spiral shell, by the thickened, reflected edge of a former aperture, after fresh deposits of testaceous matter have increased the size by adding to the growth of the shell beyond it. In this manner there are frequently many varices, or edges of former apertures, in various parts of the spire and the body whorl. They are sometimes placed at regular distances from each other, as in Harpa, fig. 419; sometimes *continuous*, as in Ranella, fig. 394; sometimes *discontinuous*, as in Triton, fig. 398; sometimes *ramose*, as in Murex, fig. 395; sometimes *simple*, as in Scalaria, fig. 351; sometimes *spinose*, as in Murex spinosus. The term *varix* has also been applied to any swelling ridge, such as that on lower part of the columella of Ancillaria, fig. 456.

VELATES. Montf. NERITINA perversa, Auct. Pl. xv. fig. 326.

VELLETIA. Gray? A genus described as differing from ANCYLLUS in being dextral. VELLETIA lacustris, ANCYLUS lacustris, Auct. Sowerby Gen. fig. 2.

VELUTINA. Fleming, 1822. *Fam.* Macrostomata, Lam.—*Descr.* Sub-globose, covered with a velvety epidermis; spire short, composed of two rapidly enlarged ventricose whorls; aperture large, sub-ovate; peritreme thin, entire, separated from the last whorl; columella tortuous, thin.—*Obs.* This shell does not resemble any other genus in the family. Northern Seas. Pl. xv. fig. 337.

VENERICARDIA. Lam. A genus composed of the shorter species of Cardita. Pl. vi. fig. 121.

VENERIRUPIS. Lam. (From *Venus* and *rupis*, a rock.) The oblong species of Venus Auct. which live in cavities of rocks and stones. This genus is united by Sowerby with some other species of Venus under the name Pullastra. V. Vulgaris, Pl. iv. fig. 97.

VENTRAL. (*Venter*, the belly.) The margin of a bivalve shell opposite the hinge. The under valve in Brachiopodous bivalves is the ventral valve. The ventral surface of an univalve spiral shell is that which faces the observer when the aperture is placed towards him. The ventral part of the whorls of symmetrical convolute shells, is the inner part, that which is nearest to the spire.

VENTRAL SIPHON. In symmetrical convolute univalves, is one placed near the inner edge of the whorls.

VENTRICOSE. (*Ventricosus.*) Swelled, rounded out, (*bombé Fr.*) as Harpa ventricosa, fig. 419.

VENUS. Auct. (*Goddess of Beauty.*) (DOSINA, Gray.) *Fam.* Marine Conchacea, Lam. Conchacea, Bl.—*Descr.* Equivalve, inequilateral, sub-globose, sub-ovate, transverse, externally rugose, striated, ribbed, cancellated or smooth; margins entire simple, close; hinge with three more or less distinct cardinal teeth, diverging from the umbones in each valve; muscular impressions two, lateral, distant; palleal impressions sinuated posteriorly; ligament external.—*Obs.* This extensive genus, including some bivalves of splendour and beauty, justifying the name given to it, may be known from Cytherea by the absence of a lateral tooth, which is found near the cardinal teeth in the latter. Artemis is distinguished not only by its beautiful form, but by the deep angular sinus in the palleal impression. Found mostly in temperate and tropical climates. A monograph will appear in No. 13 of Thesaurus Conchyliorum by the Author. Pl. vi. fig. 119. 119*a*.

VERMETUS. Adanson. *Fam.* Scalariana, lam. Cricostomata, Bl.—*Descr.* Spiral at the apex, irregularly twisted towards the aperture; aperture round, small.—*Obs.* This shell resembles the Serpulæ in general appearance, although it is regularly spiral near the apex. The animal is known to be a true mollusc, rather nearly allied to that of the genus Dentalium, which is also placed wrongly in the Lamarckian system. Vermetus Lumbricalis. Coast of Africa. Pl. xv. fig. 345.

VERMICULAR. (*Vermicularis.*) Worm-shaped, tubular serpentine. *Ex.* Vermilia triquetra, fig. 7.

VERMICULARIA. Lam. VERMETUS, Adanson; afterwards VERMETUS, Lam.

VERMILIA. Lam. A genus composed of species of Serpula, which are attached by the whole length of the shell, no part being free. Vermilia triquetra. Pl. i. fig. 7.

VERTEBRALINA. D'Orb. A genus of Microscopic Foraminifera.

VERTEX. Apex.

VERTIGO. Müll. *Fam.* Colimacea, Lam.—*Descr.* Cylindrically fusiform, sinistral, hyaline; aperture marginated, sinuated, denticulated on the inner edge; peristome sub-reflected.—*Obs.* This genus of minute land shells, resembles Pupa, but is a reversed, hyaline shell. Vertigo pusilla. Pl. xiv. fig. 293.

VERRUCA. Schum. CLITIA, Leach.

VESICA. Sw. A sub-genus of Bulinus, Sw. p. 360.

VEXILLA. Sw. A genus of "Nassinæ," Sw. thus described: "General shape of *Purpura*, the inner lip flattened and depressed; the outer, when adult, thickened, inflected and toothed; aperture wide; picta *Sw.* Chem. pl. 157. fig. 1594–5." Sw. Malac. p. 300. Pl. xxv. fig. 544.

VIRGULINA. D'Orb. A genus of microscopic Foraminifera.

VITRELLA. Sw. A sub-genus of "Bullinæ," Sw. Lardn. Cyclop. Malac. p. 360.

VITRINA. Drap. (*Vitreus*, glassy.) *Fam.* Limacinea, Lam. and Bl.—

Descr. Ovate thin, glassy, fragile; spire short; last whorl large; aperture wide, transverse; peritreme simple; columella spiral, linear.—*Obs.* This genus of land-shells is not known in a fossil state. The recent species are found among moss and grass, in shady situations. De Ferussac has divided this genus into Helicolimax, fig. 263, and Helixarion, fig. 262.

VITULARIA. Sw. A genus of "Muricinæ," Sw. thus described: "General habit of *Muricidea*, but the inner lip is depressed and flattened, as in the *Purpurinæ*; varices simple, nearly obsolete. Tuberculata, *Sw.* En. M. 419. fig. 1. (*Murex vitulinus*, Auct.)" Sw. p. 297. Pl. xxvi. fig. 553.

VIVIPARA. A generic name given by Montfort, and retained by some authors on the ground of priority for PALUDINA, Lam. on account of the animals being *viviparous*, i.e. the young being perfectly formed before they leave the ovaries.

VIVIPAROUS. See VIVIPARA.

VOLUTA. Auct. (*Volvo*, to revolve.) *Fam.* Columellaria, Lam. Angyostomata, Bl.—*Descr.* Sub-ovate, rather angulated, thick, generally tuberculated, smooth; spire short, conical, with a mammillated apex; aperture generally angulated, large, terminating anteriorly in a deep notch; columella smooth, with several plaits, of which the lowest is the largest; outer lip thickened within.—*Obs.* The genus Voluta, as left by Linnæus, is only characterized by the folds on the columella, and includes many shells which, although they agree in this respect with the genus, are yet quite opposite to each other in all other characters. Thus the Auriculæ, which are land shells, and have the aperture entire, are mixed up with others which are marine, and have a canal, as Turbinellæ, and the Fasciolariæ, and others which have merely a notch, as the true Volutes. This genus, as it is circumscribed at present, includes a great number of beautiful shells, most of which are rich in colouring. CYMBA and MELO have been separated by Mr. Broderip from the genus VOLUTA of Lamarck, for reasons stated in their respective descriptions. Fifty-eight species are described in the Monograph by the author, in Thesaurus Conchylium, Pl. xlvi. to lv. vol. 5. Our Pl. xx. fig. 443.

VOLVARIA. Lam. (*Volva*, a shuttle.) *Fam.* Columellaria, Lam.—*Descr.* Cylindrical, convolute, spirally striated; spire very short, nearly hidden; aperture narrow, as long as the whole shell; columella with three oblique plaits; outer lip dentrated.—*Obs.* The Volvariæ are only known in a fossil state, and resemble some species of Bulla in general form, but are distinguished by the plaits on the columella. V. concinna. Pl. xx. fig. 439.

VOLUTELLA. Swainson. (*A little volute.*) A genus composed of those species of MARGINELLA, Auct. which have the spire concealed, and the aperture smooth within. Fig. 438, PERSICULA of Schumacher.

VOLUTILITHES. Sw. (*Voluta*, and λιθος, *lithos*, a stone.) A genus composed of some fossil species of Voluta, which have the plaits on the pillar generally numrous, indistinct, and sometimes wanting altogether, with a pointed spire. V. spinosa, Pl. xx. fig. 436.

VOLUTION. See WHORL.

VOLVULA. Adams. Sowerby's Thesaurus, Pt. xi. 1850. A genus of Bullidæ, the shells of which are thus described: "Sub-cylindrical, beaked at both ends; spire concealed; aperture narrow; inner lip with a single obsolete fold."

VORTICIALIS. Lam. A genus of microscopic Foraminifera.

VULSELLA. Lam. (*A little tongue.*) *Fam.* Ostracea, Lau. Margaritacea, Bl.—*Descr.* Equivalve, irregular, longitudinal, compressed, oblong; umbones separated by a slight area in both valves; hinge with a large pit in the centre, containing the cartilage, the ligament being spread over the areas; muscular impressions, one on each valve, sub-central, oblong.—*Obs*. This genus differs from Ostræa in the equality of valves, and in having a hollow pait in the hinge for the cartilage. Vulsella lingulata, Pl. xi. fig. 185.

WATERING-POT. Aspergillum, fig. 44, commonly so called on account of the resemblance of its perforated termination to that of the spout of a watering-pot.

WENTLE TRAP. Scalaria pretiosa, commonly so called.

WHORL. A complete turn or revolution round the imaginary axis of a spiral shell. The last whorl is called the *body-whorl*. The whorls are described as *non-contiguous*, when they do not touch each other; *continuous*, in the opposite case. *Depressed* when they are flat. They are *angulated*, *keeled*, or coronated; *distinct*, or indistinct. they are sometimes, as in Cypræa, hidden by the last whorl.

YETUS. Adanson. CYMBA, Broderip.

XYLOPHAGA. Turton. (ξυλον, *zylon*, wood; φαγω, *phago*, to eat.) *Fam*. Tubiscolæ, Lam.—*Descr*. Equivalve, globose, closed at the back; with a large, angular hiatus in front; hinge with a small curved tooth advancing from beneath the umbones in each valve.—*Obs*. This shell, which is found in a cylindrical cavity, eaten in the wood by the animal,

resembles Teredo, but has not the shelly tube, nor the posterior hiatus. X. dorsalis, Pt. x. fig. 50, 51.

XYLOTRYA. Leach. XYLOPHAGA, Sow.

ZARIA. Gray, 1840. A division of the genus Turritella represented by T. duplicata, &c.

ZIERLIANA. Gray. The short strombiform, thick-lipped species of Mitra. M. Ziervogelii.

ZIRFÆA. Leach. 1817. Pholas crispata, without accessory valves. See Monograph of Pholas, Sowerby's Thesaurus Conchylium. No. 10, fig. 37.

ZONITES. Montf. A genus formed of Helix Algira, and other similar species with depressed spires and large umbilici; included in the sub-genus Helicella. Pl. xiii. fig. 279.

ZUA. Leach. A genus described under the word "CIONELLA." The manuscript name by Leach having them published by Gray, claims the priority.

ZURAMA. Leach. A sub-genus of Helix. H. pulchella, Auct. Gray's Turton, p. 41.

ZYZIPHINUS. Leach. MS. Gray, 1840. Tochus zyziphinus and similar species.